墨絵
Sumi-e

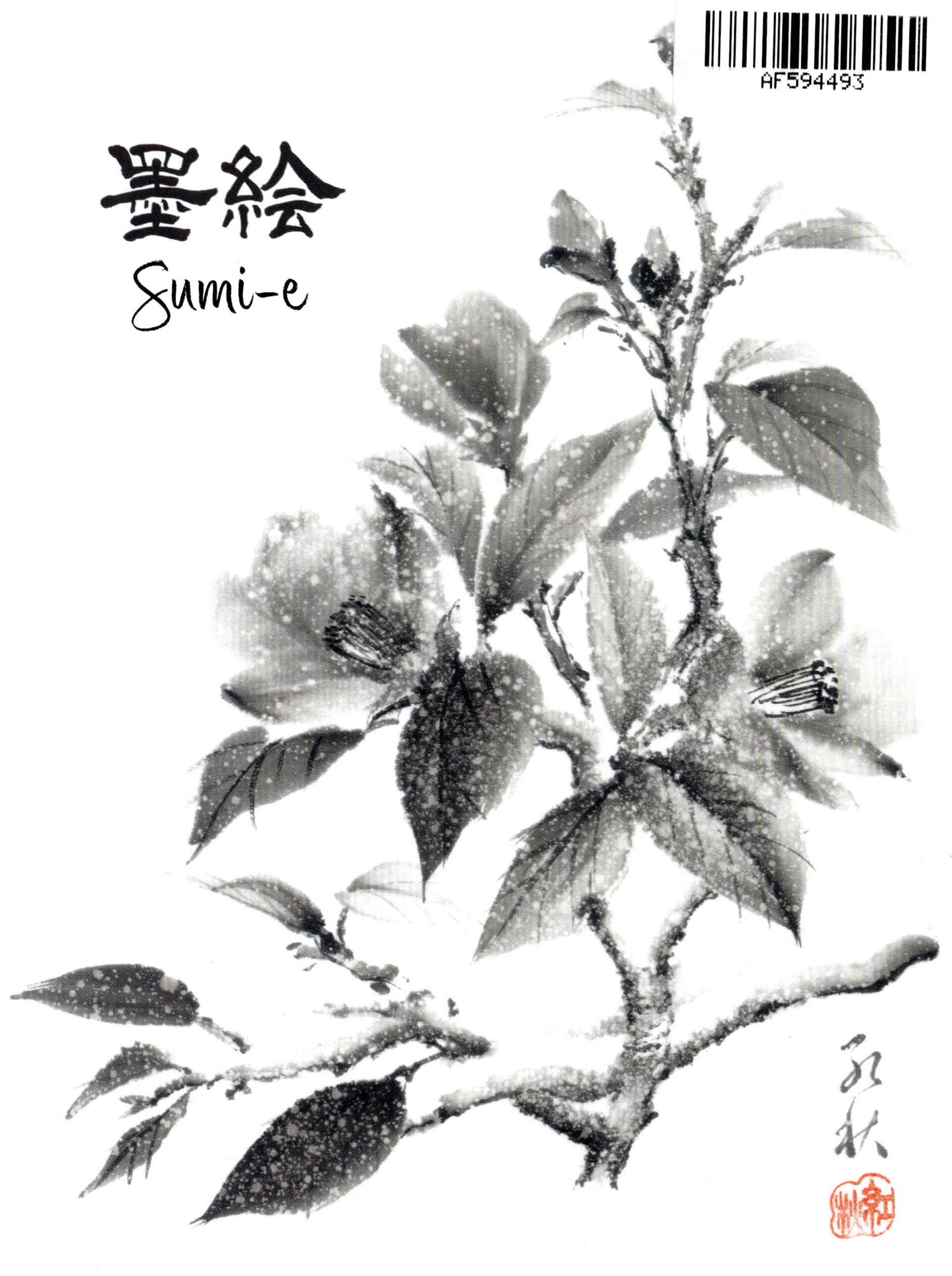

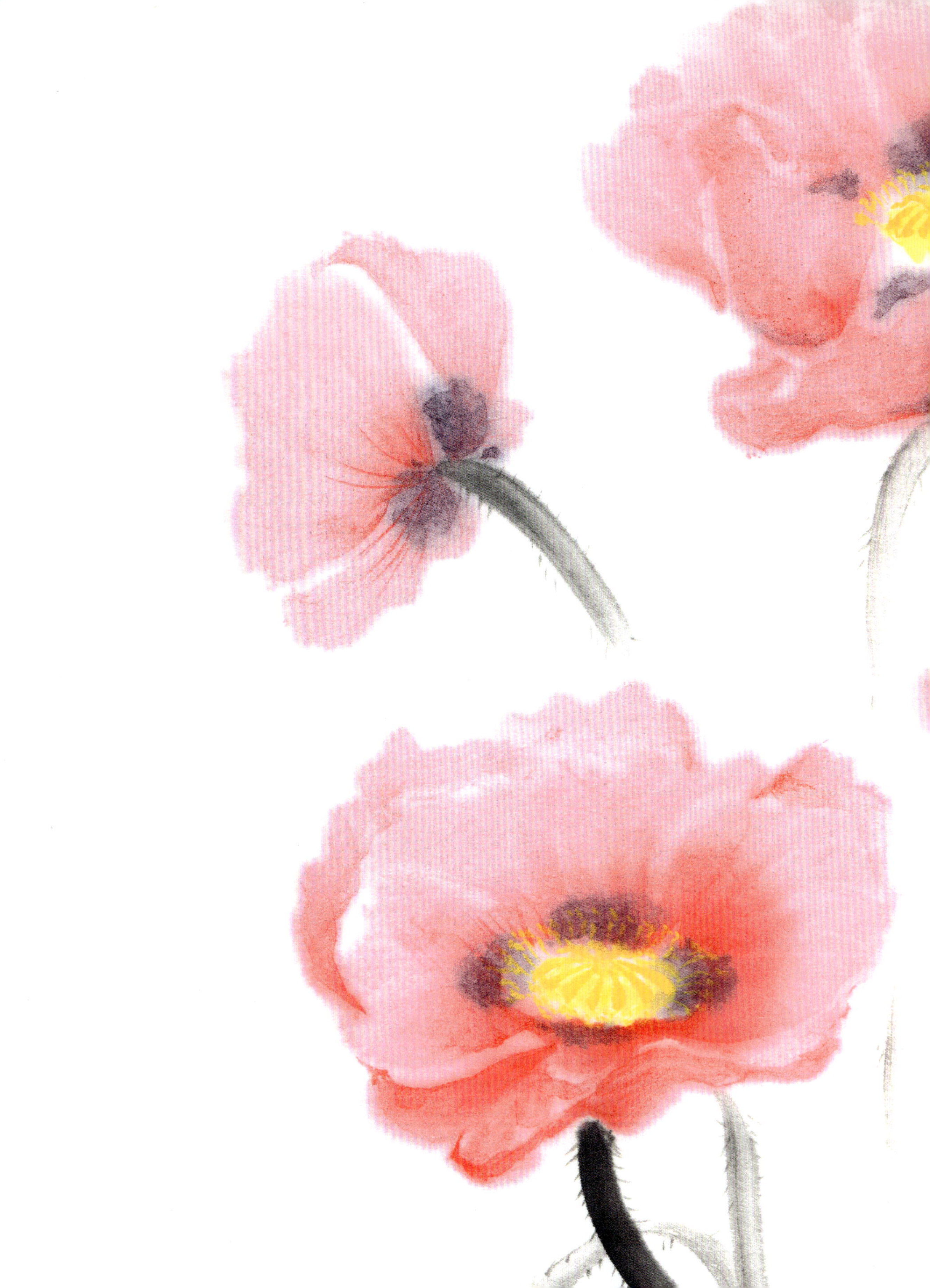

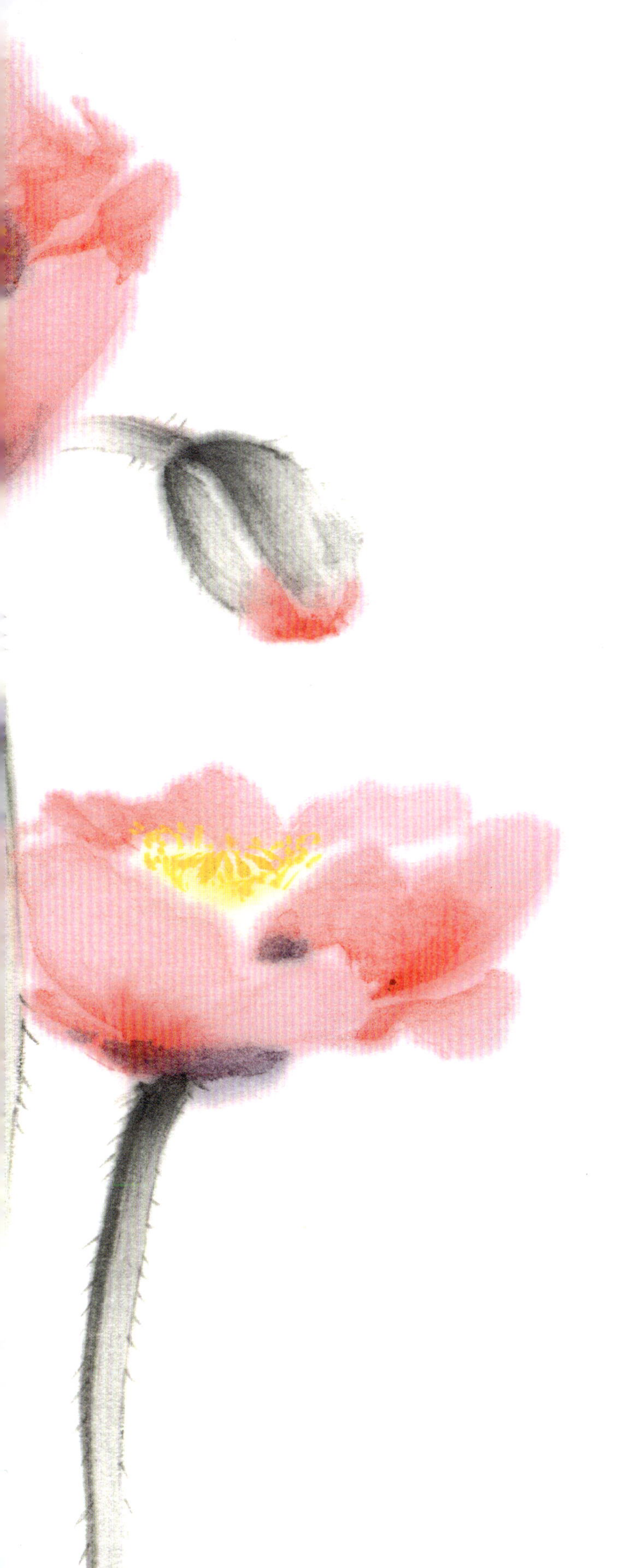

墨絵
Sumi-e

The Mindful Art of Japanese Ink Painting

AKEMI LUCAS (KOSHU)

HERBERT PRESS
LONDON • OXFORD • NEW YORK • NEW DELHI • SYDNEY

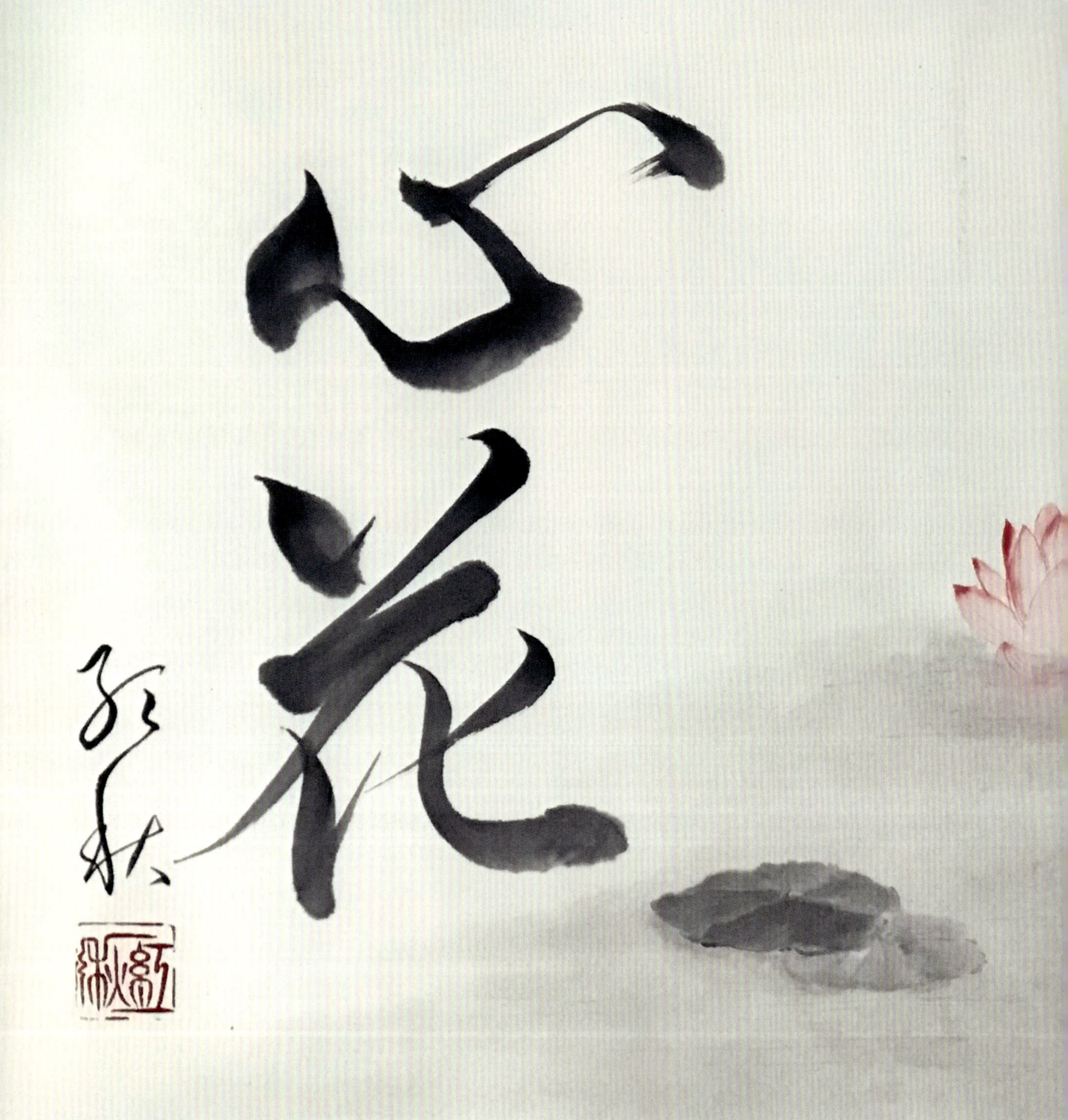

HEART OF THE LOTUS FLOWER 心花

Soon after I qualified as a calligraphy teacher, my mentor's first request was for me to paint the Buddhist proverb, 'Heart of the Lotus Flower'. 'Never forget the heart of the lotus flower', he said. Born in murky waters, the lotus flower rises with pristine petals, unspoiled. She reaches the surface and unfolds as an enlightened flower.

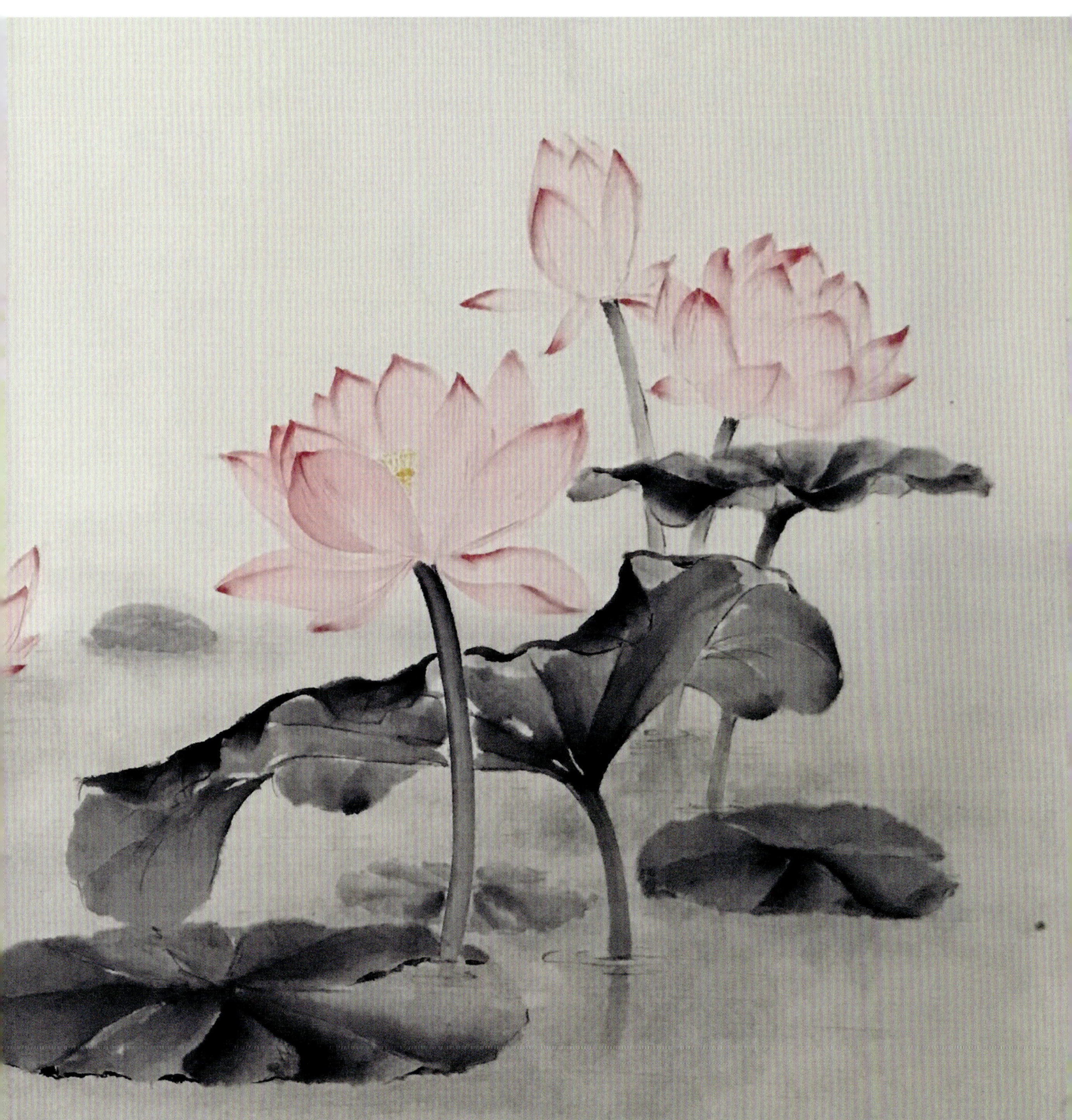

HERBERT PRESS
Bloomsbury Publishing Plc
50 Bedford Square, London, WC1B 3DP, UK
29 Earlsfort Terrace, Dublin 2, Ireland

Bloomsbury, Herbert Press and the Herbert Press logo are trademarks of Bloomsbury Publishing PLC

First published in Great Britain in 2024

A catalogue record for this book is available from the British Library
Library of Congress Cataloguing-in-data has been applied for

ISBN: 9781789941630; eBook: 9781789941623

2 4 6 8 10 9 7 5 3 1

Design by Laura Shaw Design, Inc.
Printed and bound in Turkey by Elma Basim

FSC www.fsc.org 100% From well-managed forests FSC® C164814

Acknowledgements

A special thank you to my daughters, Leanne and Matilda, for their support and contributions, and to my students for inspiring this Sumi painting book

Editing and photography: Matilda Lucas
Digital illustrations: Leanne Lucas

Contents

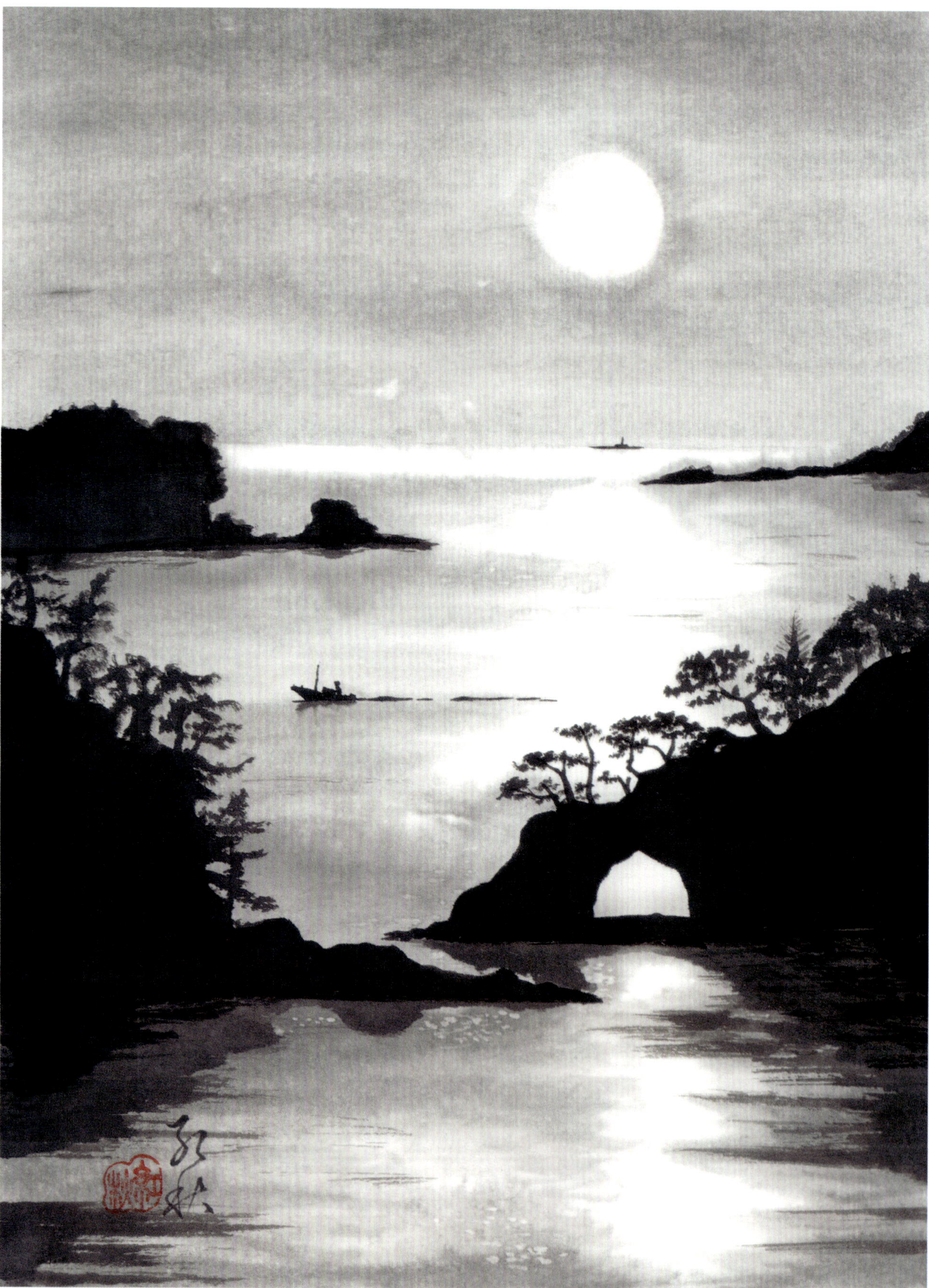

筆が奏でる音

LISTEN TO THE SOUND OF YOUR BRUSH

I STARTED CALLIGRAPHY at the age of eight. I had lost sight in my left eye, and in an effort to correct my imbalanced handwriting, my mother enrolled me in the local calligraphy school. I didn't necessarily dislike the practice, so I accepted her wishes.

With my yearning to attend dancing or singing classes quietly nestled away, I attended weekly calligraphy lessons with my sister and brother. While the other students were able to capture the correct balance with ease, I struggled. My siblings would leave class early while I stayed behind practising piece after piece until I was given my teacher's approval – a nod to say that I could go home.

As the years passed, I diligently continued my training, practising into the night while I was a university student or went to work.

However, it was only later in life that calligraphy and painting became more than mere artistic endeavours. There came a period when I couldn't bring myself to hold the brush. I was consumed by sorrow after the passing of my beloved husband when he was 36 years old. I withdrew from the world, retreating into silence and giving up on all of life's pleasures, including calligraphy and music. In my solitude, my focus shifted solely to listening to the sound of my daughter's breathing, as she was suffering from frequent fainting spells. I kept the house as quiet as possible, and her smile became my sole purpose.

It took me a couple of years to leave the darkness behind and pick up my brush again. When I finally did, a new sensation coursed through me. My brush flowed with ease and grace as I painted, and I became acutely aware of the sounds of the brush that echoed within me. I found solace, bathed in the warmth of existence. From there, slowly I was able to reclaim my life. I was grateful for my mother who took me to calligraphy school. In this stillness, I was faced with the profound truth that only by turning inward could you truly see outward.

Soon after, I learned that Zen philosophy lies at the core of calligraphy and sumi painting – everything pieced together. I became aware of the spirituality of this art form.

My passion for teaching grew, to share this art form that had given me so much. In my workshops and lessons, this message stays at the core of my teaching: to pause the day and carve out a silent space where you can look inward and paint. I hope this humble offering may guide you through your journey of creation.

HANAGURI ROCKS, KASADO ISLAND

A painting of a photograph my late husband took in 1998. I remember him waiting for the sunset, the moment the light filtered through the rocks.

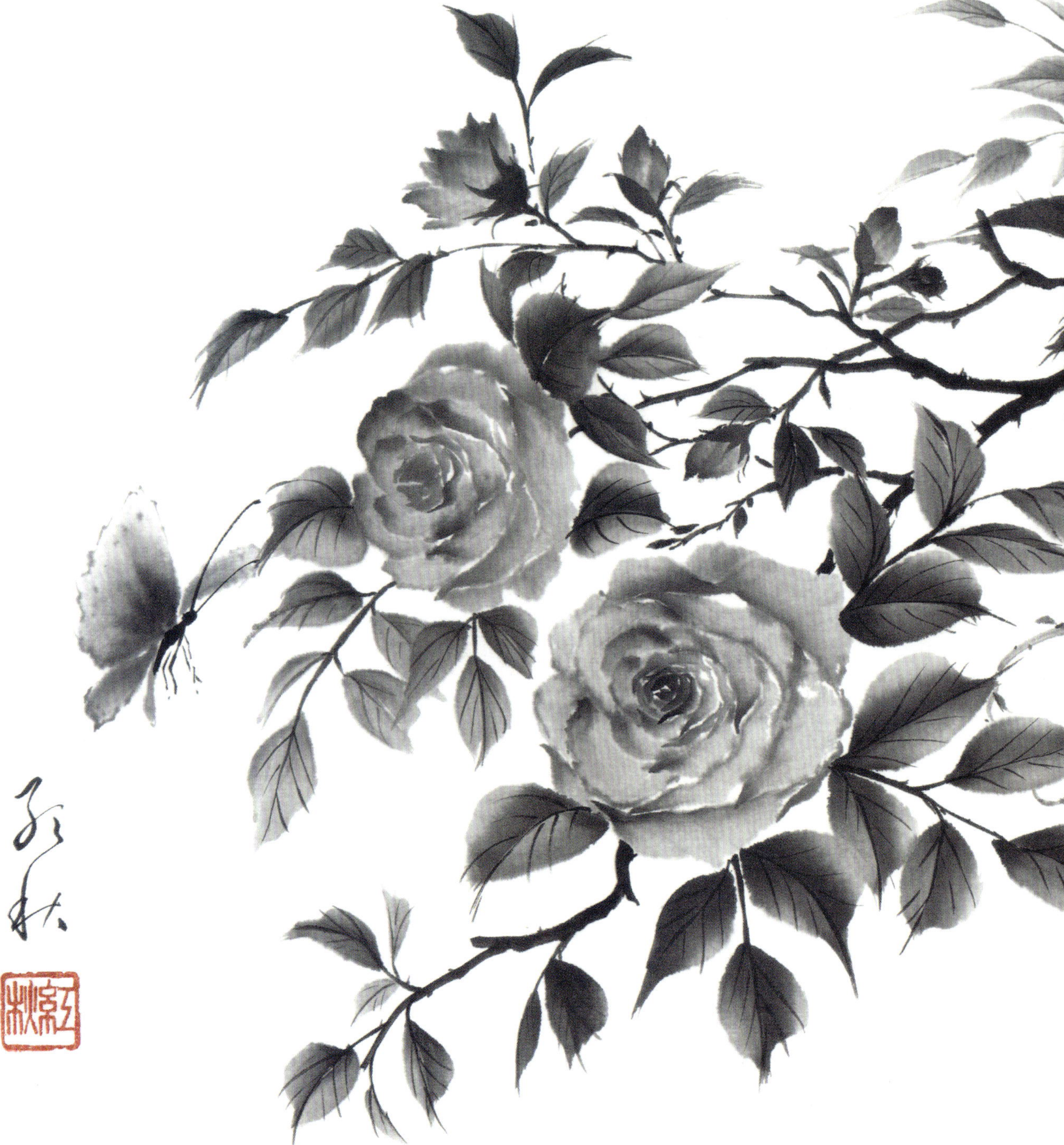

ONE TIME, ONE MEETING

一期一会

It was towards the end of my training; the final years before I qualified as a calligraphy teacher. I had acquired the technical skills that the classroom had to offer, and what was left of my training was in the realms of introspection – to look inward and create in my own space and time. My master, Seizan, asked only that I visit him to hear his stories. 'I will never repeat the same words twice', he had said.

Yet each time I visited, he would narrate the same story; the words his mentor had passed on to him unchanged. I knew the exact cadence of

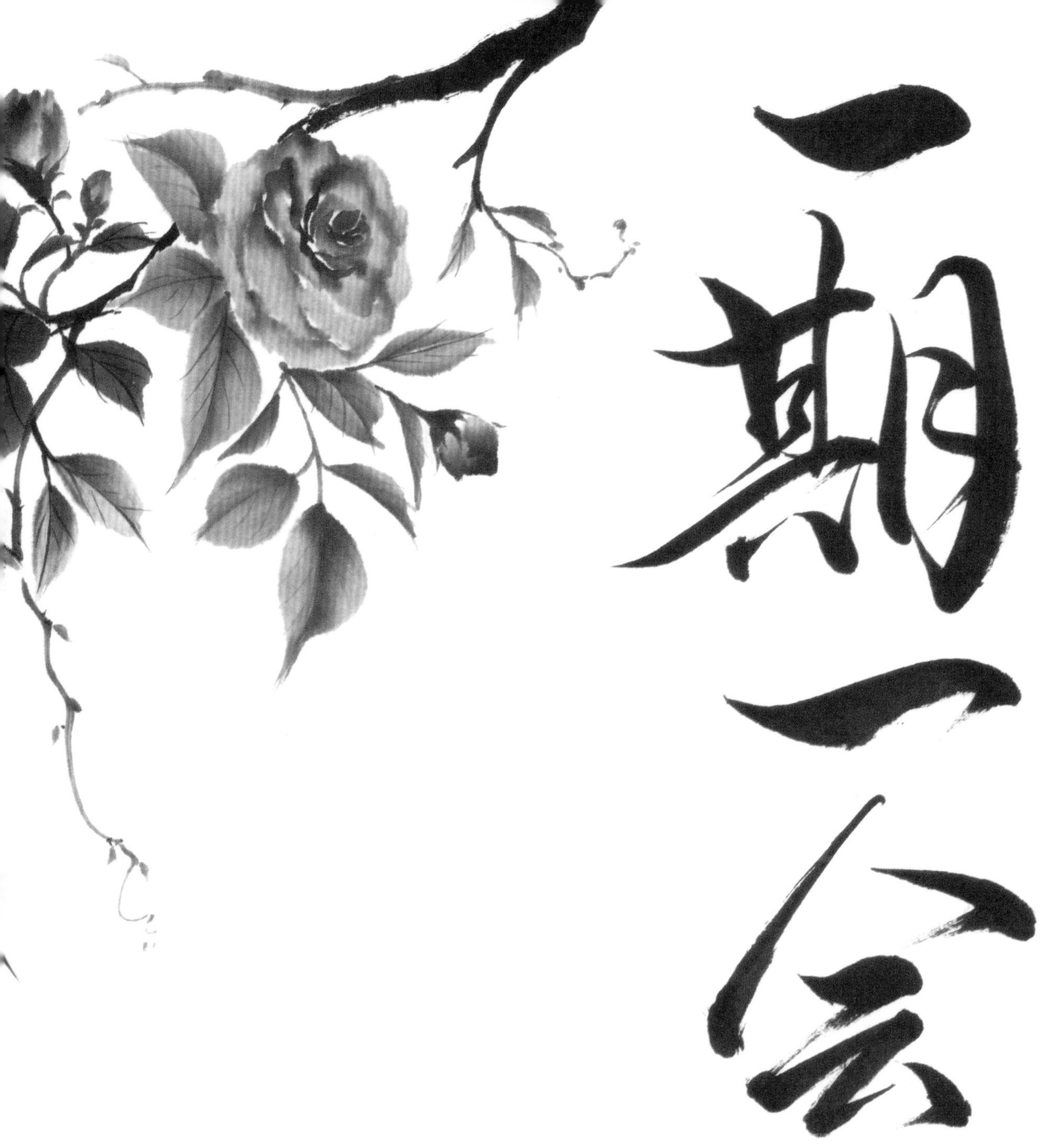

words and the very moment he would pause to take a breath. With each telling, I grew restless of these recurrent encounters, thinking my time would be better spent practising. Nevertheless, I obliged and listened.

Only retrospectively can I understand the subtleties that had eluded me back then. The season had shifted, my surroundings had changed, and I too was no longer the same person who had listened to the previous telling. Every subtle change had granted each moment a singular existence. While no longer with me, he continues to impart his wisdom: to cherish the present as no encounter will repeat in the same way.

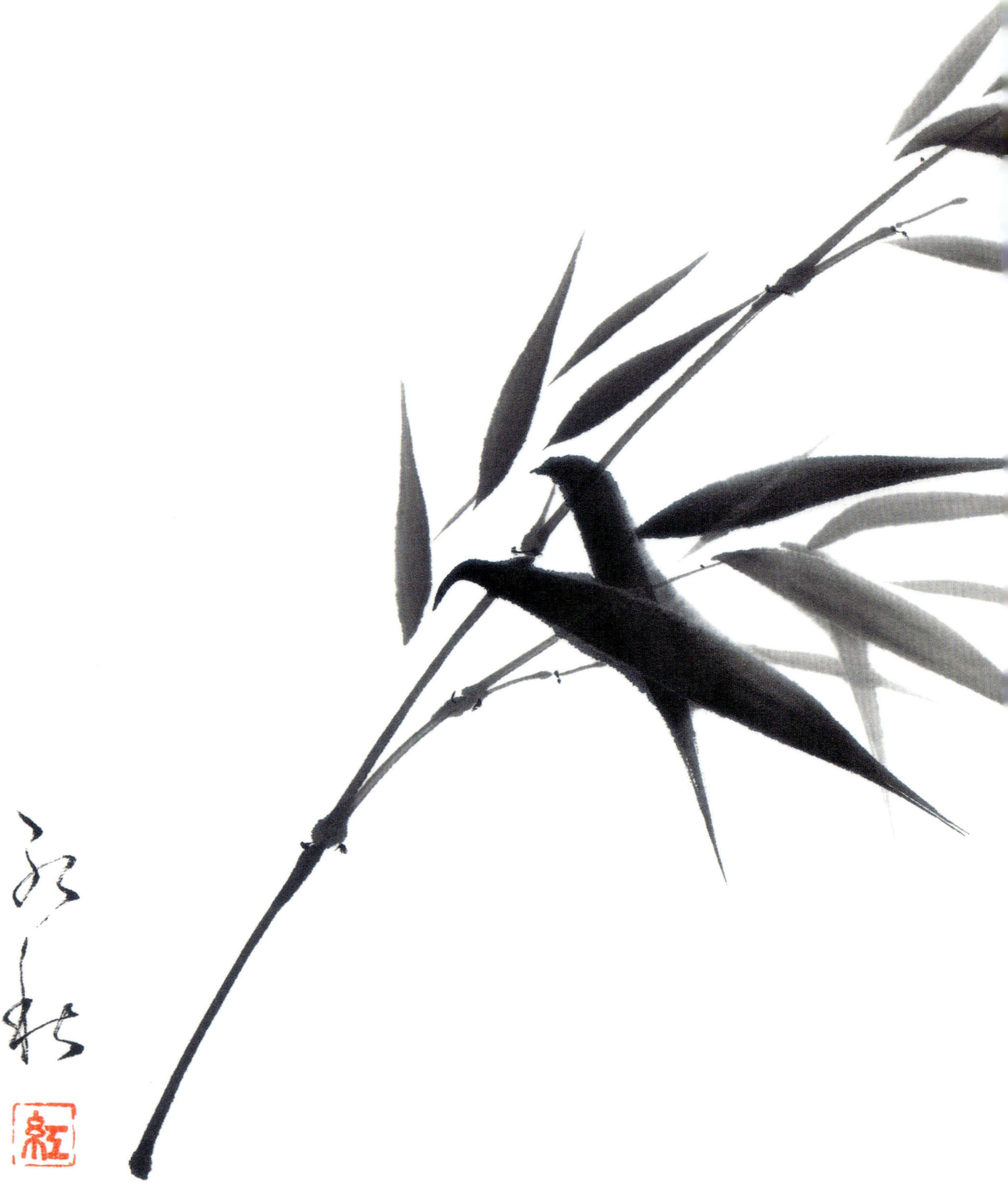

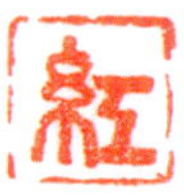
紅

水墨画

Suibokuga

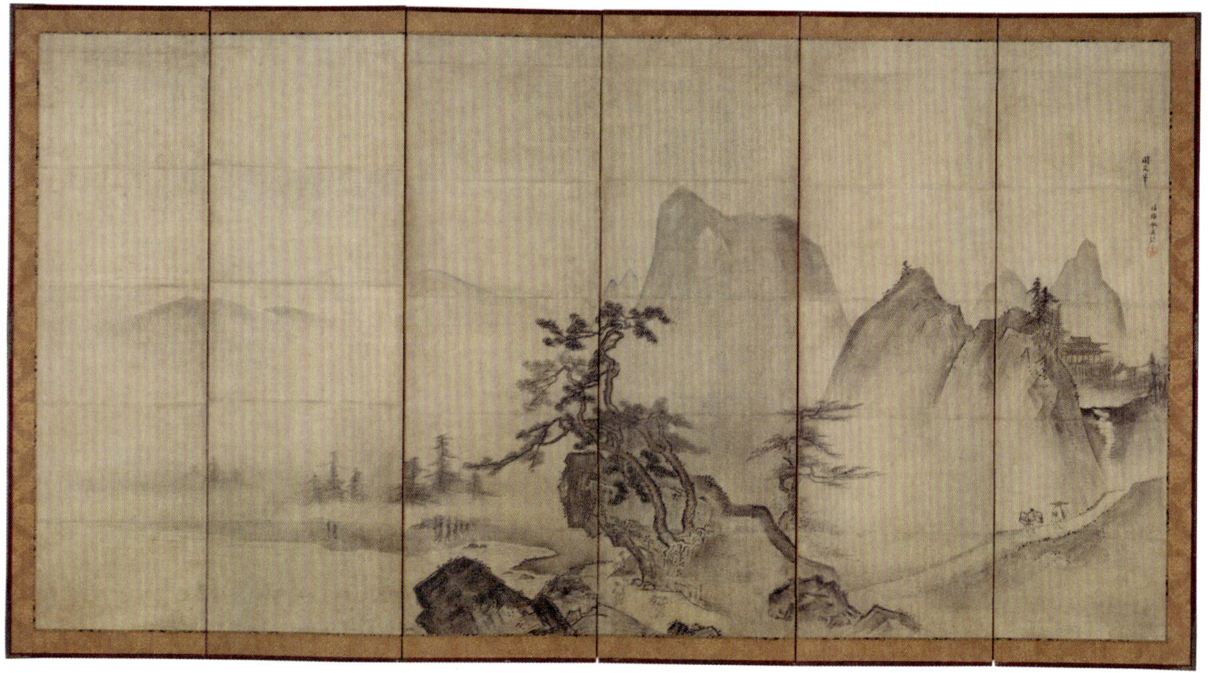

Mountain Landscape – six-panel folding screen in the style of Tensho Shubun, early to mid-fifteenth century. © The Metropolitan Museum of Art, New York, Mary Griggs Burke Collection, Gift of the Mary and Jackson Burke Foundation, 2015.

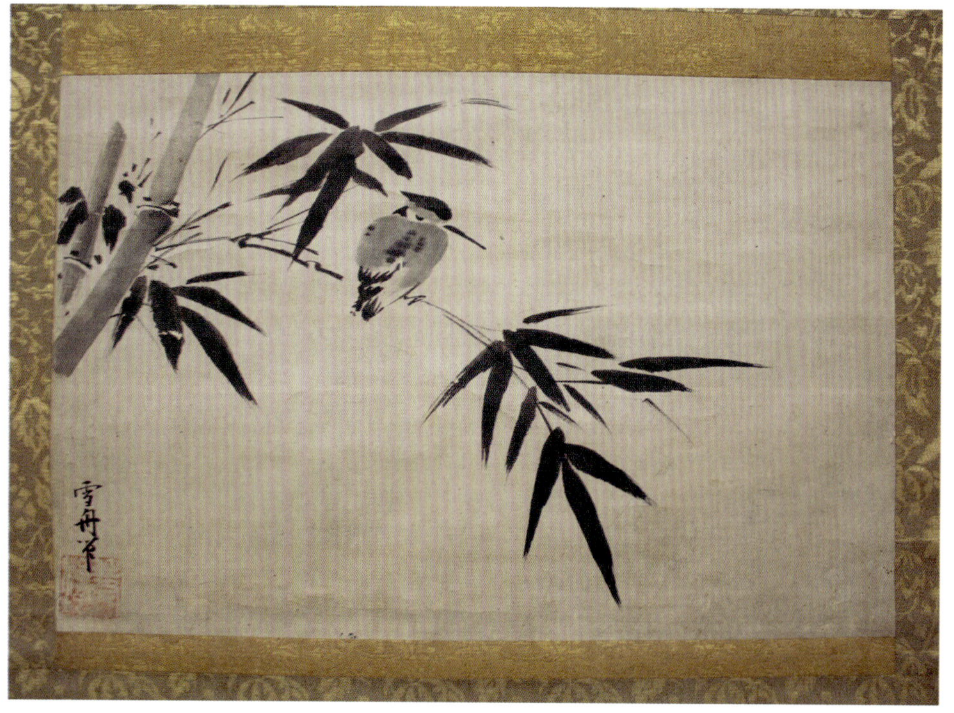

Kingfisher and Bamboo – hanging scroll in the style of Sesshu Toyo, nineteenth century. © The Metropolitan Museum of Art, New York, Charles Stewart Smith Collection, Gift of Mrs. Charles Stewart Smith, Charles Stewart Smith Jr., and Howard Caswell Smith, in memory of Charles Stewart Smith, 1914.

A SHORT HISTORY OF SUIBOKUGA

'Sumi-e' (墨絵) is a Japanese style of monochrome ink painting that uses black ink, carefully balanced with negative space, to distil and convey the essence of the subject. Its subset, 'Suibokuga' (水墨画), uses black ink washes to create a rich spectrum of shades that capture the subtle nuances of the natural world.

Originating in China during the Sung period (960–1279), Suibokuga was first introduced to Japan by Zen Buddhist monks around the end of the Kamakura era (1185–1333) and the beginning of the Muromachi period (1338–1573). However, it wasn't until the mid-fifteenth century that this art form really gained popularity in Japan, catalysed by Sesshu Toyo (雪舟等楊), a Zen Buddhist monk and skilled painter.

Born in 1420, Sesshu was enrolled at the local Houfuku-ji temple at the age of 12, when he joined the monkhood. In his late adolescent years, he relocated to Kyoto Shoukoku-ji temple where he continued his Zen training and became a disciple of the esteemed painter, Tensho Shubun (天章周文).

While his artistic talents were inherent, 1467 marked a pivotal shift; the year when Sesshu travelled to Ming Dynasty China to study ink painting techniques from the great masters while accompanying the Japanese envoy. Disillusioned with contemporary Chinese paintings, which he found devoid of spiritual sensibility, he sought solace and inspiration in the vast and numinous landscapes of the south, which he later referred to as his greatest teachers.

Upon his return to Japan, Sesshu opened an art studio in Oita before settling down in his atelier, Unkoku-an, in Yamaguchi prefecture. Here, he trained his disciples and transcribed his indelible experiences of the Chinese landscapes through his paintings; the majority of his still extant works are thought to have been produced here.

With his innovative style blending traditional Chinese painting techniques with Japanese aesthetics, Sesshu became one of the most distinguished Japanese painters of his era, and his influence can be seen in later generations of ink painters.

Infused with the contemplative practices of Zen Buddhism and a deep reverence for the natural world, Suibokuga typically captures vast, unearthly landscapes, with towering mountains and mist-laden valleys that transport the viewer to otherworldly realms. Close-up compositions that trace the veins of leaves and the gradations of petals are also commonly used, paying homage to nature's intricacies.

Through the artist's skilled, precise and simplified brushwork, the spirit of the subject is given form, using only the essential brushstrokes and colours. As the renowned Tang dynasty art historian, painter and calligrapher Zhang Yanyuan (張彥遠) said, 'If by using ink a painter can allude to the five colours, we say that he has grasped the mind. But if an artist's mind is fixed on true colours, the essence of things will escape him.'

The true mastery of ink lies not in the imitation of colours, but in the artist's ability to evoke the essence of the subject through its subtle shades. In the simplicity of black ink, the artist is free to reveal their inner self and capture the 'mind'.

KEY FEATURES OF SUIBOKUGA

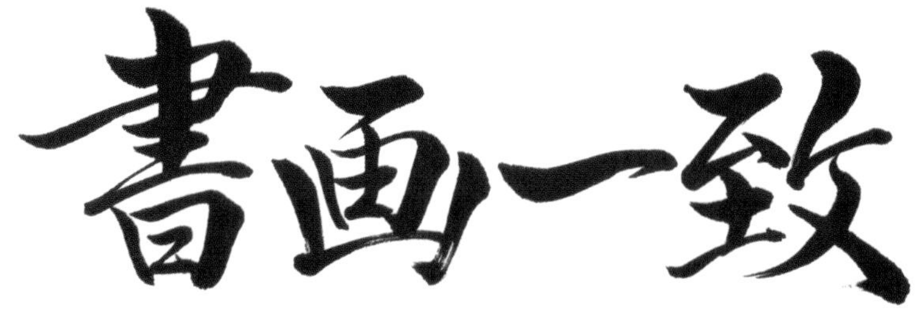

SHOGAICCHI (書画一致)

The unity of Shodo (Japanese calligraphy) and Suibokuga

This Zen Buddhist teaching holds that calligraphy and painting are one and the same. More than mere artistic endeavours, they are also paths to enlightenment. To practise 'Shogaicchi' is to lose oneself in the act of creation.

SHAI (写意)

To express not what one sees but what one feels

In Suibokuga, 'Shai' is the use of abstract forms and spiritual intuition to capture the essence of the subject. This stands in contrast to the concept of 'Shajitsu' (写実), which is to paint a realistic representation of the subject.

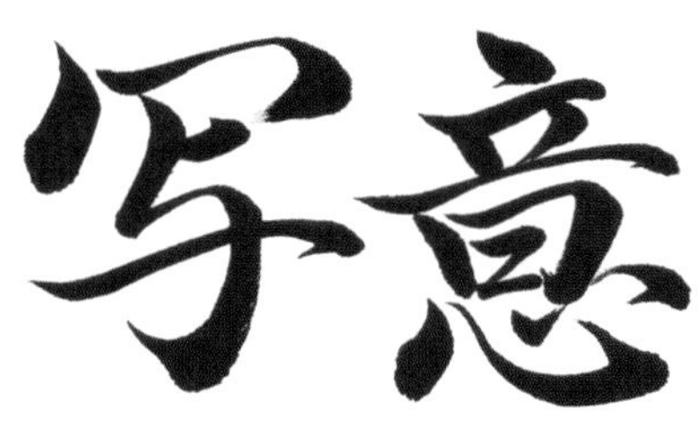

MA (間)

Emptiness or negative space

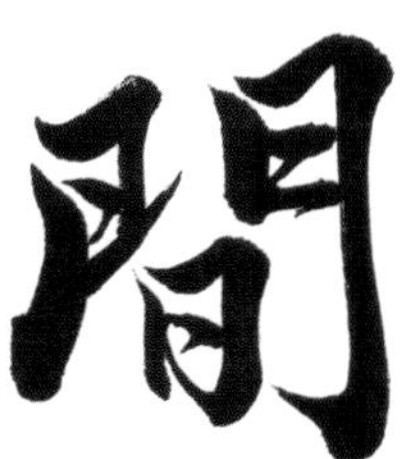

The Zen concept 'Ma' denotes the space that exists between objects. It is deeply ingrained in Japanese culture and can be observed in daily life, from the pause in a conversation to a silent interlude in a musical piece.

Ma is particularly important in calligraphy and Suibokuga, where the vitality of each brushstroke can only be observed by virtue of the emptiness that lies in between. When used effectively, it can create depth, form and balance that flows through the painting and transcends the confines of the paper.

ISSHIN (一心)

One mind

The Zen principle 'Isshin' refers to a state of focused attention, and is deeply intertwined with the practice of Zazen, or seated meditation.

In calligraphy and Suibokuga, it is a moment of complete immersion, where the artist's entire being is attuned to the present moment and the brush flows of its own accord. By bringing the same awareness cultivated during Zazen to the act of creation, the artist can express their innermost self.

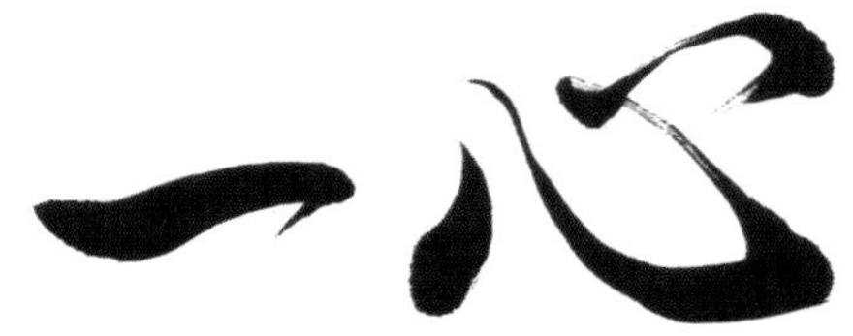

HISSEI (筆勢)

Brushwork

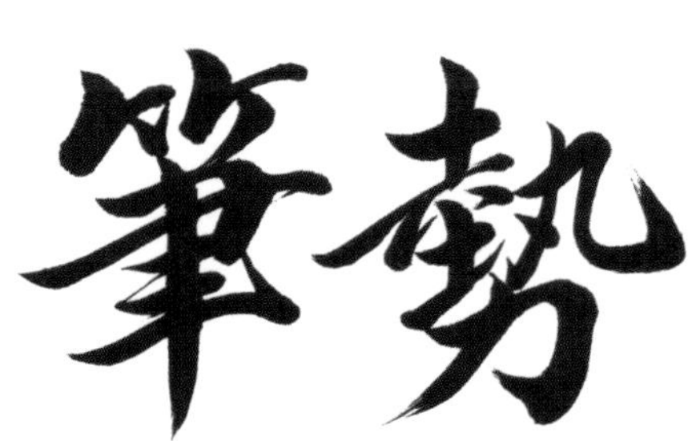

'Hissei' is the use of speed, rhythm and pressure control to facilitate the seamless and uninterrupted flow of energy through the brush. It is a technique that demands dedication to practise the same stroke a thousand times over, until the brush can be controlled with the same dexterity as moving a limb. Once the brush touches the paper, the mark it leaves is irreversible, making mastery of 'Hissei' essential for the artist to imbue their works with both strength and sensitivity.

CHOUBOKU (調墨)

Ink control

'There are five colours in ink' ('墨に五彩あり'). This well-known adage in Suibokuga embodies the idea that the skilful control of ink density, the wet or dry application of the brush and the manipulation of water can express all the colours, tonal values and nuances found in nature. Achieving this level of expression is to master 'Chouboku', such as kasure (broken lines), nijimi (bleeding), bokashi (ink blurring), and the use of different ink shades and gradations.

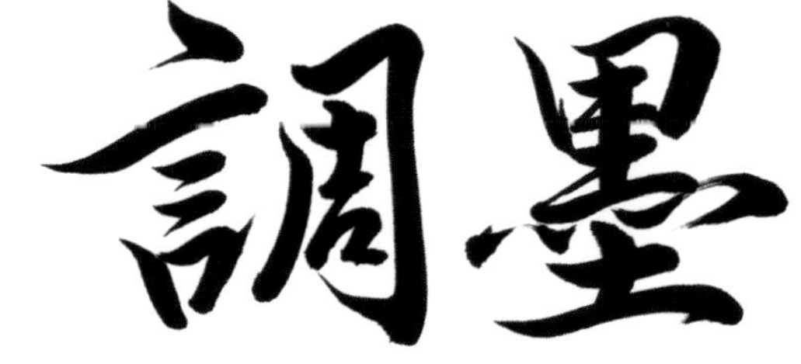

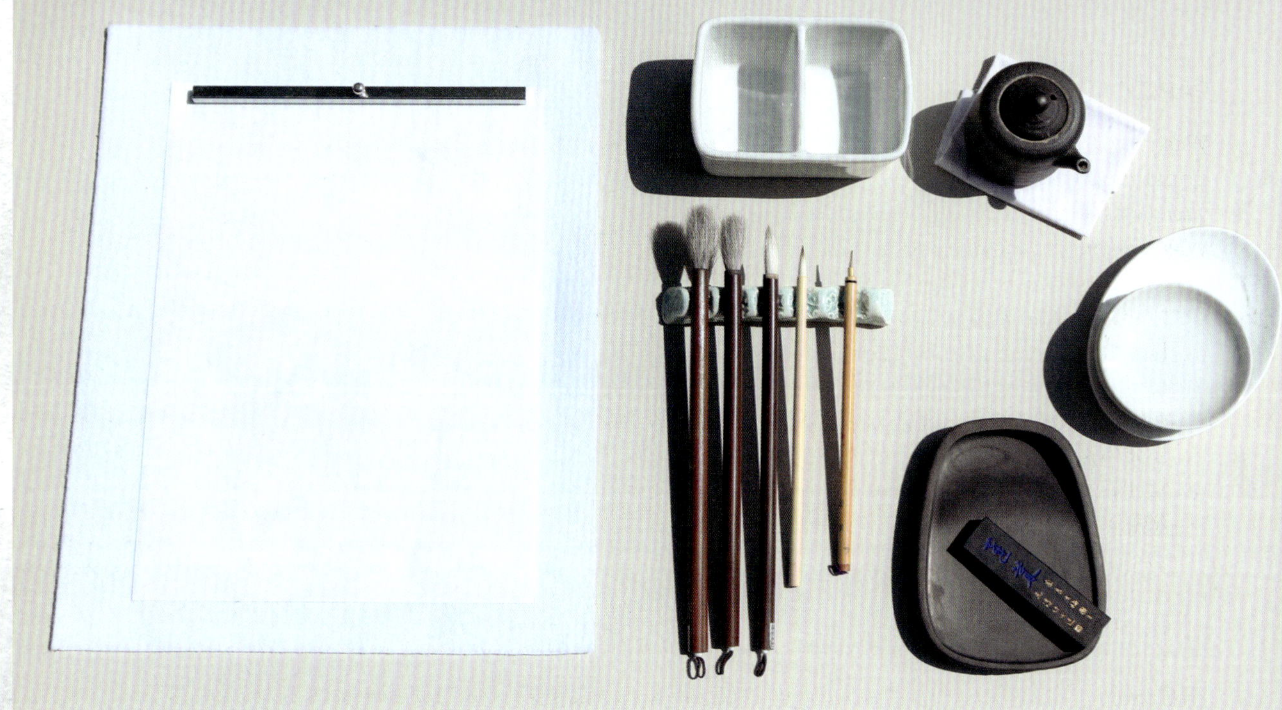

MATERIALS

The four essential tools used in calligraphy and Suibokuga, also referred to as the 'Four Treasures of the Study' (文房四宝), are:

- **PAPER** (Kami/Shi; 紙)
- **BRUSH** (Fude/Hitsu; 筆)
- **INK** (Sumi/Boku; 墨)
- **INKSTONE** (Suzuri/Ken; 硯)

In addition to the 'Four Treasures of the Study', the exercises covered in this book will require the following materials:

- Felt cloth to place underneath the paper and absorb excess water and ink (Shitajiki; 下敷き).
- Paperweight to stabilise and hold the paper in place (Bunchin; 文鎮).
- Jar of water to wash the used brushes (Hissen; 筆洗).
- Three or more small plates to mix and dilute the ink with water and create different shades of grey. It is recommended to use white plates as they provide better visibility for determining the density of the inks (Ezara; 絵皿).
- Flat plate to blend the ink for Chouboku (ink control) and reshape the brush.
- White cloth or kitchen towel to wipe excess ink from the brush and control the ink density.
- Water pot to provide a source of clean water, which is then transferred to the Ezara to create different shades of ink.

Following the layout in the image above, place the paper on the felt shitajiki, and then use the paperweight to hold it in place. If you are right-handed, place the brushes, inkstone, inkstick, plates, water and white cloth towards the right of the paper. If you are left-handed, place them towards your left.

PAPER

Washi (和紙) refers to paper made from traditional Japanese manufacturing methods using a variety of long natural fibres. Common types of Washi paper include:

- **KOZO PAPER** (Kozoshi/Choshi; 楮紙) – made from the inner bark of the kozo (mulberry) tree.
- **GANPI PAPER**/Ganpishi (雁皮紙) – made from the gampi plant.
- **MITSUMATA PAPER** (Mitsumatashi; 三椏紙) – made from the inner bark of the mitsumata shrub.
- **ASA PAPER** (Asashi/Mashi; 麻紙) – made from the inner bark of the hemp plant.

There are also various papers made from a combination of different plant fibres and raw materials.

Another commonly used paper is Gasen paper (Gasenshi; 画仙紙), which refers to the Japanese imitation of Chinese Xuan papers (Senshi). These Xuan papers are traditionally made from blue sandalwood, as well as rice, bamboo, paper mulberry and other fibres. In Japan, it is now made from a blend of various fibres including mitsumata, kozo, rice straw and bamboo.

Both within and across these categories, there is a notable variation in the characteristics of the paper, including its thickness, absorbency and tensile strength, which profoundly impacts how the ink spreads and interacts with the fibres, as well as how the colour is expressed.

When choosing paper, the key properties to consider are the paper's ability to accentuate nijimi, sujime and tonal gradations. Experiment with various paper types and explore how the same ink effect manifests differently on various papers. Most of the artworks in this book have been painted on Kozo-shi and Gasenshi, sized 333 x 242 mm (approximately B4).

Nijimi (滲み)

Nijimi, or the bleeding effect, refers to the diffusion of ink beyond the original brush-stroke when a wet brush is applied to paper. To test for nijimi, drop a few water droplets onto the paper – if the water disperses immediately, it is high nijimi.

Sujimi (筋目)

Sujimi refers to the effect of visual separation that occurs when ink touches and repels. This creates a white streak in between the strokes that cannot be painted over, known as Mu (無).

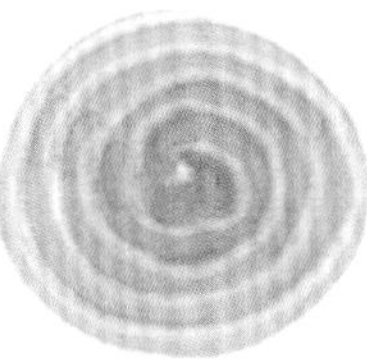

KEY POINTS

- Japanese paper suppliers often provide information about the level of nijimi the paper allows, which can guide the selection process. Beginners should select papers labelled moderate nijimi, as excessive nijimi can make ink control challenging.
- In addition to traditional paper, mixed-pulp and synthetic papers are useful for brush technique and ink control practice and are readily available and affordable. Steer clear of printing or Western watercolour paper, as they typically have low absorbance, which restricts the desired nijimi, sujime and tonal gradations.
- Washi has one smooth side and one slightly rough side. While the smooth side of the paper is traditionally used for Suibokuga painting for its greater absorption effects, depending on the paper type, the rough side can yield better results.

BRUSHES

The brush handle is typically crafted from bamboo, and the bristles are made from a combination of animal hair - such as goat, horse or weasel hair - or synthetic fibres. Each type of hair has a specific ink capacity and when bundled together, creates brushes of various textures (soft, medium and hard), shapes and sizes. The mixed-hair brush - which is made from a combination of hard hair for the core surrounded by soft hair - is particularly versatile and can be used for both delicate and bold strokes.

Mastery of the brush requires an intimate understanding of its characteristics and capabilities - the various brush types, their absorbency, flexibility and how they interact with different types of paper. This understanding develops through experimentation and forms part of the creative process.

For the exercises outlined in this book, it is recommended to use at least three brushes with varying tip lengths:

1. ŌFUDE (大筆): a medium or large brush with 3.0–4.5cm-length bristles, for example, the tsuketate-fude.
2. KOFUDE (小筆): a small brush with 1.6–2.0cm-length bristles, for example, the sakuyo-fude.
3. MENSOU-FUDE (面相筆): an even smaller and thinner brush with 1.0–1.5cm-length bristles, for example, the menso-fude.

All the exercises in this book have been completed using using the three brush types outlined below. While the menso-fude is useful for detailed and precise brushwork, the tip of the kofude can also be used.

Tsuketate-fude (付立筆)

A mixed-hair brush commonly made with a combination of soft, flexible sheep hair and hard deer, horse and racoon dog hairs. It has great absorbency and was fashioned for the tsuketate-hou technique (see p. 32), which involves painting without outlines or contours.

Sakuyo-fude (削用筆)

The sakuyo-fude is a smaller brush, typically made with a core of strong weasel and white racoon dog hair, surrounded by soft goat hair. As a mixed-hair brush, it is flexible, absorbent, easy to control and suitable for creating thin and wide lines through pressure control.

Menso-fude (面相筆)

A small brush designed with a sharp tip, typically made from hard weasel, badger or deer hair. Originally intended for drawing thin lines on dolls' faces to define the eyebrows and other delicate features, this brush is suited for painting fine, precise lines.

If possible, invest in Japanese or Chinese brushes and avoid Western watercolour paintbrushes.

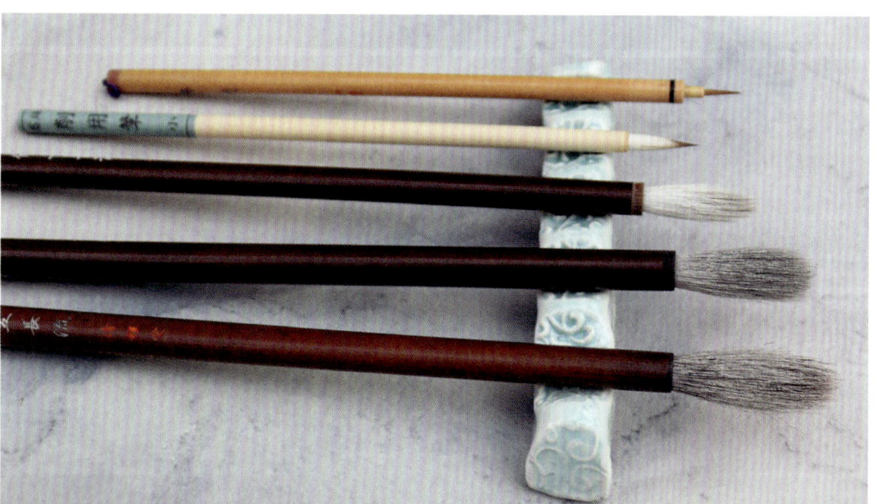

BOTTOM TO TOP Three tsuketate-fude brushes, a sakuyo-fude brush and a menso-fude brush.

INK

The first step in painting is to grind the inkstick on an inkstone to produce freshly ground ink, also known as sumi. This process of ink preparation is considered a form of meditative practice, cultivating awareness and preparing the mind for painting.

The inkstick is a compressed mixture of vegetable or pine soot, fragrance and nikawa glue (traditional, natural Japanese adhesive made from the skin and bones of animals), and can be broadly categorised into shouenboku and yuenboku.

Shouenboku (松煙墨)

An inkstick made from burnt pinewood soot with a matte finish. The freshly ground ink typically yields a distinctive bluish-black hue, highly valued for its ability to evoke soft, mysterious landscapes.

Yuenboku (油煙墨)

An inkstick crafted from a blend of rapeseed or camellia soot and glue with a lustrous finish. Once ground, it typically produces ink with a rich, brownish-black hue and smooth consistency, which is particularly favoured for capturing warmth and nostalgia.

There are other forms of classification. For example, inksticks are categorised into Wasumi (和墨) inksticks made in Japan, and Touboku (唐墨) inksticks made in China. It is generally thought that Chinese inksticks are harder, due to the manufacturing process and higher animal glue content.

In addition, inksticks can be categorised into old and new. The animal glue in sumi deteriorates over time; this ageing and withering of sumi ink changes the viscosity and gives old ink a deeper, richer colour, which is highly sought after.

While bottled ink is useful for beginners to practise, it typically uses synthetic resin as an adhesive and lacks the depth that freshly ground ink can offer.

INKSTONE

The inkstone, the last of the 'Four Treasures of the Study', is used to grind the inkstick into liquid ink. Most commonly handcrafted from slate, the inkstone is ground and polished by inkstone artisans by methods that have been passed down from generation to generation.

The inkstone consists of a flat surface (known as 'oka'; 陸) for grinding and a reservoir (known

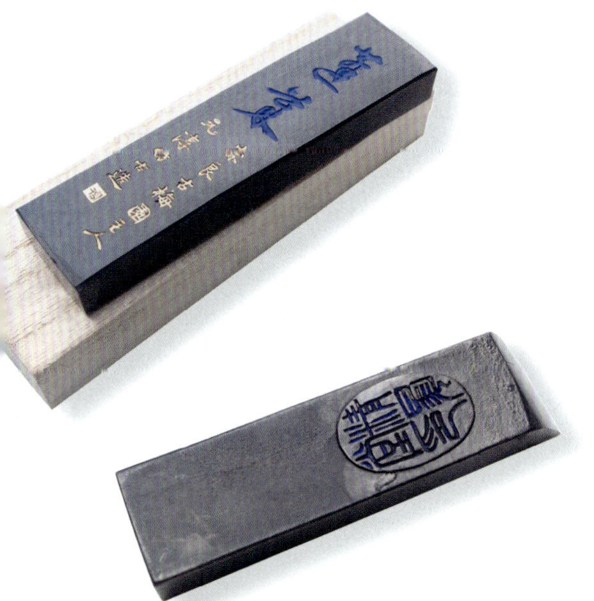

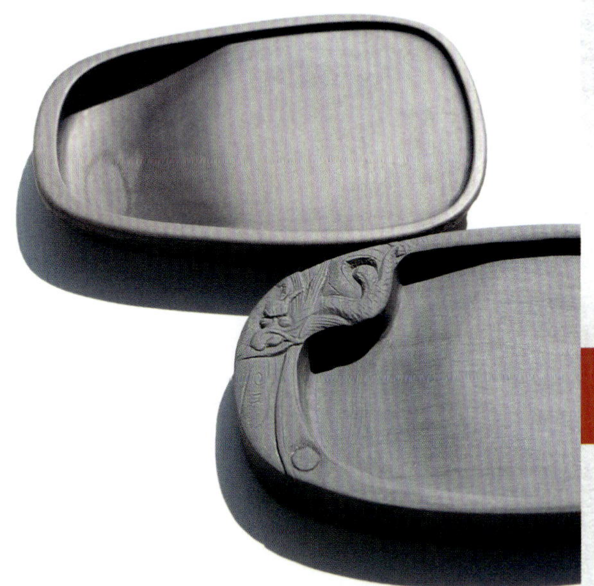

as 'umi'; 海) for holding water. The flat surface of the inkstone has a slightly coarse texture, which is referred to as Houbou (鋒鋩). Different inkstones vary in stone hardness and have a different texture and density of Houbou; this in turn affects the colour and texture of the freshly ground ink.

Inkstones can be broadly categorised into Waken and Touken:

Waken (和硯)

Inkstones made in Japan. A few of the most noble include Akama, Ogatsu and Amehata, which are produced in different prefectures.

Touken (唐硯):

Inkstones made in China. A few of the most highly regarded include the Duan and She inkstones.

As a general principle, Chinese inkstones are harder with a stronger Houbou than their Japanese counterpart. To avoid scratching and damaging the Houbou of the inkstone, the inkstick should be softer than the inkstone. It is therefore advisable to use Japanese inksticks with Japanese inkstones, and Chinese inksticks with Chinese inkstones. Within these categories, Shouenboku is typically harder than Yuenboku, therefore Shouenboku should be used with a harder inkstone. Understanding the relationship between the inkstone and inkstick, and how one can complement the other, is essential as you develop your practice.

The flat surface of the inkstone can also be useful for certain ink effects, which we will cover in later chapters. Students using bottled ink won't require an inkstone – instead, use a flat plate for the ink control techniques.

HOW TO GRIND THE INKSTICK

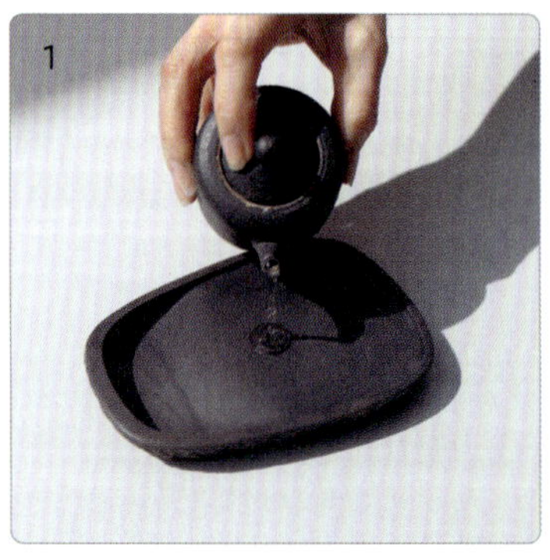
1

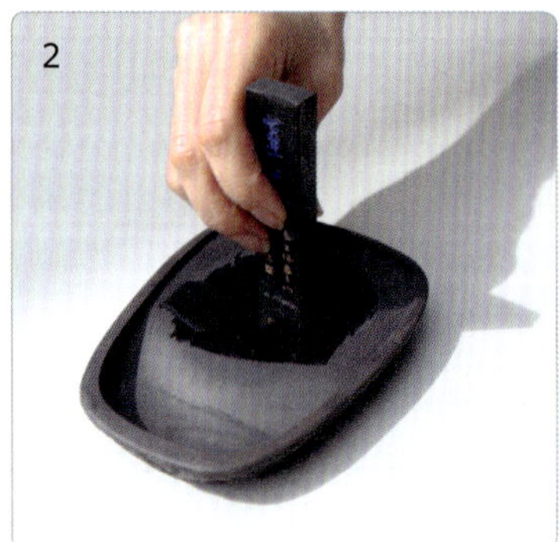
2

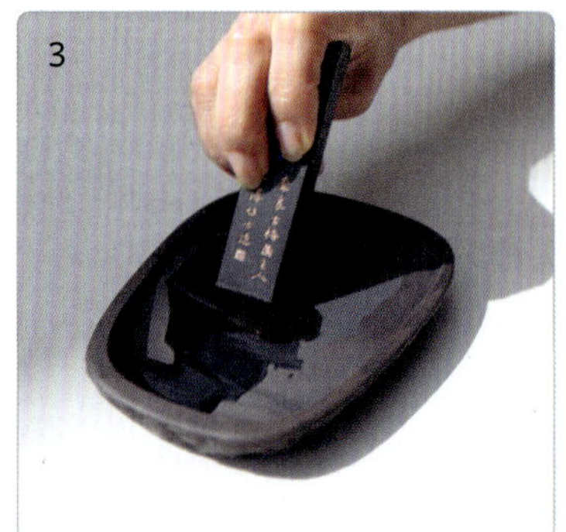
3

1. Begin by pouring approximately a teaspoon of clean water onto the flat surface ('oka') of the inkstone.

2. Hold the inkstick upright or at a slight angle, and slowly grind against the flat surface of the inkstone in a circular motion or along a straight line, maintaining a consistent speed and pressure. Continue this motion until the ink becomes thick and glossy in appearance. Add another teaspoon of water and repeat this step (adjust the amount of water according to the amount of ink desired).

3. Once enough ink has been made, use the inkstick to push the ink into the reservoir ('umi'). The freshly ground ink is referred to as **nouboku**, and it is the darkest and richest shade of ink.

BASIC TECHNIQUES

CHOUBOKU (INK DENSITY)

Chouboku (調墨) is a technique used to create distinct shades of ink washes. The process involves taking nouboku (dark ink), either freshly ground or bottled, and diluting it with water to create various shades of grey. Here we will prepare nouboku (dark), chuboku (medium-dark), tanboku (light) and goku-tanboku (very light).

1. Pour an equal volume of water into three separate plates.

2. Dip the tip or one-third of the brush in **nouboku** (濃墨).

3. Transfer the brush to the first plate and stir in the water to create **chuboku** (中墨). Wash the brush in clean water and remove excess water.

4. Dip the brush completely in chuboku, then transfer the brush to the second plate and stir in the water to create **tanboku** (淡墨).

5. Wash the brush again, dip the brush completely in tanboku, then transfer the brush to the third plate and stir in the water to create **goku-tanboku** (極淡墨).

6. Finally, check how the various ink densities appear on the paper.

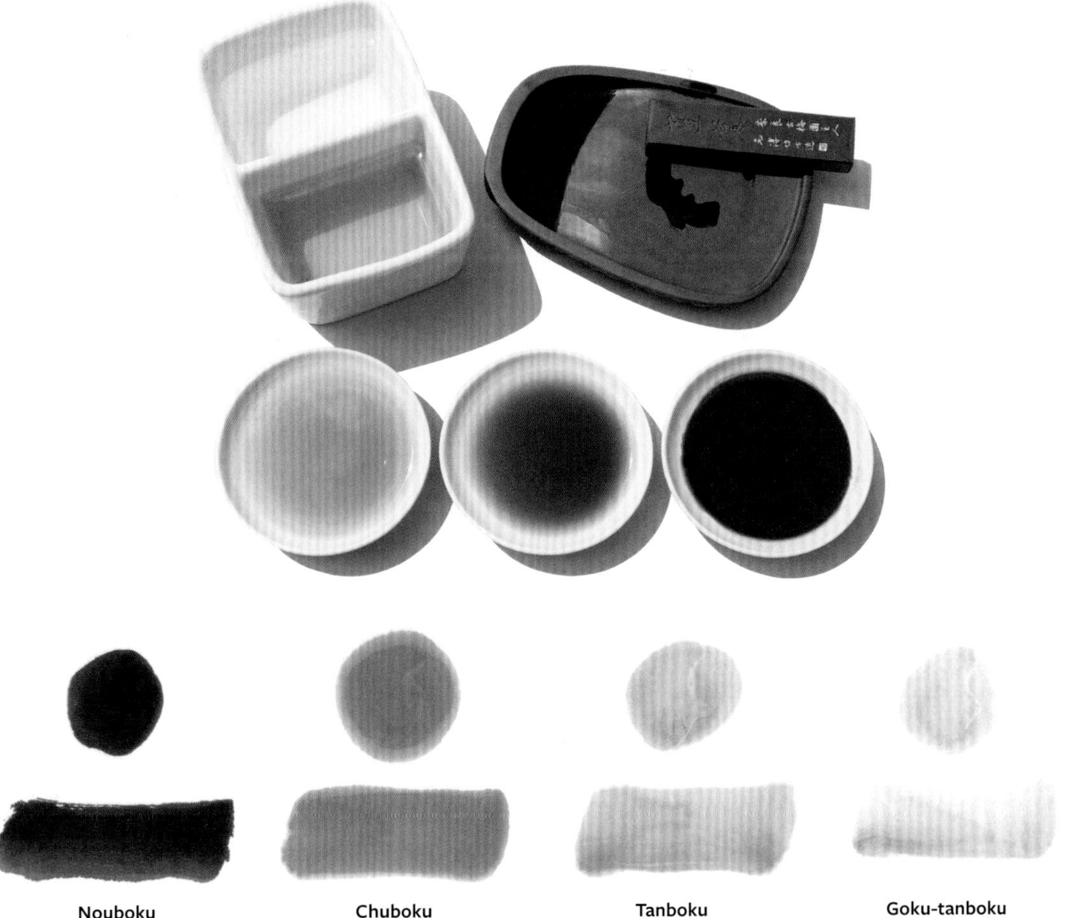

Nouboku **Chuboku** **Tanboku** **Goku-tanboku**

POSTURE AND BRUSH GRIP

In Suibokuga, achieving the desired brush-strokes and expressions is as dependent on the unity between body and mind as it is on practising the proper techniques. This requires a mindful focus on the inward sensations, including breath, posture and correct brush positioning.

Assume an upright posture, ensuring that your spine, neck and head are aligned. Let go of the tension in your fingers and clear your mind as you hold your brush. The two primary methods for holding the brush are soukou-hou and tankou-hou, and the two main methods for positioning the arm are kenwan-hou and teiwan-hou.

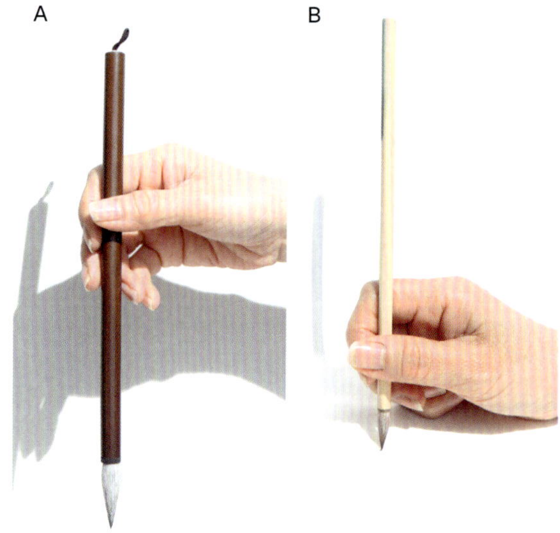

A. *Soukou-hou* (双鉤法)

Position the thumb, index finger and middle finger in front to grip the brush, and place the ring and little fingers at the back for support. This technique stabilises the brush and allows for greater control, particularly for larger movements.

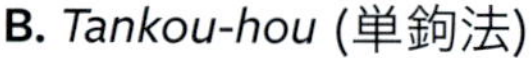

B. *Tankou-hou* (単鉤法)

Position the thumb and index finger in front to grip the brush, and place the middle, ring and little fingers at the back for support. This technique is commonly used when working with a small brush. Hold the brush where the bristles join the handle.

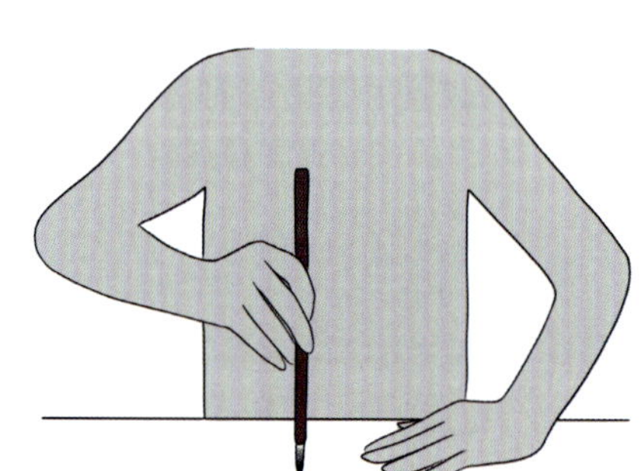

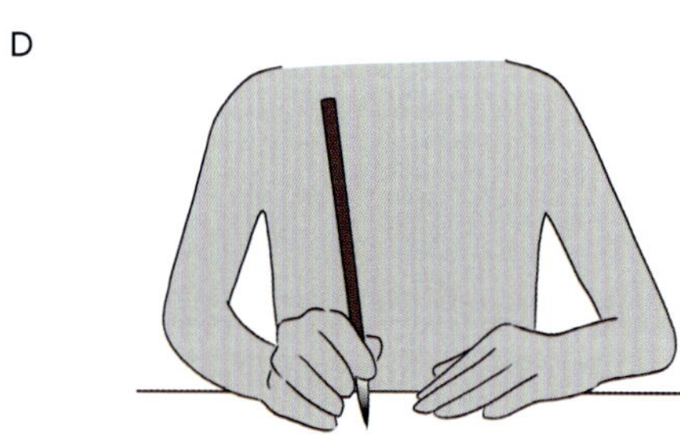

C. *Kenwan-hou* (懸腕法)

Lift the elbow midway between the table and the shoulder. This position allows for more freedom and ease when executing larger, broader movements.

D. *Teiwan-hou* (提腕法)

Rest the wrist gently on the table. This position allows for greater stability and control over the brush when executing smaller, more precise movements.

BRUSH MOVEMENT

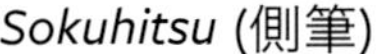

Chokuhitsu (直筆)

In chokuhitsu, the tip of the brush should run through the centre of the line. Combining this movement with pressure control can create varied lines, from uniform and linear lines of even thickness to wavy lines of uneven thickness.

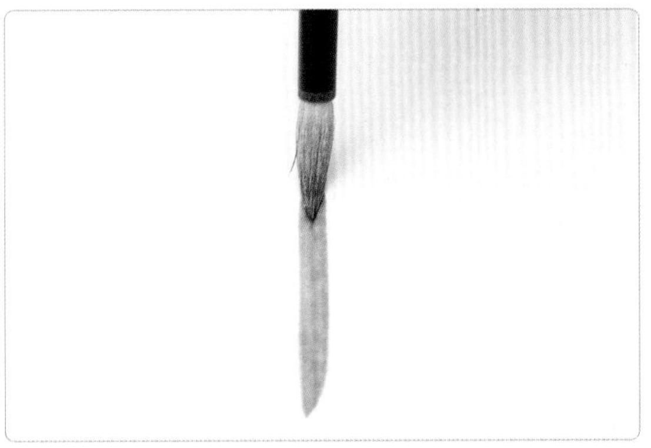

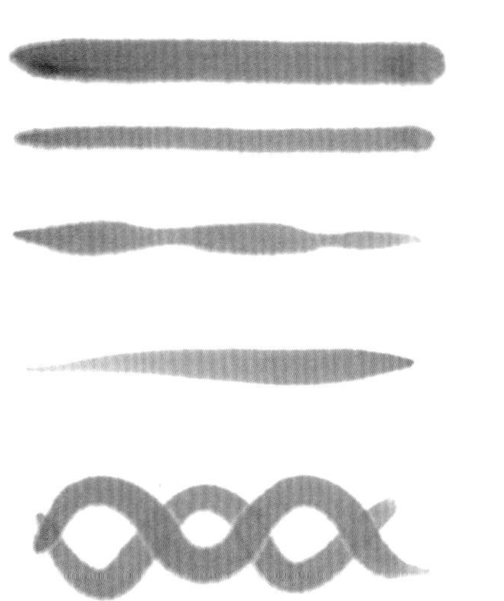

Sokuhitsu (側筆)

In sokuhitsu, the tip of the brush should mark one edge of the line. By adjusting the angle of the brush, the speed and the ink application, you can create various expressions.

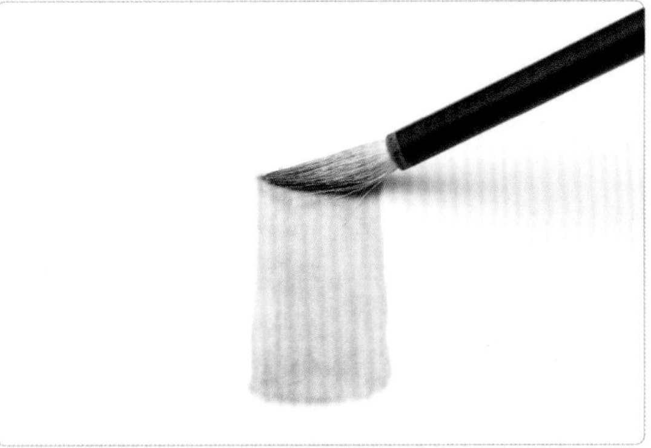

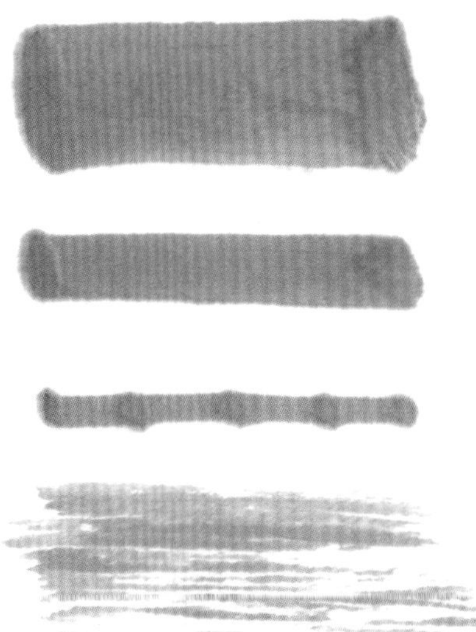

Hansokuhitsu (半側筆) *or 'semi-sokuhitsu'*

The brush is held in half-chokuhitsu and half-sokuhitsu. This technique allows you to create lines in various angles.

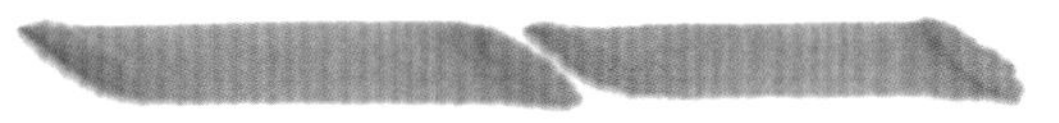

CHOUBOKU (INK CONTROL) AND BRUSH TECHNIQUES

Combining chokuhitsu and sokuhitsu techniques with chouboku (ink control) can convey an array of tones and nuances within a single stroke, producing various effects including sakiguma, kataguma, uchiguma, sotoguma, ryoguma, soft ryoguma, sanboku-hou, motoguma, haboku-hou and kasure, which we cover here.

Sakiguma (先隈)

Load the brush with tanboku, dip the tip in nouboku and paint a line in chokuhitsu. The resulting stroke should have a dark tip and transition smoothly from dark to light.

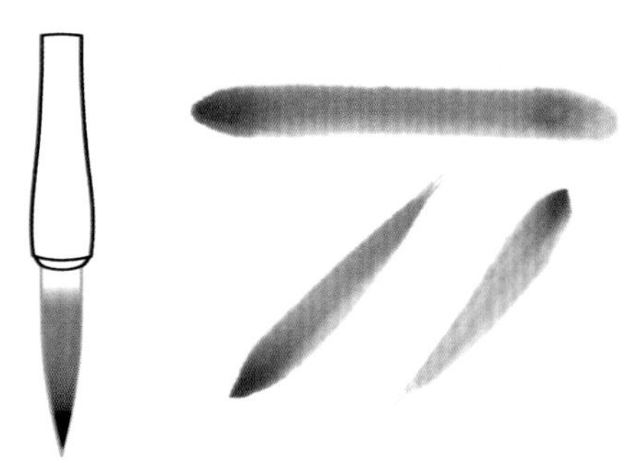

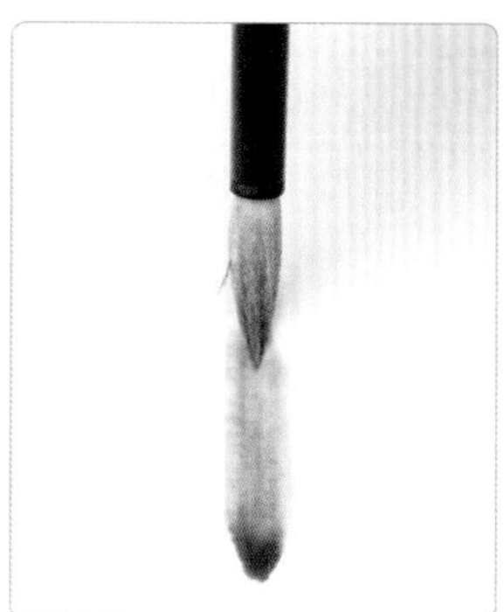

Kataguma sokuhitsu (片隈)

Prepare the brush in the same way as for sakiguma and paint a line in sokuhitsu. The resulting stroke should have one dark side, which is referred to as kataguma.

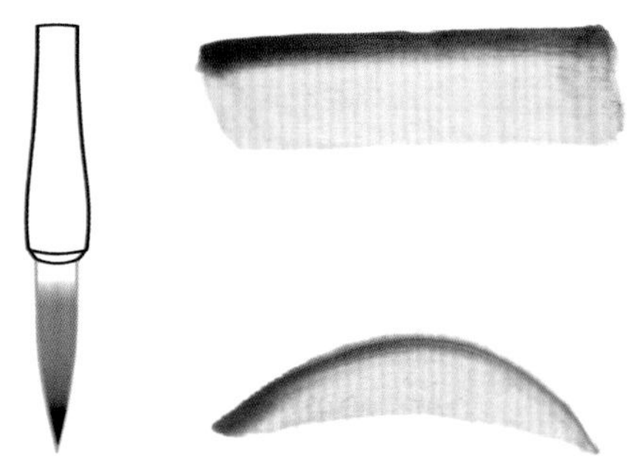

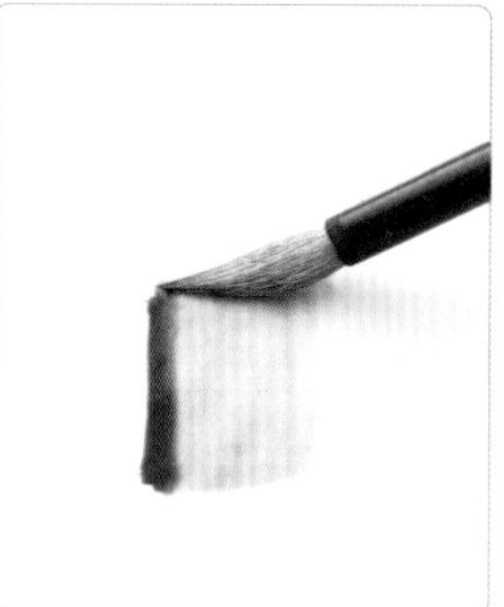

Kataguma chokuhitsu (片隈)

Load the brush with tanboku and flatten using the plate or your fingers. Rotate the brush 45 degrees and slide one edge against the oka of the inkstone to apply nouboku. (For those without an inkstone, prepare a thin, even layer of nouboku on the surface of a flat plate for this technique.) Paint a line in chokuhitsu. The resulting stroke should have one dark side.

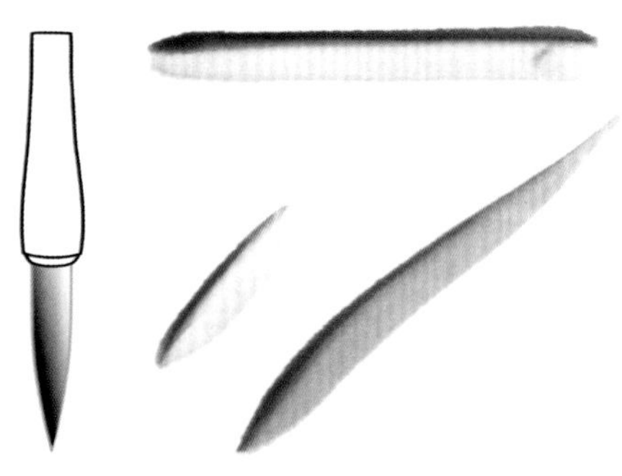

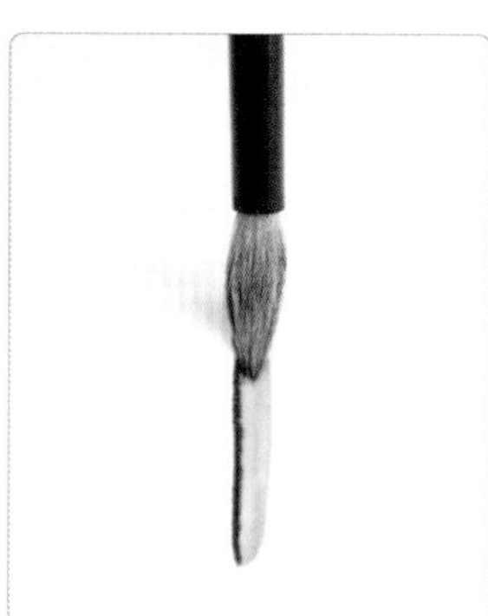

Uchiguma (内隈)

Prepare the brush in the same way as for the kataguma chokuhitsu and paint a line with the darker edge of the brush facing outwards. With this technique, you can create sharp, clear borderlines. It is particularly useful for painting spherical objects.

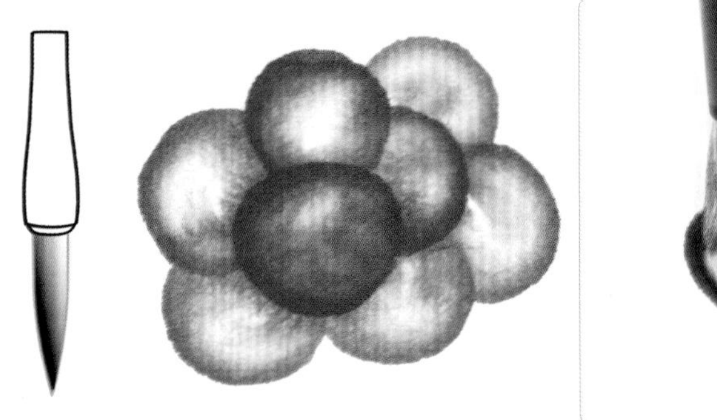

Sotoguma (外隈)

Prepare the brush in the same way as for the kataguma chokuhitsu and paint a line with the darker edge of the brush facing inwards. With this technique, you can create a darker inner ring, surrounded by a blurred lighter outer ring. It is often used to paint the moon.

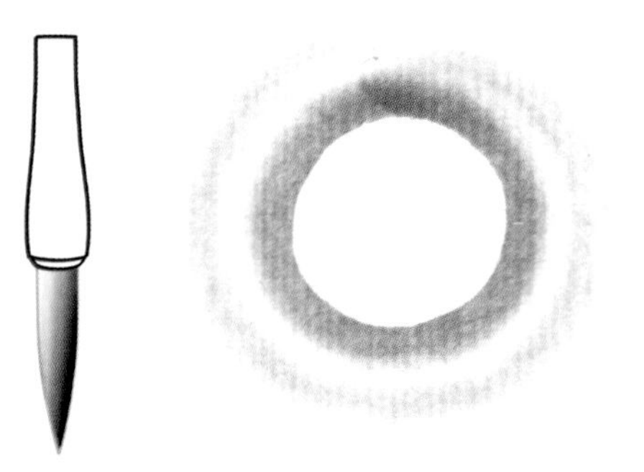

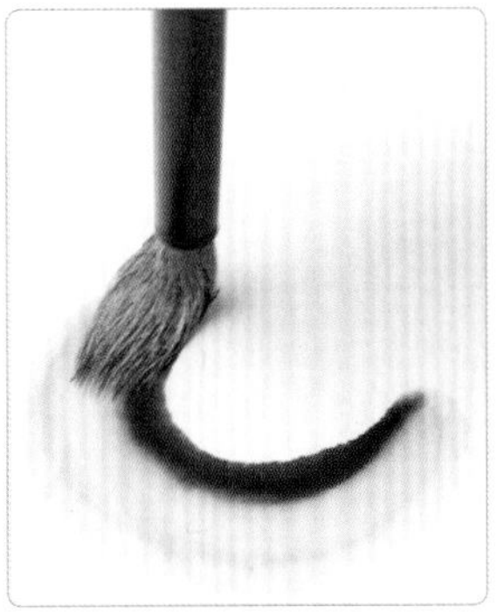

Ryoguma (両隈)

Load the brush with tanboku and flatten using the plate or your fingers. Rotate the brush 45 degrees and apply nouboku by sliding both edges of the brush against the oka of the inkstone (for those without an inkstone, prepare a thin, even layer of nouboku on the surface of a flat plate for this technique). Paint a line in chokuhitsu. The resulting stroke should have two dark sides.

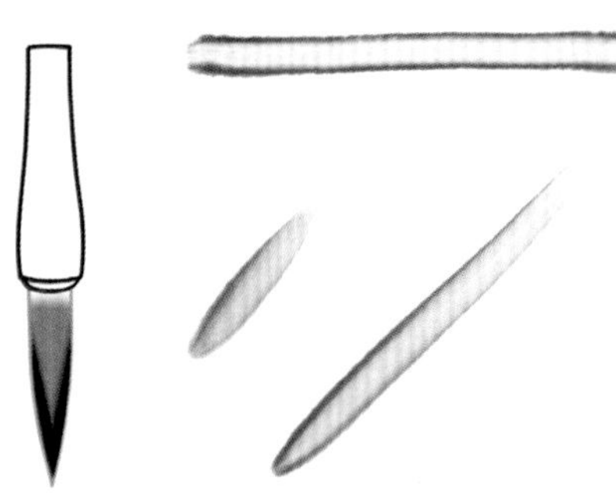

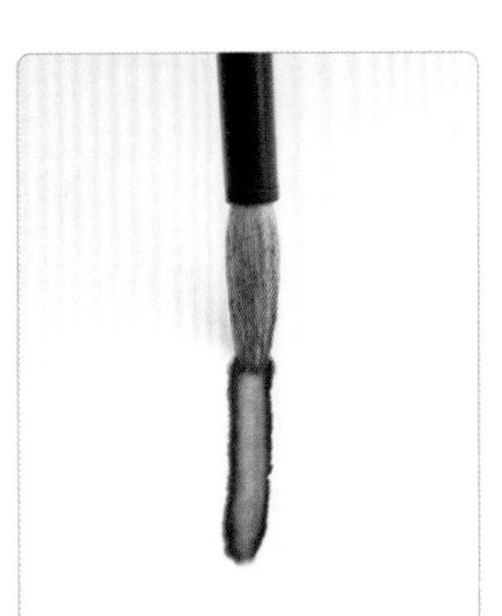

Soft ryoguma (淡い両隈)

The soft ryoguma technique prepares the brush with a darker upper section and a lighter lower section. It is particularly suited for painting thin leaves and petals, such as orchid petals, chrysanthemum petals and bamboo leaves.

1. Load the brush with chuboku and remove any excess ink by running the brush against the side of a plate or cloth.

2. Press one side of the brush onto the flat surface of the inkstone (oka), which should hold nouboku from the ink preparation step. If you are using bottled ink, use a flat plate with nouboku instead.

3. Lift the brush from the inkstone and flip it over to the other side, with the dark side facing up.

4. Paint a line, ensuring that the light side of the brush is in contact with the paper throughout each stroke.

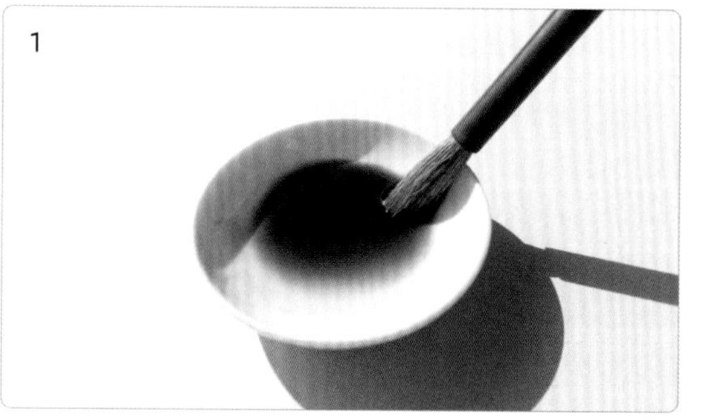

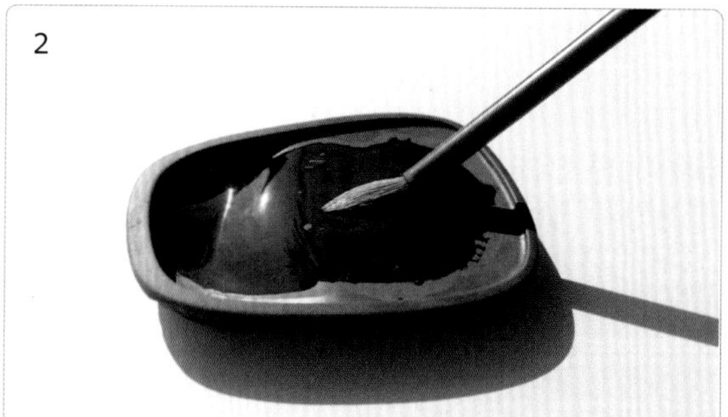

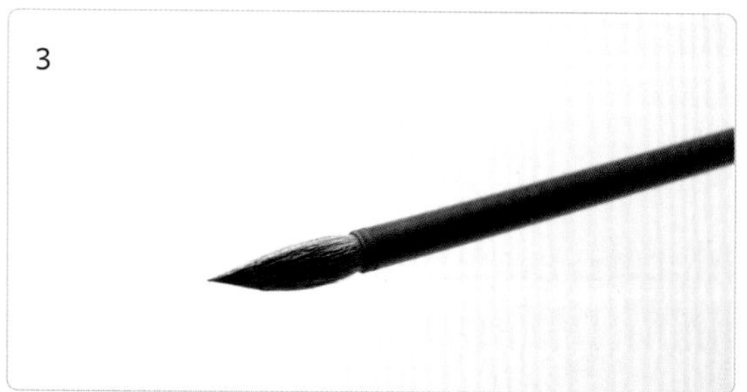

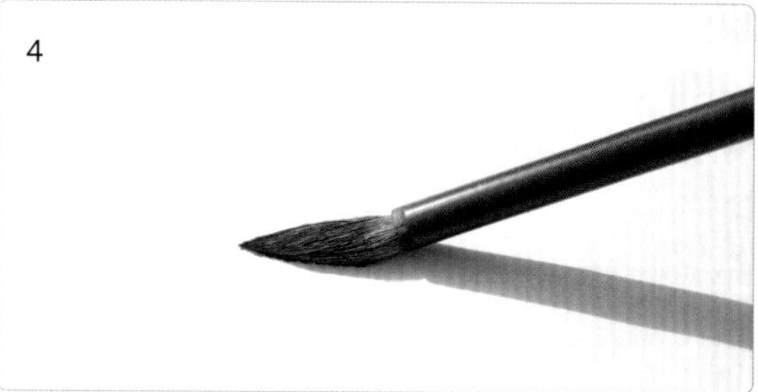

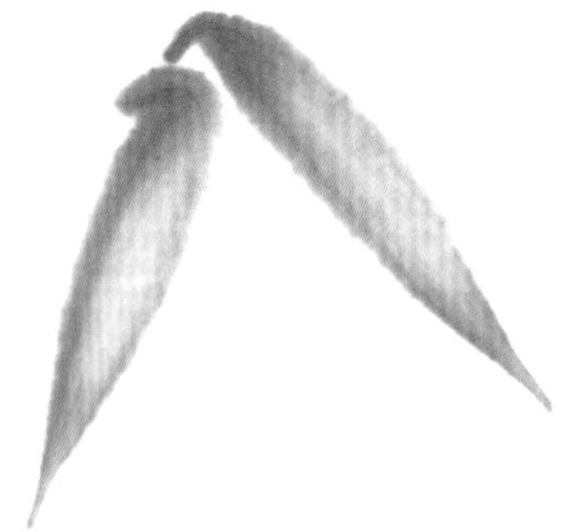

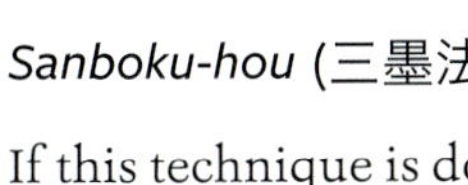

Sanboku-hou (三墨法)

If this technique is done correctly, you will see a gradient of light to dark within the line, which is referred to as sanboku-hou ('the three-ink technique').

1. Submerge the whole brush in tanboku and gently wipe off excess ink with a cloth.
2. Apply nouboku to the tip of the brush.
3. Turn the brush against a flat plate, pushing side to side to blend in the ink.
4. Dip the very tip of the brush in the nouboku again, then paint a line.

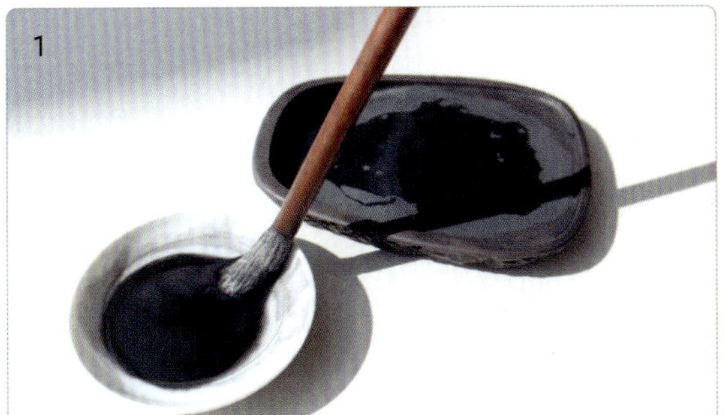

1

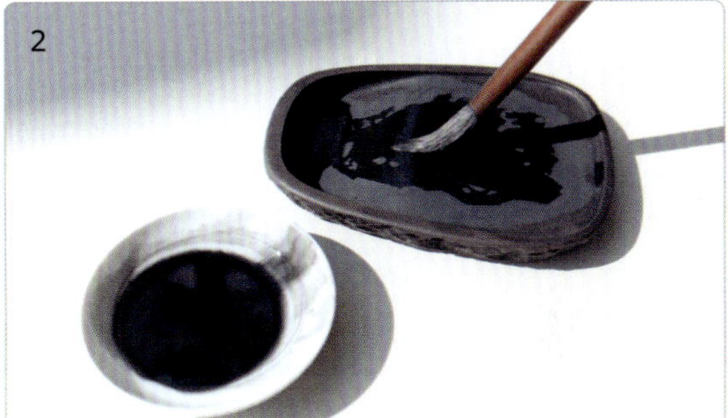

2

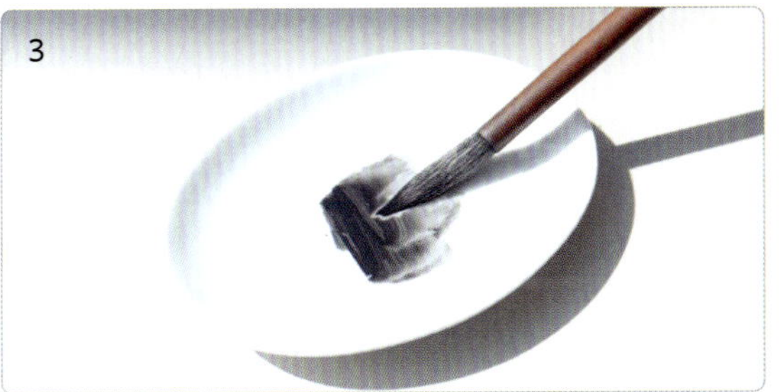

3

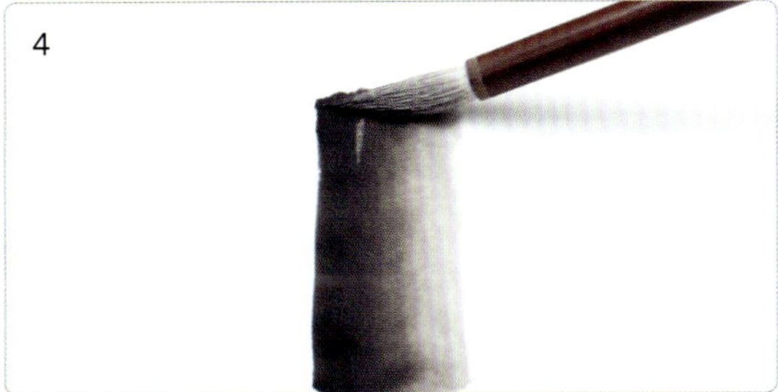

4

KEY POINTS

- In steps 1 and 2, we applied tanboku and nouboku respectively, however any shade of ink can be used, whether that is goku-tanboku, tanboku, chuboku or nouboku. The key element is having two separate shades of ink.
- Sanboku-hou can be prepared with the whole brush as outlined above or using only two-thirds or one-half of the brush to create a more concentrated gradient effect.

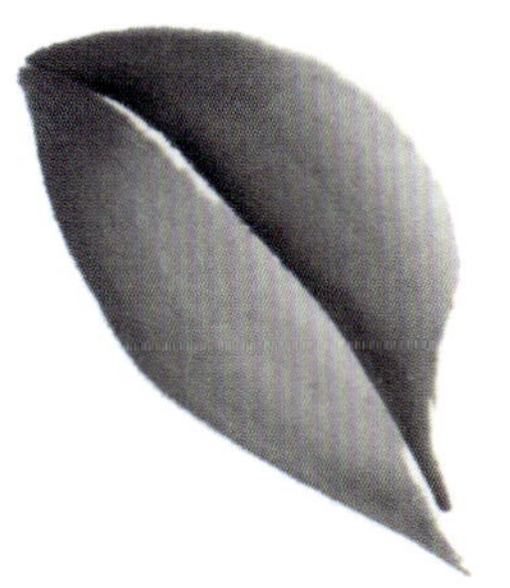

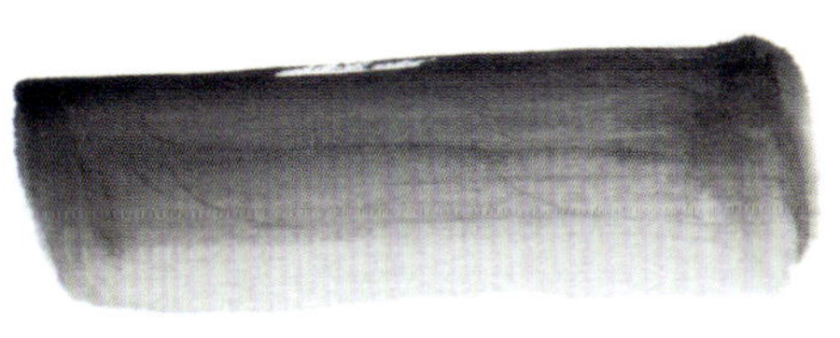

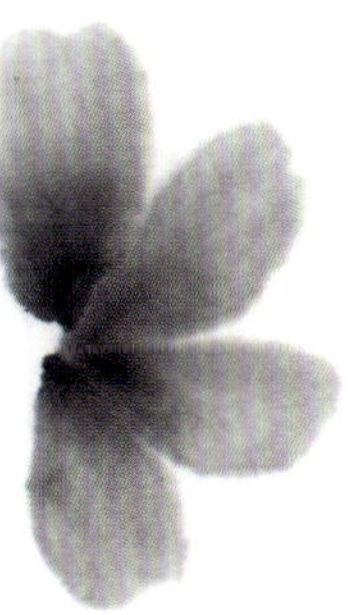

Motoguma (元隈)

The motoguma technique creates the same ink gradation as sanboku-hou, but uses darker ink for the root of the brush and lighter ink for the tip.
It is very effective at capturing round objects.

1. Load the brush with nouboku, ensuring the bristles are fully submerged in the ink (this can be done with other shades of ink, depending on the desired effect).

2. Wash the tip (approximately one-third) of the brush in a jar of clean water.

3. Optional: to enhance the motoguma effect, hold the brush upside down for a while and allow the ink to accumulate at the base of the brush. If necessary, gently wipe the brush with a cloth to remove excess water.

4. Paint a line, ensuring that the full surface of the brush touches the paper (painting in sokuhitsu enhances the motoguma effect).

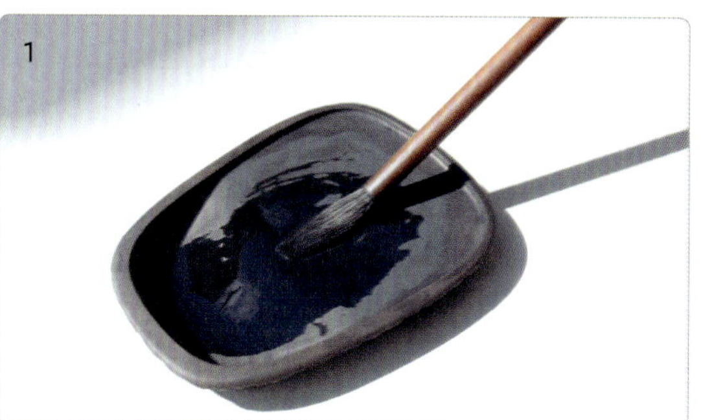
1

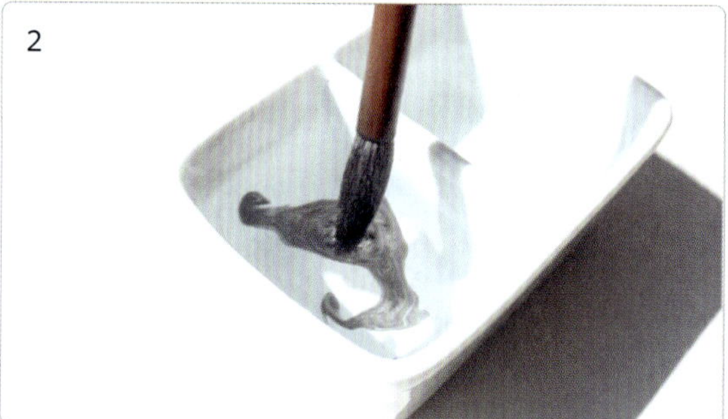
2

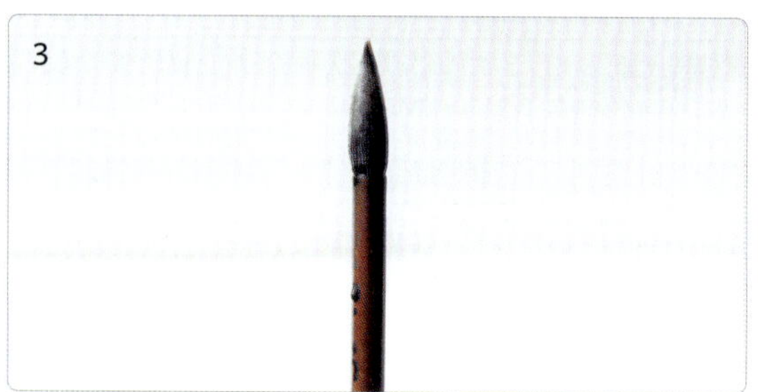
3

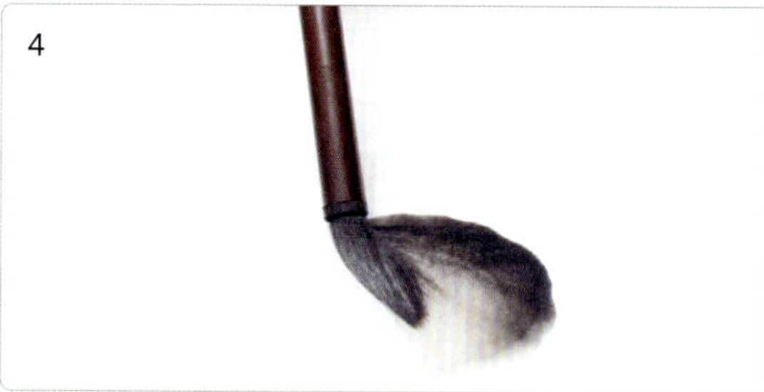
4

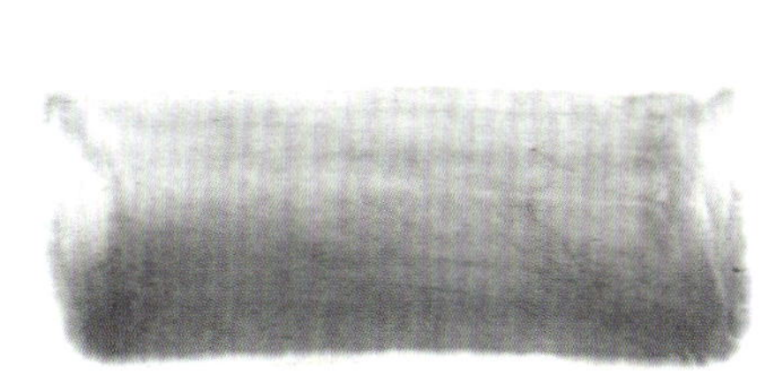

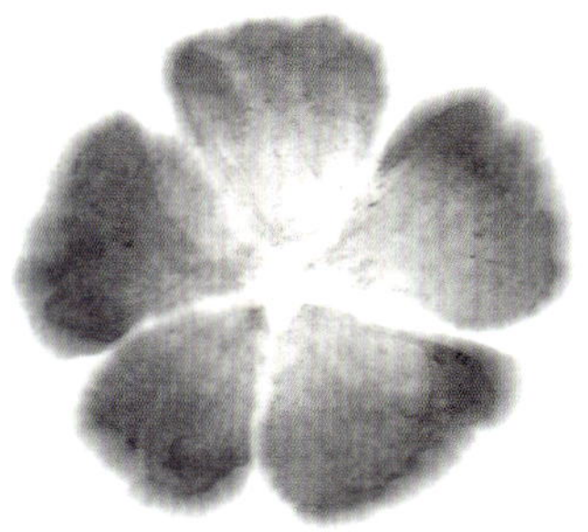

JUNPITSU-HOU & KAPPITSU-HOU

In Suibokuga, there are wet-brush techniques (junhitsu-hou) such as haboku-hou, which are effective at capturing soft and smooth lines, and dry-brush techniques (kappitsu-hou) such as kasure which are effective at capturing rough and coarse lines.

Junpitsu-hou

Haboku-hou (破墨法)

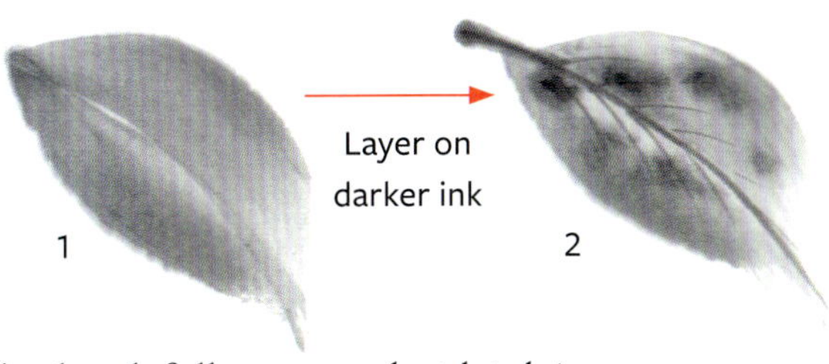

This technique involves painting with light ink and applying an additional layer of darker ink while the paper is still wet. This creates a natural bleeding effect, known as nijimi (see p. 19).

As an additional step, once the ink is dry, paint the veins using the tip of the kofude in darker ink.

Other wet-brush techniques involve painting with a brush fully saturated with ink/water or painting on a wet piece of paper to enhance the nijimi (bleeding) or bokashi (blurring) effects, which will be introduced on p. 123.

Kappitsu-hou

Kasure (掠れ)

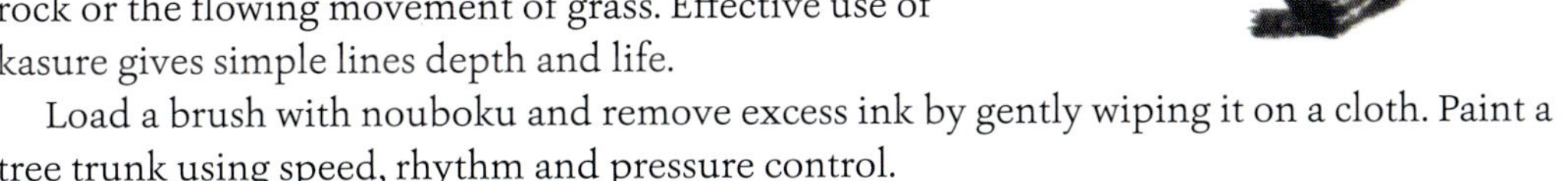

A technique that involves painting with a dry brush and creating coarse, broken and asymmetrical strokes. It is commonly used to capture elements of the natural world – the gnarled bark of a tree, the rough surface of a rock or the flowing movement of grass. Effective use of kasure gives simple lines depth and life.

Load a brush with nouboku and remove excess ink by gently wiping it on a cloth. Paint a tree trunk using speed, rhythm and pressure control.

Alternatively, load a brush with nouboku, remove excess ink and reshape the bristles to twist or spread out:

Nejiri-fude (ねじり筆)

A painting technique using a brush with dry, twisted bristles.

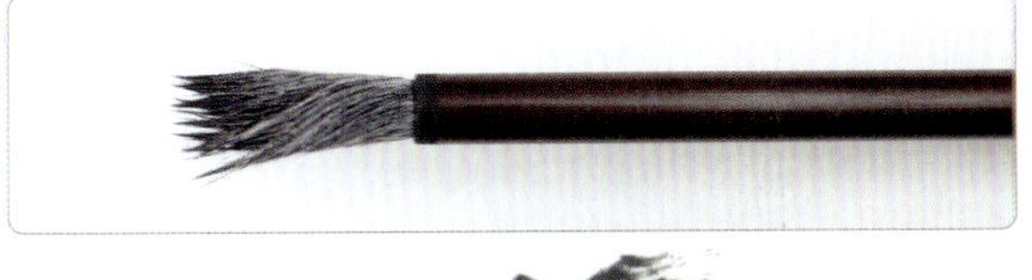

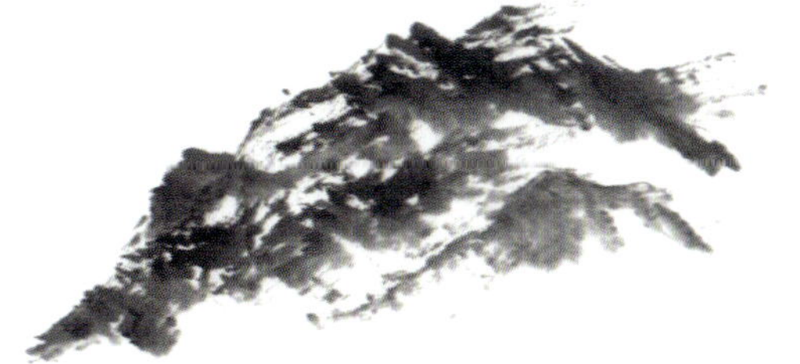

Wari-fude (割筆)

A painting technique using a brush with dry, spread-out bristles.

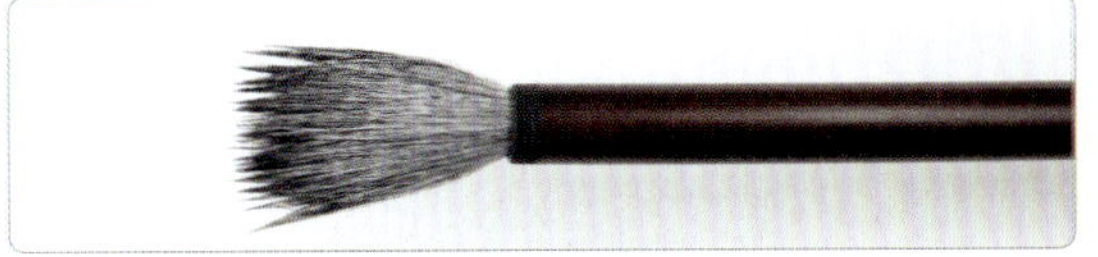

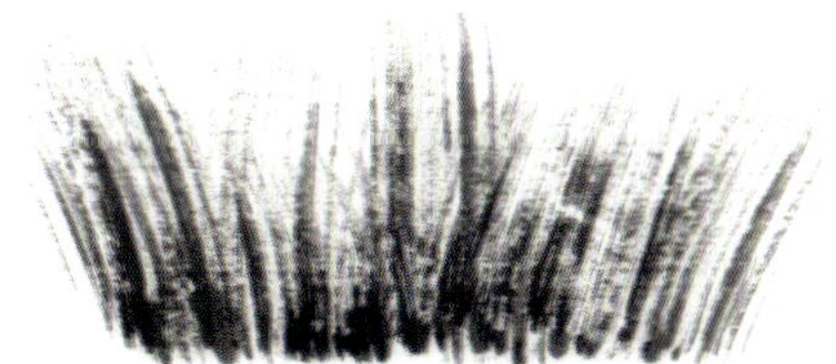

BASIC EXPRESSIONS

Senbyou-hou (線描法) /
Kouroku-hou (鉤勒法)

This method of drawing utilises outlines and contours. The form and shape of the subject are expressed through fine, controlled lines painted with the tip of the brush. You can create an artwork using solely senbyou-hou/kouroku-hou, or in combination with shading and colour.

The plum flower petals and chrysanthemum below exemplify senbyou-hou/kouroku-hou.

Tsuketate-hou (付立法) /
Mokkotsu-hou (没骨法)

This method of drawing does not use outlines or contours. Instead, the form and shape of the subject are expressed through shading and layering. It is commonly used in Suibokuga to create fluid and soft ink effects and requires the careful manipulation of the ink density and mastery of the sokuhitsu and chokuhitsu brush movements.

The plum flower petals, branches and chrysanthemum below exemplify tsuketate-hou/mokkotsu-hou.

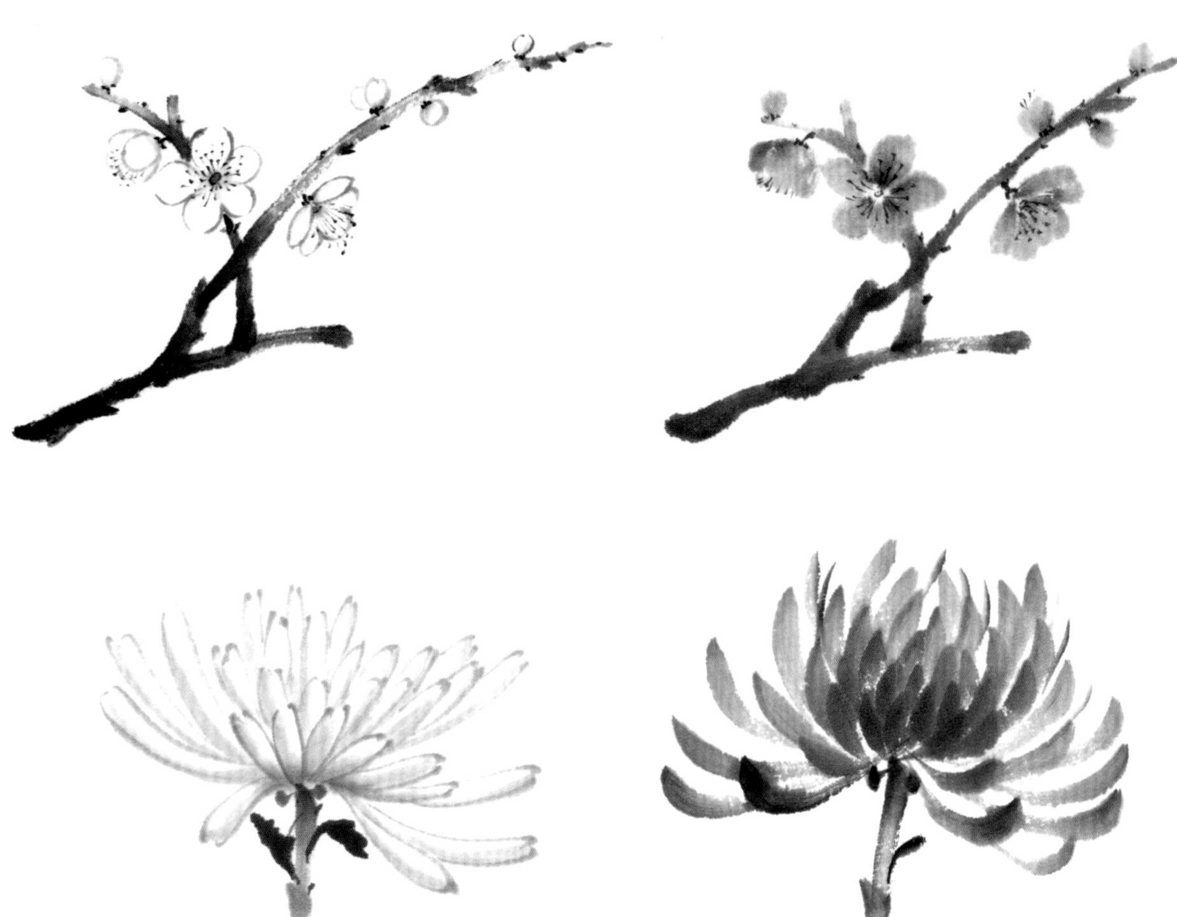

RINGA PRACTICE

The Ringa (臨画) practice involves faithfully studying and copying skilled painters' artworks to gain insight into various aspects such as brushwork, ink control techniques and compositional principles. Through this seemingly simple practice, you can refine your skills, absorb the techniques of experienced painters and eventually develop your own distinctive style.

A specific method used in Ringa practice involves tracing the compositional skeleton of the artwork in charcoal and creating a draft line drawing, known as Atari (あたり), which can be used as a guide before painting. Creating Atari is a valuable way to study other artists' work, as well as to build up the composition for your own artwork.

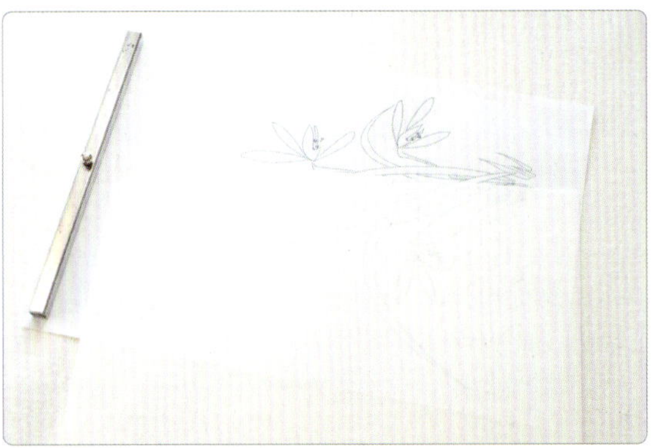

1. Place the sample artwork under the sheet of paper and trace over the key lines of the artwork with charcoal (mokutan) to create Atari.

I recommend following the same stroke order with charcoal as instructed for the brush stroke order.

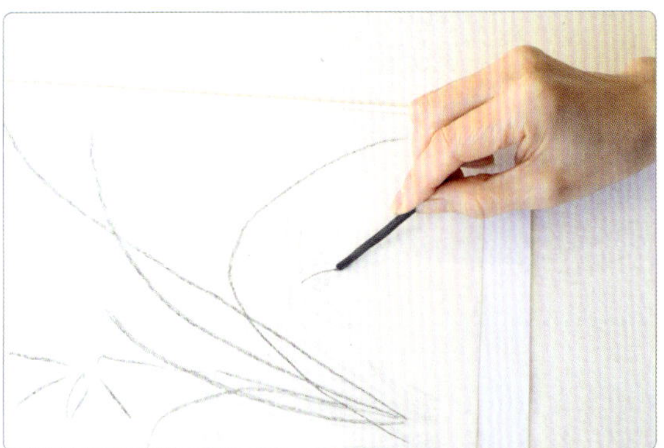

2. After tracing the lines, remove the sample artwork and position it next to the atari.

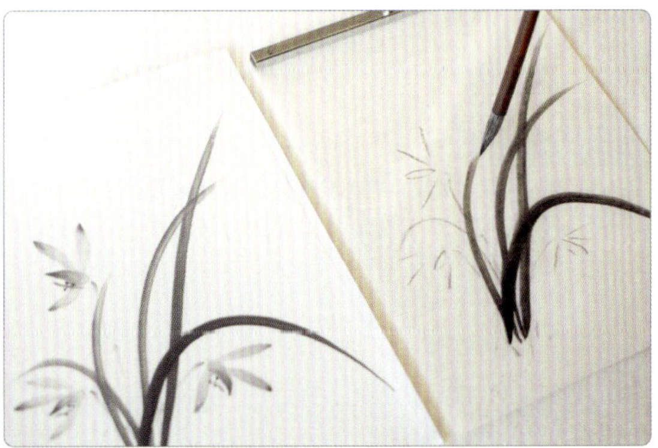

3. Paint over the traced lines with ink and focus on building hissei (speed, rhythm and energy flow – see p. 17). Practise until the brush movements flow naturally and spontaneously.

COMPOSITIONAL PRINCIPLES

In Suibokuga, the Ringa practice is crucial for studying the artworks of skilled painters and developing an understanding of the key compositional principles. Once you feel comfortable with the brush movements and techniques acquired, start developing your own compositions.

Here are some guidelines to follow that I use in my practice:

1. **IMMERSE:** choose the subject of your painting and explore it in its natural ecosystem - take photos, make sketches or search online to gather references.

2. **CLARITY:** clearly define the primary and secondary subjects to bring focus to your composition.

3. **OBSERVE:** plan your composition and sketch a rough outline. Observe and study the subjects from various angles and sketch them separately, allowing for more options for your final composition.

4. **SPACE:** the space that exists between, known as 'Ma', is a key pillar of your composition. It is not necessary to extract and include every detail, the aim is to capture the essence and paint what you experience or feel, referred to as 'Shai' (see p. 16).

5. **DEPTH:** even when painting close-up botanical artworks, try to express depth within the scene by incorporating a focal point, and distinguishing the foreground, midground and background.

6. **SHITAE:** once you have decided on a composition, create a final sketch ('shitae') with charcoal or pencil. Make sure to include space for the seal and signature in your composition.

7. **BUILD:** isolate the subjects and practise the brush movements and ink effects separately before combining. Adjust the layout, size, balance and ink effects as you build up your composition. If necessary, use Atari tracing for guidance.

8. **FINALISE:** when finalising your artwork, focus on chouboku ('ink control'), hissei ('brush control') and isshin ('one mind') as discussed on pp. 16–17. These elements will give each stroke vitality. If possible, minimise the use of the Atari tracing to allow the brush to move spontaneously.

四君子

Shikunshi

'The Four Gentlemen'

THE WILD ORCHID, bamboo, chrysanthemum and plum blossom are collectively referred to as Shikunshi or 'The Four Gentlemen'. It is a traditional motif in Suibokuga that captures the moral character of each plant and the human virtues: purity, integrity, nobility and perseverance, respectively. Each plant represents a distinct season, uniting as a quartet to symbolise the seasonal oscillations of nature and the ephemeral yet cyclical stages of human life.

Encompassing the fundamental brush movements and ink control techniques, mastery of Shikunshi serves as a foundational element in learning Suibokuga.

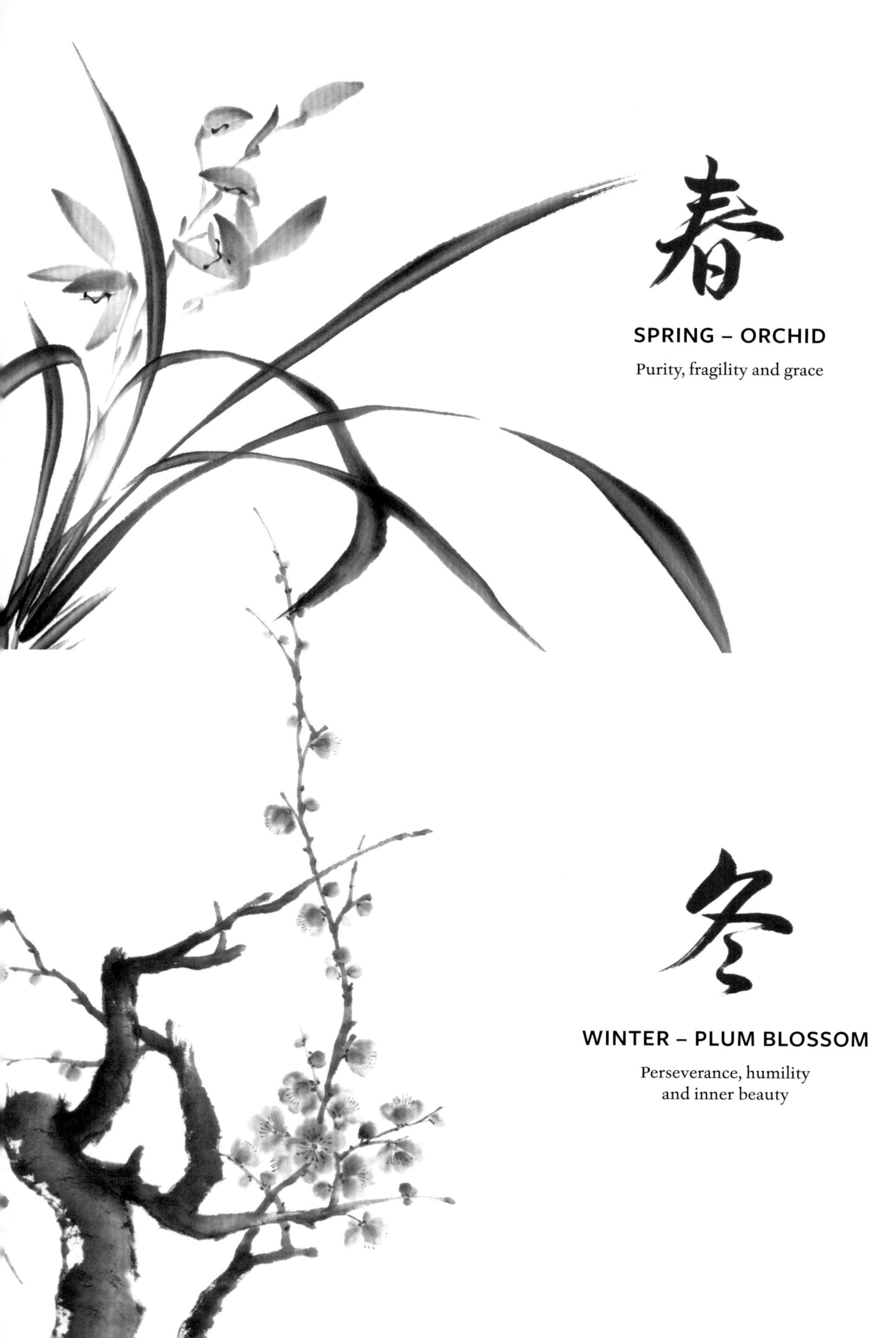

春

SPRING – ORCHID

Purity, fragility and grace

冬

WINTER – PLUM BLOSSOM

Perseverance, humility
and inner beauty

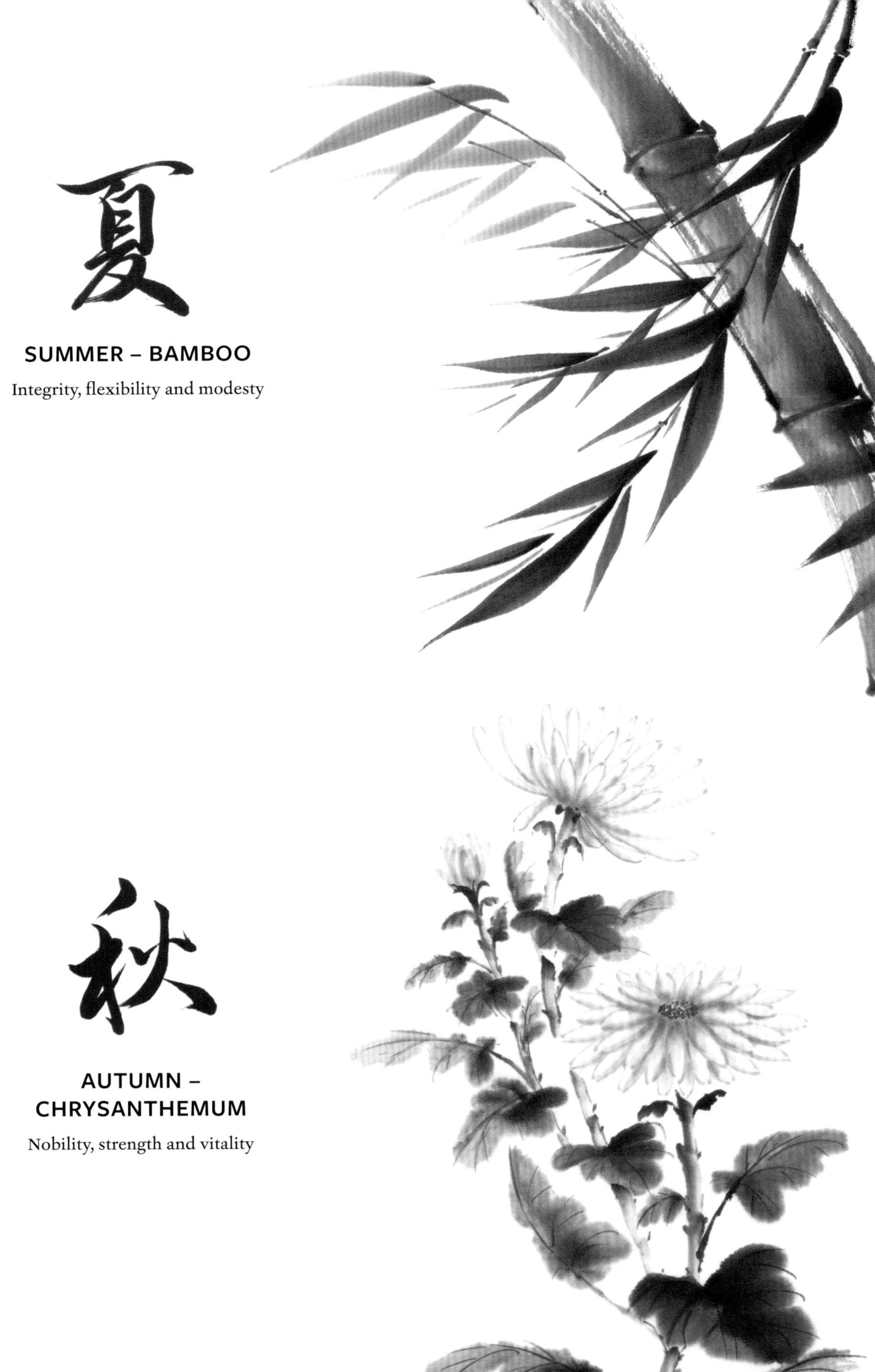

夏

SUMMER – BAMBOO

Integrity, flexibility and modesty

秋

AUTUMN – CHRYSANTHEMUM

Nobility, strength and vitality

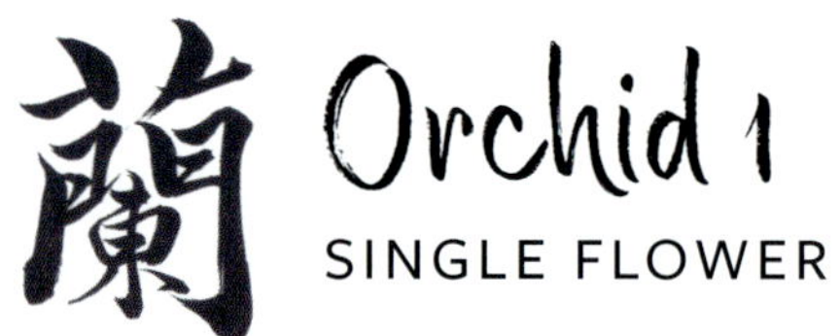

蘭 Orchid 1

SINGLE FLOWER

AS THE FIRST STAGE of Shikunshi, the orchid is associated with spring and symbolises a noble character, purity and elegance. In this artwork, you will learn the fundamental brushstrokes and compositional principles to paint the orchid that you can later apply to other Suibokuga subjects. This guide will cover brush techniques, pressure control and ink effects.

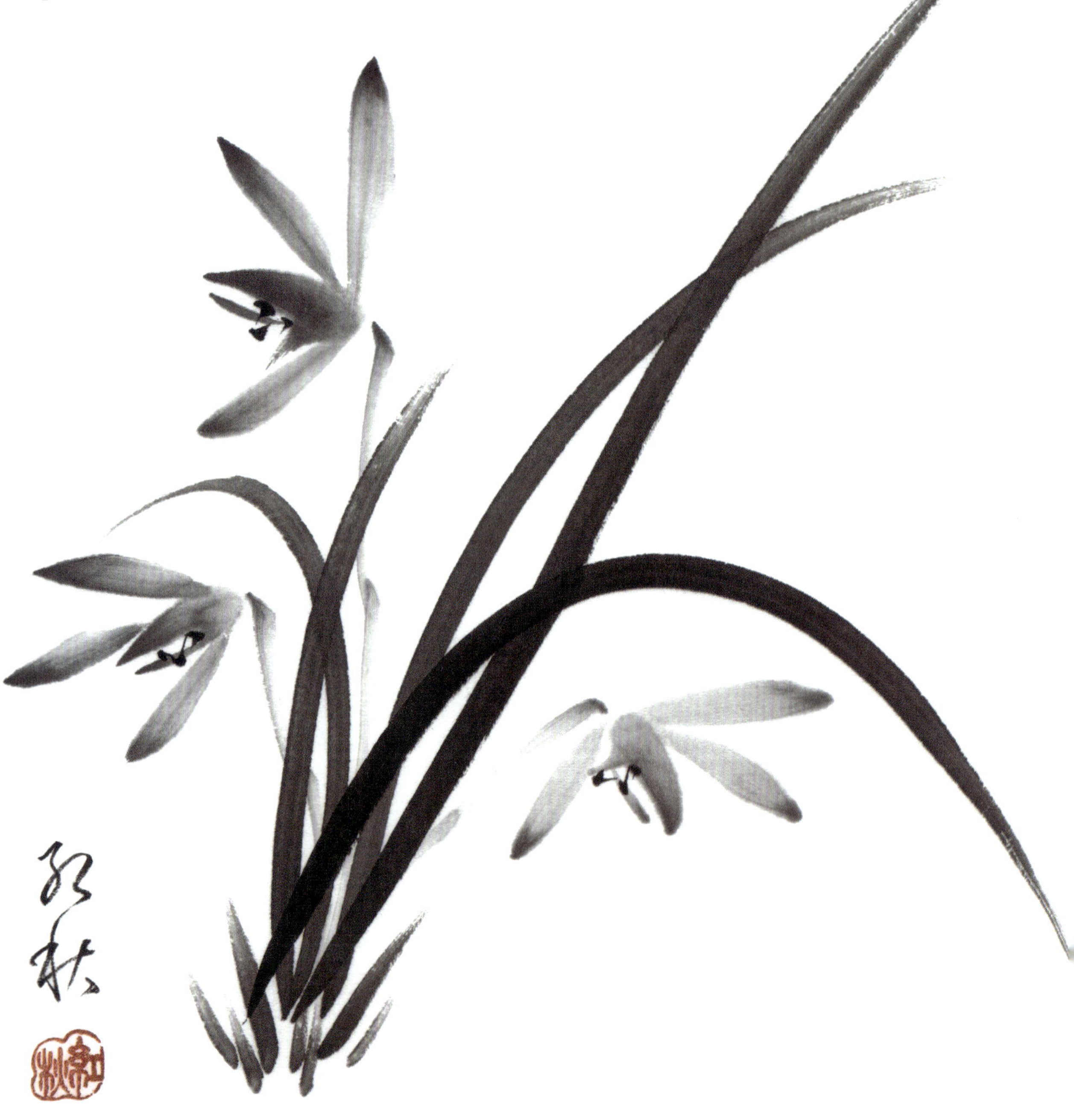

ORCHID LEAVES

Load the ōfude with chuboku and prepare the tip with nouboku. Depending on the desired ink effect, proceed directly to step 2 for sakiguma, or blend the brush for sanboku-hou before continuing (see pp. 26 and 29).

Hold the brush just above the midpoint, making sure it is perpendicular to the paper. With your spine straight and your body relaxed, raise your elbow just below the shoulder in kenwan-hou (see p. 24).

1. Gently press the tip of the brush on the paper (A), and in chokuhitsu (see p. 25), exert consistent pressure as you push the brush upwards (B). For a curved line, rotate from your wrist and arm to create an arch. Gradually lighten the pressure as you reach the end of the line (C), and swing the brush away from the paper to create a pointed ending that mimics the natural shape of the leaf.

2. Repeat these steps and practise creating leaves of varying lengths, widths and directions.

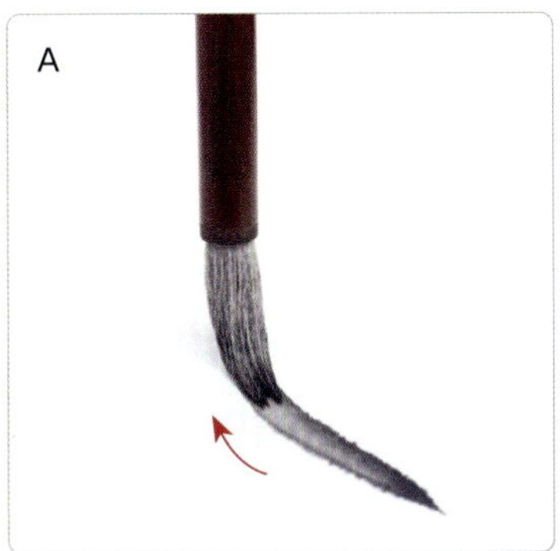

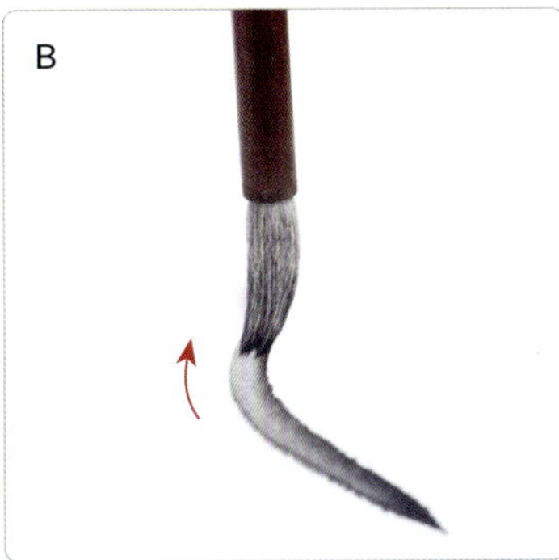

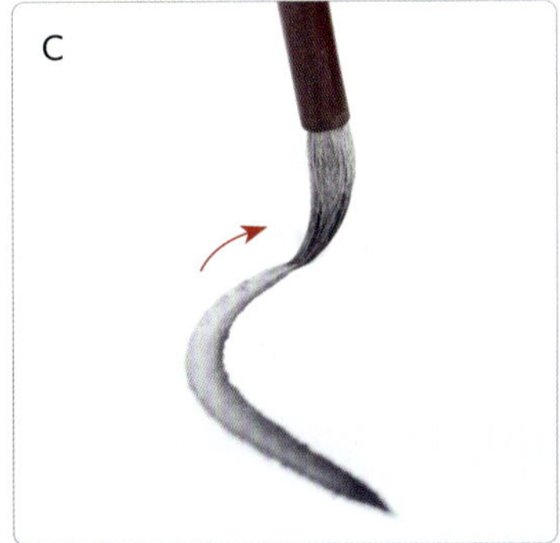

KEY POINT
After loading the brush with ink, paint leaves 1–5 without reapplying ink between the strokes. Each leaf will appear a different shade, introducing depth into your painting.

Practise painting each leaf in a bottom-up stroke from the base to the tip. Once you feel confident with the brush movements, bring the leaves together following the five-leaf arrangement, starting with leaf 1.

The base of the leaves should be positioned in the left corner, each occupying a unique spot on the ground line. From there, the leaves should disperse outwards with leaf 1 crossing over leaves 2 and 3, and leaf 4 crossing over leaf 5 (make sure the leaves don't run parallel to each other).

To begin with, trace over the sample artwork ('Atari') on p. 169 and practise painting over the charcoal to develop a sense of the right composition.

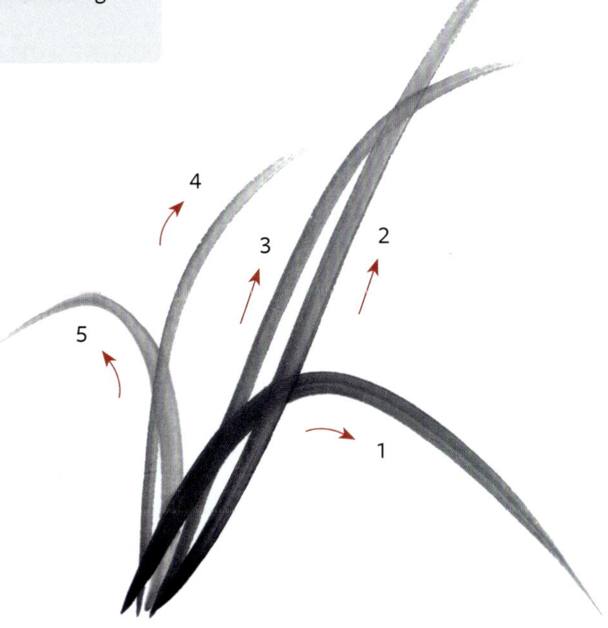

ORCHID FLOWERS

The open orchid flower is typically composed of five or seven petals. Load the ōfude with tanboku, prepare the tip with chuboku and use sakiguma or sanboku-hou to create a unique gradient effect within each petal.

1. In chokuhitsu, press the body of the brush diagonally towards the bottom-right corner of the paper, followed by a slight lift. With the tip of the brush still in contact with the paper, twist and flick.

2. Using just the tip of the brush, press slightly and swing to create a thin line running parallel.

3. Landing from the tip of the brush, gently press the body and follow the line towards the focus point. Lift the brush and swing as you reach the focus point to create a tapered ending.

4. Repeat these steps for the remaining two petals.

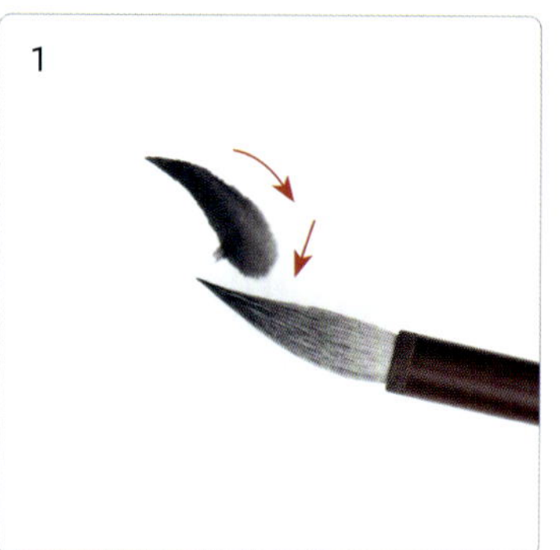

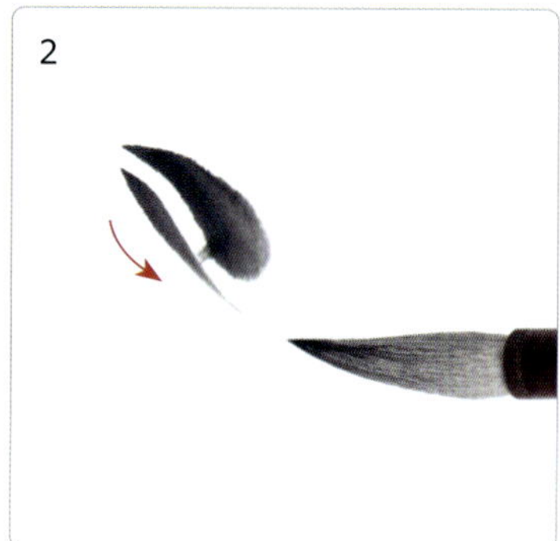

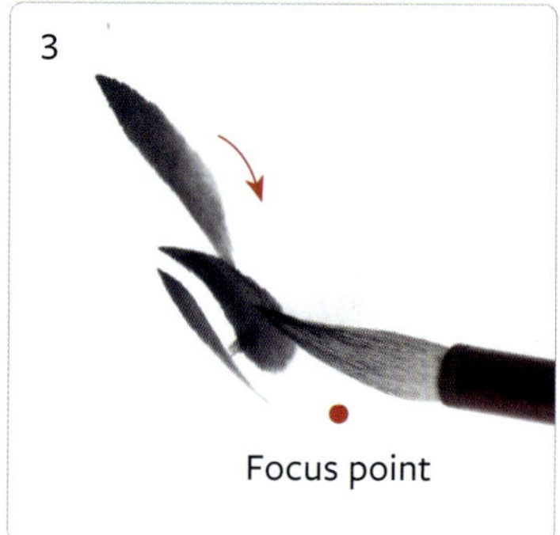

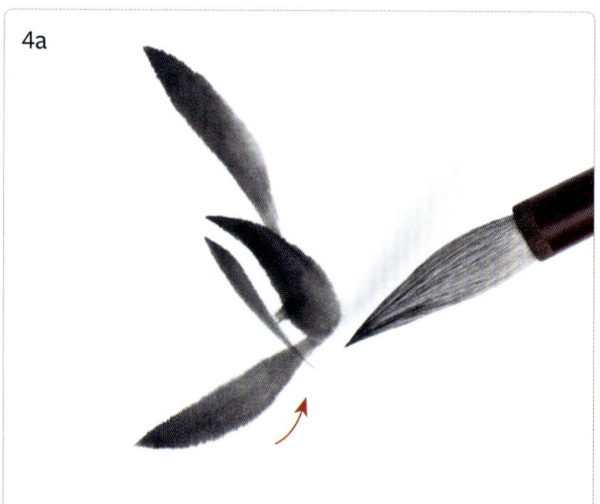

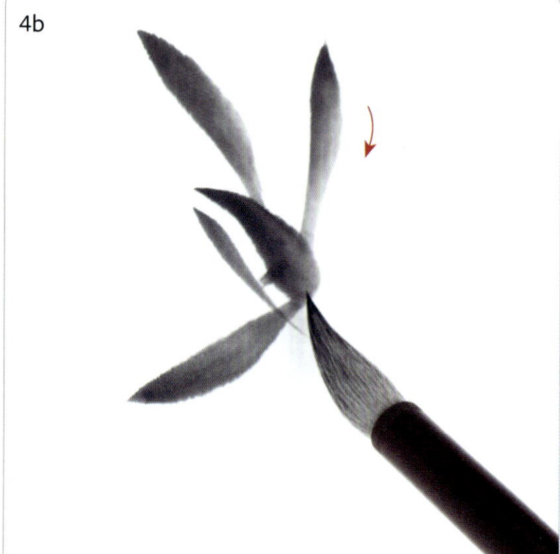

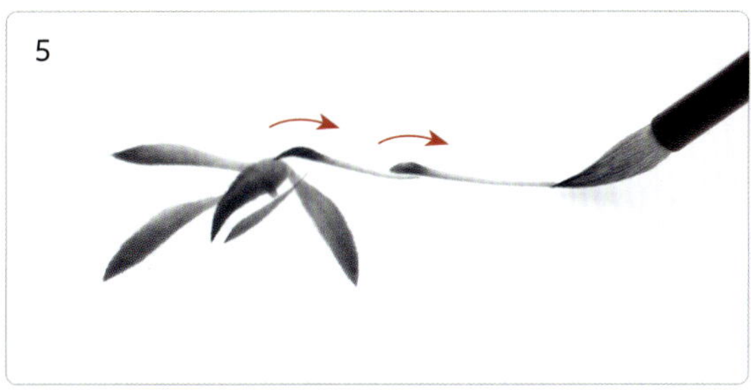

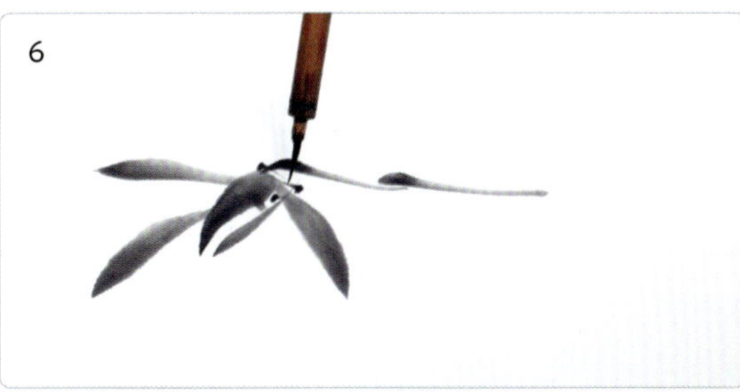

5. Hold the brush upright, position the tip at the focus point and push downwards in chokuhitsu to paint the stems in two strokes.

6. Load the menso-fude or kofude with nouboku and paint three dots around the centre petals to form the stamen. These dots resemble the character 'kokoro' (meaning 'heart') in running style calligraphy and are referred to as tenshin (点心). It is the final touch that places the heart inside the flower, equivalent to putting the eyes on the statue of Buddha.

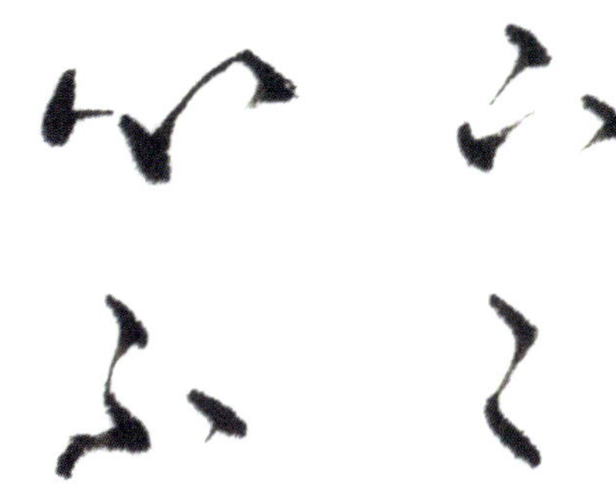

KEY POINT
After preparing the brush with ink in step 1, paint one orchid flower without reapplying ink between the strokes.

Practise the orchid flower blooming in different directions.

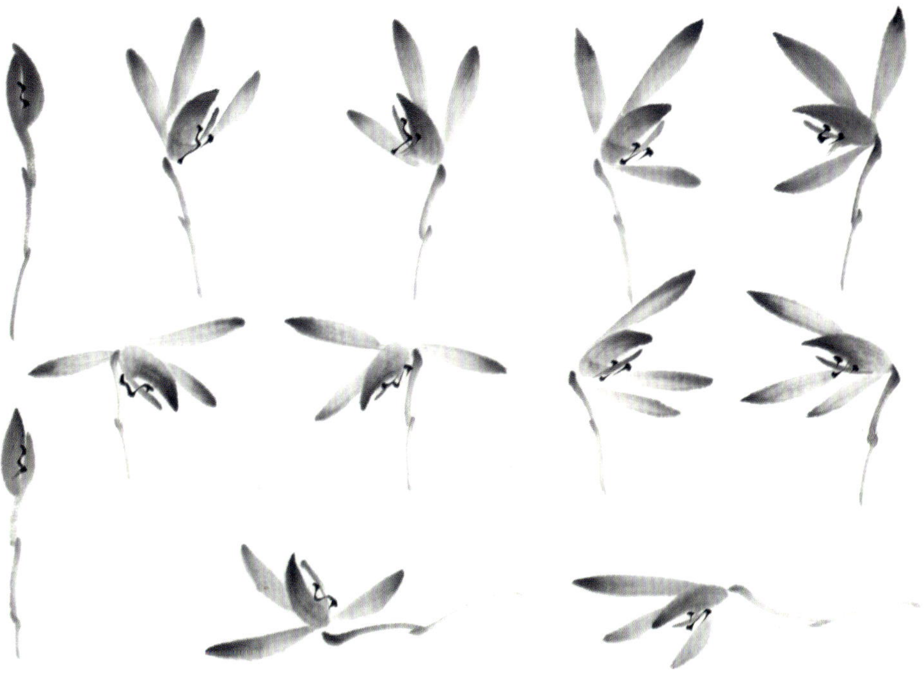

Bring together the various elements in the following order: the leaves, flowers, stems and finally, add tenshin.

蘭 Orchid 2

MULTI FLOWER

BUILDING ON THE SKILLS covered for the single flowering variety, here we will paint the multiflowered orchid. We will delve into more advanced techniques for controlling brush pressure and explore the use of two ink effects: kataguma and ryoguma.

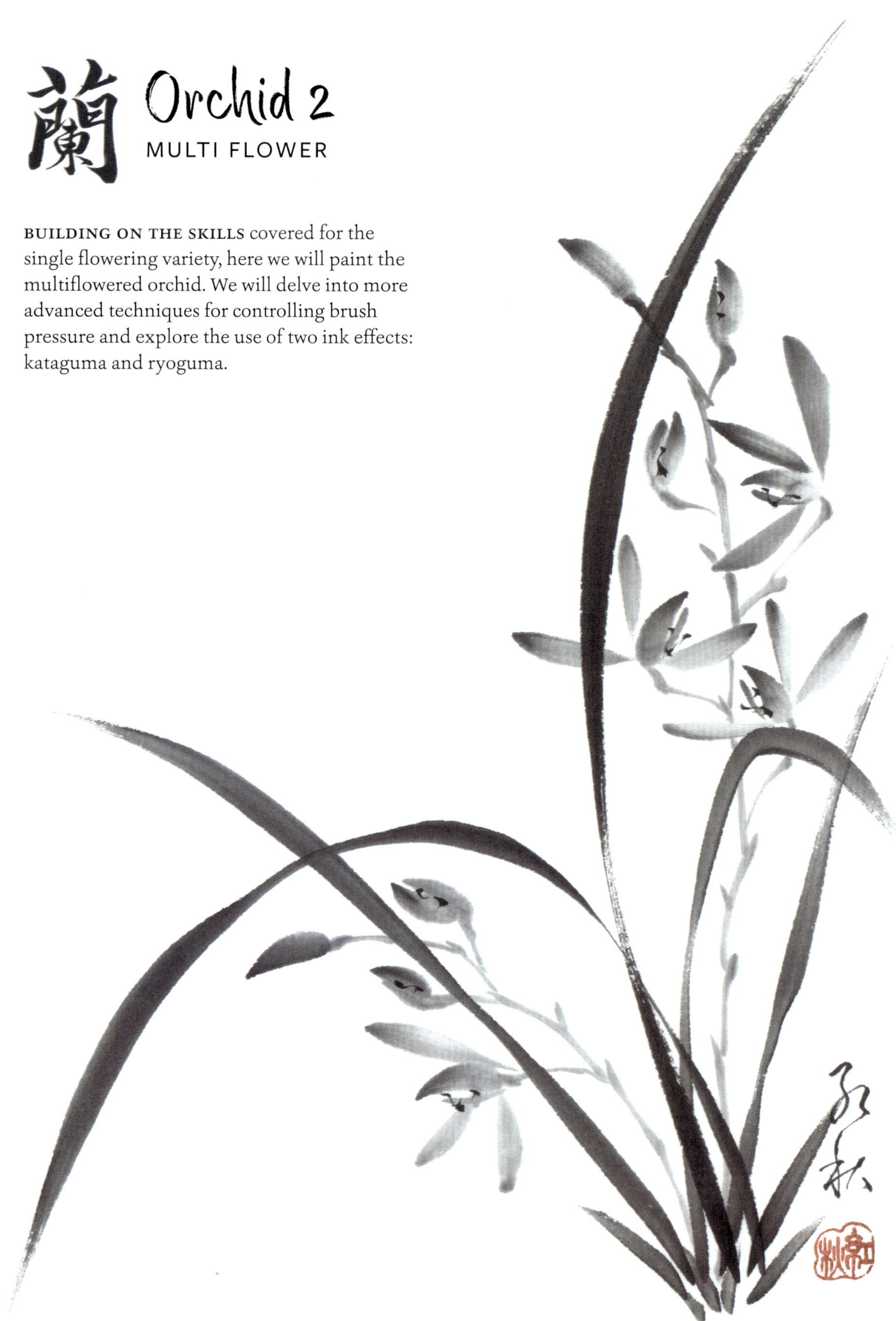

ORCHID TWISTED LEAVES 1

Load the ōfude with chuboku, the tip with nouboku and blend in preparation for san-boku-hou (see p. 29).

1. Starting with leaf 1, press the tip of the brush on the bottom of the paper. In chokuhitsu, apply pressure to create a thicker line for the base of the leaf.

2. As you approach the midpoint of the leaf, gradually lighten the pressure by lifting the brush away from the paper. This will appear as a twist in the shape of the leaf. Reapply the pressure and repeat the process of gradually lifting the brush as you reach the end of the line.

3. Finish by swinging the brush away from the paper to create a tapered ending. As you follow the curvature of the line, try to maintain a consistent speed to achieve a smooth line.

4. Repeat these steps for the remaining leaves, following the five-leaf arrangement.

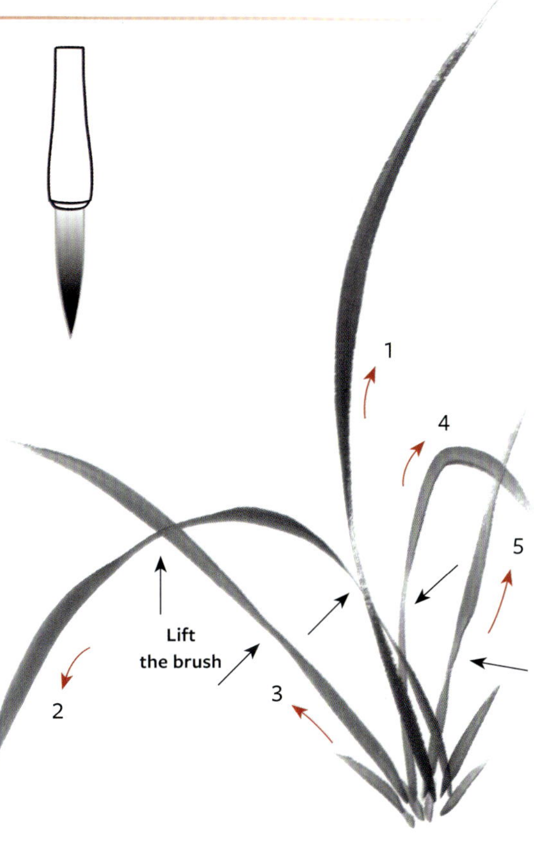

Paint the five leaves in kataguma (left) or ryoguma (right), depending on the desired ink effect (see pp. 26 and 27).

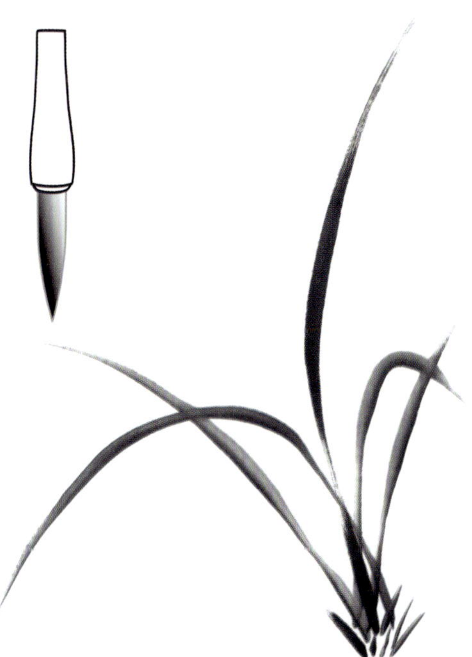

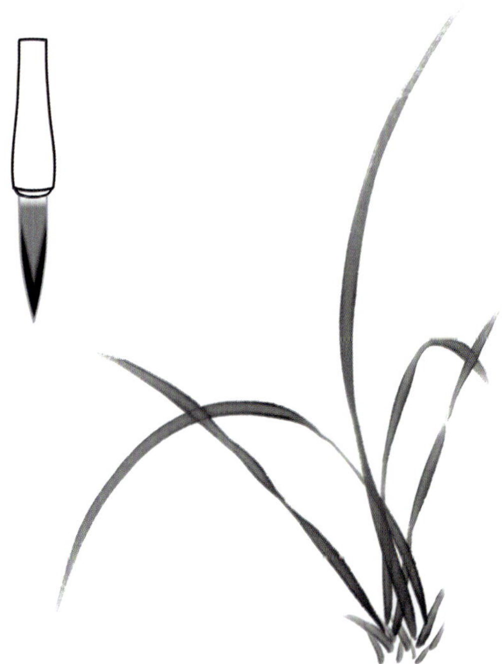

ORCHID FLOWERS

Load the ōfude with tanboku and prepare the tip with chuboku. Depending on the desired ink effect, proceed directly to step 1 for sakiguma, or blend the brush for sanboku-hou before continuing (see pp. 24 and 26).

1. To create the first orchid bud, gently press the body of the brush downwards in chokuhitsu. Lift the brush slightly, and using just the tip, paint a thin line for the stem.

2. Follow the same technique to paint the open bud.

3. Paint the open flower, as practised on pp. 40–1.

4. With the tip of the brush, paint a stem running through the centre, connecting the open flower and buds together.

5. Load the menso-fude with nouboku and paint the tenshin for the open bud and flower.

Work from the top downwards without reapplying ink between the strokes. Naturally, the flowers towards the base of the stem will appear lighter.

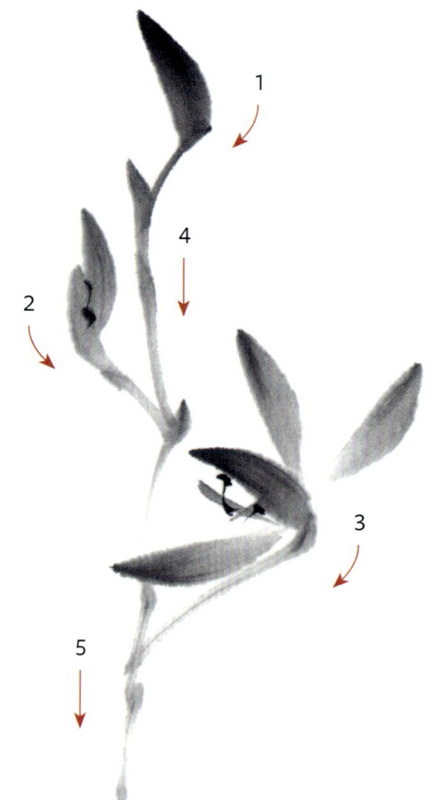

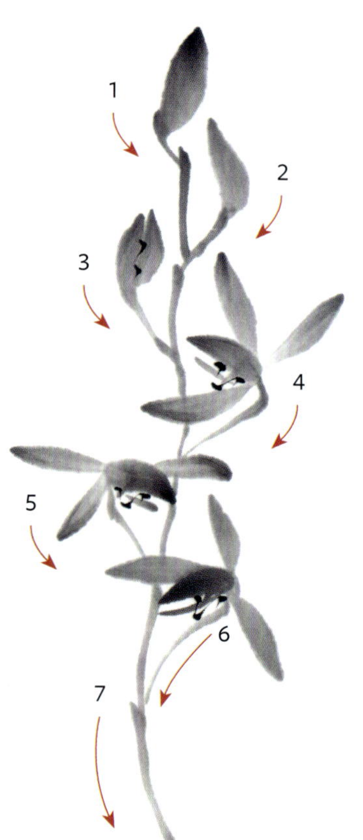

Paint multiple buds and flowers sprouting from the same stalk, ensuring balance by incorporating varying angles, sizes and gradations of ink.

Once you are confident with the brush movements for the leaves and flowers, bring them together following the arrangement displayed on p. 42.

Bring together the various elements in the following order: the leaves, flowers, stems and, finally, add tenshin.

KEY POINT
Paint the leaves with a darker shade of ink, and the flowers with a lighter shade. This will bring the leaves to the fore, capture the light colours of the petals and create depth in the painting.

ORCHID TWISTED LEAVES 2

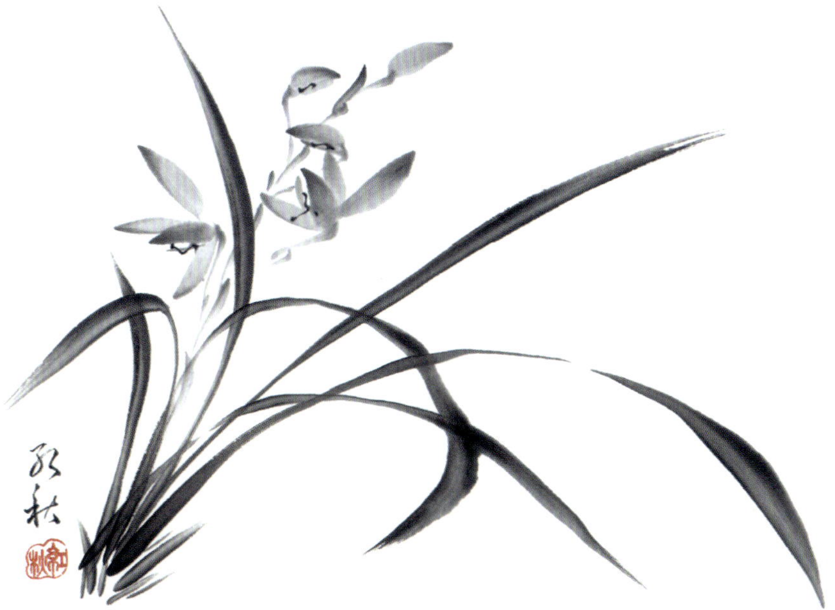

Here, we introduce another technique for creating an expressive twist in the leaf. As you approach the midpoint of the leaf, gradually reduce the pressure on the brush by lifting it away from the paper. When you reach the peak, flip the brush over and follow the curvature of the line with the other side of the brush.

The kataguma technique is particularly effective in illustrating this method.

For variation 1, the darker side of the brush traces the lower section of the leaf, however, once you flip the brush over at the peak, the darker side of the brush traces the upper section of the leaf (refer to the illustration below).

For variation 2, the darker side of the brush traces the upper section of the leaf to begin with and switches after the peak.

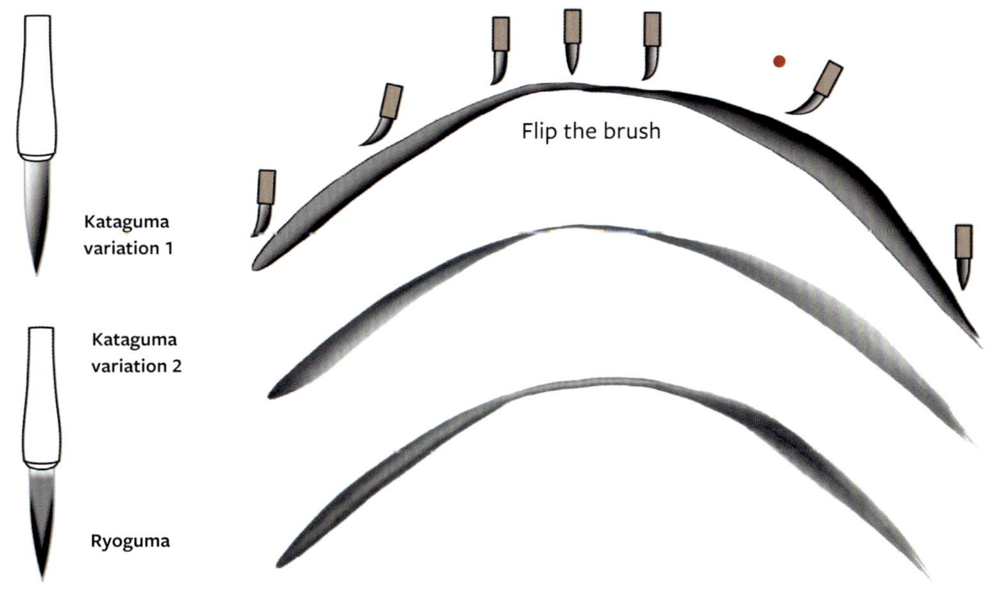

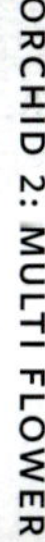

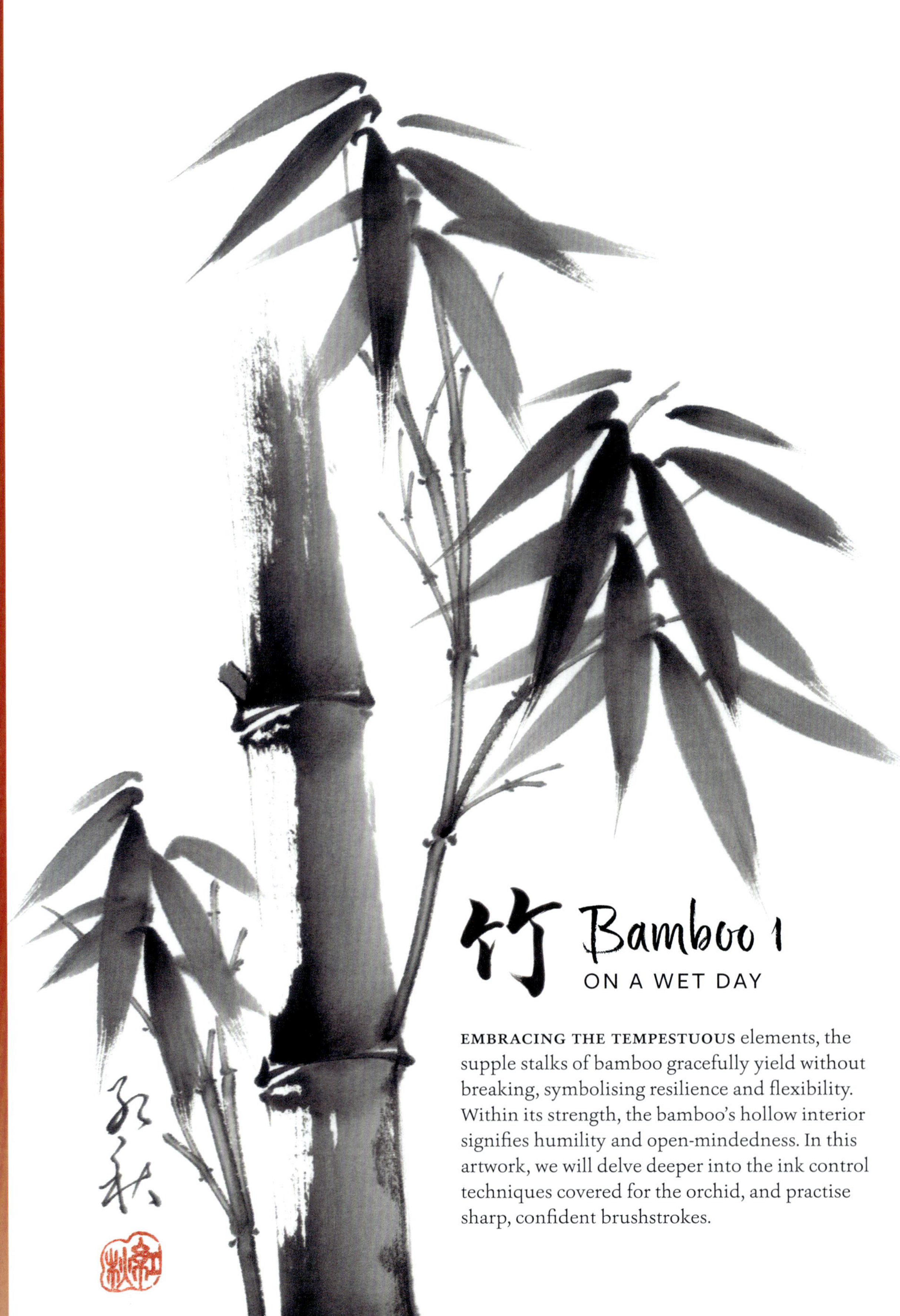

竹 Bamboo 1

ON A WET DAY

EMBRACING THE TEMPESTUOUS elements, the supple stalks of bamboo gracefully yield without breaking, symbolising resilience and flexibility. Within its strength, the bamboo's hollow interior signifies humility and open-mindedness. In this artwork, we will delve deeper into the ink control techniques covered for the orchid, and practise sharp, confident brushstrokes.

BAMBOO CULM

Load the ōfude with chuboku, the tip with nouboku and blend in preparation for sanboku-hou.

To paint a line in sokuhitsu, lower the angle of the brush until the side of your hand glides smoothly across the paper, while engaging your arm and hinging from the elbow for controlled movements.

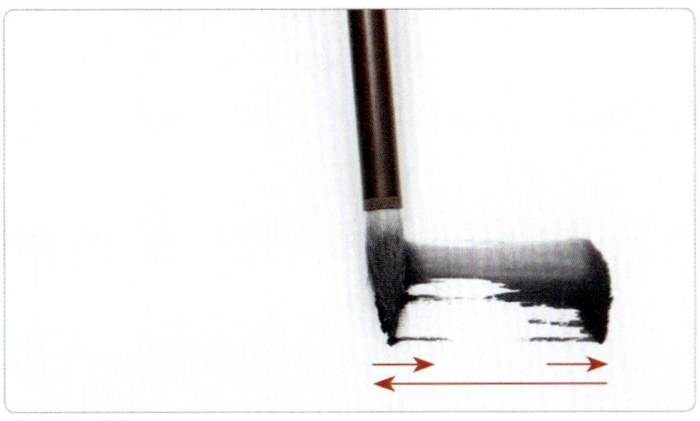

1. Position the brush at the bottom of the paper, apply a slight downward pressure (indicated by the arrows) and slide upwards with a swift, energetic movement to create the first segment of the bamboo culm. Without lifting the brush, apply a slight downward pressure to mark the first node.

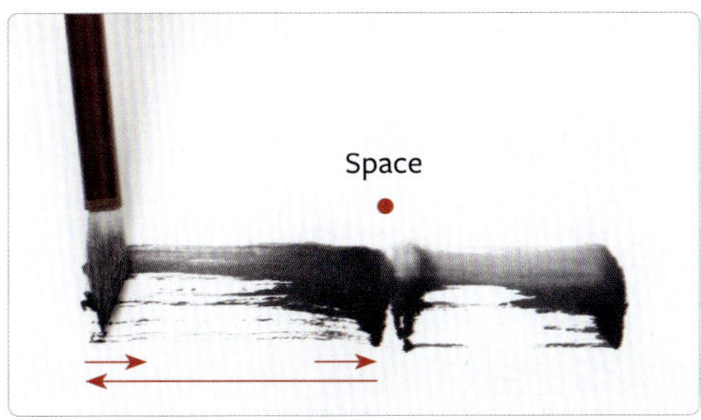

2. Without reapplying ink, leave a small space and paint the second segment. Maintain the same brush positioning and techniques as before and ensure this segment is longer than the previous one. Once again, in a continuous motion, apply a slight downward pressure to mark the second node.

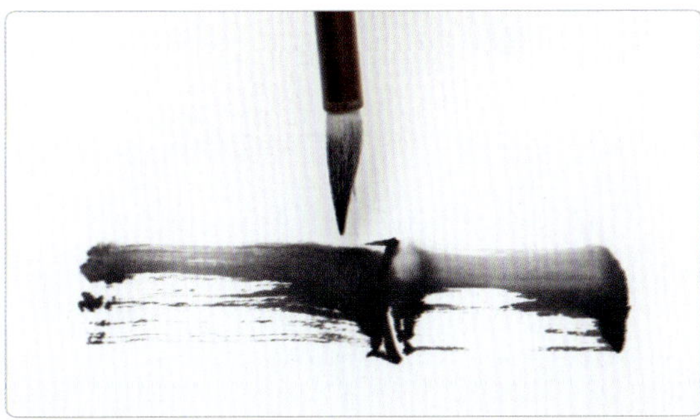

3. Once the ink has dried, we will mark the nodes to segment the culm. Prepare the tip of the brush with nouboku and paint two adjoining dots that bridge over the blank space. Repeat this step to mark the second node.

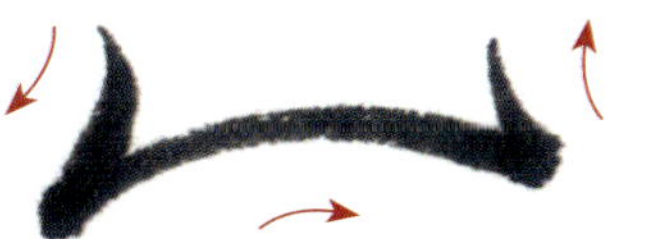

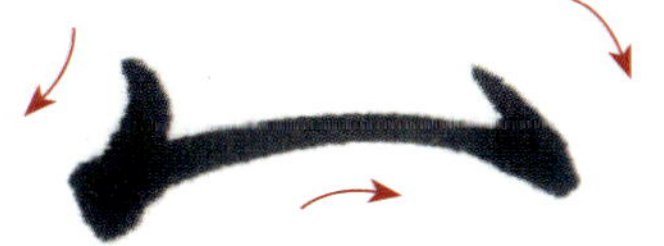

BAMBOO BRANCHES

The branch typically grows from the culm, just above the node.

Load the ōfude with chuboku, run both sides across nouboku for ryoguma, and paint a sharp line in chokuhitsu to create the branch. Alternatively, use sanboku-hou.

1. Similar to the culm, the branches are also segmented by distinct nodes. As you reach the branch node, apply a slight downward pressure without lifting the brush.

2. Without reapplying ink, and maintaining the same brush positioning, push upwards to continue the branch.

3. To mark the nodes, paint two adjoining dots that bridge over the blank space. For twigs, paint two detached dots.

4. For the final touch, load the kofude with chuboku or nouboku and paint the smaller twigs. This step should be completed after painting the leaves. To create sharper lines, hold the brush in tankou-hou and position the arm in teiwan-hou (see p. 24).

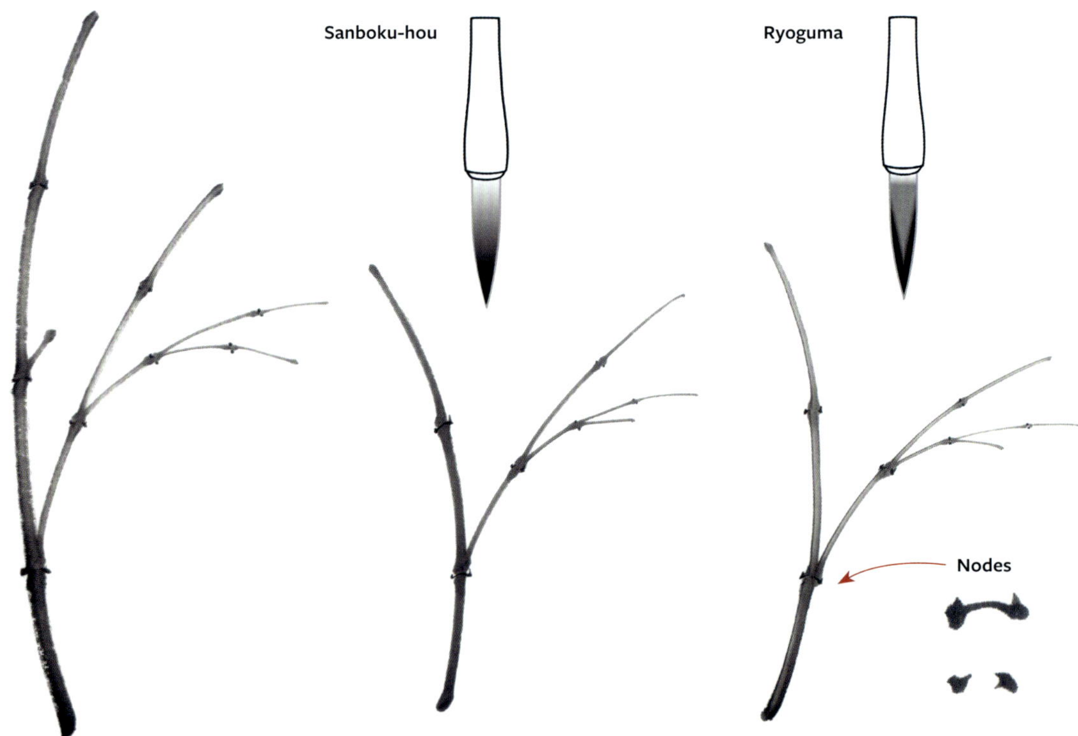

KEY POINTS

- Embody the strength and resilience of the bamboo and infuse your painting with energy and momentum.
- Refine your sanboku-hou practice to effectively capture the natural curvature of the bamboo culm.
- Begin by applying a generous amount of ink and avoid reapplying ink between the segments to achieve a kasure effect.

BAMBOO LEAVES: ON A WET DAY

To paint the bamboo leaves, follow a similar technique as in painting the orchid flower petals (see p. 40) but using sharper, stronger brushstrokes. One subtle distinction is the addition of a small hook at the leaf's base where it meets the branch, resembling the shape of a bird's beak. During rainfall, bamboo leaves bow downwards.

Load roughly two-thirds of the ōfude with chuboku, gently wipe off any excess ink and add a touch of nouboku to the tip of the brush. Depending on the desired ink effect, proceed directly to step 1 for sakiguma, or blend the brush for sanboku-hou before continuing.

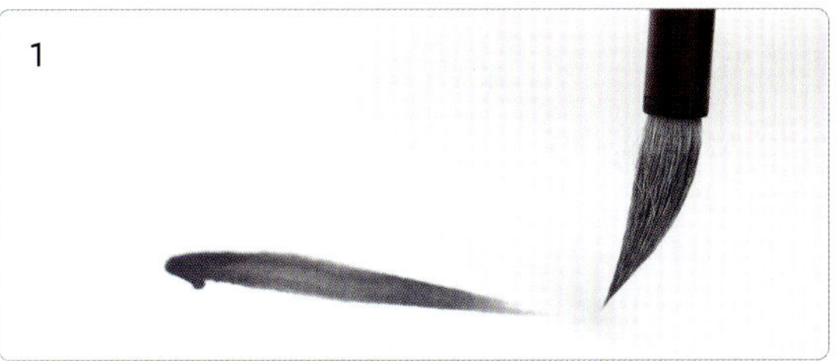

1. Hold the brush in chokuhitsu. Push the tip upwards to fashion a slight hook, then tilt the brush downwards and apply pressure to create the main body of the leaf. Perform a swift swing, pushing the handle towards the paper to create a sharp tip of the leaf.

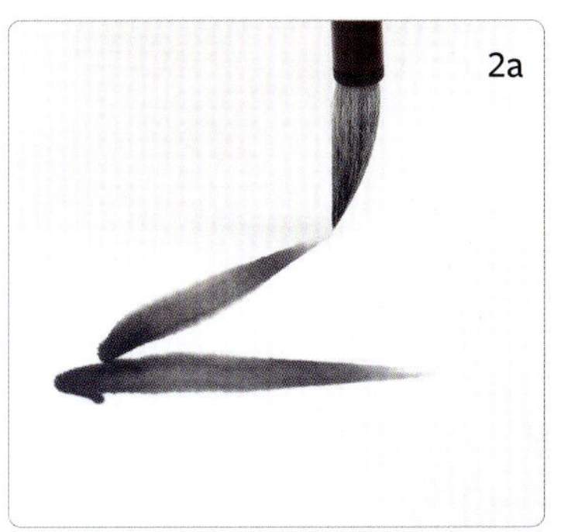

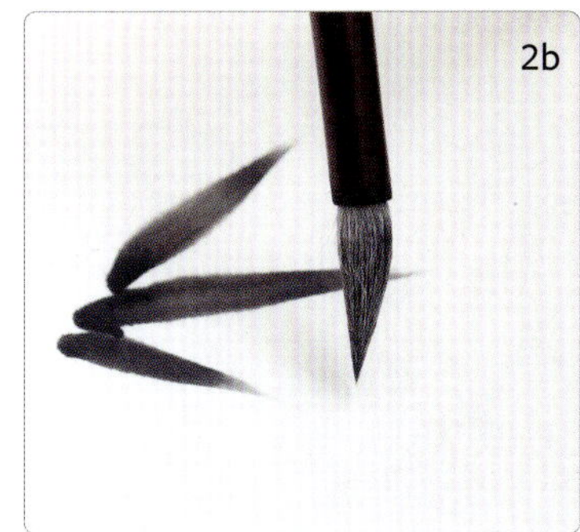

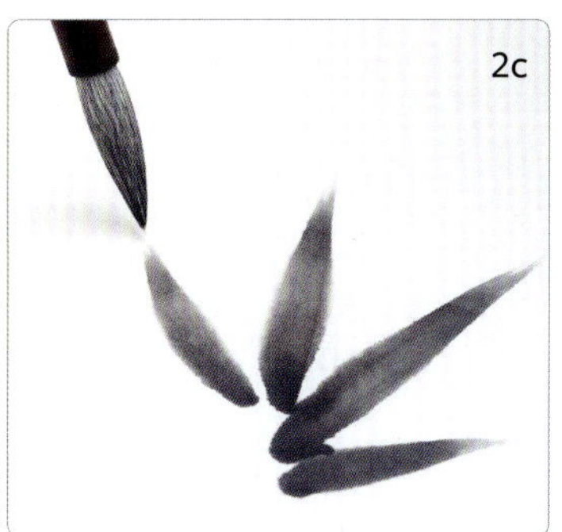

2. Following the same technique, paint the second, third and fourth leaves without reapplying any ink. Refer to the sample images below and introduce variety in both the length and orientation of your leaves to infuse a sense of balance. Be mindful of the negative space in between.

3. Paint the upper leaves first, followed by the bottom leaves, without reapplying ink.

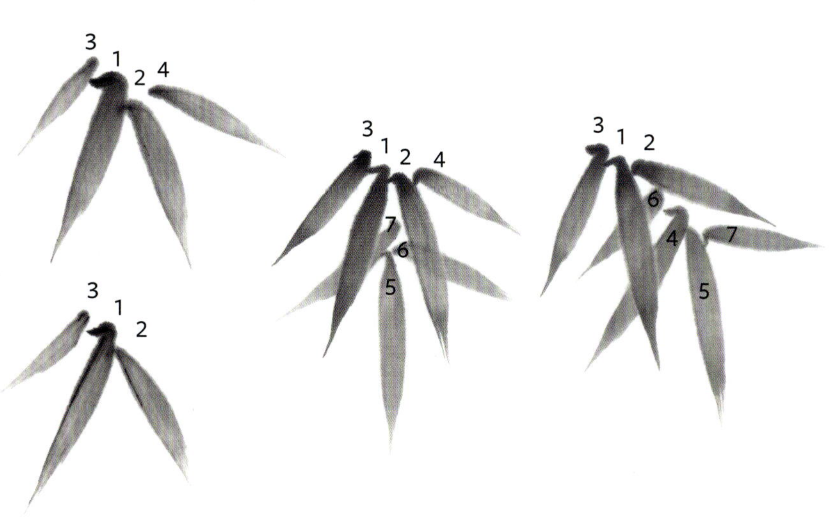

Bring together the various elements in the following order: the bamboo culm, primary branches, leaves (right middle, top middle, left bottom), twigs and finally, the nodes.

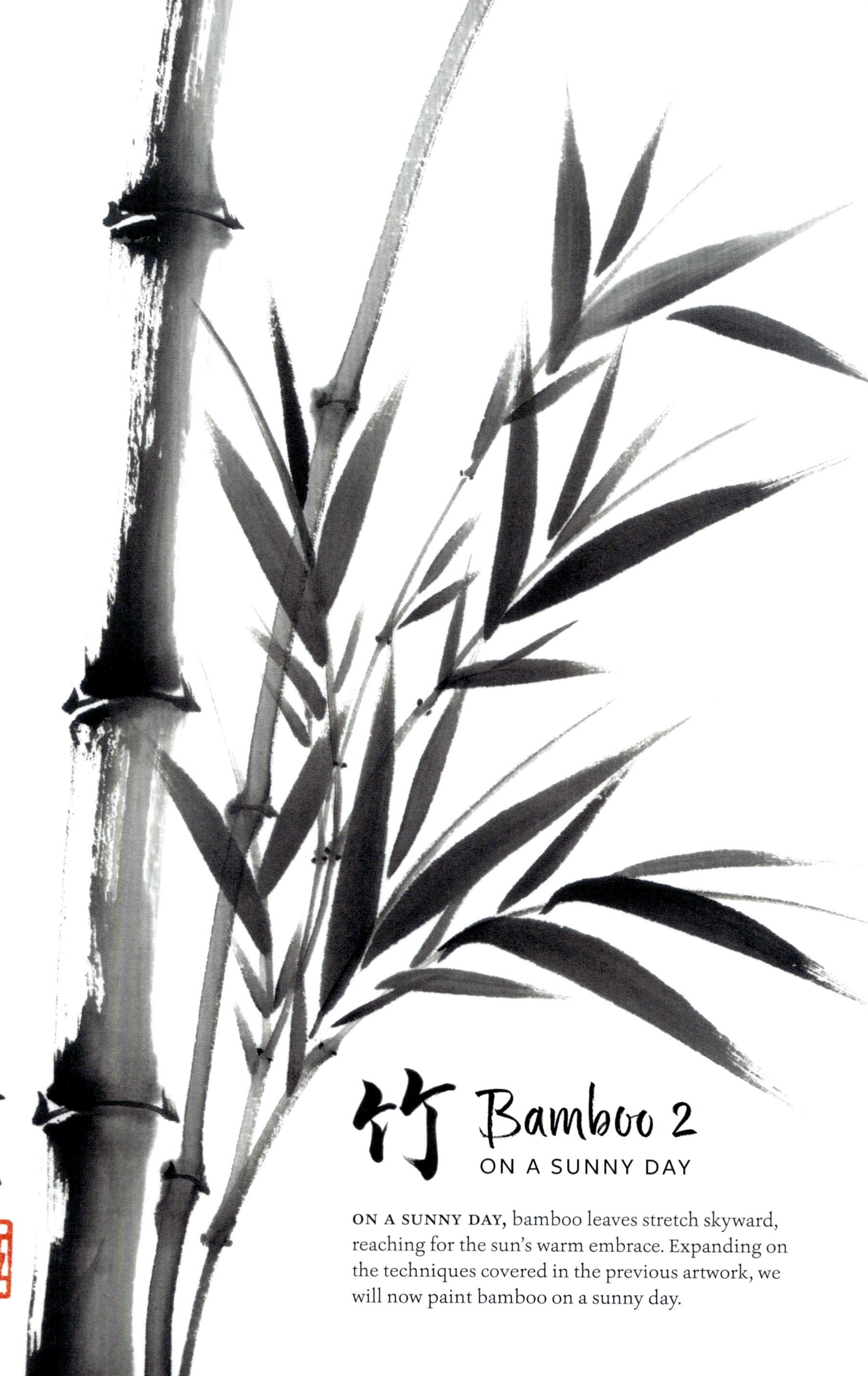

竹 Bamboo 2

ON A SUNNY DAY

ON A SUNNY DAY, bamboo leaves stretch skyward, reaching for the sun's warm embrace. Expanding on the techniques covered in the previous artwork, we will now paint bamboo on a sunny day.

BAMBOO LEAVES: ON A SUNNY DAY

Load roughly two-thirds of the ōfude with chuboku, the tip with nouboku and blend in preparation for sanboku-hou, as on p. 49. Alternatively, prepare the brush for sakiguma.

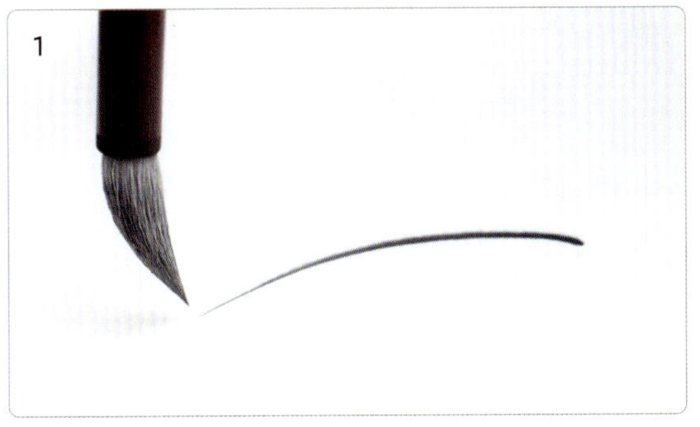

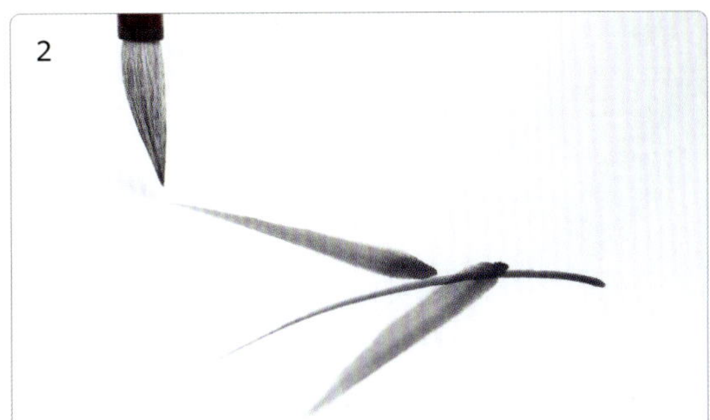

1. To paint the centreline that represents the end of the twig, use the tip of the brush to create a thin, sharp line in one swift bottom-up stroke.

2. For the leaves, use the body of the brush to paint a line in chokuhitsu in one swift bottom-up stroke. Swing the brush at the end to create a sharp, tapered ending.

3. Paint three to four smaller leaves of different sizes.

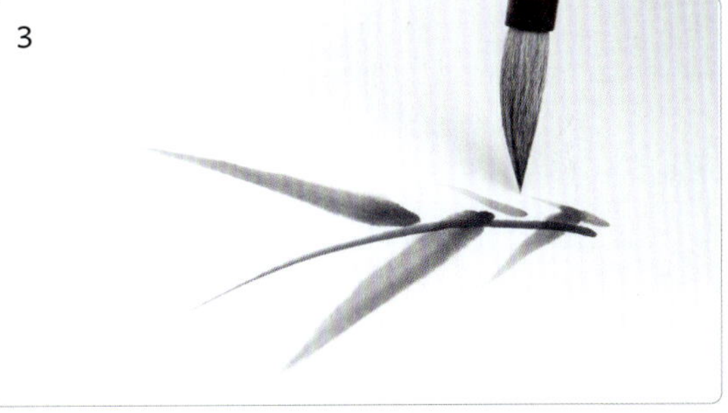

Explore variations while following this general arrangement.

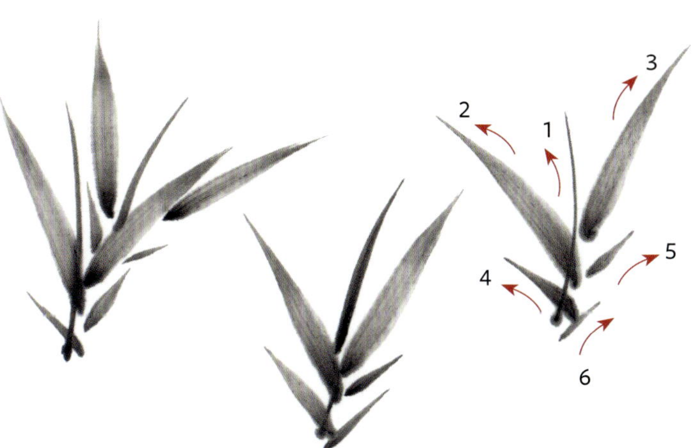

KEY POINTS

- Bamboo leaves seldom sprout symmetrically along the stem. Embrace this inherent asymmetry through the careful use of space and varying leaf sizes and placements along the stem.
- If the bristles of the brush spread out while painting a sequence of leaves, use the flat plate or your fingers to reshape and point the tip of the brush without reapplying ink.

Bring together the various elements in the following order: the primary bamboo culm, branches on the very right-hand side, leaves, and finally the branch in between in a lighter shade of ink to bring the leaves to the foreground.

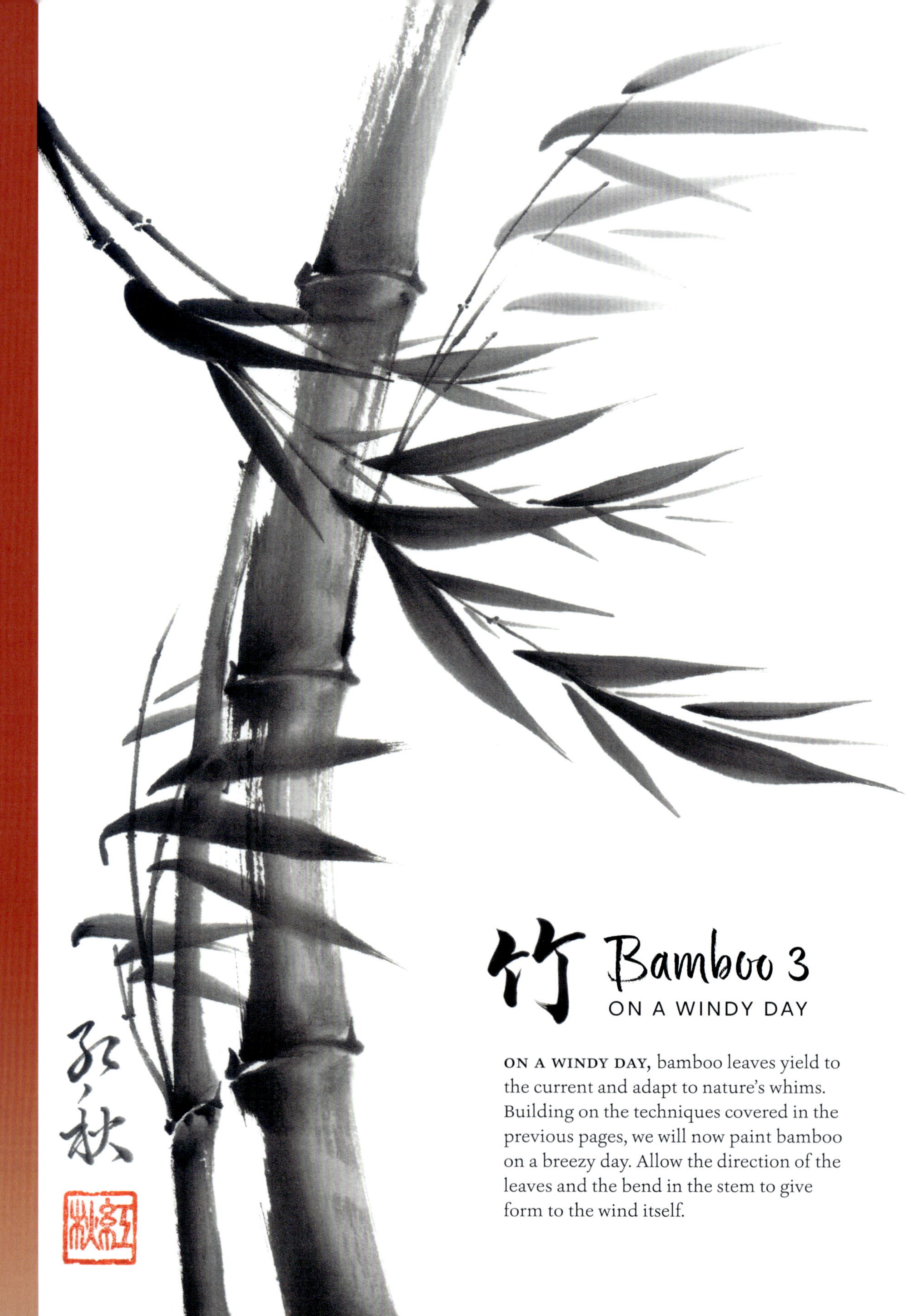

竹 Bamboo 3

ON A WINDY DAY

ON A WINDY DAY, bamboo leaves yield to the current and adapt to nature's whims. Building on the techniques covered in the previous pages, we will now paint bamboo on a breezy day. Allow the direction of the leaves and the bend in the stem to give form to the wind itself.

BAMBOO LEAVES: ON A WINDY DAY

Load roughly two-thirds of the ōfude with chuboku, the tip with nouboku and blend in preparation for sanboku-hou, as on p. 49. Alternatively, prepare the brush for sakiguma.

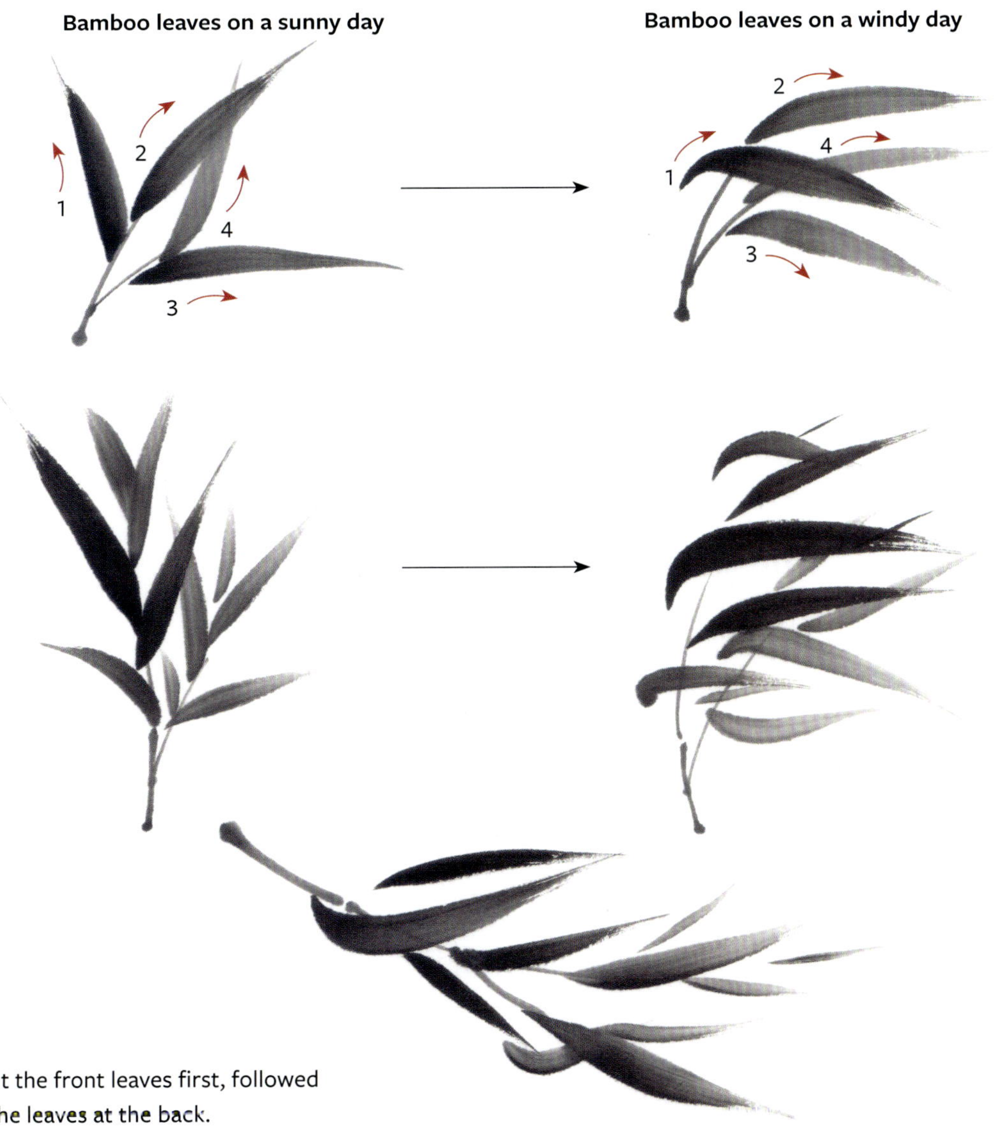

Paint the front leaves first, followed by the leaves at the back.

Bring together the various elements in the following order: the primary bamboo culm, the branches and leaves that enter the frame from the top left, the branches and leaves in the bottom left and, finally, the background leaves in a lighter shade of ink. Before painting the leaves, ensure that the ink of the culm is moderately dry.

KEY POINTS

- Create a slight bend in the culm, branches and twigs, and allow the leaves to sway in the same direction, marking the course of the wind.
- Elongate the leaves to create sharper endings and incorporate fluid, curving brushstrokes to convey the gentle sway of the leaves.

菊 Chrysanthemum 1

WHILE THE NEIGHBOURING flowers dissolve in the cold autumn air, the chrysanthemum blooms with unwavering vitality. It symbolises the virtue to withstand all adversities and embodies the ideals of nobility and elegance. It can even be found adorning the imperial seal, bearing testament to its majestic allure. In this artwork, we will paint the chrysanthemum florets in senbyou-hou.

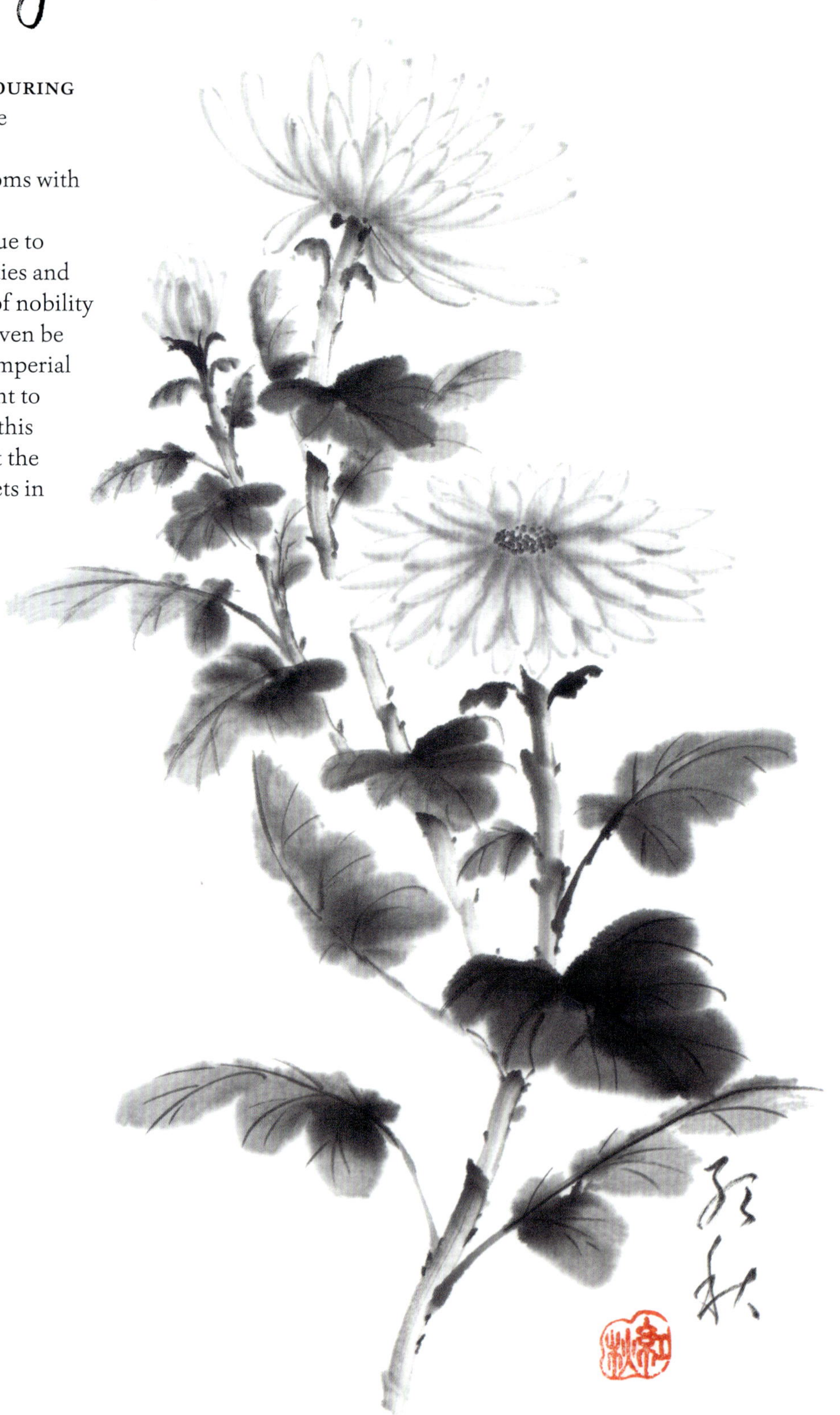

CHRYSANTHEMUM FLOWER: SENBYOU-HOU

In this artwork, we will depict the chrysanthemum's ornate bloom in senbyou-hou/ kouroku-hou. By skilfully outlining the florets and harnessing the interplay of negative space, this technique is particularly effective in capturing the delicate hues of light-coloured florets, such as white and yellow.

Load the kofude with tanboku or chuboku, hold it upright and paint the outlines of the florets in chokuhitsu.

Front-facing tilted flower A

1. Begin by painting small dots in the centre to represent the disc florets. Next, paint each ray floret in two brushstrokes. Paint a line from the centre outward, applying a light pressure that incrementally increases, then flicking the brush inwards at the end of the line. Mirror the same line on the other side to form one downward-facing ray floret. Repeat this step using the same pressure control to create two downward-facing florets.

2. Repeat step 1 to create two more florets of a similar length, facing downwards . . .

3. . . . Followed by four smaller florets facing upwards/away from you.

4. Repeat the previous steps to add more florets positioned under the first layer. Adjust the length and angle of the florets according to the composition outlined in the image on the left.

5. Finally, shade in the centre with goku-tanboku to introduce depth.

Side-facing flower B

1. Applying the same brush techniques as before, begin by painting shorter, upward-facing ray florets from the centre outward.

2. Layer on three florets in between to build up the structure of the flower.

3. Paint two long florets from the centre reaching sideways to the left and right.

4. With symmetry and balance in mind, layer longer florets behind the existing ones.

5. Finally, shade in the centre with goku-tanboku. Paint two dots to represent the calyx of the flower (refer to p. 58 for the stem).

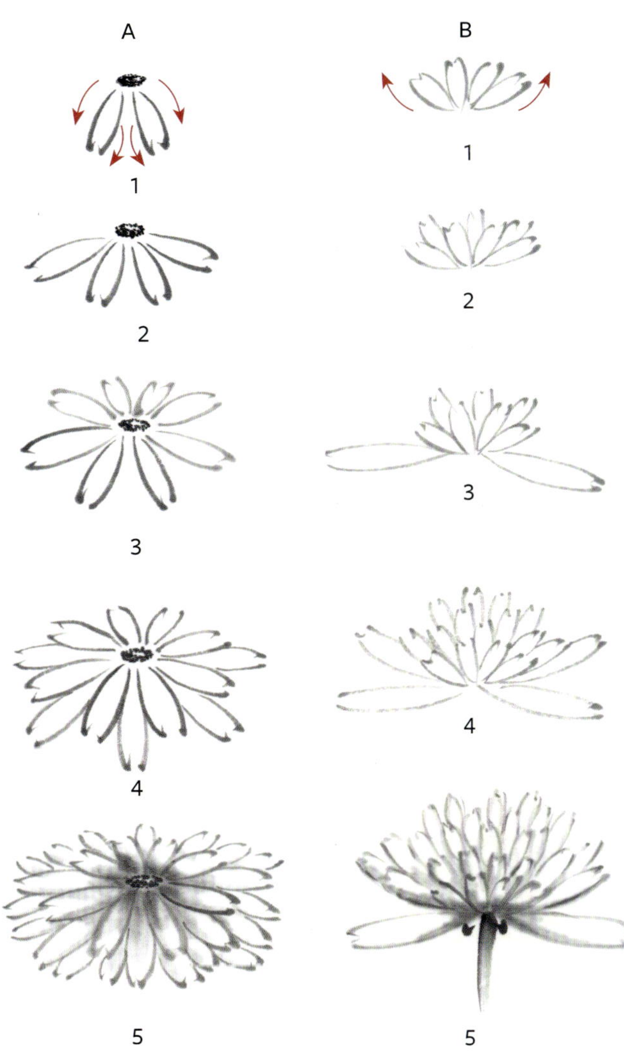

CHRYSANTHEMUM LEAVES

Load the ōfude with chuboku, the tip with nouboku and blend in preparation for sanboku-hou.

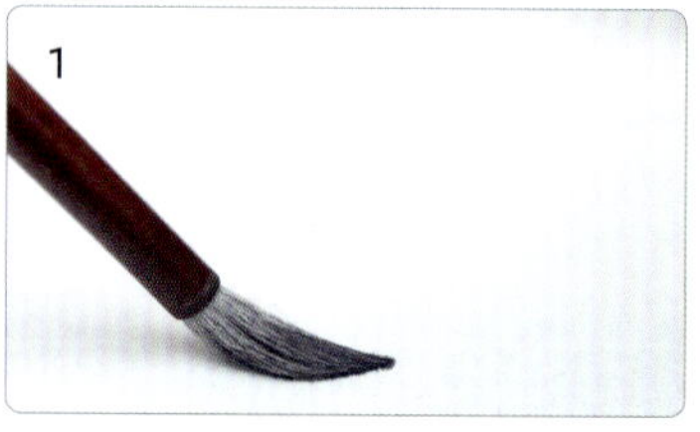

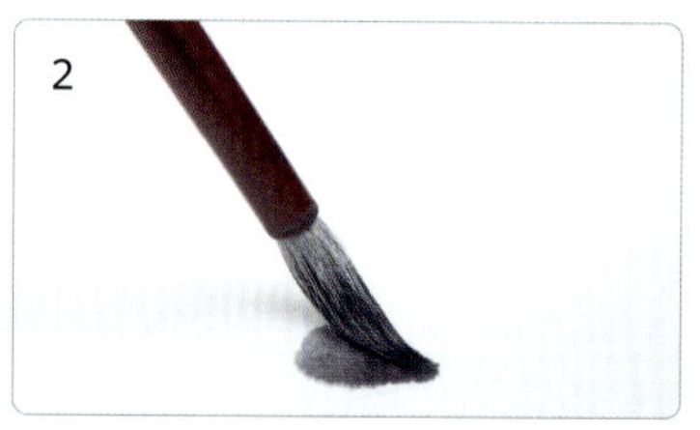

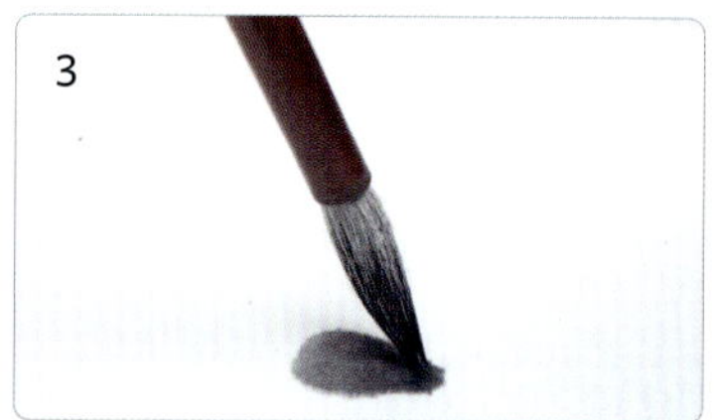

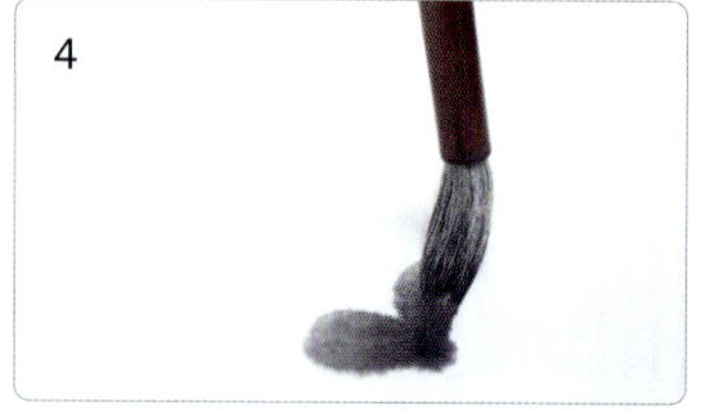

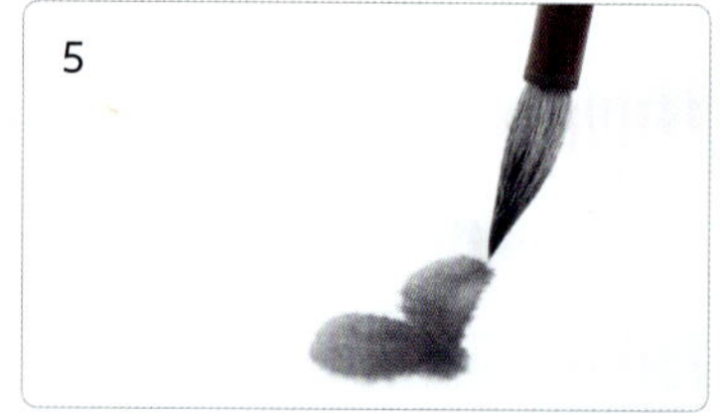

Front-facing leaf (A)

1. Press down the body of the brush while maintaining focus on the tip.

2. Tilt sideways.

3. Lift the brush, and after a slight turn . . .

4. . . . Press downwards again, tilt and push sideways.

5. At the end of the line, lift the brush to create a rounded finish. Repeat steps 1– 4 for the other side of the leaf.

6. Once the ink is moderately dry, load the kofude with nouboku and paint the veins, starting with the centreline. For the veins, try lifting the brush as you reach the end of the line to create a tapered ending.

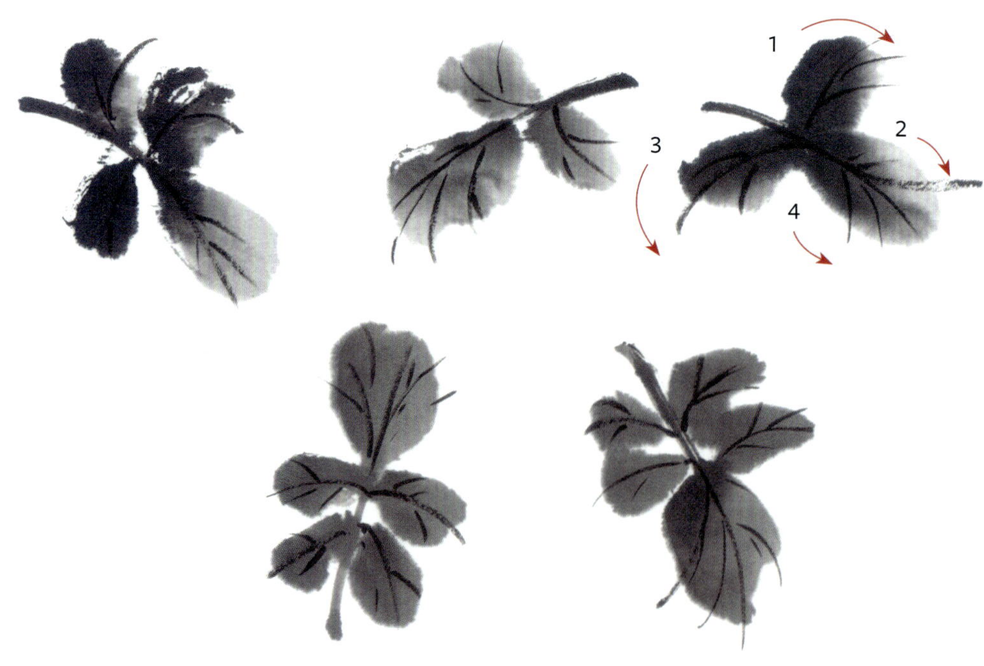

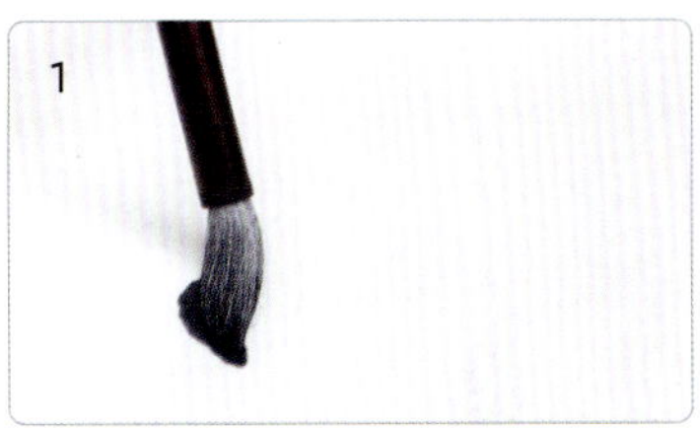

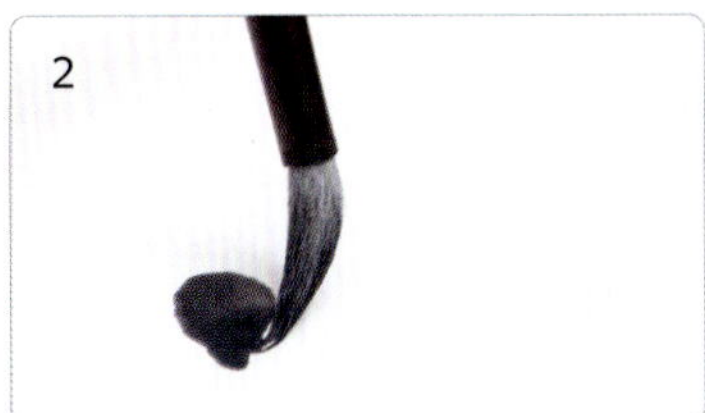

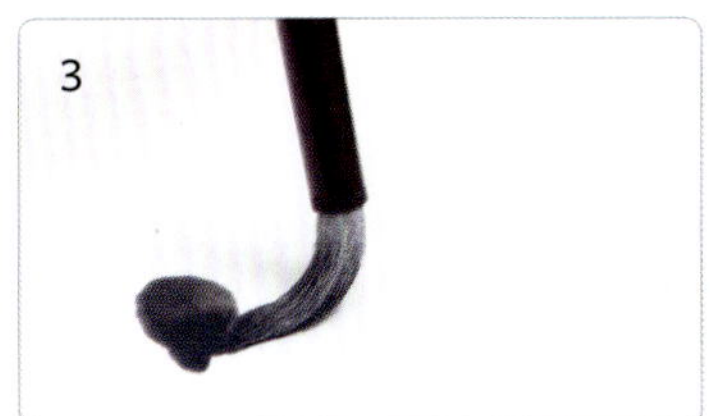

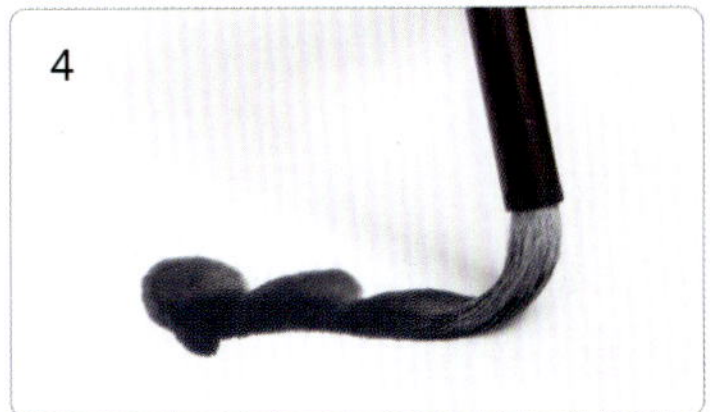

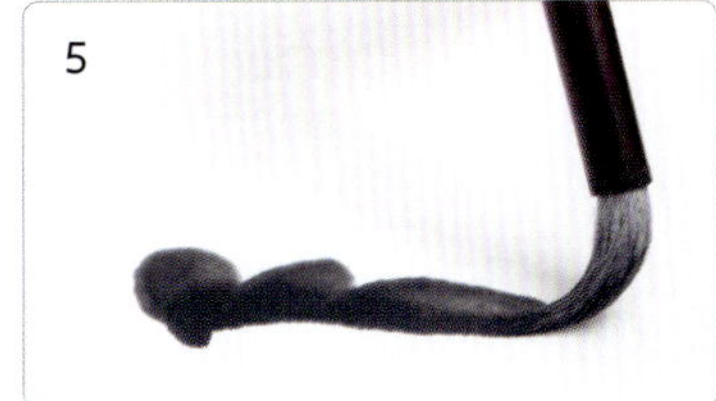

Side-facing leaf (B)

The side-facing leaf is composed of three interconnected segments.

1. Landing from the tip of the brush, press down with full pressure and tilt sideways.

2. Lift the brush, and after a slight turn . . .

3. . . . Press downwards again, tilt and lift.

4. Press downwards again, tilt and push sideways.

5. At the end of the third segment, lift the brush to create a rounded finish.

6. Again, paint the veins once the ink has moderately dried, starting with the centreline that runs through the bottom, followed by the smaller veins.

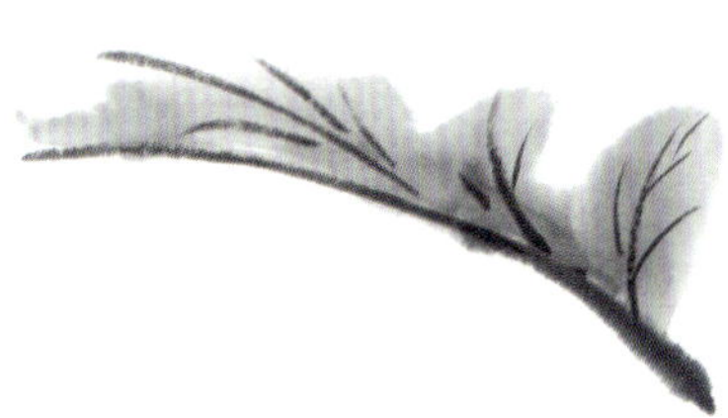

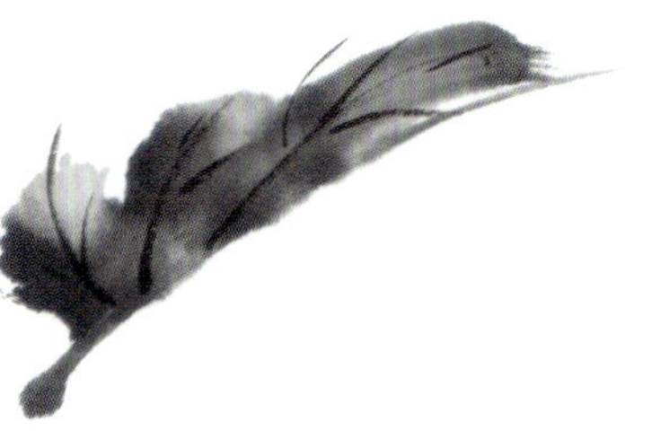

Front-facing tilted leaf (C)

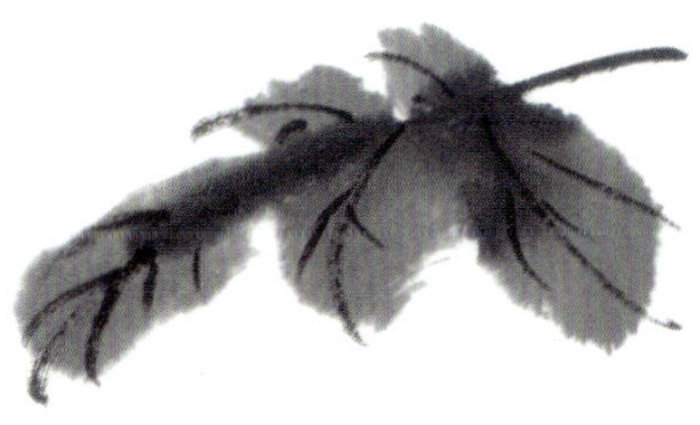

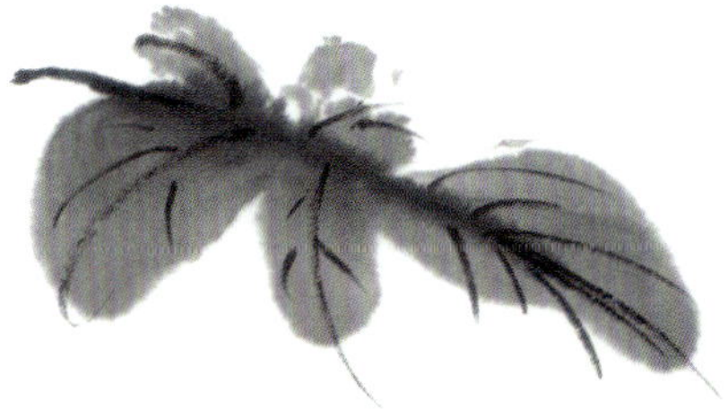

CHRYSANTHEMUM STEM

Load the ōfude with chuboku, the tip with nouboku and blend in preparation for sanboku-hou. Alternatively, load the ōfude with chuboku, run both sides across nouboku for ryoguma.

Hold the brush upright and position it at the centre point at which the florets emerge. In chokuhitsu, paint the stem in a long, flowing movement towards the bottom of the page.

For additional detail, pause the stroke at regular intervals, lift the brush and then continue with a slight overlay to create the axillary buds.

To complete the artwork, paint small dots asymmetrically on both sides of the stems to represent additional axillary buds.

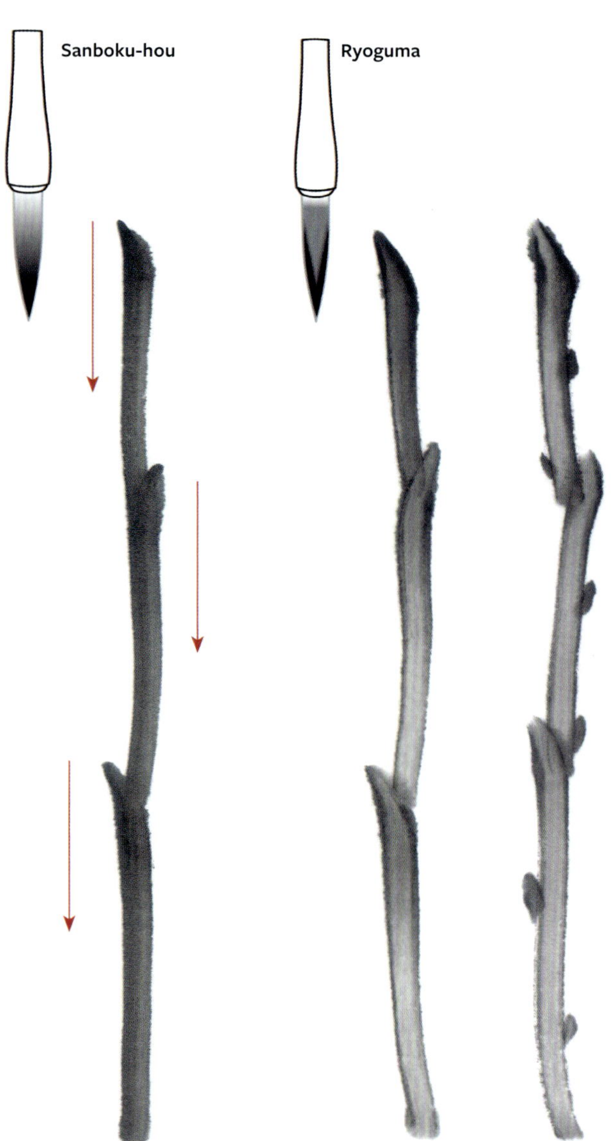

Bring together the various elements in the following order: the two primary flowers and bud, foreground stem (remember to leave a blank space within the stem to accommodate the front leaves), background stem in a lighter shade of ink, foreground leaves and, finally, background leaves in a lighter shade of ink.

KEY POINTS

- To enhance your painting, introduce variety. Consider positioning the leaves at different angles, allowing them to overlap, or experimenting with various sizes to infuse your artwork with movement.
- To create visual separation and direct focus on the flower, use different shades of ink for the florets, differentiating them from the leaves.
- While introducing variety, ensure that the elements work harmoniously together. Step back occasionally to evaluate your progress and make necessary adjustments.

菊 Chrysanthemum 2

IN THIS ARTWORK, we will paint the chrysanthemum florets and leaves in tsuketate-hou. This technique is particularly versatile, and, when paired with ink density control, can be used to express the diverse palette of chrysanthemum blossoms. Lighter shades of black ink allude to the soft, luminous white and yellow florets, while darker shades suggest the vivid orange, pink or purple florets.

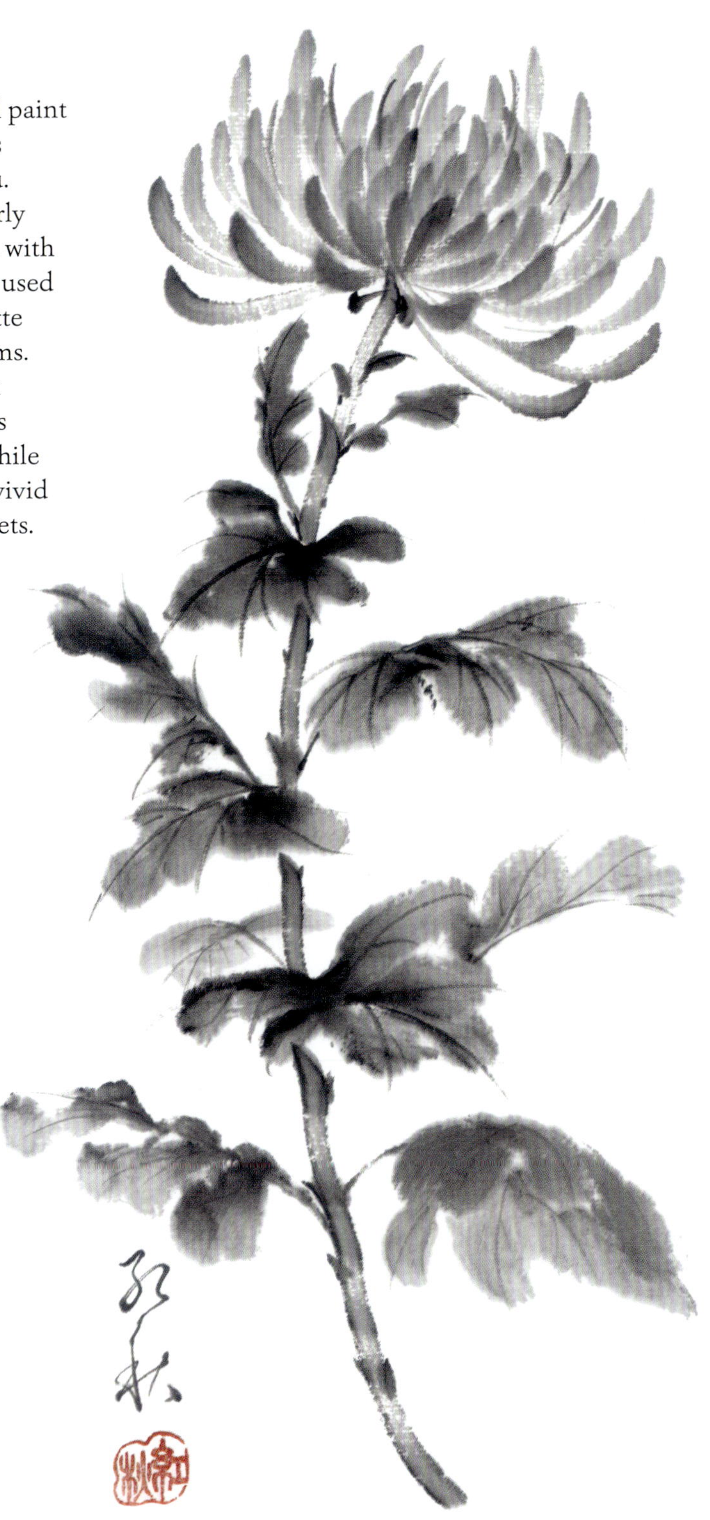

CHRYSANTHEMUM LEAVES AND FLOWERS: TSUKETATE-HOU

Use the image below as a guide and practise painting another variation of the chrysanthemum leaves:

Leaf variations

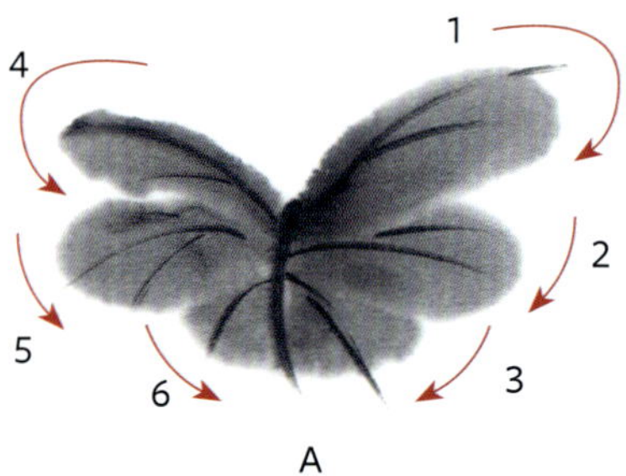

A

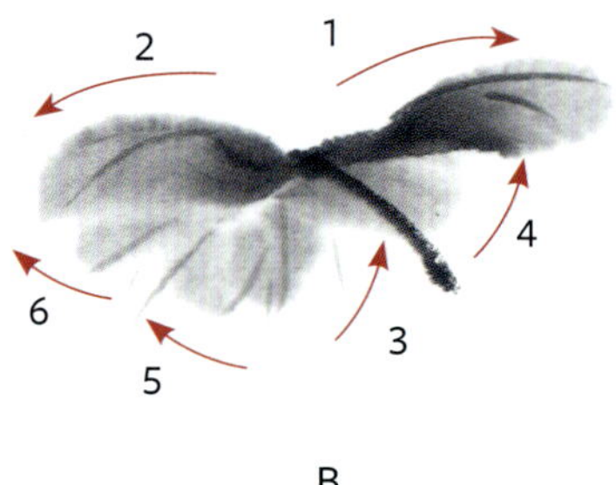

B

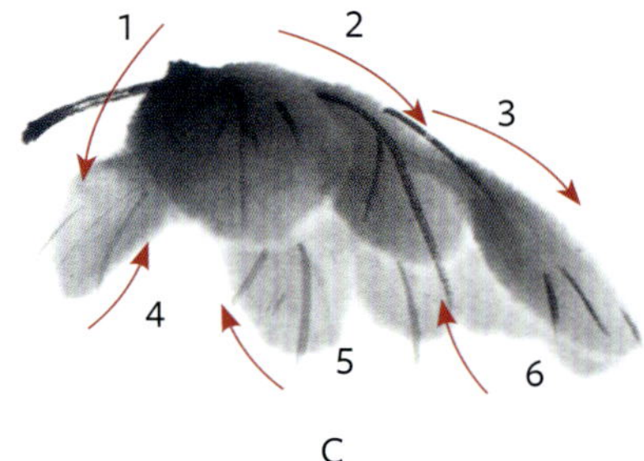

C

For leaf (A), paint the upper right segment followed by the two lower segments, then follow the same order on the left side. For leaves (B) and (C), paint the upper segments of the leaf first using a darker shade of ink (this represents the front side), followed by the lower segments of the leaf in a lighter shade (this represents the rear side).

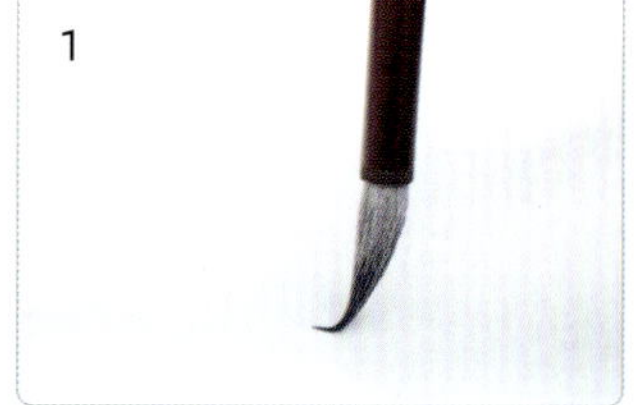

Petal practice

Before painting the chrysanthemum flower in tsuketate-hou, it is important to learn how to turn the brush in chokuhitsu to create curved lines.

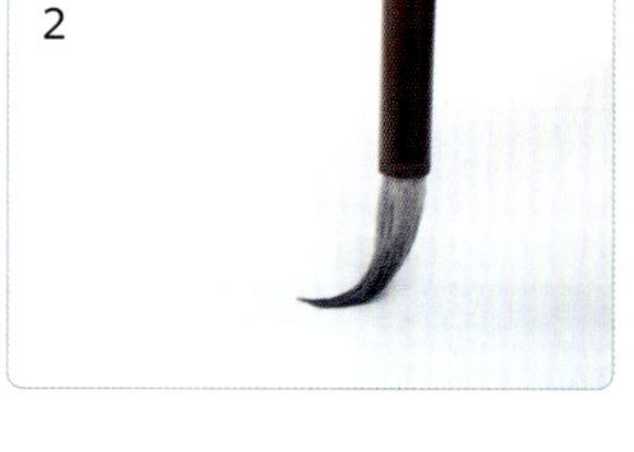

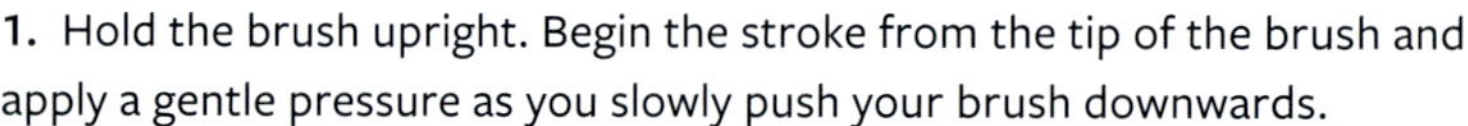
1. Hold the brush upright. Begin the stroke from the tip of the brush and apply a gentle pressure as you slowly push your brush downwards.

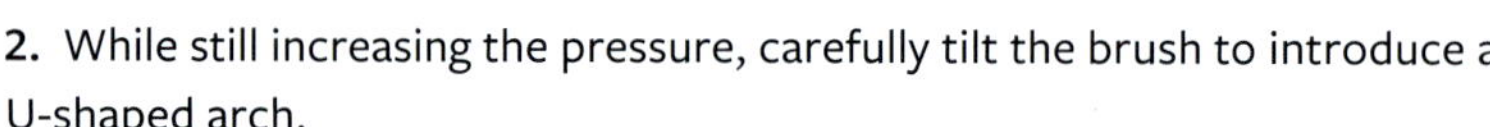
2. While still increasing the pressure, carefully tilt the brush to introduce a U-shaped arch.

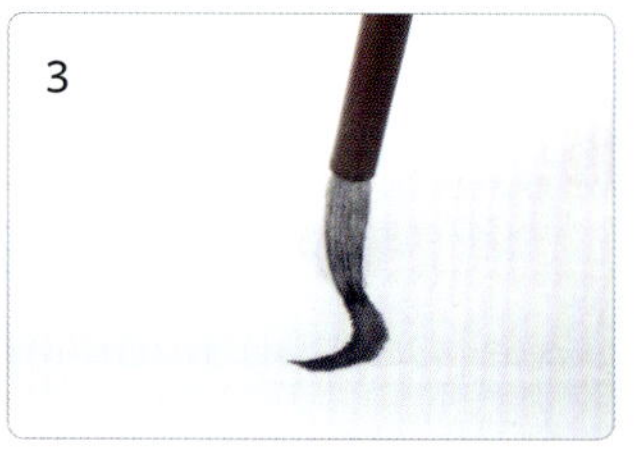

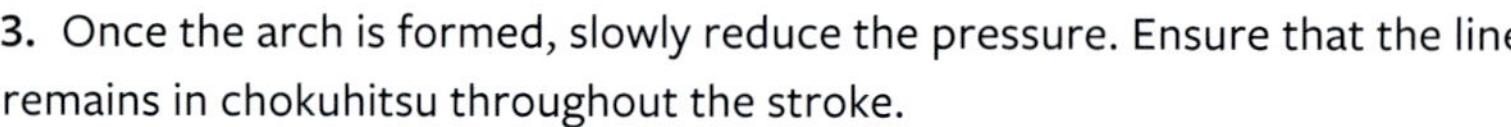
3. Once the arch is formed, slowly reduce the pressure. Ensure that the line remains in chokuhitsu throughout the stroke.

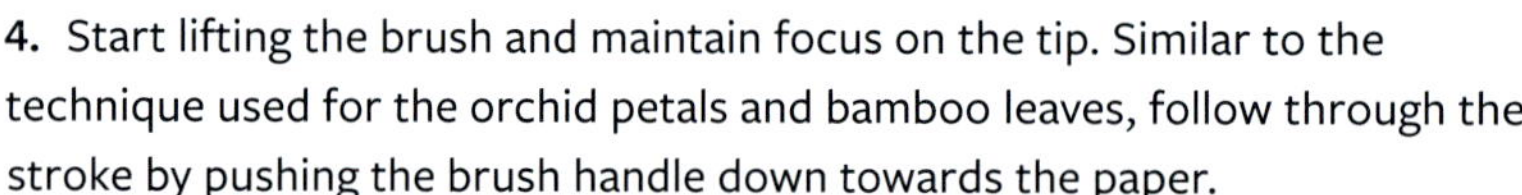
4. Start lifting the brush and maintain focus on the tip. Similar to the technique used for the orchid petals and bamboo leaves, follow through the stroke by pushing the brush handle down towards the paper.

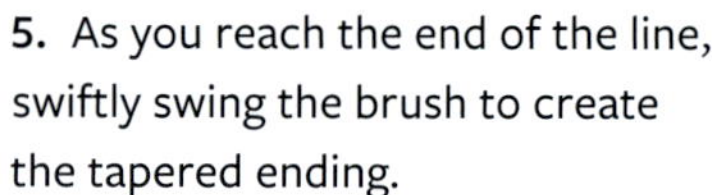
5. As you reach the end of the line, swiftly swing the brush to create the tapered ending.

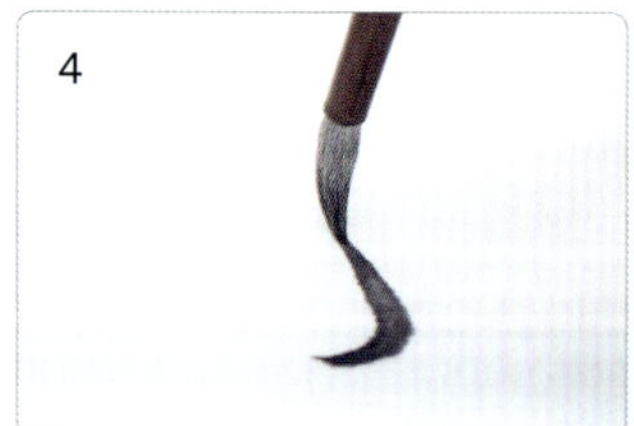

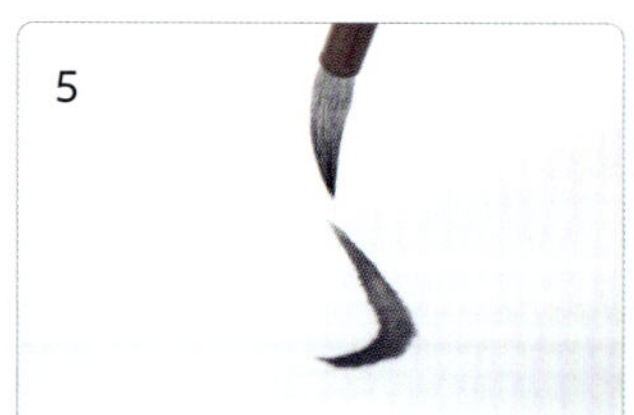

Flower

Load the ōfude with tanboku, the tip with chuboku and blend in preparation for sanboku-hou.

1. Begin by painting three short top-down strokes in chokuhitsu to create the centre florets.

2. Paint two florets on the left-hand side and another two on the right-hand side. This brush movement is similar to the technique used to paint the orchid petals.

3. Once the first layer is complete, paint more florets in between, again moving the brush towards the centre point. Remember that with sanboku-hou, the ink should gradually become lighter as you paint. If you paint over the first row, there will be minimal bleeding.

4. Continue to paint additional layers of florets behind.

5. Now, utilise the brush techniques covered on the previous page to paint some longer florets from the outside to the centre on both sides. Reapply nouboku to the tip of the brush for sanboku-hou and start from the front florets. Focus on maintaining core balance, rather than perfect symmetry.

6. Layer on additional florets behind the existing ones. These will naturally appear lighter. Next, use nouboku to paint two dots by the receptacle to represent the calyx.

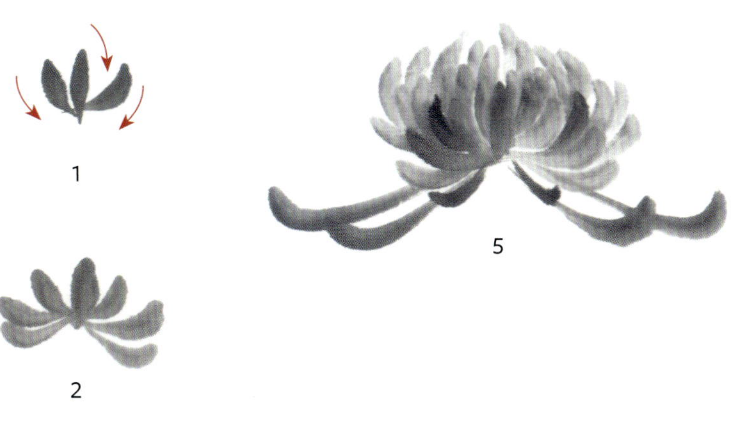

1

2

5

Finally, prepare the brush in either sanboku-hou or ryoguma and paint the stem.

7. Optional: paint thinner side-facing florets in between to enhance your expression (as shown on p. 59).

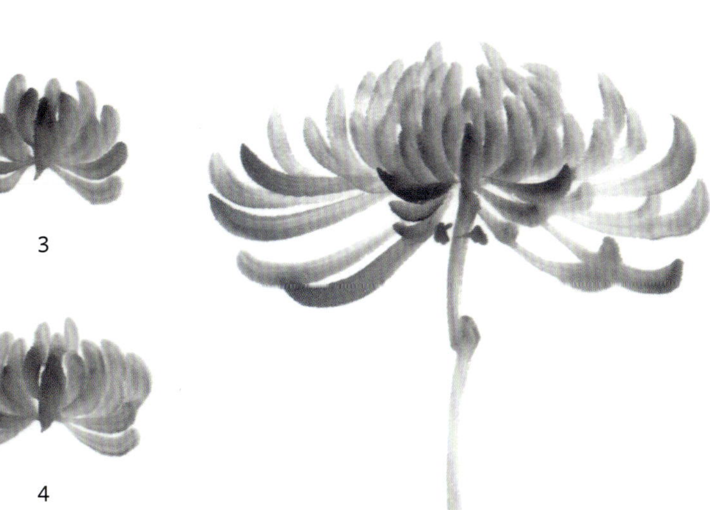

3

4

6

Bring together the various elements in the following order: the primary flower, stem (remember to leave a blank space within the stem to accommodate the front leaves) and leaves.

菊 Chrysanthemum 3

EXPANDING ON THE brush techniques covered in the previous two artworks, follow the composition on this page to paint the multi-flowered chrysanthemum in soft ryoguma.

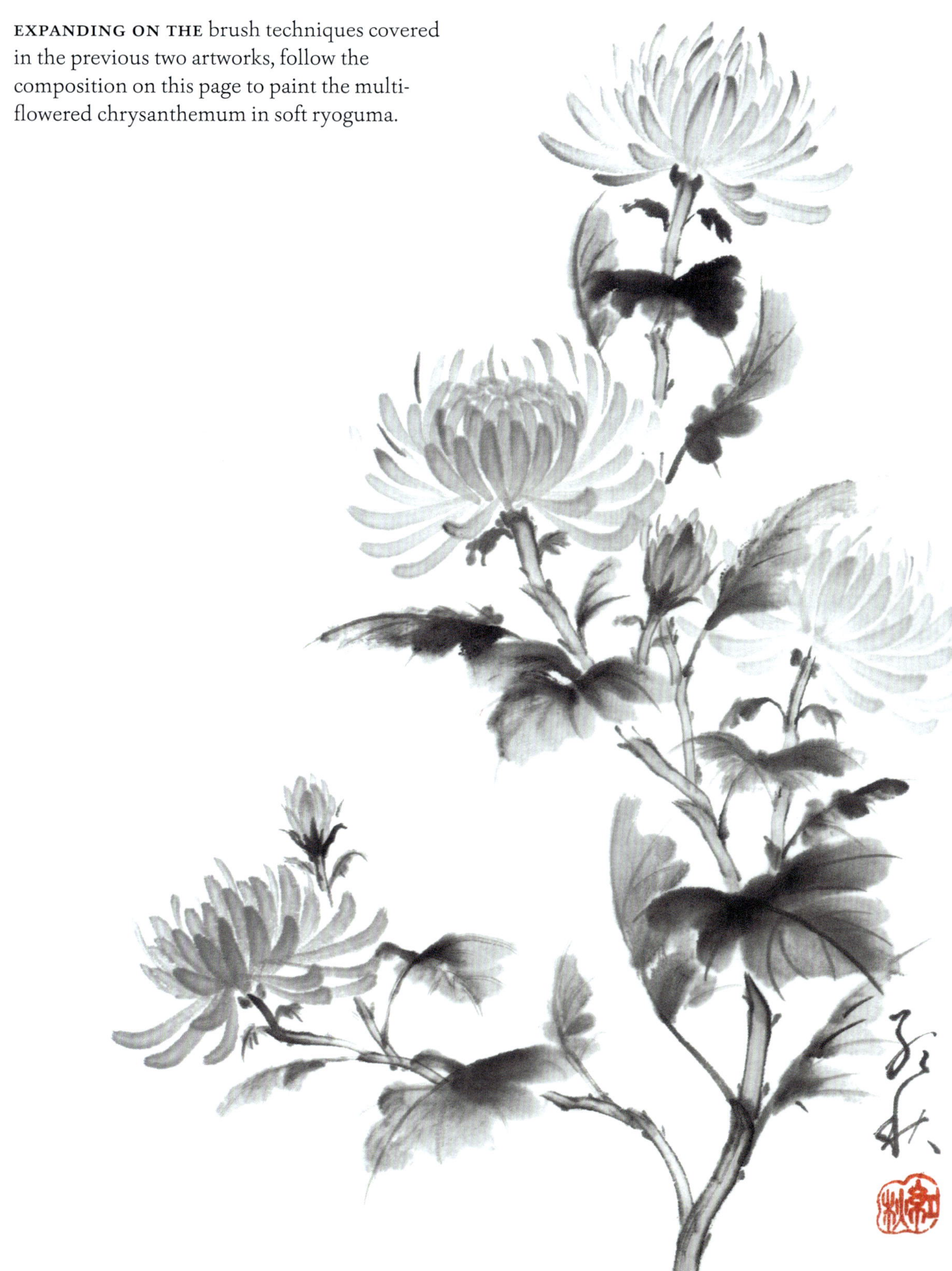

CHRYSANTHEMUM FLOWERS USING DIFFERENT INK TECHNIQUES

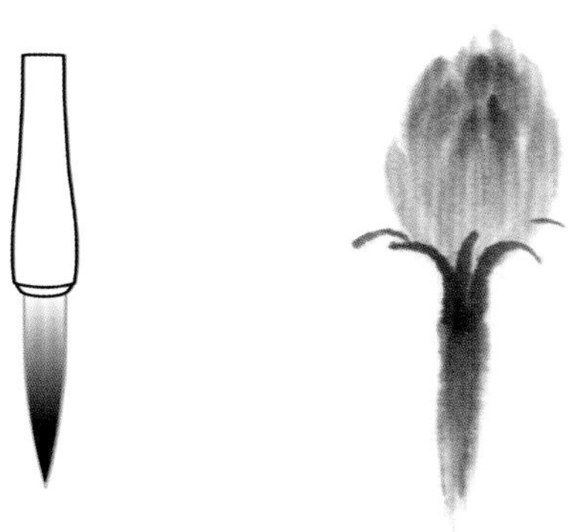

Bud in sanboku-hou

Paint the calyx in nouboku first, followed by the petals in sanboku-hou, using the same brush movements as painting the inner florets of the chrysanthemum bloom.

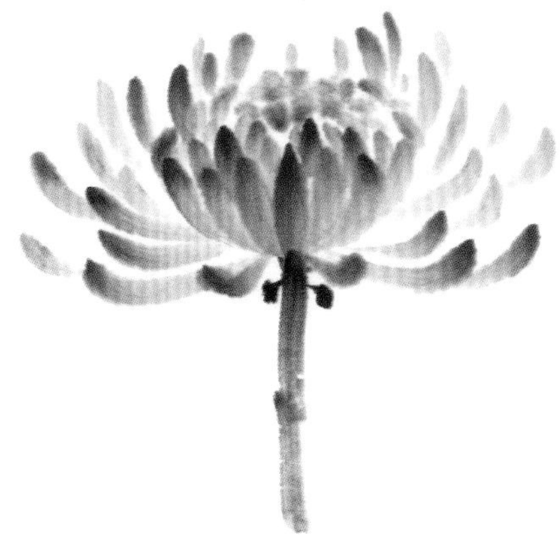

Closed chrysanthemum in sanboku-hou

Follow the steps to paint the chrysanthemum bloom outlined on p. 61. However, when you reach step 4, position the brush with the tip facing down towards the centre point, and gently tap the tip of the brush to complete the centre florets that curl inwards. Next, proceed with steps 5 and 6.

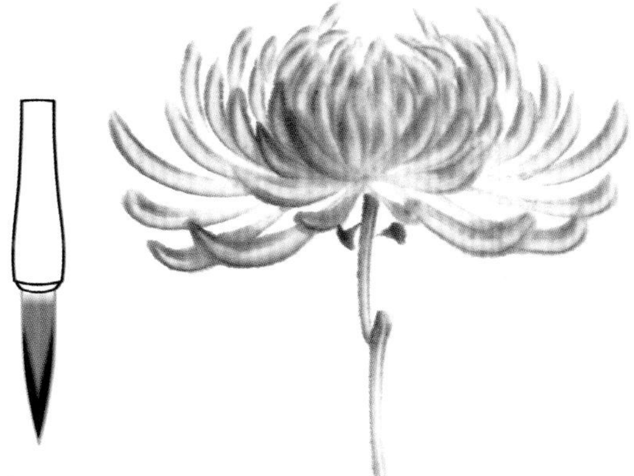

Open chrysanthemum in ryoguma (see p. 27).

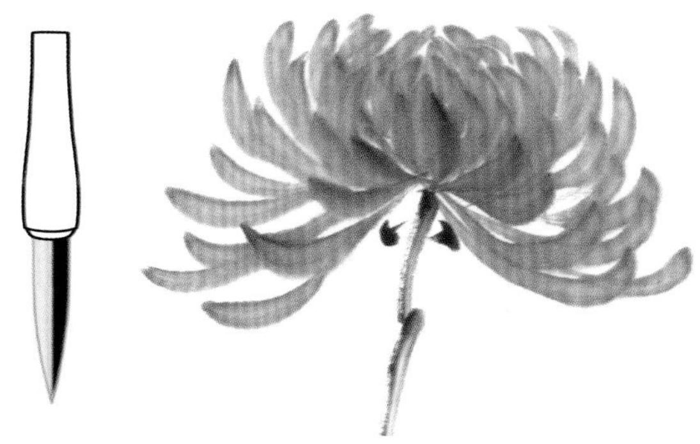

Open chrysanthemum in soft ryoguma

The soft ryoguma technique (see p. 28) creates softer colour edges in the florets compared to the ryoguma technique.

KEY POINTS

- The artwork on p. 62 uses soft ryoguma, however, you can explore the various brush techniques covered on this page (sanboku-hou, ryoguma or soft ryoguma) and choose a style that resonates with you.
- Take your time and savour the journey of creation.

Bring together the various elements in the following order: the flowers and buds, stems (remember to leave a blank space within the stems to accommodate the front leaves) and leaves.

梅 Plum Blossom 1

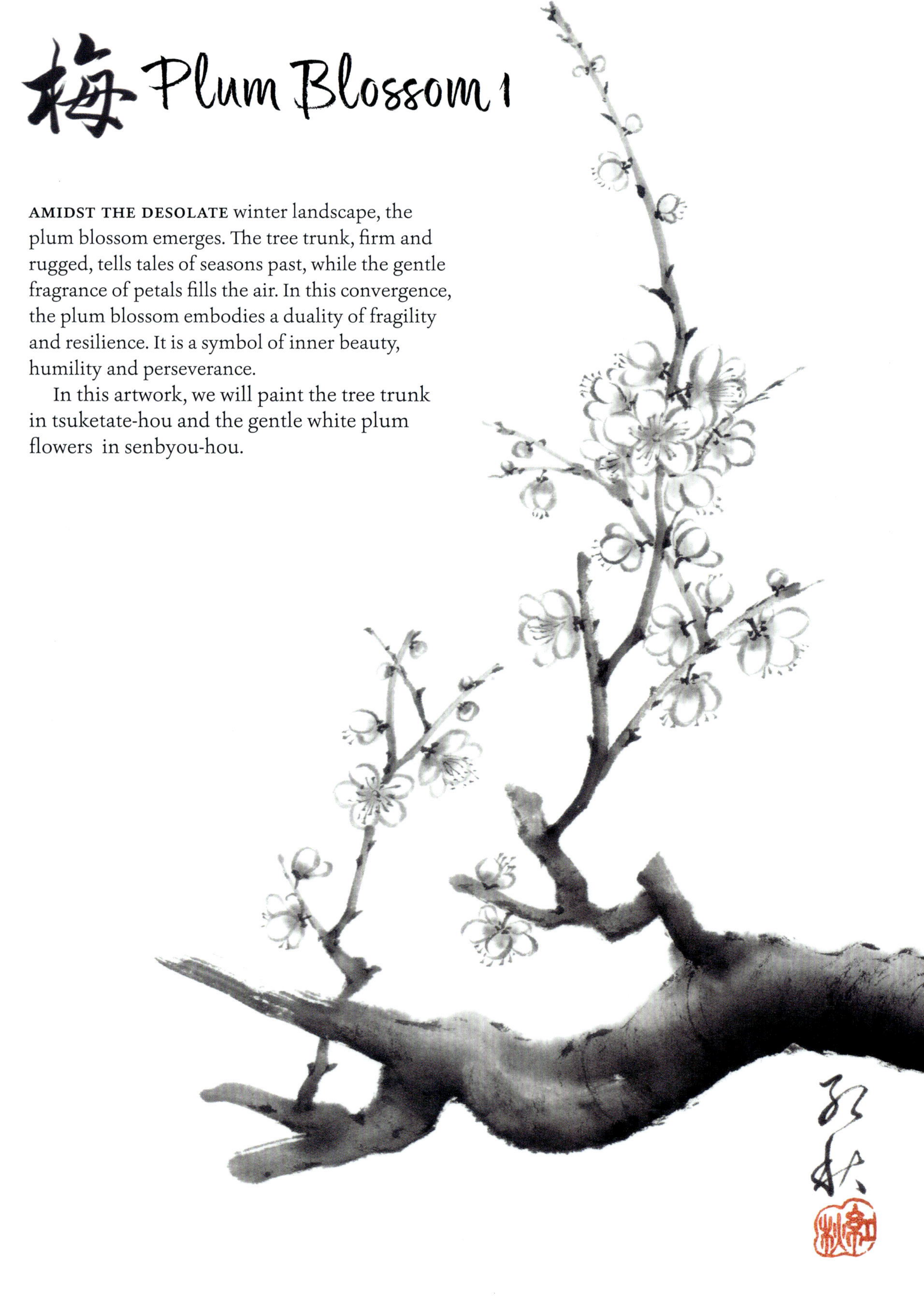

AMIDST THE DESOLATE winter landscape, the plum blossom emerges. The tree trunk, firm and rugged, tells tales of seasons past, while the gentle fragrance of petals fills the air. In this convergence, the plum blossom embodies a duality of fragility and resilience. It is a symbol of inner beauty, humility and perseverance.

In this artwork, we will paint the tree trunk in tsuketate-hou and the gentle white plum flowers in senbyou-hou.

PLUM BLOSSOM TREE TRUNK

Load the ōfude with chuboku, the tip with nouboku and blend in preparation for sanboku-hou. Use dynamic movements of the whole brush to paint the main tree trunk in sokuhitsu and the twigs and branches in semi-chokuhitsu, then chokuhitsu.

Unlike the straight and sleek lines of the bamboo culm, the plum tree trunk appears weathered and winding. Practise the following steps and build up the techniques to paint the plum tree trunk:

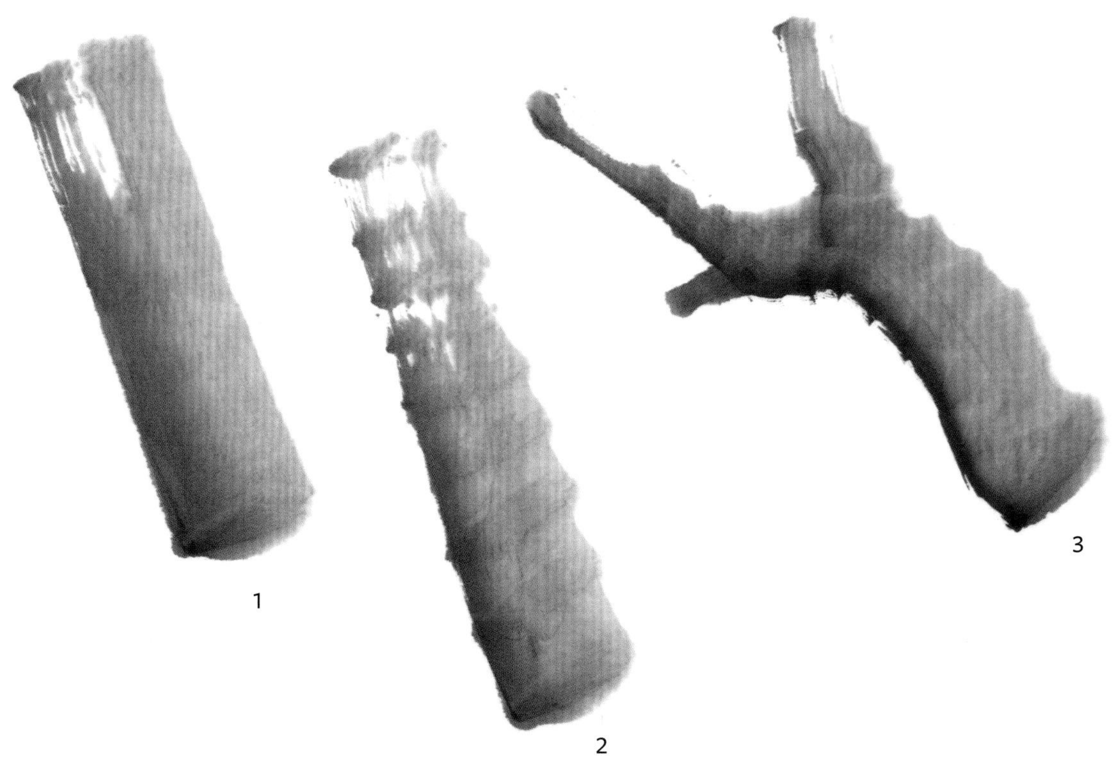

1. Straight line: create a straight and strong line in sokuhitsu, similar to the bamboo culm (p. 47). Maintain consistent pressure throughout the stroke.

2. Straight line with varied pressure: apply the technique from step 1, but introduce changes in pressure along the line with several quick, irregular pauses. Make sure the pauses are short to avoid ink bleeding.

3. Irregular line: apply the technique from step 2, but incorporate bends at a few locations. This stroke will mimic the natural irregularity found in the plum tree trunk. As you move up the branch, transition from sokuhitsu to semi-sokuhitsu to create thinner lines. Practise painting the tree trunk and branches from different angles until you feel comfortable.

Load the ōfude with chuboku, the tip with nouboku and blend in preparation for sanboku-hou. Adopting similar techniques used to paint the bamboo culm, hold the brush in sokuhitsu, lowering the angle. The tip of the brush should point towards the bottom of the paper, allowing the darker side to shade the lower portion of the tree trunk. Apply pressure with the whole brush and control the speed of your stroke, alternating between fast and slow movements.

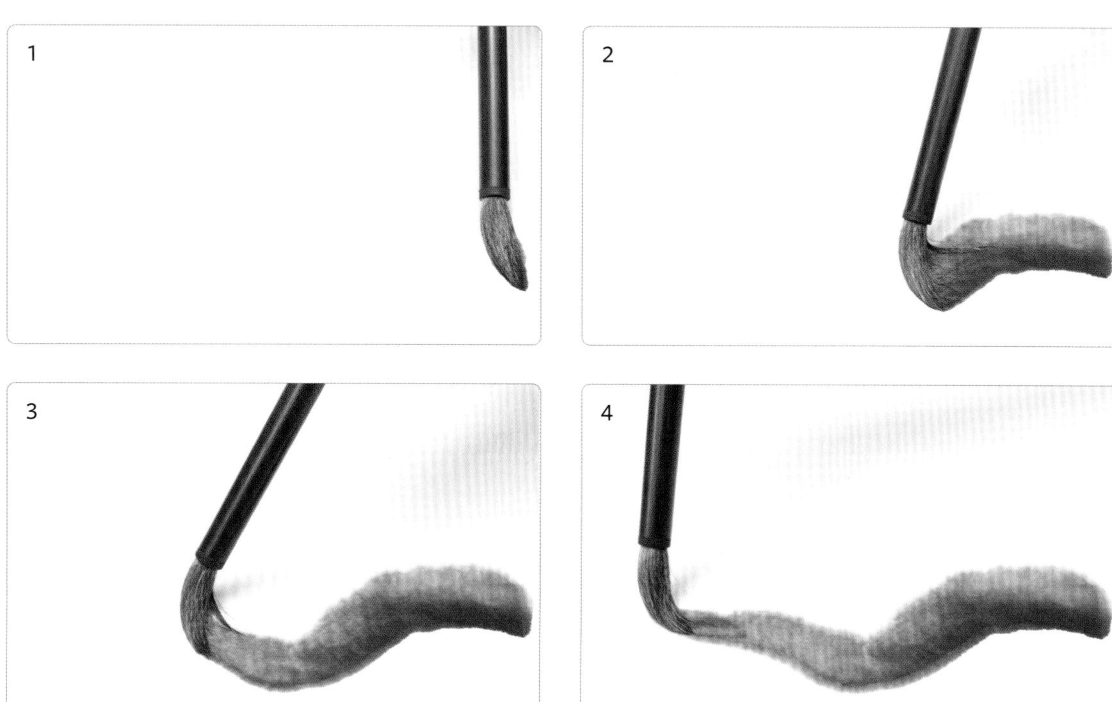

When preparing the brush for sanboku-hou, make sure to remove excess ink and complete the stroke without reapplying ink. Naturally, the kasure (dry brush) effect will show, which is particularly effective in capturing the weathered, textured appearance of the plum tree bark. As you reach the end of the main tree trunk, lift the brush swiftly to create a broken, tapered ending. To create thinner tree trunks, lift the brush and adjust the angle accordingly.

The branch collar (the junction between the tree trunk and branch) appears slightly swollen and bulbous. To paint this feature and create a seamless and organic transition from trunk to branch, gently push the brush inward, embed the stroke into the original trunk and then paint the branch.

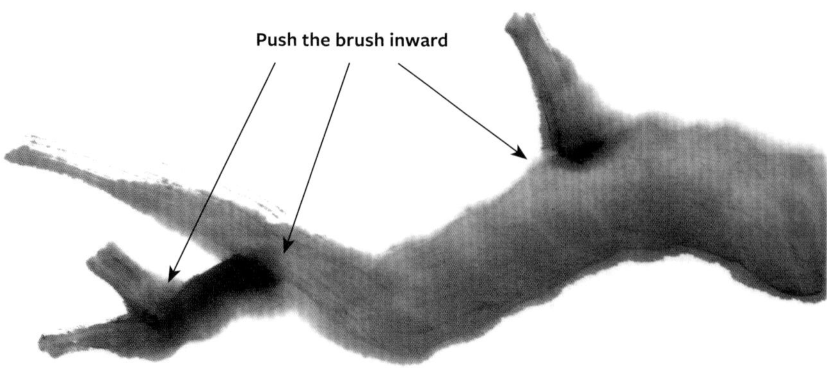

PLUM BLOSSOM BRANCHES AND TWIGS

'Nyoji' (女字)

The term 'Nyoji' derives from the combination of two characters: 'Nyo' (女) meaning 'woman', and 'Ji' (字), meaning 'letter'. Traditionally, Suibokuga students are taught to incorporate 'Nyoji' when depicting the tree trunks and branches of a plum tree, as the interlacing and crossing of these tree trunks and branches often resemble the shape of the character '女'.

Keep the '女' character in mind and cross two or three branches over in your painting.

As you reach the tip of each branch, reduce the pressure to create thinner lines.

Paint dots along the branches and twigs to represent the axillary buds.

For the final touch, use the nejiri-fude or wari-fude (dry brush) techniques to give the tree trunk a rugged organic finish (see p. 31). Load the kofude with nouboku then spread out the bristles of the brush with your fingertips or a cloth. Paint softly curved lines, following the natural contours of the trunk, while keeping in mind its cylindrical nature. Start with a light touch and gradually build up the texture.

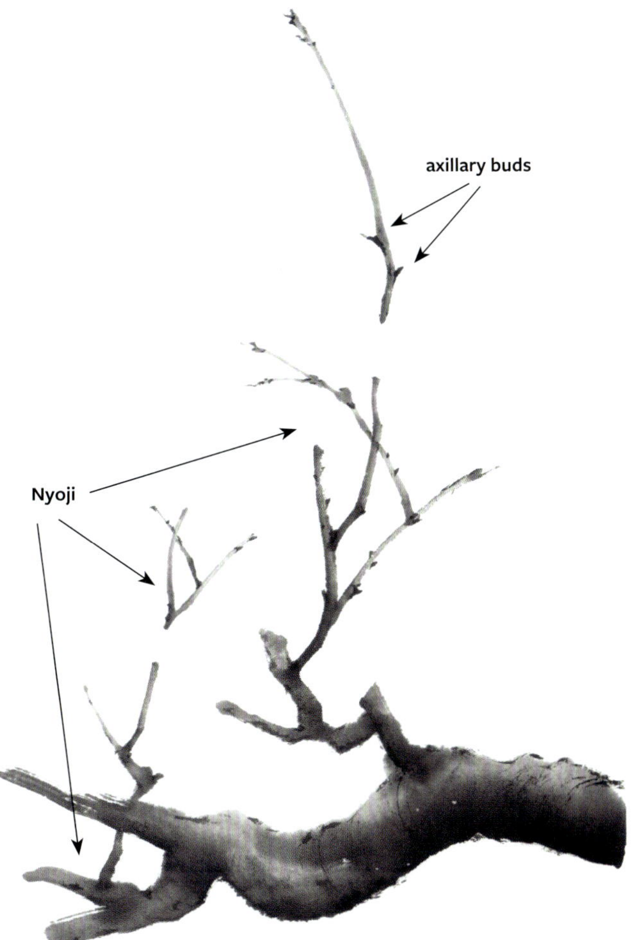

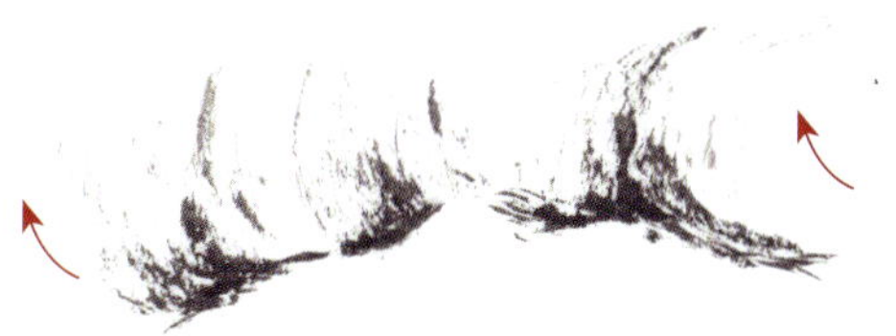

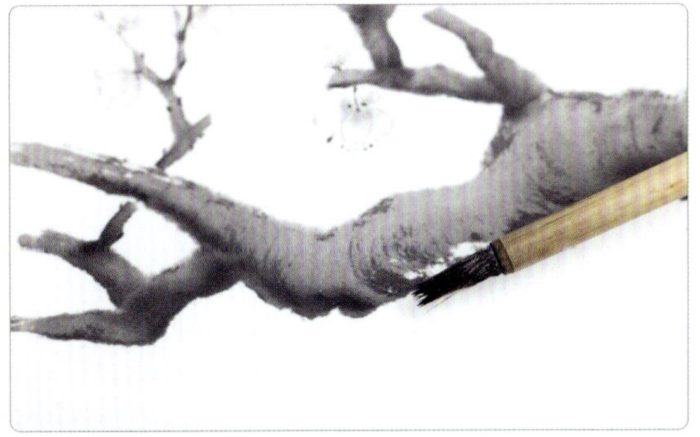

KEY POINTS

- To embody the resilience and strength of the plum tree, use darker shades of ink while maintaining the 'three layers' of sanboku-hou.
- Embrace the kasure effect as it appears naturally to create broken, asymmetrical lines; facilitate the effect by removing excess ink and painting the line in one continuous, swift stroke.

PLUM BLOSSOM FLOWER: SENBYOU-HOU

Load the kofude with tanboku and hold it upright.

Front-facing flower (A)

1. Start by painting a small circle in the centre, using the tip of the brush. This will serve as a guide to balance the five round petals evenly.

2. Paint a round shape for the first petal, either in one or two strokes, using a lighter pressure near the centre.

3. Add two more petals on the opposite side.

4. Place the final two petals in between the existing petals. Following this order will help achieve a balanced arrangement of petals around the centre point.

5. Load the menso-fude or the tip of the kofude with nouboku or chuboku, and with a gentle flick, paint thin, dark lines from the outside inwards to represent the long pistil and stamens. Once the ink is moderately dry, apply goku-tanboku to the centre.

A B

1

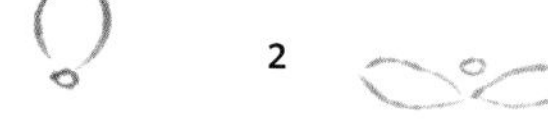

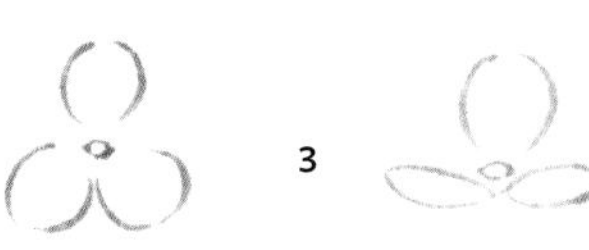

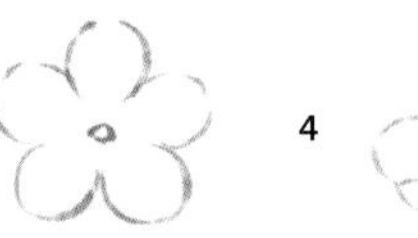

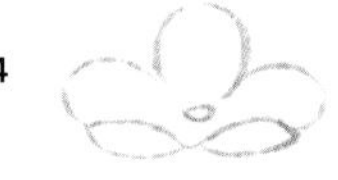

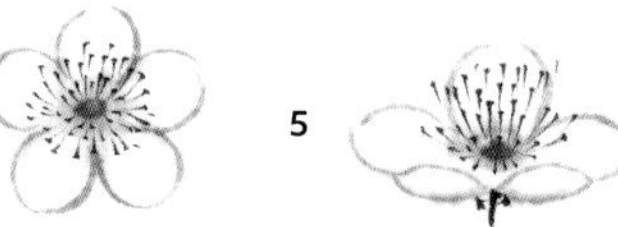

Front-facing tilted flower (B)

1. Follow step 1 for flower A.

2. Paint two flat, oval-shaped petals underneath the circle on both sides.

3. Paint one round petal in the middle.

4. Paint two more round petals in between the existing petals.

5. Follow step 5 for flower A. Finish by painting the calyx in darker ink.

Practise painting the plum blossom flowers from different angles.

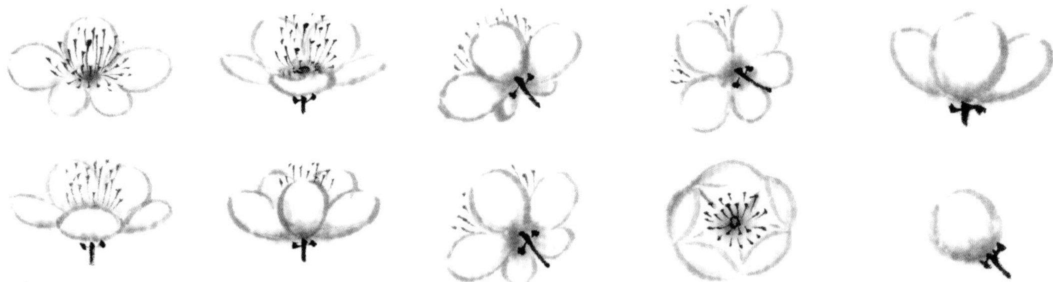

Bring together the various elements in the following order: the main plum tree trunk, branches, plum flowers and buds, axillary buds and twigs. Finish off by painting the weathered texture of the tree bark using the nejiri- or wari-fude technique.

KEY POINT

Unlike other woody plants, the plum blossom tree shows unique flowering patterns, where the flowers and buds bloom directly on the branches and the twigs, and often gather in clusters. Keep these characteristics in mind when painting the plum blossom tree.

梅 Plum Blossom 2

IN THIS ARTWORK, we will use light, delicate strokes to paint the plum blossom petals in tsuketate-hou. Similar to the chrysanthemum blossoms, we will use the shade of ink to allude to the colour of the petals: darker shades of ink to depict the red plum flower, known as 'kobai' (紅梅) and lighter shades to depict the white plum flower, known as 'hakubai' (白梅).

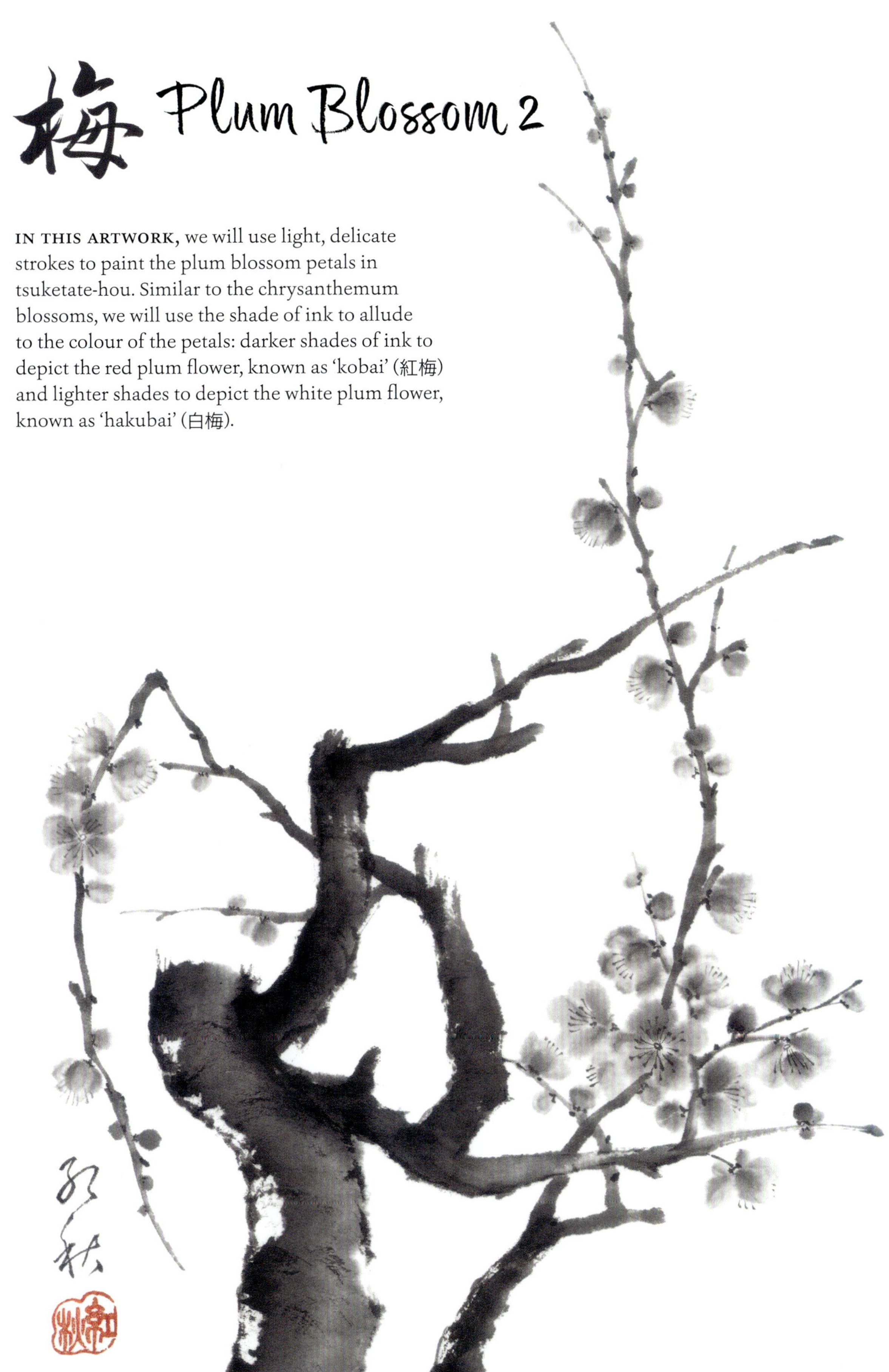

PLUM BLOSSOM FLOWER: TSUKETATE-HOU

Follow the same flower shape and arrangement as covered in Plum Blossom Flower: senbyou-hou artwork on p. 68, and experiment with different ink effects. Incorporating sanboku-hou, for example, creates a natural gradation within each petal, featuring a darker centre where the pistil and stamens cast shadows.

Load a smaller ōfude with goku-tanboku, the tip with chuboku and blend in preparation for sanboku-hou.

Front-facing flower (A)

1. Start by painting a small circle in the centre with the tip of your brush.
2. To paint the first petal, point the tip of the brush towards the centre, and press the body of the brush downwards and sideways to create an oval shape in one stroke.
3. Using the same technique, paint two more petals around the centre point.
4. Place the final two petals in between the existing petals.
5. Once the ink is moderately dry, load the menso-fude or tip of kofude with chuboku and paint the pistil and stamens as before.

Front-facing tilted flower (B)

1. Follow step 1 for flower A.
2. Point the tip of the brush towards the centre, and paint two flat oval-shaped petals underneath the circle, on both sides.
3. Using the same technique, paint one round petal in the middle.
4. Paint two more oval petals in between the existing petals.
5. Follow step 5 for flower A. Finish off by painting the calyx in nouboku.

A B

1

2

3
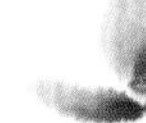

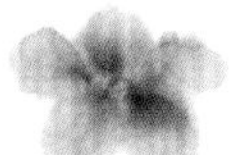
4
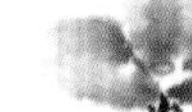

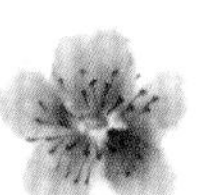
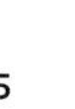
5
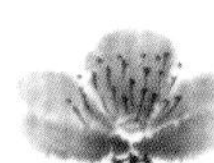

Practise painting the plum blossom flowers from different angles.

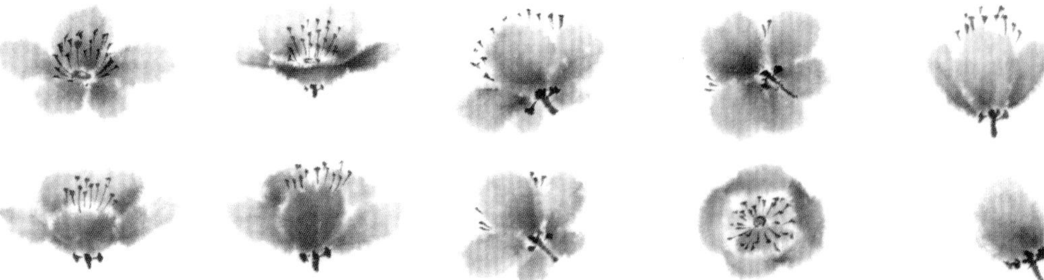

Bring together the various elements in the following order: the main plum tree trunk, branches, plum flowers and buds, axillary buds and twigs. Finish by painting the weathered texture of the tree bark using the nejiri-fude or wari-fude technique.

墨彩画

Bokusaiga

The allure of colour

IN THE PREVIOUS CHAPTER, we explored 'The Four Gentlemen' and learned the fundamental brush techniques and compositional principles that form the backbone of Suibokuga. In the remaining artworks, we will build upon these techniques to paint flowers, fruits, vegetables, insects, birds and fish.

So far, we have focused solely on Suibokuga, which is one subset of Sumi-e and is characterised by its predominantly monochrome style of painting, featuring minimal or secondary use of colour. However, another subset of Sumi-e is Bokusaiga, where 'boku' represents ink and 'sai' means colour. Bokusaiga broadens the palette by embracing the use of colour as a means to complement and enhance the sumi ink, while using the same brush and ink control techniques as Suibokuga.

In Sumi-e, paintings that incorporate colour are typically more ornate compared to their monochromatic counterparts, depending on how the colour is utilised. Nevertheless, across the various subsets of Sumi-e, the allure lies in capturing the essence of the subject and the addition of colour should not distract from the main principles of Sumi-e.

For the following artworks, we will paint various subjects, simultaneously exploring the principles of colour use in Sumi-e.

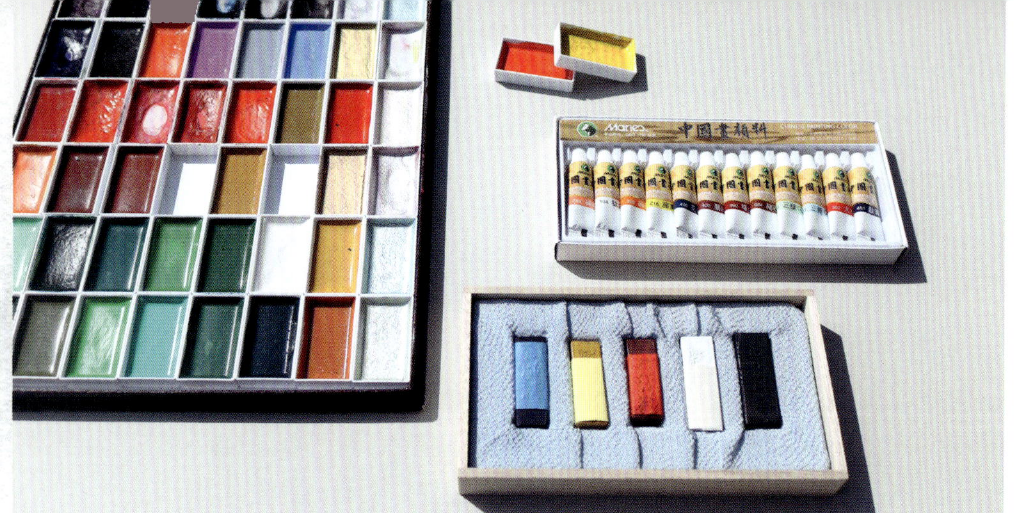

LEFT TO RIGHT Gansai paint, Saienboku and Chinese paint.

COLOURED INKS

There are several types of coloured ink that you can use for Bokusaiga, depending on the desired effect, accessibility and affordability.

Saienboku

Saienboku is the coloured counterpart of the traditional Japanese shouenboku inkstick and can create a wide range of shades, from subdued colours tailored to Japanese aesthetic preferences to brilliant primary colours. This medium can also be blended with black sumi ink to deepen and intensify the colours.

While many coloured paints use gum arabic as their primary adhesive, Saienboku contains nikawa glue (a traditional, natural Japanese adhesive made from the skin and bones of animals). This alters the ink's viscosity and allows for the creation of three-dimensional effects that are not easily achievable with other types of ink. Saienboku can be used in a similar manner to sumi ink, but is unique in that it enables the full expression of brush marks and enhances the nijimi and gradation effects.

Gansai paint

A more accessible and affordable option, Gansai paint is a traditional Japanese pan watercolour renowned for its versatility and ease of use. It is characterised by the vibrant, soft colours it produces, which resemble the colours found in nature.

Gansai paints are typically bound by a combination of nikawa glue, gum arabic, sugar syrup, starch and other ingredients. The inclusion of nikawa glue (although minimal compared to Saienboku) in Gansai paint helps minimise bleeding and prevents fading. To further minimise bleeding and fading, additional nikawa glue can be applied, either directly to the paper or mixed with the Gansai paint.

Compared to Western watercolour paints, Gansai paints are highly pigmented and opaque. Although Western watercolours can be used if necessary, they tend to create more transparent washes that do not interact as well with Japanese paper. Additionally, Western watercolours are traditionally bound with gum Arabic, which means a higher likelihood of bleeding and colour fading, compromising the high degree of ink control that is preferred in Sumi-e.

Chinese paint

This is another option for Bokusaiga, as it is generally more affordable and accessible outside of Japan. This type of paint typically contains a higher amount of adhesive compared to Gansai paint, which provides better control over ink density, allowing for the creation of a spectrum of colours, from light and transparent to rich and opaque. Again, with Chinese paint, the addition of nikawa glue can mimic the effects achieved with Saienboku.

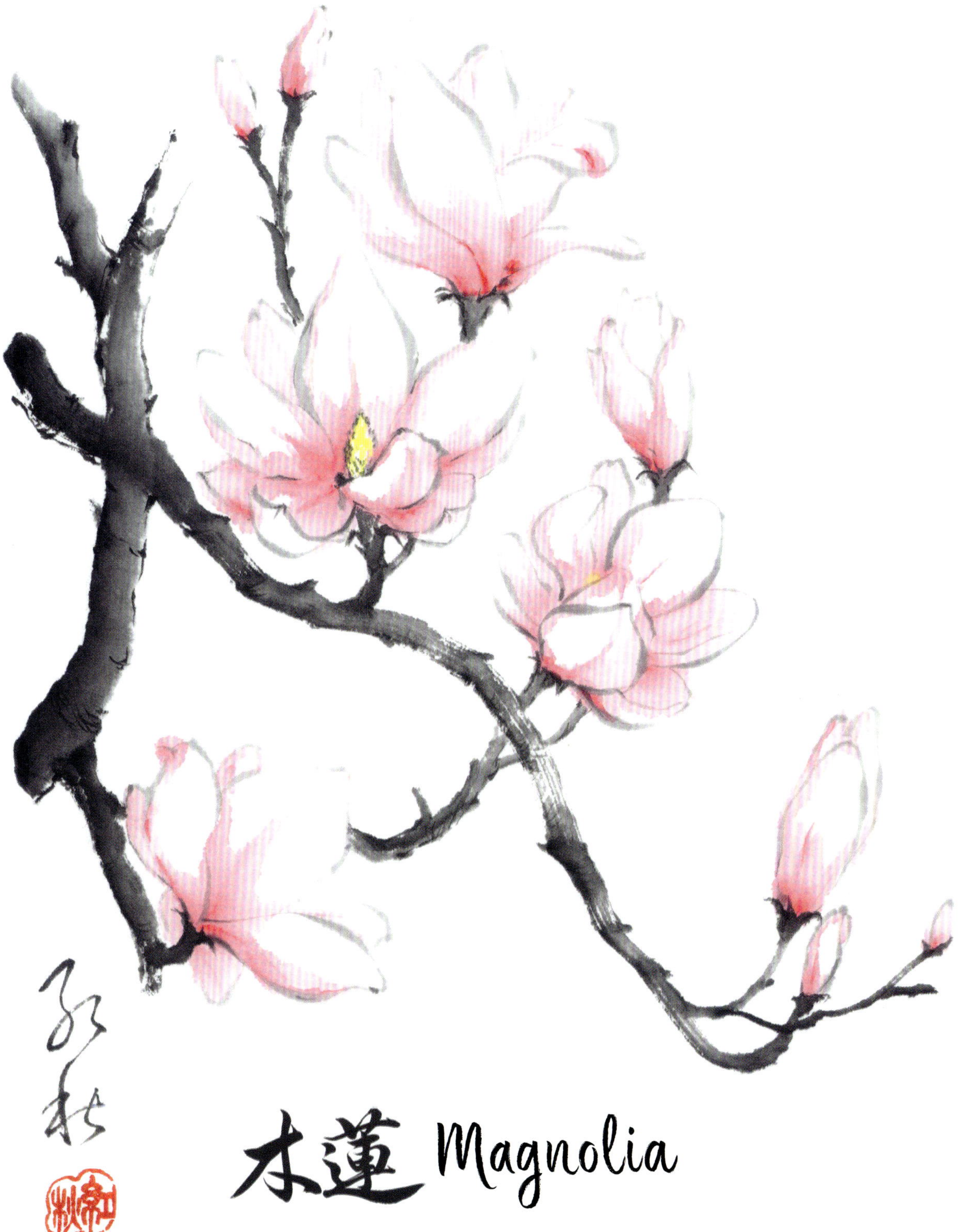

木蓮 Magnolia

IN THIS ARTWORK, we will paint the Japanese magnolia bloom in senbyou-hou, the same technique employed in painting the chrysanthemum and plum blossom. We will introduce variations in pressure control and colour to capture the essence of the magnolia's lush, delicate tepals as they unfurl.

MAGNOLIA FLOWER

Load the kofude with tanboku and paint in senbyou-hou.

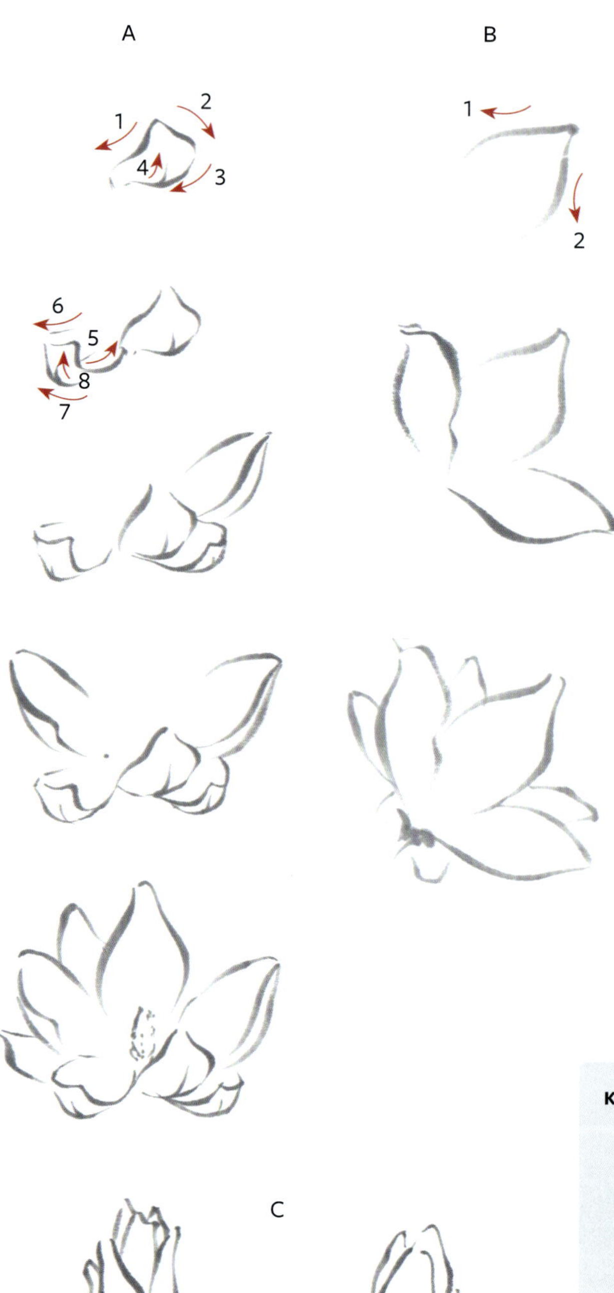

Front-facing tilted flower (A)

Draw the outline of the centre front tepal in four strokes, following the arrows for guidance. Use the tip of the brush and apply a slight pressure where the lines appear thicker. Repeat the same technique to build the front tepals first, followed by the side and back tepals. For the final touch, paint a faint outline for the pistils and stamens in the centre.

Side-facing flower (B)

Following the same brush movements as in painting flower A, create another variation of an open flower. Start by painting the front tepals, followed by the side then the back tepals.

Bud (C)

Following the same brush movements as in painting the open flower, create thinner tepals that curl inwards for the bud.

Load the brush with chuboku and paint the receptacle where the flower meets the branch.

KEY POINTS

- Once you have outlined the magnolia bloom and buds in senbyou-hou, the addition of lighter sumi ink or colour can enhance the form and expression of the flower. The key principle of senbyou-hou is to express using simple lines, so it is essential not to detract from this simplicity when incorporating colour.
- When painting with colour, make sure you use a new or clean brush that does not contain any black ink residues.

To apply colour in sanboku-hou, we must first create two shades of colour.

To create the darker shade of pink:

1. Begin by pouring a few drops of clean water into the ezara.

2. Load the ōfude with water and remove excess water to avoid dripping.

3. Dip the brush into the red paint/ink from the palette, paint tube or inkstone and transfer it to the ezara.

4. Rinse the brush in clean water and, again, remove excess water.

5. Dip the brush into the white paint/ink, transfer to the same ezara and blend to create a pink shade. This pink shade is the colour equivalent of 'chuboku' or medium-dark ink. Adjust the levels of red and white paint, depending on the desired shade.

To create the lighter shade of pink:

6. Prepare another ezara with a teaspoon of water.

7. Load the brush with the pink 'chuboku' from the first ezara and transfer it to the new ezara. This will create a diluted shade; the colour equivalent of 'goku-tanboku'.

This method will apply when creating different coloured shades for subsequent artworks.

Colour use

Load the ōfude with very light pink ink and the tip with medium-dark pink. Blend in preparation for sanboku-hou, and gently wipe the brush with a cloth.

Place the tip of the brush towards the centre of the tepals, press down and gently swing the brush upwards towards the tip of the tepals. This technique will create a natural gradation of colour within each tepal. Add subtle accents of pink to the tepals in the back.

Apply the colour sparingly to bring out the simplicity of the lines and complement the white of the petals.

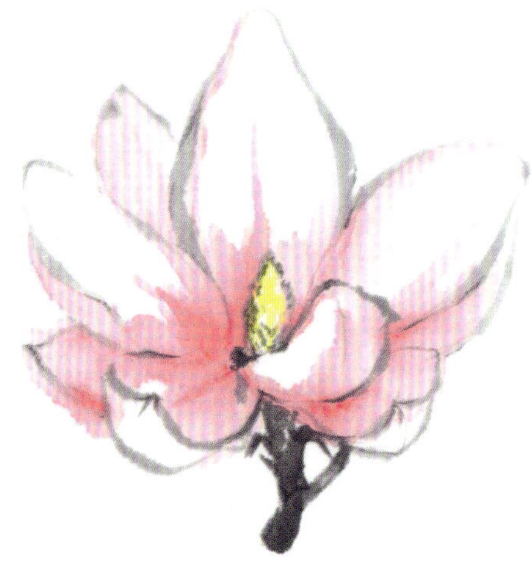

To colour in the centre pistils and stamens, prepare a damp brush and apply yellow paint directly from the palette without additional dilution.

Branches and twigs

A distinguishing feature of the magnolia tree is its thin branches, curving form and silvery bark. To capture these characteristics, we will adapt the techniques used to paint the plum blossom tree to paint the magnolia branches and twigs.

1. Load the ōfude with chuboku, the tip with nouboku and blend in preparation for sanboku-hou. Remove excess ink to enable the kasure effect.

2. Start creating a line in semi-sokuhitsu for the broader sections of the branch, and gradually transition to chokuhitsu to create the thinner branches and sharper twigs. While executing the strokes, embrace an irregular rhythm with pauses at regular intervals and variations in speed to mimic the organic growth of the branches.

3. For the final touch, load the kofude with nouboku and use the nejiri-fude technique to paint softly curved lines that follow the cylindrical contours of the branches. Let the rhythm of the branch guide your strokes, pay attention to the pauses in the branch's structure and paint axillary buds at these points (see p. 67).

Bring together the various elements in the following order: the main branches, outline of the flowers and buds, twigs and details (texture of the bark, axillary buds). Finally, apply colour.

向日葵 Sunflower

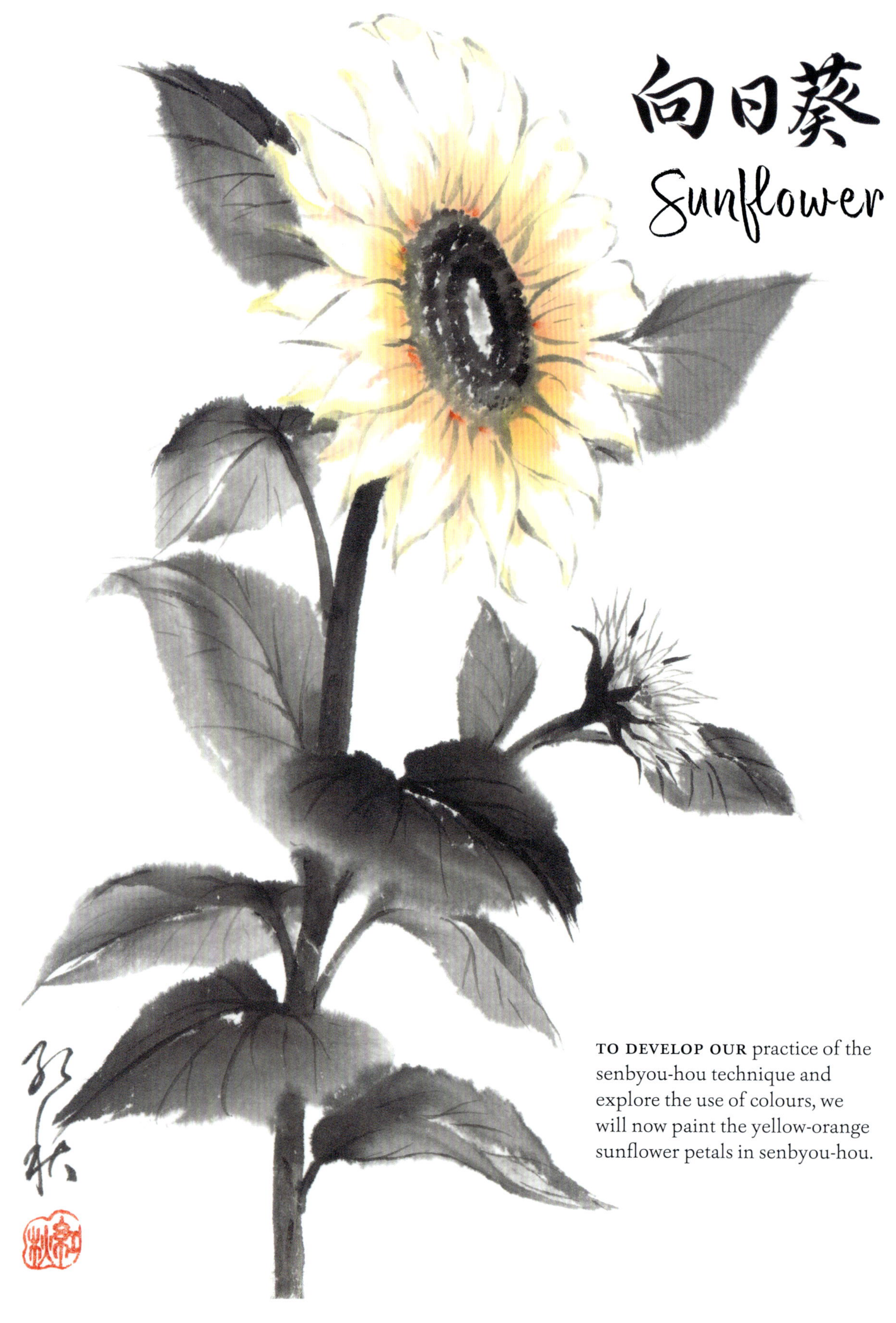

TO DEVELOP OUR practice of the senbyou-hou technique and explore the use of colours, we will now paint the yellow-orange sunflower petals in senbyou-hou.

SUNFLOWER FLORETS

The sunflower head is composed of many small flowers; the black-brown disc florets cluster in the centre in a spiral formation, surrounded by a ring of larger, bright yellow-orange ray florets that resemble petals.

Load the ōfude with tanboku, the tip with nouboku and blend just the tip of the brush (approximately 5mm).

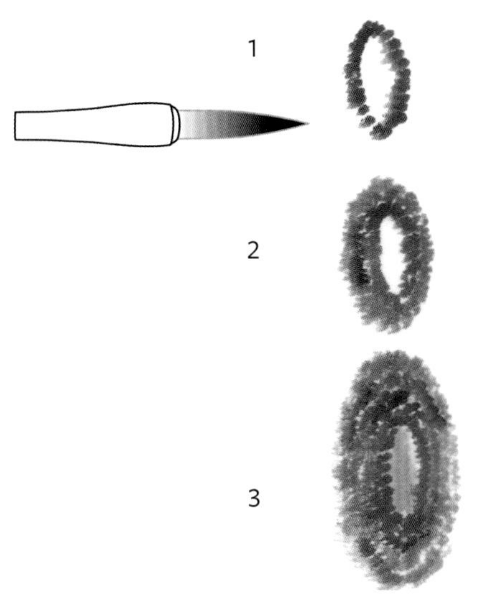

1. Begin by painting the disc florets that form the centrepiece of the sunflower. Paint dots by tapping the tip of the brush on the paper (alternatively use the kofude), forming an oval ring. This technique will create a natural gradation within each disc floret, with the upper half being darker than the lower half.

2. From the centre outwards, use the same brush movements to build around this ring. For this step, it may be easier to position the paper in landscape.

3. Once the disc florets are dry, apply goku-tanboku to the very centre.

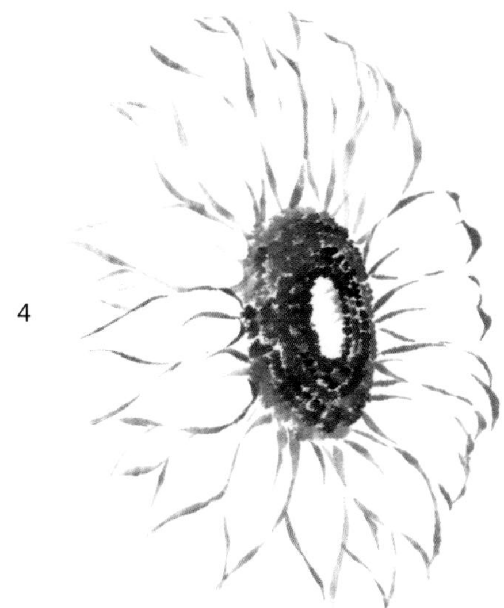

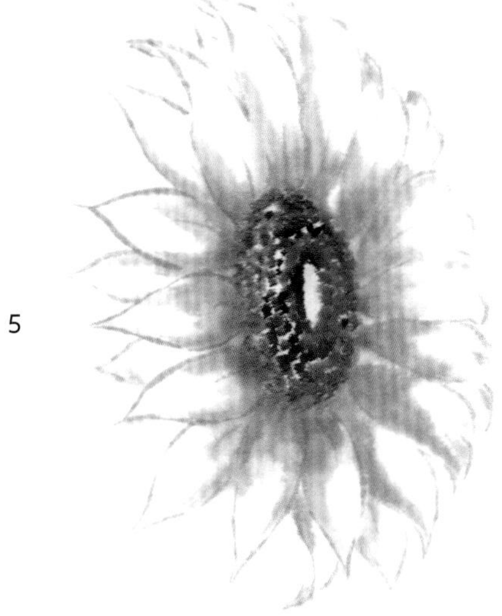

4. Load the kofude with tanboku and paint the outline of the ray florets, one by one. Employ the same brush techniques and pressure control as in painting the magnolia flower (see p. 74).

5. Load the ōfude with goku-tanboku and shade in the base of each ray floret (similar to the shading of the magnolia tepals). To introduce a further contrast, apply an additional layer of tanboku or chuboku while the goku-tanboku is still wet – this method of creating a nijimi effect refers to haboku-hou (see p. 31).

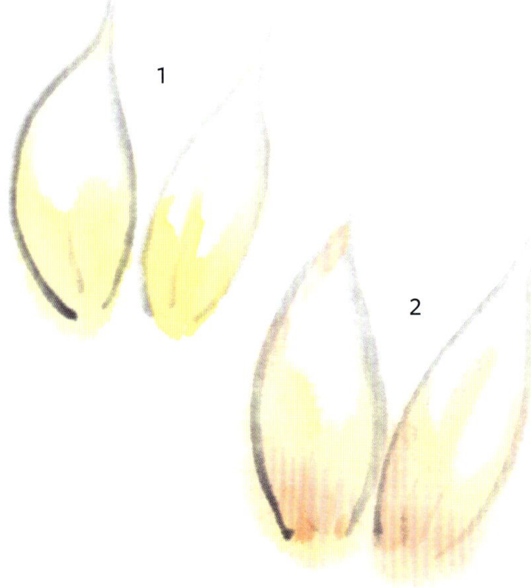

Colour use

Prepare two colours of ink: a light yellow and a medium-dark orange.

1. Load the ōfude with light yellow ink, the tip with medium-dark orange ink and blend in preparation for sanboku-hou.

Place the tip of the brush towards the base of the ray floret, press down and gently swing the brush toward the tip of the floret.

This technique will create a natural gradation of colour, with a darker shade at the base that gradually fades.

2. To introduce a further contrast, apply an additional layer of orange ink at the base of the ray floret, while the previous layer is still wet.

Bud

1. Load the kofude with nouboku and begin by painting the calyx.

2. In senbyou-hou, paint thin, short ray florets in the front.

3. Paint dots for disc florets.

4. Proceed to paint the petals at the back.

Colour use

To depict the younger buds, use either a light touch of yellow ink or continue in black sumi ink.

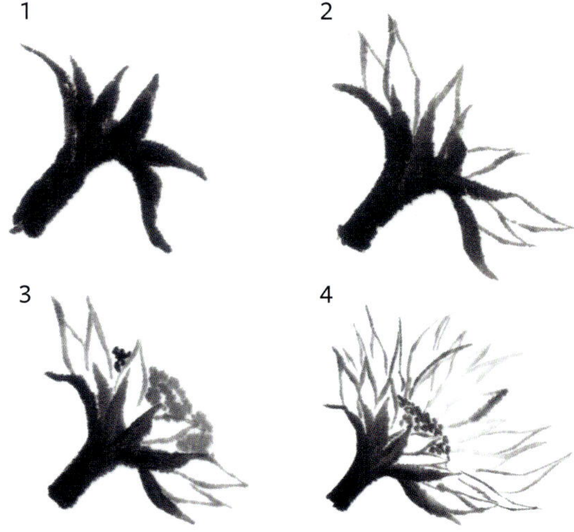

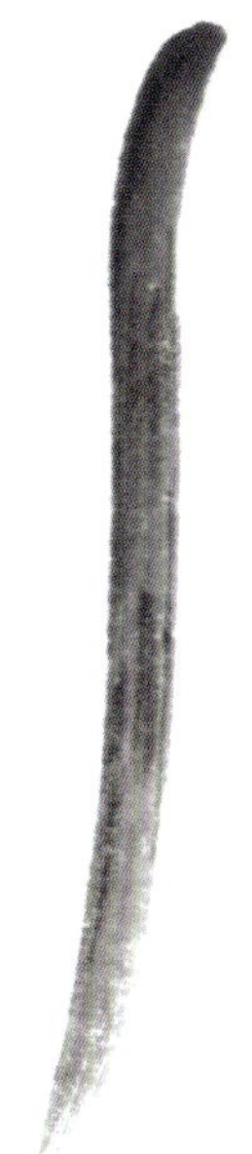

Stem

The sunflower stem stands tall and erect; its surface covered in coarse hairs.

Take the ōfude and gently flatten the brush against the palette or with your fingers.

In chokuhitsu, create a wide strong stem extending from top to bottom.

To capture the textured and hairy stem, use the wari-fude or nejiri-fude technique (see p. 31) with nouboku to create faint lines on the stem.

SUNFLOWER LEAVES

The sunflower leaves are large and broad, arranged alternately on the stem.

Load the ōfude with chuboku, the tip with nouboku and blend in preparation for sanboku-hou.

In tsuketate-hou, paint each leaf in two full strokes. Position the tip of the brush towards the centre vein to darken this area. Begin with the brush positioned in sokuhitsu, tilting it to create a round structure. Without lifting the brush, transition to chokuhitsu and gently swing to create a pointy ending. Mirror the same stroke on the other side, forming a heart-shaped leaf. Once the ink is moderately dry, load the kofude with nouboku and paint the veins, similar to the chrysanthemum leaves. Begin with the centre vein and paint additional lines dispersing outwards.

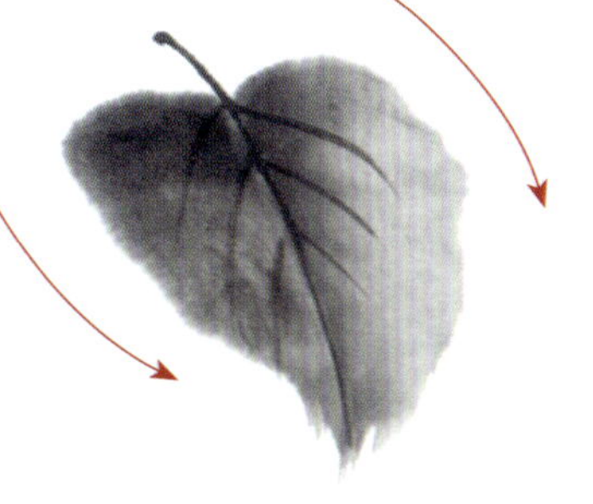

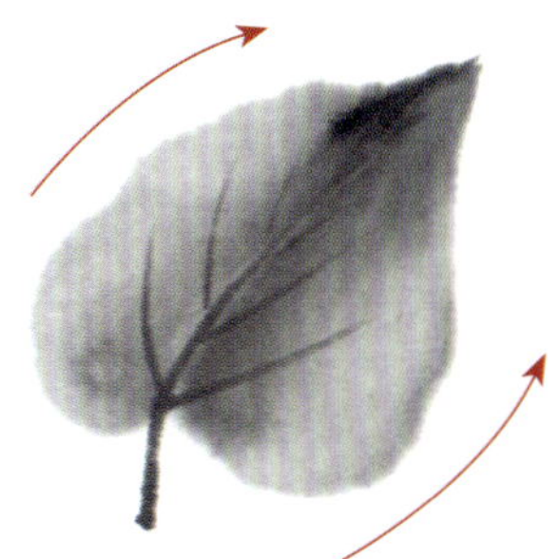

Practise painting the leaves from different angles.

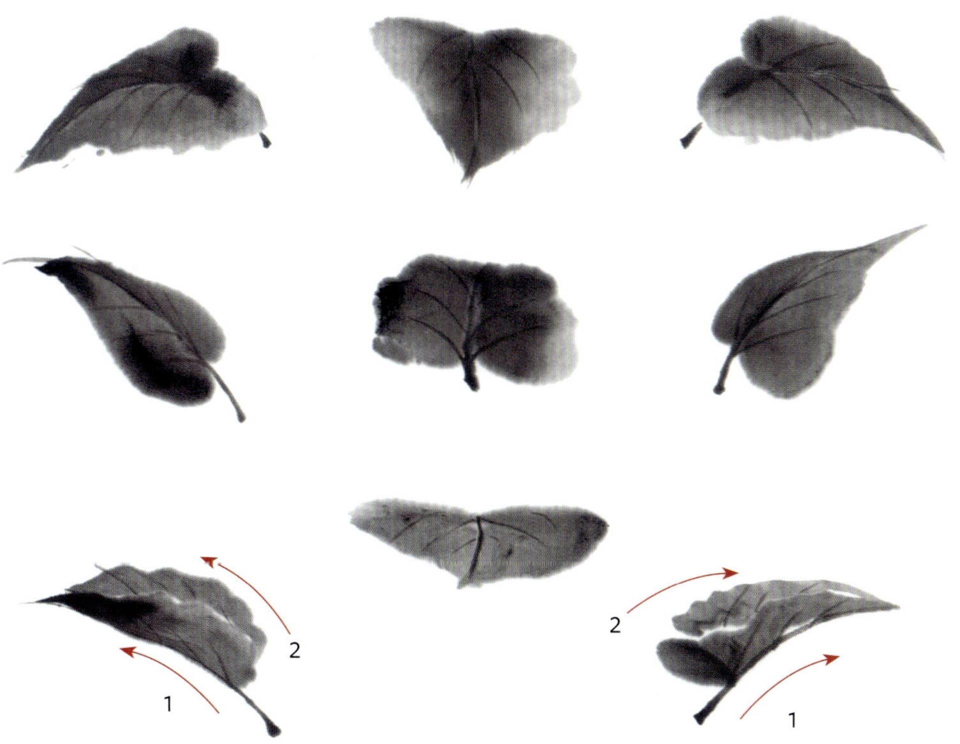

Bring together the various elements in the following order: the disc florets, outline of the flower petals and buds, front leaves, stems, secondary leaves, details (texture of the stem, veins of the leaves) and, finally, colour.

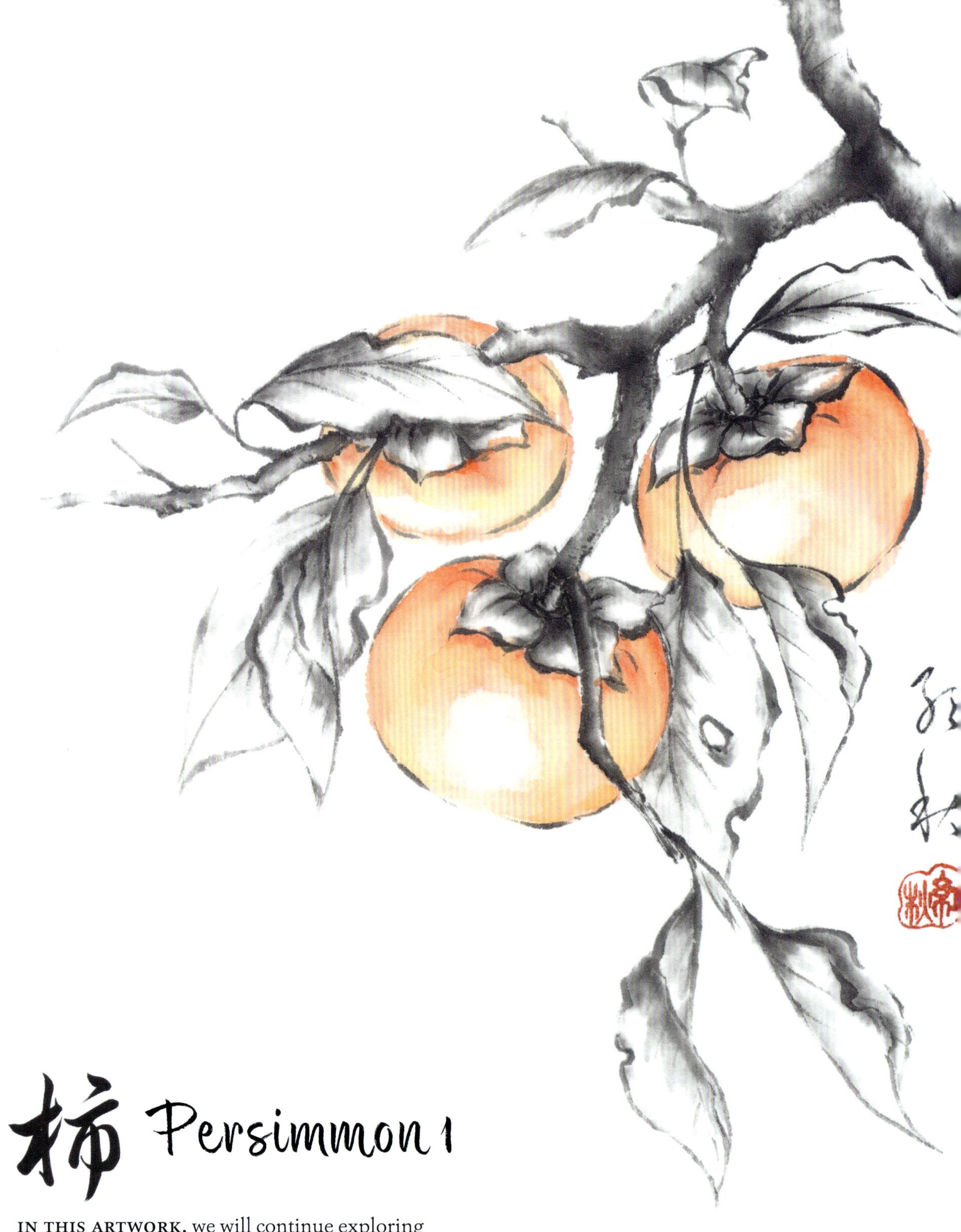

柿 Persimmon 1

IN THIS ARTWORK, we will continue exploring the senbyou-hou technique to paint the persimmon fruit and leaves.

PERSIMMON FRUIT: SENBYOU-HOU

1. Load the kofude with tanboku or chuboku and use controlled movements to paint the centre leaves. Start by painting two circular rings in the centre. Next, with the tip of the brush pointed towards the outer ring, paint each leaf in two strokes. For additional details, paint a few curved lines at the base of each leaf to depict the natural folding.

2. Paint the spherical outline of the persimmon with the tip of the brush and let it sit to dry.

3. Optional: to shade in the persimmon, first apply a layer of either water or goku-tanboku, then layer on tanboku. The initial layer of water or goku-tanboku will allow you to conceal the sujime brush marks from the second layer. Make sure to avoid painting the whole surface of the persimmon with the same shade of ink. While image 3 uses minimal shading, there is an option to increase shading and leave a roughly circular space to highlight the spherical shape and mimic the light reflecting off the glossy surface (see the fruits on p. 80).

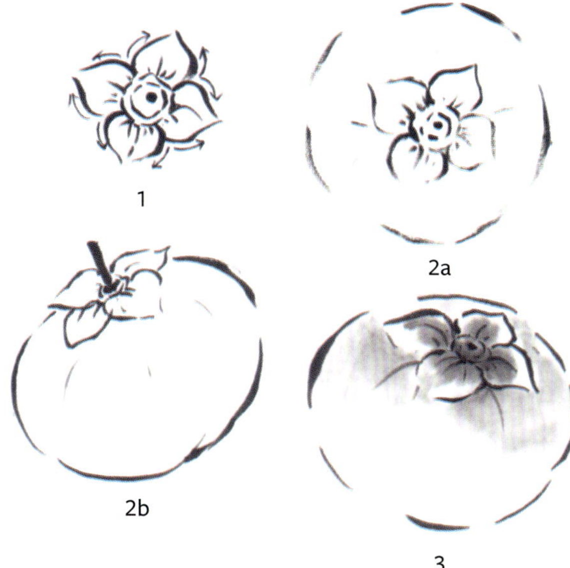

KEY POINTS

When shading in a large surface area in multiple strokes, each stroke can create the sujime lines (see p. 19). While this effect can be desirable for certain painting styles, our aim here is to avoid sujime by adopting either of the following two methods:

- Firstly, paint with as few strokes as possible, use light ink (goku-tanboku or tanboku) and ensure the tip of the brush traces the outline of the fruit.
- Secondly, ensure that the paper (where you plan to paint the fruit) is damp before ink application: apply water to the paper with a brush, gently blot away any excess water with a cloth, then proceed with applying the ink.

Colour use

To apply colour to the persimmon, repeat step 3 with light yellow ink instead of goku-tanboku and orange ink instead of tanboku (refer to the image on p. 80).

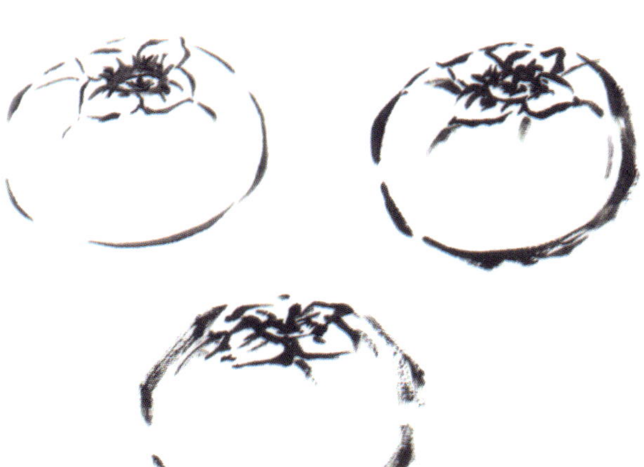

Different expressions in senbyou-hou

The persimmon fruit typically has a flattened spherical shape. While preserving the simplicity of the senbyou-hou technique, use pressure and speed variation and imperfect lines to express the unique features of each fruit.

PERSIMMON LEAVES: SENBYOU-HOU

Load the kofude with chuboku and, with the tip of the brush, paint the outline of the leaf followed by the veins. Lighten the pressure as you reach the tip of the leaf to create a tapered line.

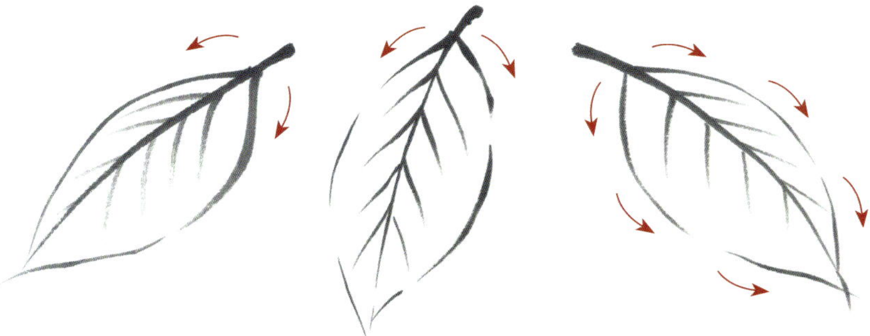

Practise the various angles and positioning of the persimmon leaves.

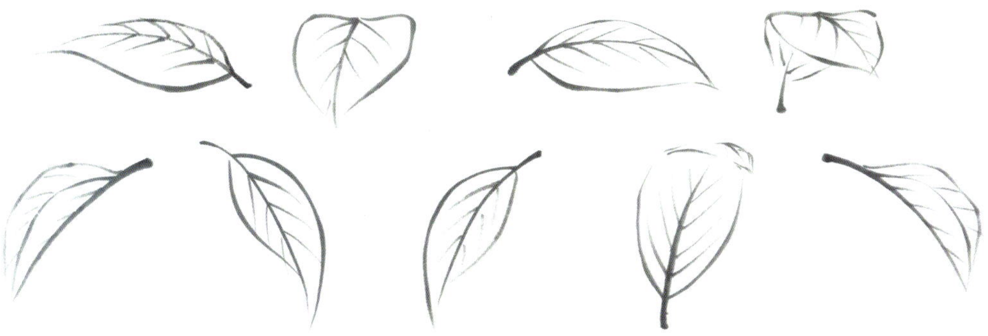

Incorporating these variations into your painting will allow you to effectively capture the natural fall and movement of the leaves.

Further expressions

Use haboku-hou for shading (see p. 31). First paint a layer of goku-tanboku around the base or centreline, and while the ink is still wet add some darker ink to create a natural bleed.

Senbyou-hou, which makes use of fine lines and pressure control, is particularly suited for capturing details. For instance, convey seasonal changes by painting dried or holey leaves.

Paint the persimmon tree following the same techniques and brush movements as with the magnolia tree.

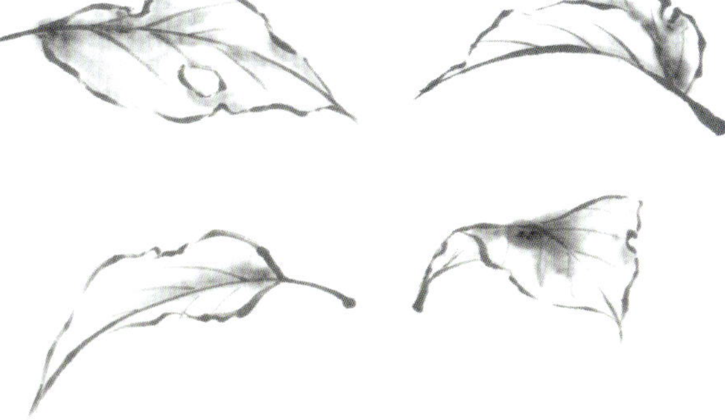

Bring together the various elements in the following order: the main branch, persimmon fruits, leaves, sumi shading, colour and, finally, the details (texture of the tree).

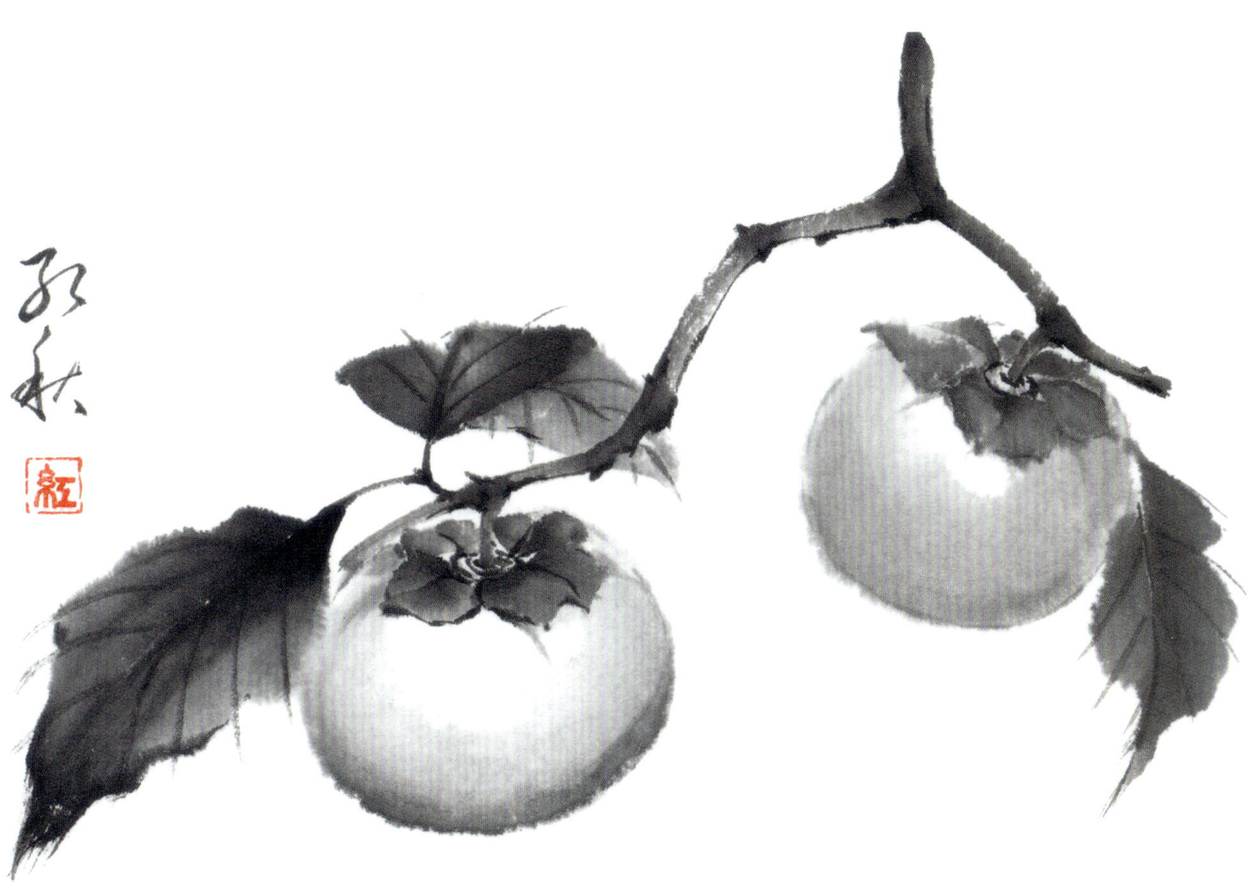

柿 Persimmon 2

IN THIS SECTION, we will explore a simple composition and use motoguma (see p. 30) to paint the persimmon in tsuketate-hou. We will then paint some vegetables and fruits to develop our motoguma practice.

PERSIMMON LEAVES: TSUKETATE-HOU

Load the ōfude with chuboku, the tip with nouboku and blend in preparation for sanboku-hou.

Similar to the sunflower leaves (see p. 79), paint each leaf in two strokes. Position the tip of the brush towards the centre vein to darken this area. Begin with the brush positioned in semi-sokuhitsu. Without lifting the brush, swiftly transition to chokuhitsu and swing the brush to create a sharper ending. Mirror the same stroke on the other side.

To accentuate the three-dimensional appearance of the leaves, apply shading to specific regions of the leaf, for example: the front or rear, the base or tip, or the centreline or margin.

Once the ink is moderately dry, load the kofude with nouboku and paint the centre veins followed by veins dispersing outwards from the centreline.

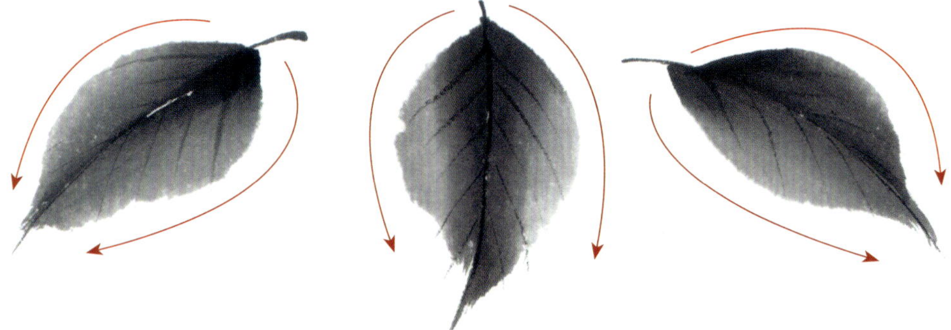

Practise painting the leaves from different angles.

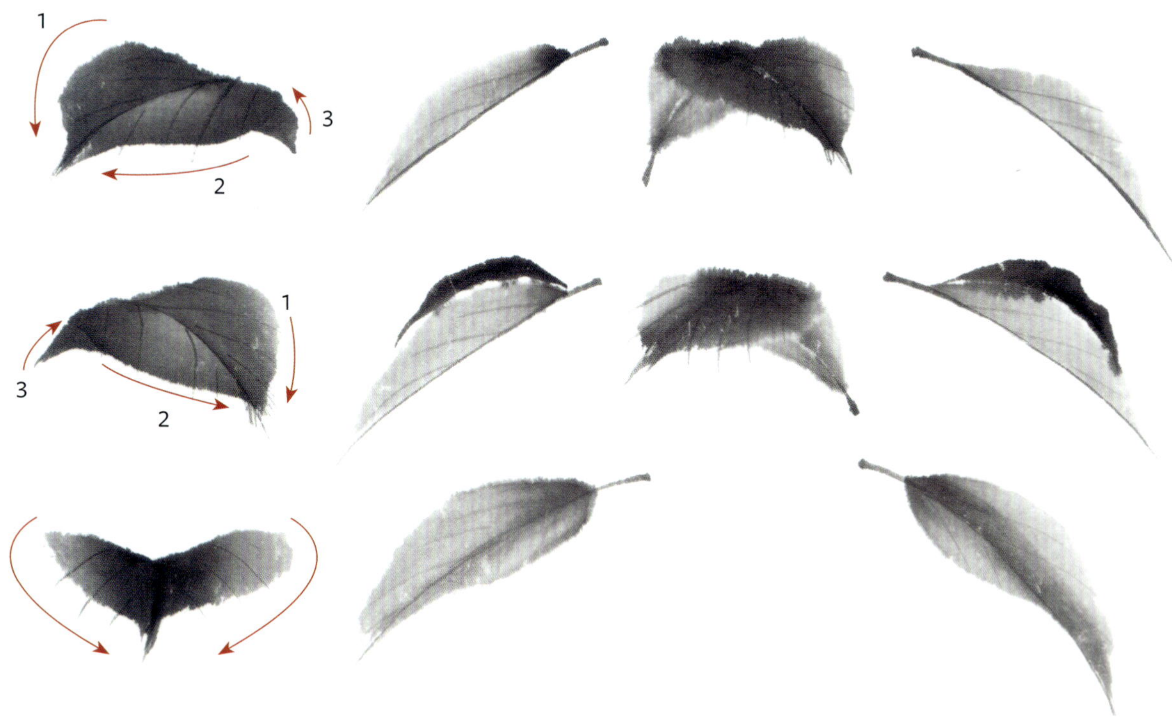

PERSIMMON FRUIT: MOTOGUMA

The motoguma technique (see p. 30) is particularly useful for capturing the spherical shape of the persimmon fruit.

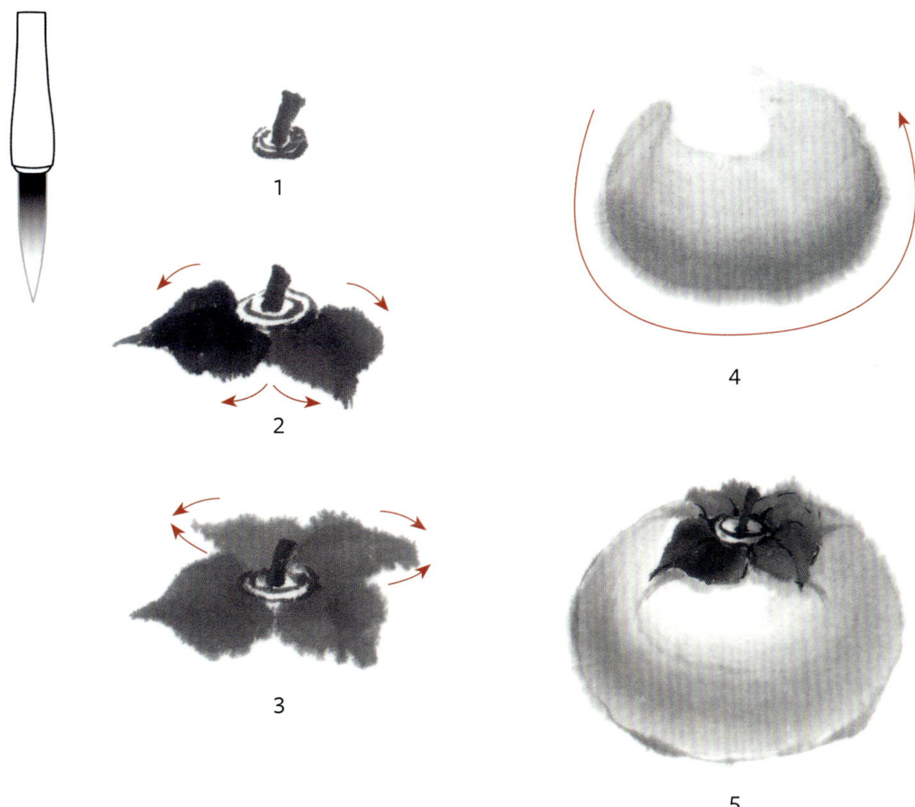

1. Load the kofude with nouboku and paint the centre stem and two surrounding rings.

2. Load the brush with chuboku, the tip with nouboku and blend in preparation for sanboku-hou. Paint the front leaves, using two strokes for each leaf . . .

3. . . . Followed by the back leaves.

4. Wash the ōfude and load with chuboku, ensuring full saturation, then carefully wash the tip of the brush in water (approximately one-third of its length). Hold the brush in reverse, allowing gravity to assist in creating a natural gradation from light to dark ink in the bristles (if painting a larger persimmon, this step may require a larger brush). With the tip of the brush facing towards the centre stem, press the body of the brush down onto the paper, and push it sideways to form a full crescent shape. This stroke should be completed in one continuous movement. To clarify the brush sweep in this image the stem has been omitted – but it would ordinarily be in place before this stroke

5. Optional: to accentuate the spherical shape, paint a faint outline of the persimmon body with the tip of the brush. Ensure that the shade of ink selected blends in with the fruit body.

Bring together the various elements in the following order: the main branch, persimmon fruits, leaves and, finally, the details (texture of the tree).

MOTOGUMA PRACTICE: FRUITS AND VEGETABLES

The motoguma technique (see p. 30) is also effective at capturing smooth-edged objects. Below, you will find a tomato, paprika and aubergine painted in motoguma.

First, load the ōfude with nouboku and paint the stem. Second, prepare the brush for motoguma and paint the body of the vegetable or fruit, following the arrows for guidance.

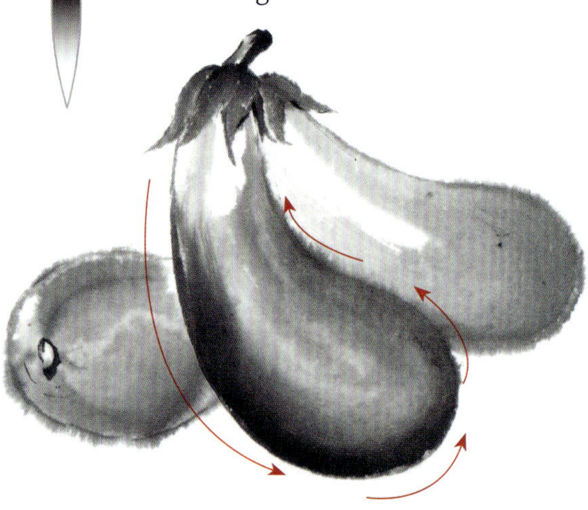

Aubergine

First paint the aubergine calyx in nouboku using the kofude.

Next, prepare the brush for motoguma. The aubergine body should be painted in one continuous stroke, with the base of the brush tracing the margins and following the curvature of the vegetable.

Paprika

First paint the paprika calyx in nouboku using the kofude.

Next, prepare the brush for motoguma. Create each paprika segment in one continuous stroke, with the darker base of the brush marking the edge.

Start with the segments closest to you.

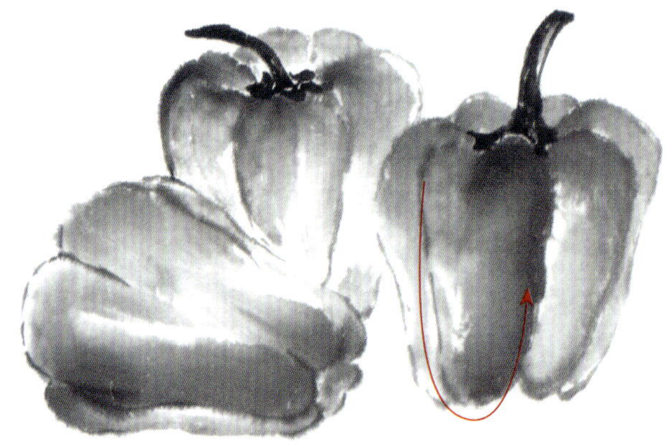

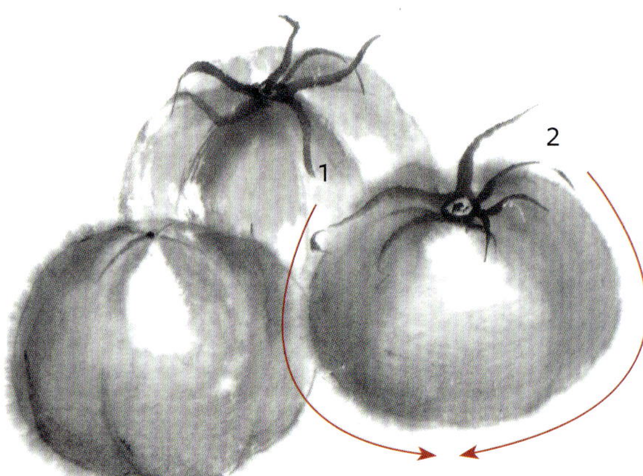

Tomato

First paint the tomato calyx in nouboku using the kofude.

Next, prepare the brush for motoguma. Paint the body of the tomato in two strokes, again, with the base of the brush marking the margins.

クロッカス
Crocus

FROM THIS ARTWORK FORWARD, we will focus solely on tsuketate-hou. Here, we will paint the crocus flower using the sakiguma brush application to create a kataguma effect (see p. 26).

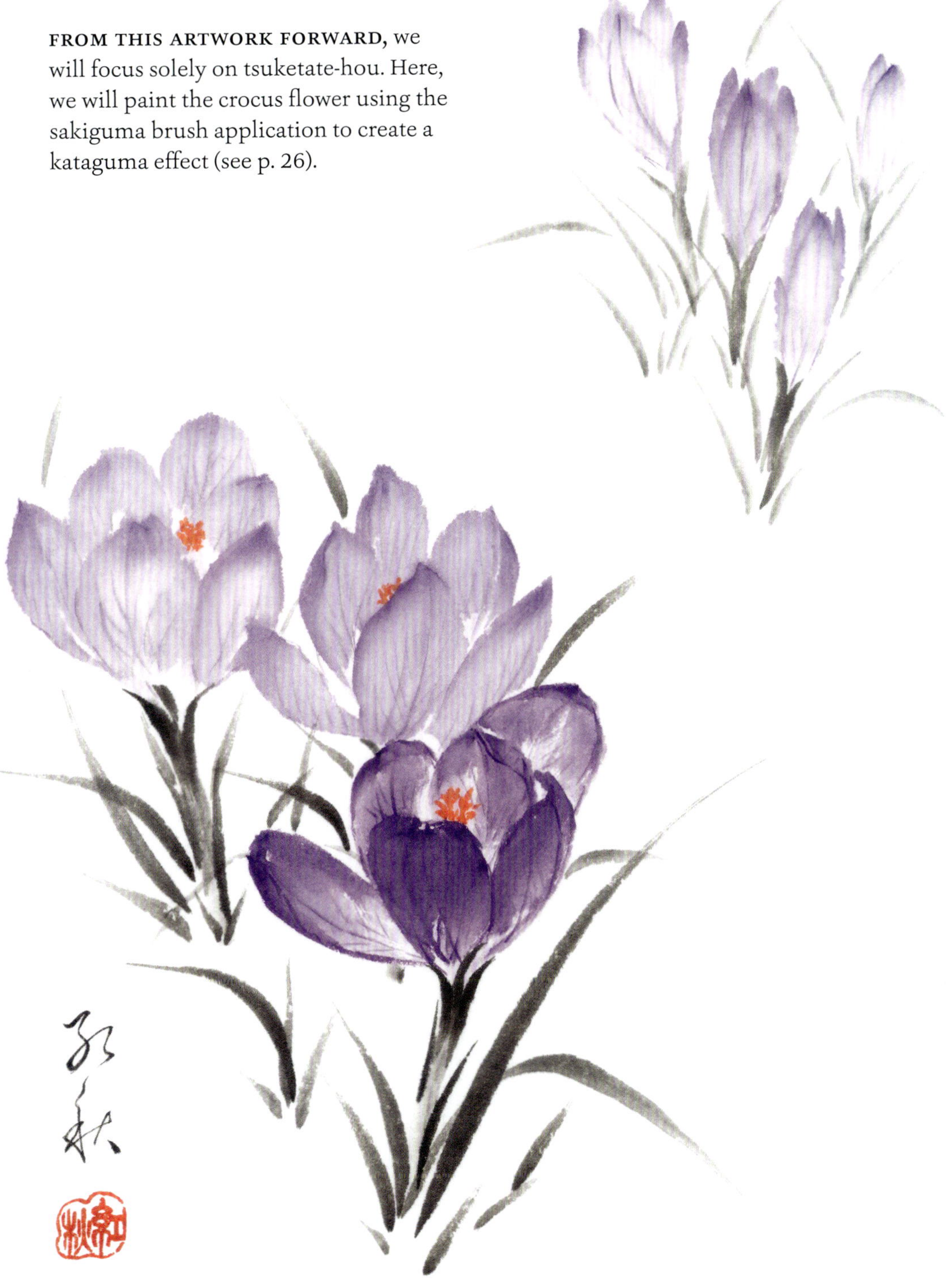

CROCUS FLOWER

Load the ōfude with tanboku and the tip with chuboku for sakiguma.

1-17. Paint the centre-front petal in two top-down strokes. Beginning at the tip of the petal, apply pressure and follow through the stroke with the tip of the brush tracing the outline of each petal to create the kataguma effect. Lift the brush as you reach the base.

Repeat these steps to build the side and back petals. For the back petals, use a lighter shade of ink to convey depth.

18. With the tip of the brush, paint three top-down strokes in nouboku to signify the receptacle. Use a swift motion and create a tapered ending. Wash the brush, apply tanboku, flatten the bristles using your fingers or the side of the plate, and then paint the lower half of the stem.

19. Switch to the kofude or menso-fude and paint the veins on each petal. Paint the veins bottom-up and centre-outward, in a swift motion to ensure they taper off as they reach the petal margins. Using the same brush with nouboku, paint dark dots to represent the stamen.

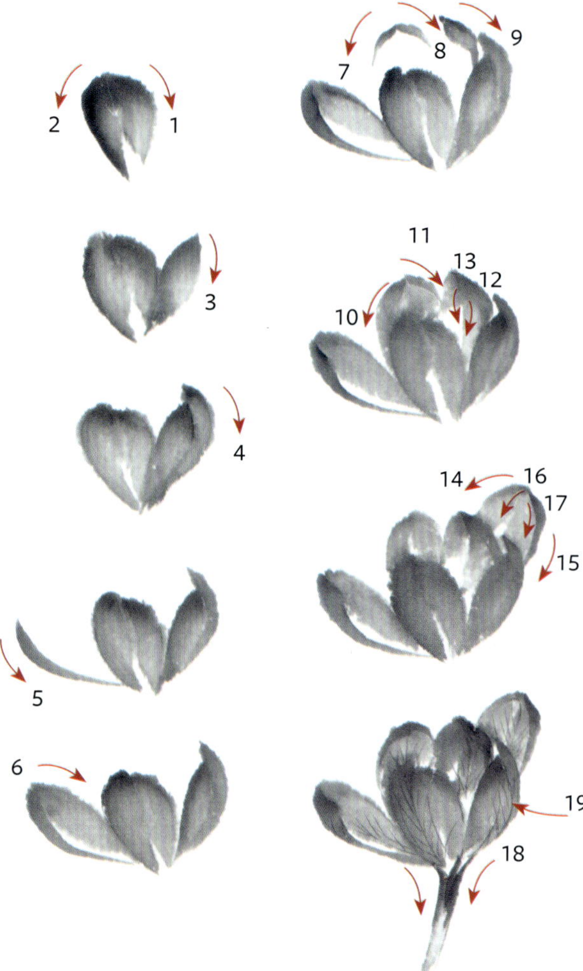

Leaves

To paint the crocus leaves, follow the same brush movements and techniques as with the orchid leaves (see p. 39), but with shorter and lighter brushstrokes.

Bring together the various elements in the following order: the foreground and background flowers followed by the foreground and background leaves.

Colour use

For the petals, load the brush with a mixture of diluted purple and white ink, prepare the tip with undiluted purple ink and blend for sanboku-hou. For the stamens and pistils, prepare the brush with undiluted orange ink.

KEY POINTS

- Use variation in flower size and placement, as well as different shades of ink to depict distance.
- The foreground flowers on the left-hand side should be larger and darker, and the background buds on the right-hand side should be smaller and lighter.
- The same principle applies to the leaves, with larger, darker leaves for the foreground, and smaller, lighter leaves for the background.

芥子 Poppy

IN THIS ARTWORK, we will paint the poppy flower, capturing its fragile, ethereal petals. This particular artwork uses Saienboku for colour.

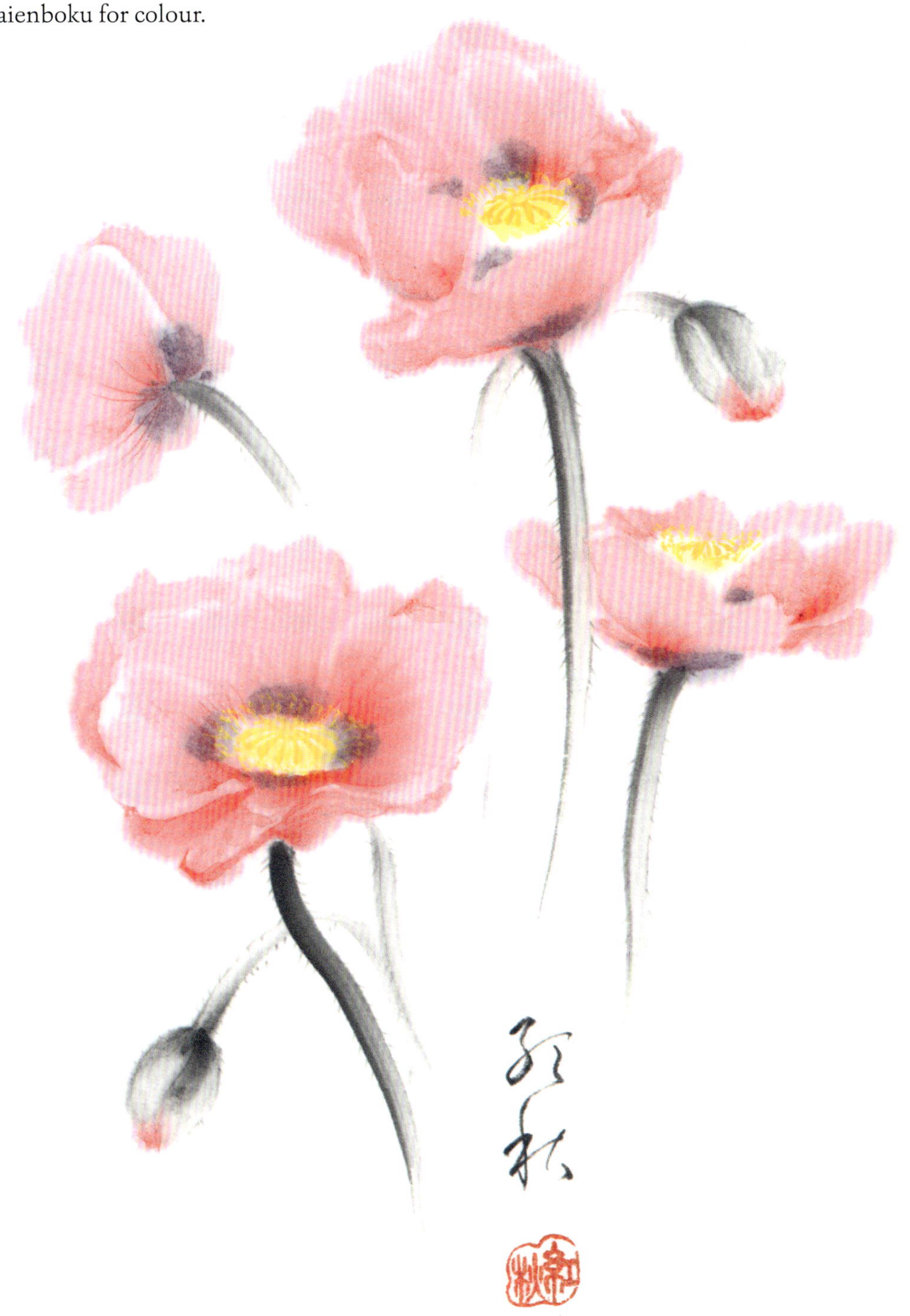

POPPY FLOWER

Flower (A)

1. Prepare the kofude with nouboku and paint the pistil that forms a circular disc in the centre of the flower.

2. Load the ōfude with tanboku, the tip with chuboku and blend in preparation for sanboku-hou. With the tip of the brush pointed upwards, paint a wavy line that forms the drooping front petal.

3. With the tip of the brush pointed towards the centre, push your brush upwards in sokuhitsu following the arrow. With the brush prepared in sanboku-hou, this will create a natural gradient effect, with the centre parts of the flower appearing darker than the outer edges.

4. Paint the remaining petals in sokuhitsu, with the tip of the brush pointed towards the centre of the flower for each stroke. Use a gentle up-and-down motion to create the soft, undulating edge of the petals.

5. Paint one or two petals underneath to create layers.

6. Load the kofude with nouboku and paint the stamens. Once the ink is moderately dry, add patches of darker ink around the base.

7. Poppy flowers typically have one blossom per stem. Flatten the ōfude and paint the stem in chokuhitsu in one continuous, flowing stroke. Finally, switch back to the kofude and paint small dots along the stem to represent the coarse hairs.

Flower (B)

Apply the same techniques to paint another arrangement of the poppy flower.

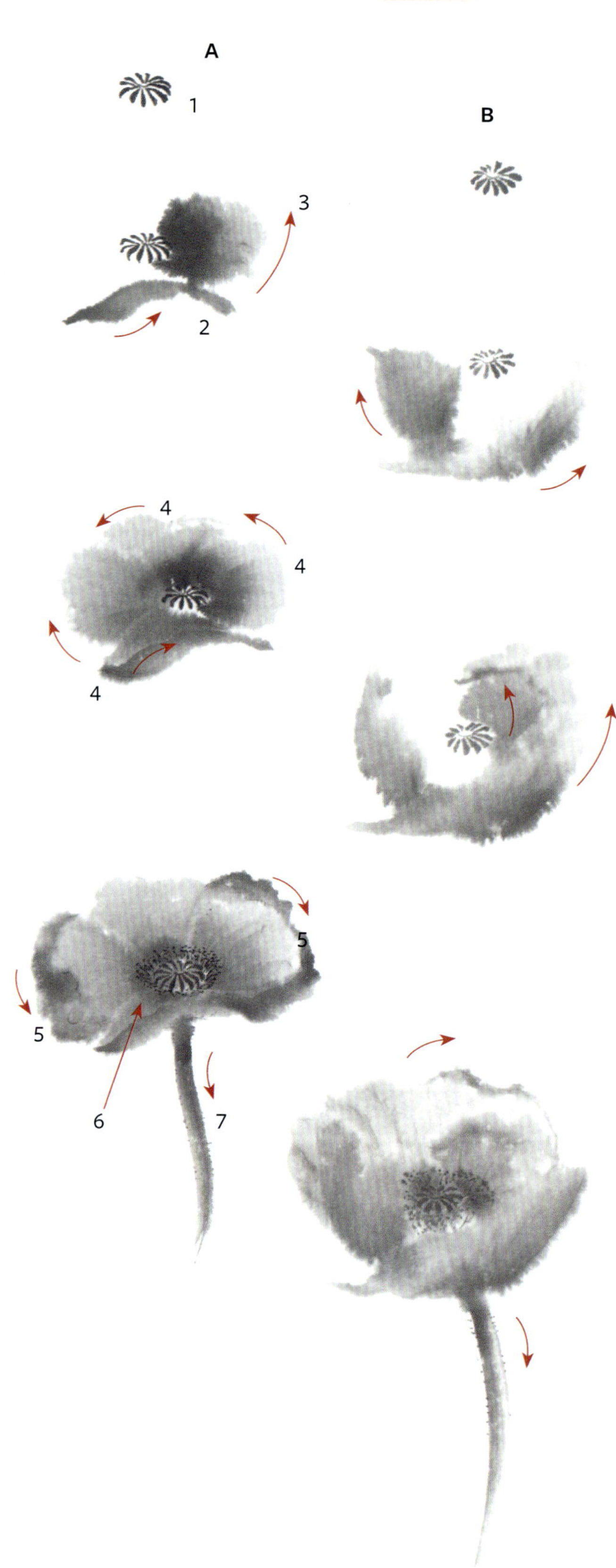

Colour use

Paint the pistil that forms a circular disc in the centre of the flower in yellow ink.

For the petals, load the brush with light pink ink, prepare the tip with medium-dark pink ink and blend for sanboku-hou.

Create a shade of purple ink for the coloured patches on the petals.

Variation 1

When painting the petals, point the tip of the brush towards the centre of the flower, creating a natural gradient effect with a darker centre (in the same way as flowers A and B on p. 90).

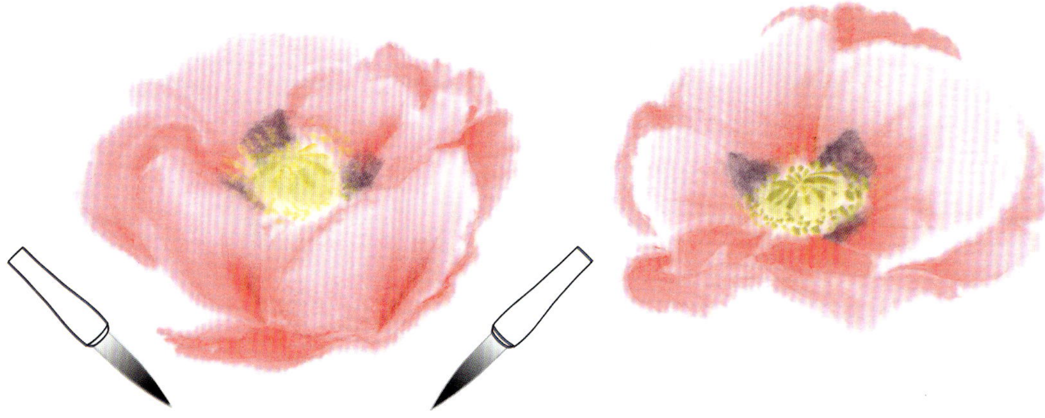

Variation 2

Follow the same steps used to create flower variation 1, with one modification. Point the tip of the brush towards the outer edge of the petal, creating a lighter centre and a darker outer edge. Use a gentle up-and-down motion of the tip of the brush to create the soft undulating edges of the petals.

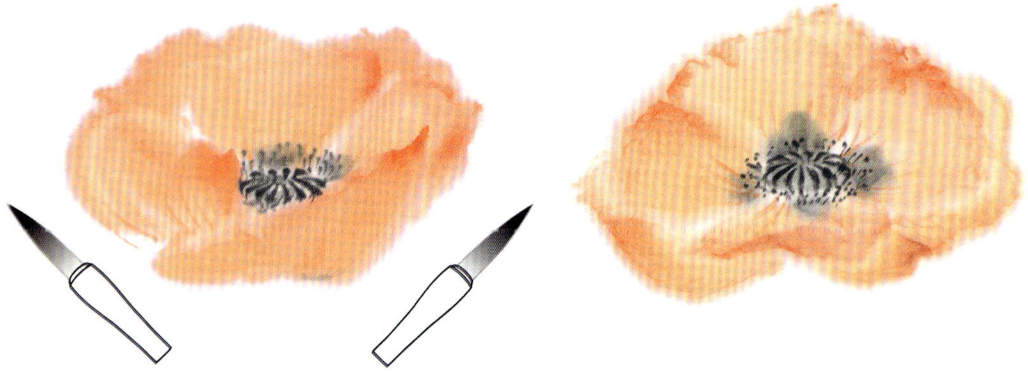

KEY POINT

As illustrated in the sample images above, the direction of the brush can significantly influence the colour gradations, the softness of the petal edge and the feathery texture. Experiment with both of these methods and select one based on artistic preference and ease of ink control.

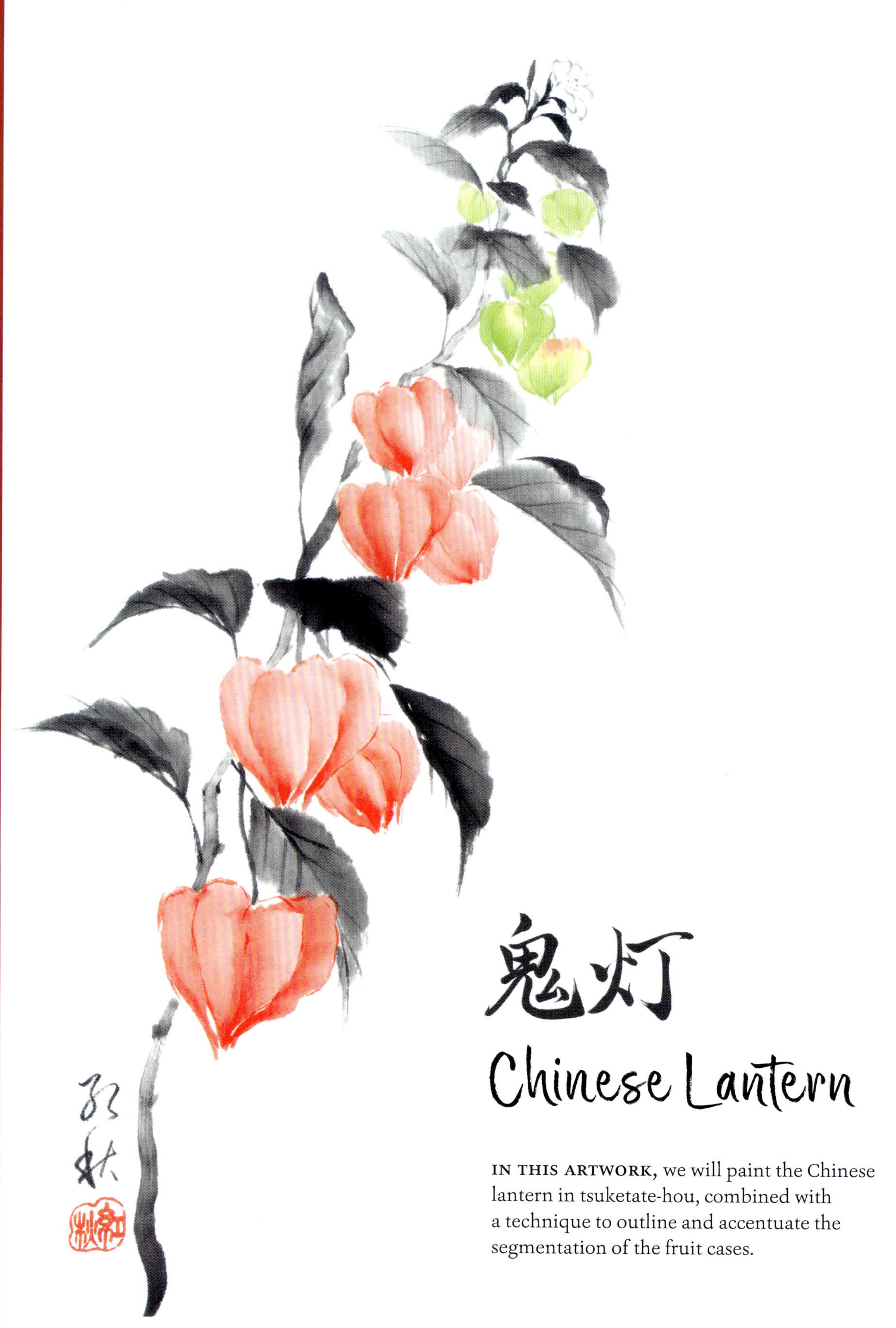

鬼灯
Chinese Lantern

IN THIS ARTWORK, we will paint the Chinese lantern in tsuketate-hou, combined with a technique to outline and accentuate the segmentation of the fruit cases.

CHINESE LANTERN FRUITS

The distinguishing feature of the Chinese lantern is the orange-red, lantern-shaped papery pod that encases the fruit and flower.

Sanboku-hou

Load the ōfude with tanboku, prepare the tip with nouboku and blend for sanboku-hou.

1. Paint the segments of the Chinese lantern fruit case one by one. With the tip of the brush pointing downwards, gently press and push the brush upwards in semi-sokuhitsu while incrementally increasing the pressure. As you near the top of each segment, apply full pressure with the body of the brush to create a thicker, rounded finish. The ink effects created by sanboku-hou introduce a natural separation between the segments.

2. Repeat the previous steps to paint three additional segments on the right-hand side. Here, you can introduce variation by painting the segments in a different order, from either left to right, right to left or starting from the centre outward.

3. Load the menso-fude or kofude with chuboku or tanboku, and finish off by outlining each segment to accentuate the separation.

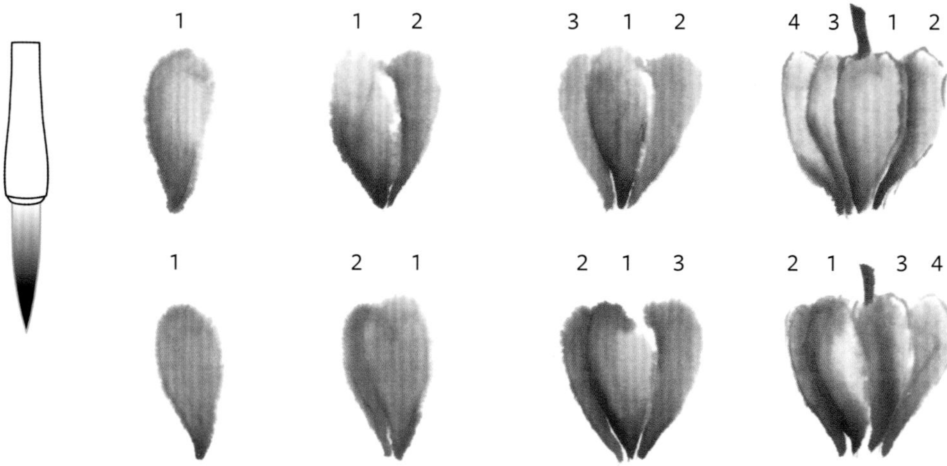

Motoguma

The motoguma technique (see p. 30) can also be used to paint the Chinese lantern fruit cases.

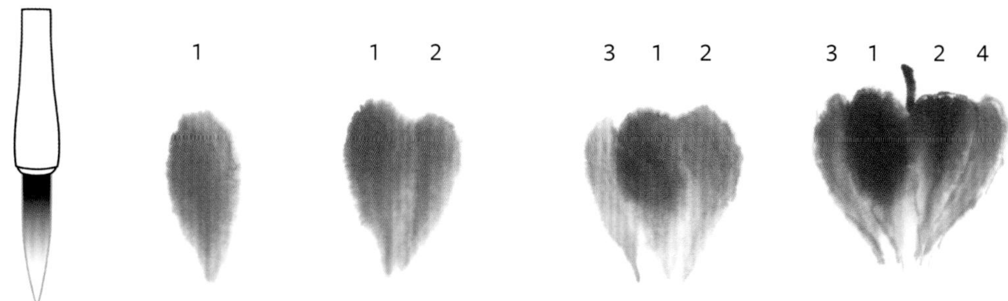

Colour use

To paint the fruit cases, load the brush with light orange-red ink, prepare the tip with dark orange-red ink and blend for sanboku-hou.

Optional: towards the top of the stem, paint several younger fruit cases that exhibit a gentle green hue. Prepare the brush for sanboku-hou using two shades of green ink.

CHINESE LANTERN LEAVES

Chinese lantern leaves are soft and ovate with gently crenated edges.

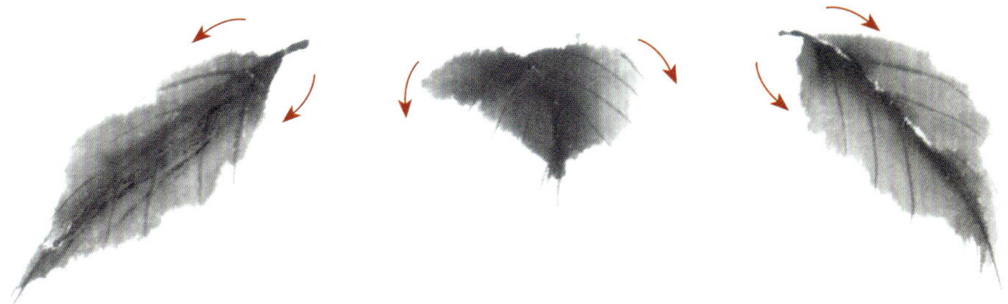

Load the ōfude with chuboku, the tip with nouboku and blend in preparation for sanboku-hou.

We will apply a similar technique as used to paint the persimmon leaves, but with changes in pressure control to accentuate the crenated edges. Start with the tip of the brush pointed towards the centre of the leaf and push the brush along the centreline, while pressing the body of the brush down at intervals.

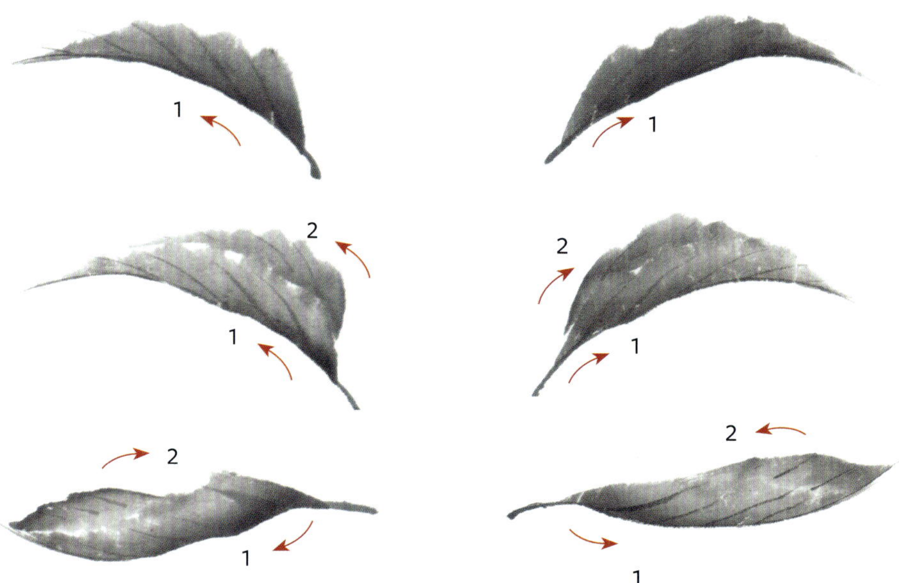

Stem

For the stem, take the ōfude and remove excess ink to enable the kasure effect. Paint a bottom-up line in chokuhitsu, embracing an irregular rhythm, pausing at intervals and varying the speed to give structure to the stem. Gradually reduce the pressure to create a lighter finish towards the top of the stem.

For additional detail, load the kofude with tanboku and paint a white open flower at the top of the stem in senbyou-hou.

Bring together the various elements in the following order: the fruit cases, stem, leaves, flower (optional), and finally, the details (leaves, veins and fruit case outlines).

KEY POINT
Again, use different sizes and shades of ink to create a sense of depth. The flower cases and leaves should become smaller and lighter towards the top of the stem.

菖蒲 Iris

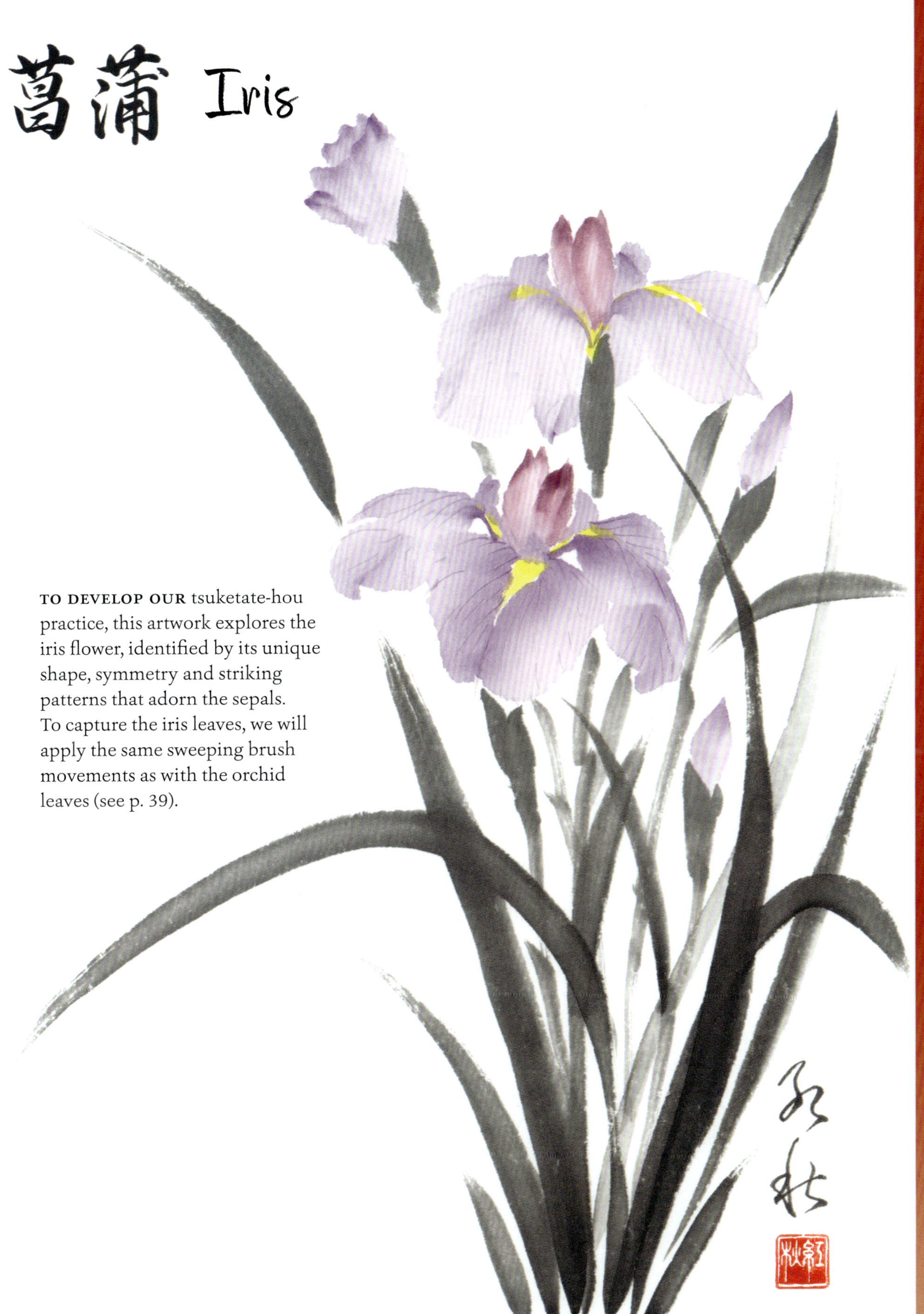

TO DEVELOP OUR tsuketate-hou practice, this artwork explores the iris flower, identified by its unique shape, symmetry and striking patterns that adorn the sepals. To capture the iris leaves, we will apply the same sweeping brush movements as with the orchid leaves (see p. 39).

IRIS FLOWER

The iris flower is typically composed of three petals that gracefully curve upwards, and three sepals (resembling petals) that droop softly downwards and are adorned with delicate veins and yellow patches.

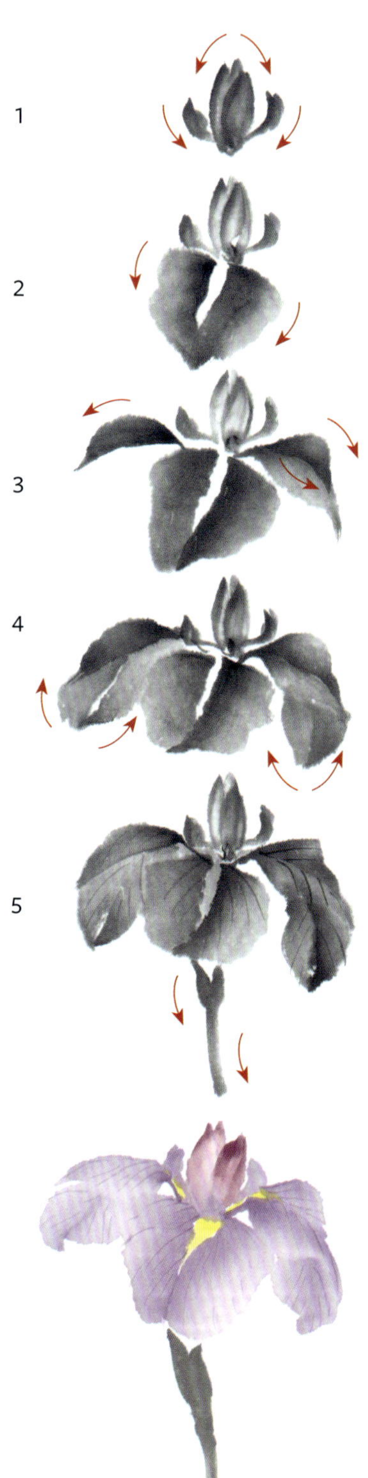

Flower A

Load the ōfude with tanboku (or a diluted mixture of purple, red and white, if using colour) and prepare the tip with nouboku (or an undiluted mixture of purple and red) for sakiguma.

1. Begin by painting the three curved petals in the centre, pushing the brush in a top-down motion. Use two strokes for the front petal, and one stroke each for the petals in the back. Next, paint the style arms surrounding the centre petals, again in a top-down curved stroke.

Wash the brush and load with tanboku (or a diluted mixture of purple and white), ensuring the core is fully saturated with ink, then remove excess ink. Apply nouboku (or undiluted purple) to the tip of the brush and blend for sanboku-hou. Now, we will paint the large surface of the iris sepals.

2. With the tip of the brush pointing towards the centre, paint the centre sepal in two top-down strokes. Leave a blank space between the two strokes, where we will later shade in.

3. For the side sepals, paint the upper section in one or two top-down strokes (and repeat for the sepal on the other side).

4. Prepare the brush for sanboku-hou using lighter shades of ink. Paint the lower section of the side sepal in two bottom-up strokes (and repeat for the other sepal).

5. Once the ink is moderately dry, shade in the centreline of the sepals with tanboku (or yellow). Once dry, load the kofude with chuboku (undiluted purple) and paint the veins. Finish off by painting the stem in chuboku.

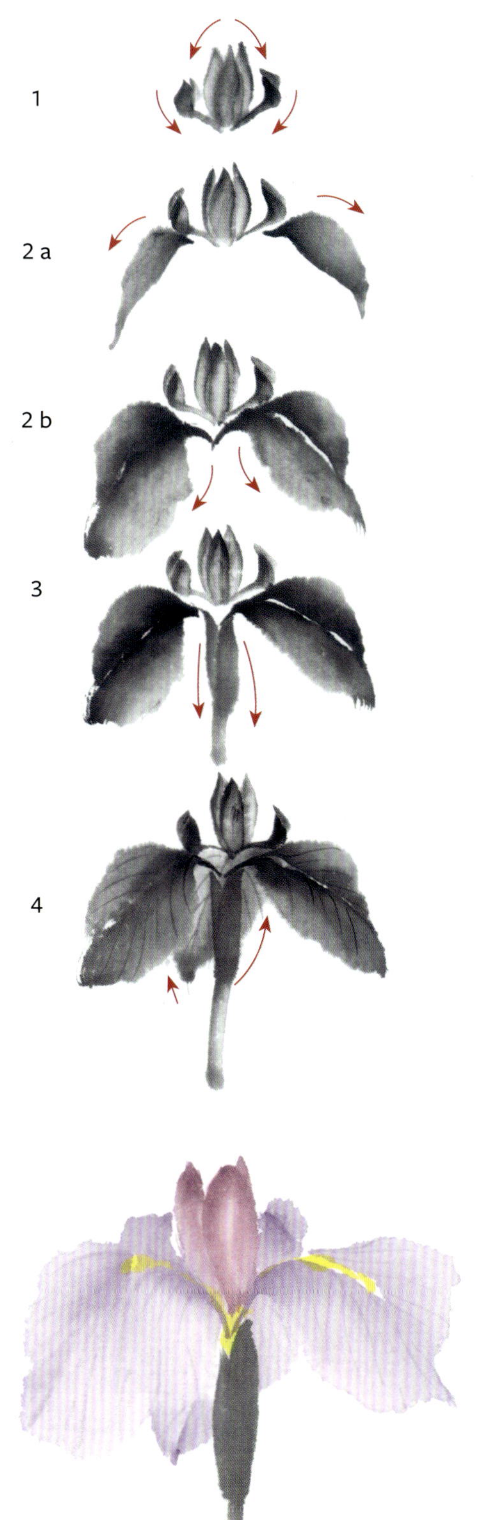

Flower B

1. Repeat step 1 of flower A to paint the centre petals and style arms.

2. For this variation, paint the side sepals first in two strokes for each sepal.

3. Load the brush with chuboku and paint the stem.

4. Once the ink is moderately dry, prepare the brush for sanboku-hou using lighter shades of ink, and paint over the stem to create the background sepal in two strokes.

Closed bud

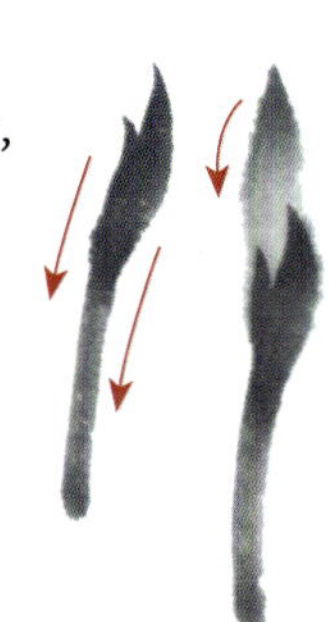

Begin by painting the stem in chuboku in a top-down motion. Next, prepare the brush for sakiguma using lighter shades of ink. Paint the closed bud in one swift stroke, while focusing on the tip of the brush. While the exact shade of ink may vary, the stem should appear darker than the petals.

Open bud

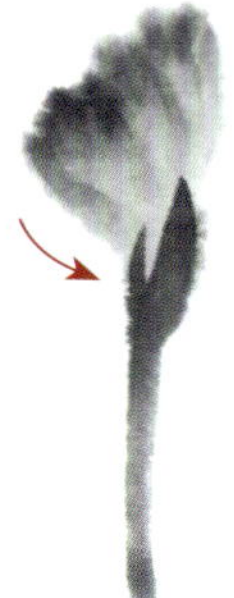

Follow the same steps as with the closed bud, however, instead of lifting the brush off the paper, slide it up and down to fashion a wavy feathery edge.

Leaves

Paint the iris leaves using the same techniques and brush movements as with the orchid leaves (see p. 39), but with wider and thicker brushstrokes. Prepare the brush for sanboku-hou, using chuboku and nouboku for the front leaves, and tanboku and chuboku for the back leaves.

Bring together the various elements in the following order: the flower heads and respective stems, the buds and respective stems, leaves and, finally, the details (veins and petal patches).

薔薇 Rose 1

FOR THIS ARTWORK, we will paint the side-facing rose in tsuketate-hou.

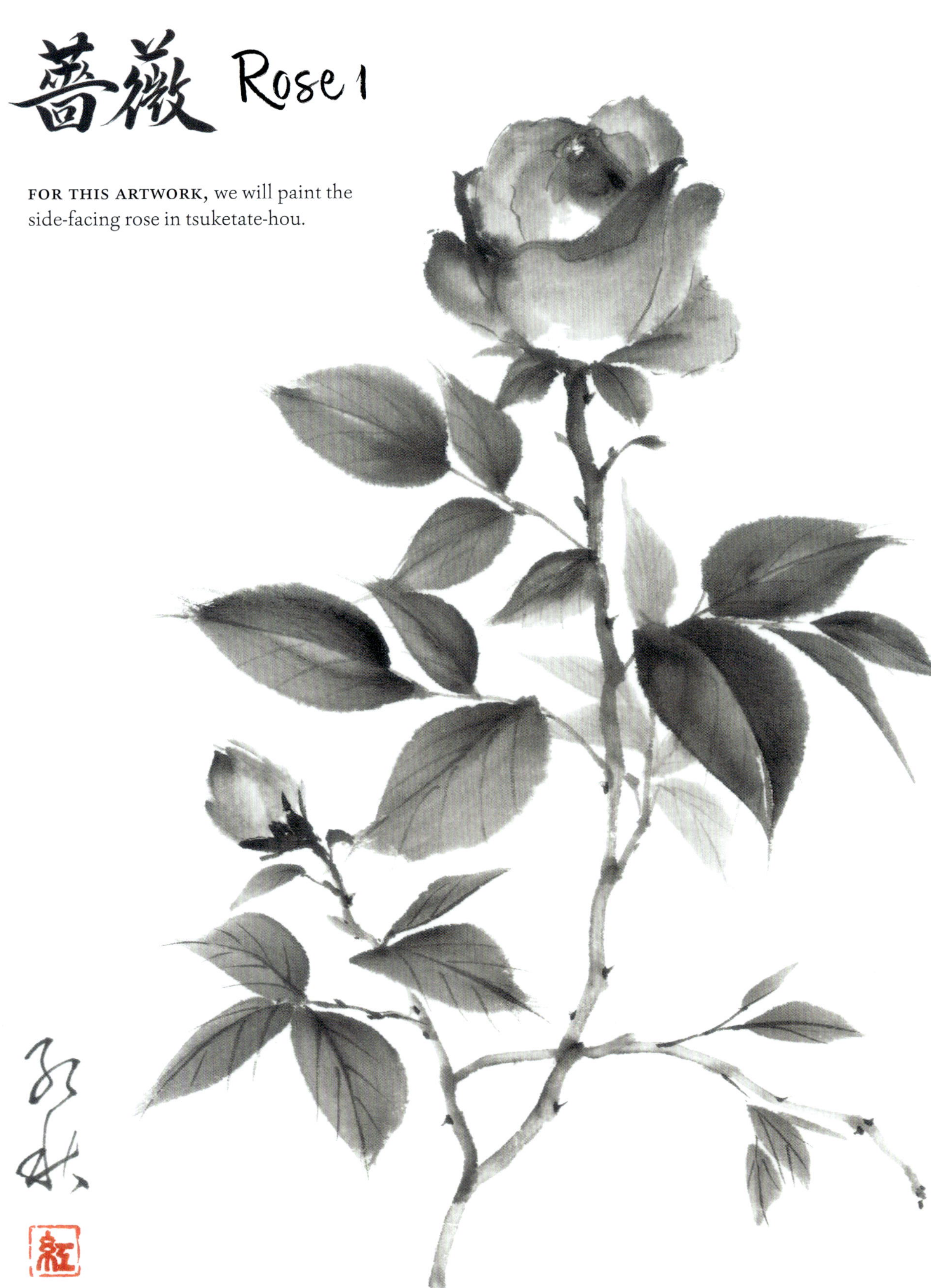

ROSE FLOWER

Flower practice

1. Prepare the brush for sanboku-hou and practise the sokuhitsu movement, pivoting from the tip of the brush.

2. Starting with the central petals, use alternating strokes from the left and right to build up the spiral formation of the rose.

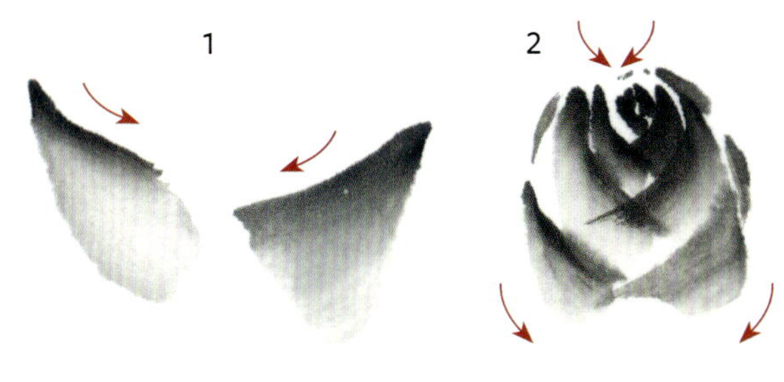

Side-facing flower

1. Load the ōfude with tanboku, prepare the tip with chuboku or nouboku and blend for sanboku-hou. With the tip of the brush, paint the centre petals in two strokes.

2–11. Paint the petals that layer in a spiral formation, following the image on the right and using the arrows for guidance. Paint the outmost petals in broader strokes that envelop the centre petals. Try to capture the delicate, velvety texture of the petals.

12–13. Paint the calyx and stem in nouboku.

Finally, switch to the kofude and paint the thorns in nouboku. Embed the stroke in the stem, then use a swift flick from the stem outwards.

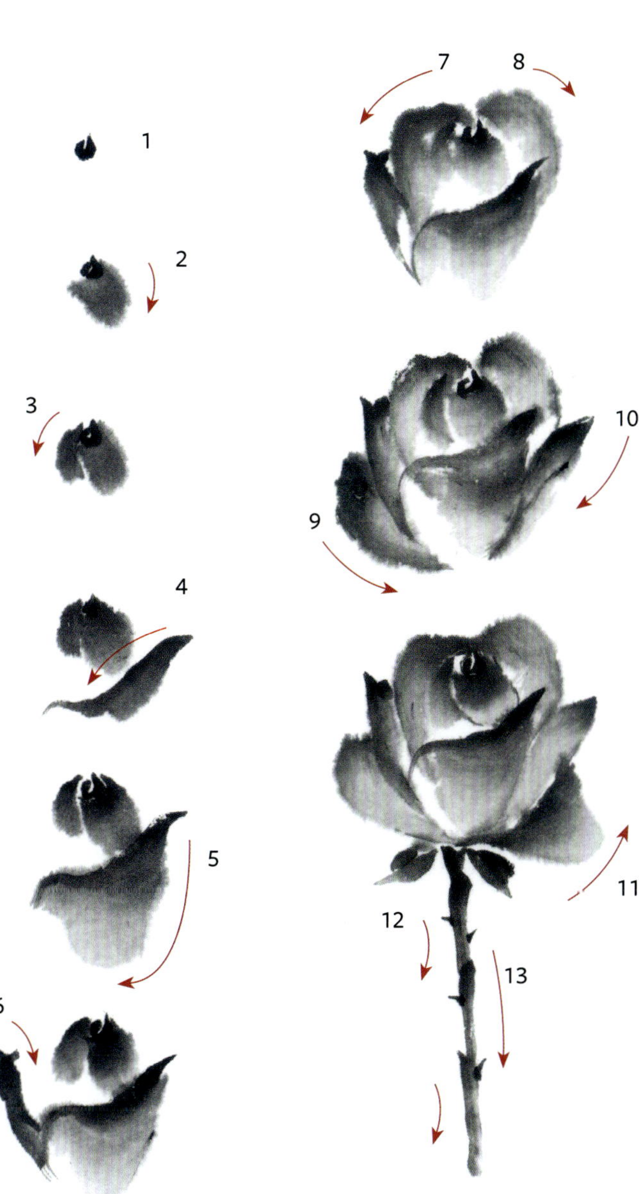

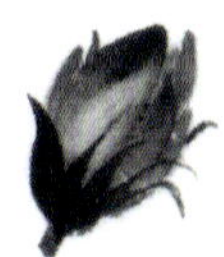

Buds

For the buds, first paint the calyx in nouboku. Second, prepare the brush for sanboku-hou using lighter shades of ink and paint the petals.

ROSE LEAVES

Again, in sanboku-hou, paint the leaves in various formations and angles. Follow the same principles and techniques as with the persimmon, sunflower and Chinese lantern leaves, but create leaves that are shorter and more ovate. You have the option to paint the veins in chuboku or nouboku.

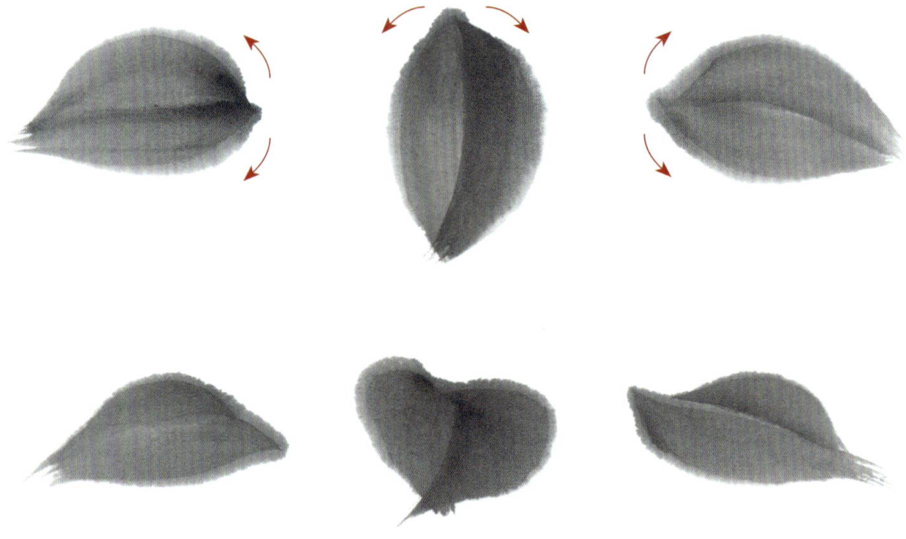

Arrange the leaves symmetrically along the central rib.

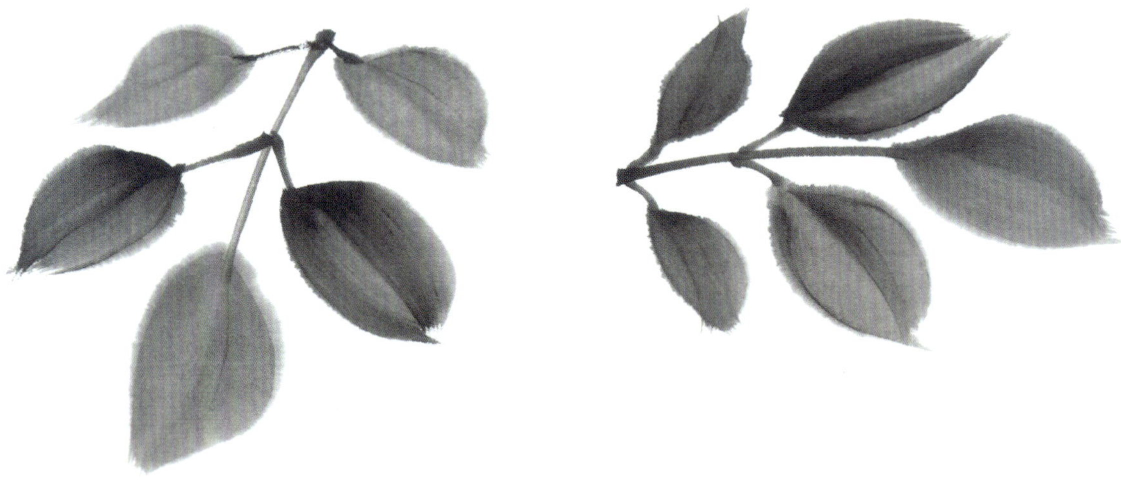

Bring together the various elements in the following order: the flower head, stem, leaves, bud and, finally, the details (thorns on the stem and veins on the leaves). Before painting the background leaves in a lighter shade, make sure that the stem is moderately dry to avoid bleeding or blurring.

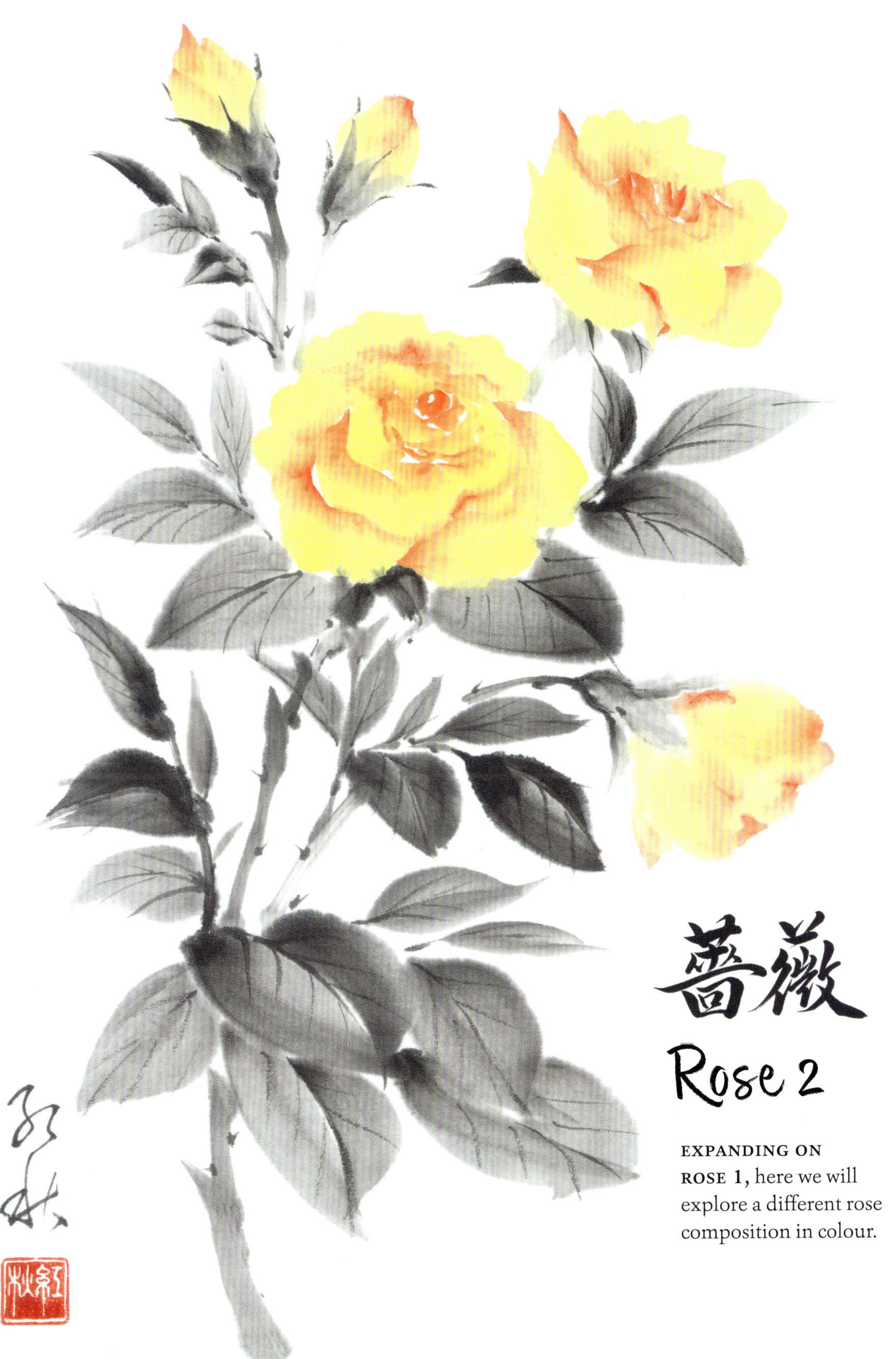

薔薇
Rose 2

EXPANDING ON ROSE 1, here we will explore a different rose composition in colour.

ROSE FLOWER

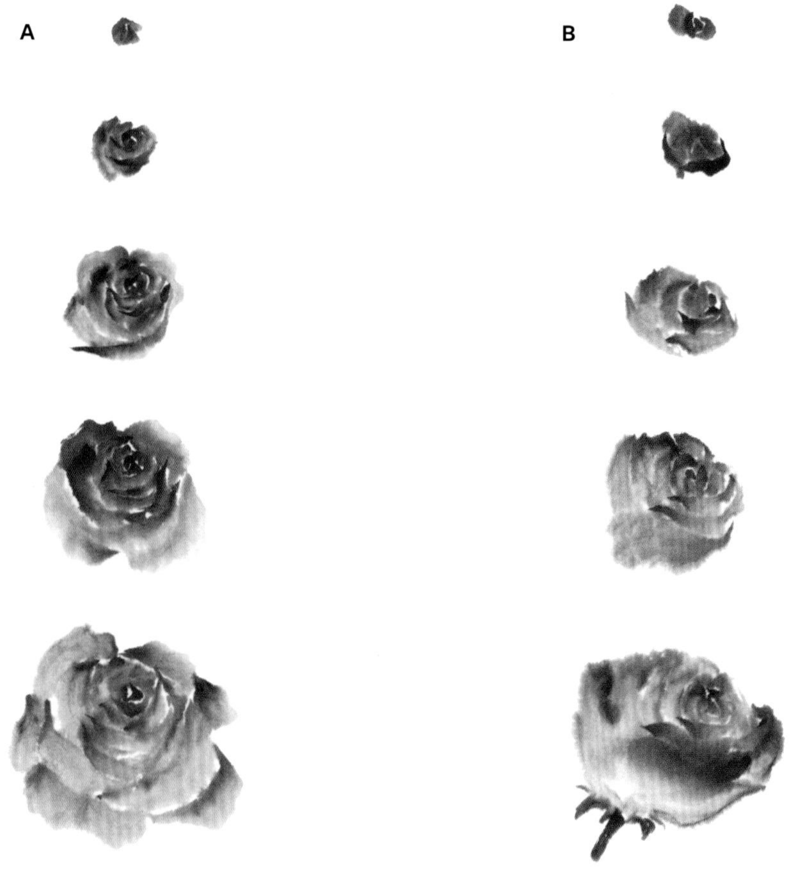

Front-facing flower (A)

1. Load the ōfude with tanboku, prepare the tip with chuboku and blend for sanboku-hou. With the tip of the brush, paint the centre petals in two strokes.

2. Paint the second layer of petals. With the tip of the brush directed towards the centre and positioned in sokuhitsu, paint the undulating curves of the rose petal by gently pushing the brush up and down, then flicking the brush to create a tapered ending.

3. Repeat this movement for the surrounding petals, increasing the pressure to create wider brushstrokes, especially for the outermost front petals.

Front-facing tilted flower (B)

For this variation, ensure that the front petals are even wider.

Colour use

Roses come in a wide array of colours – use multiple shades within each brushstroke to enhance your expression. The sample image on p. 101 showcases the application of sanboku-hou with three different shades of ink: a gentle yellow, a medium yellow-orange and a dark orange. Load the brush with light yellow ink, prepare the tip with medium yellow-orange ink and blend for sanboku-hou. Before proceeding to paint, apply dark orange to the tip of the brush.

Bring together the various elements in the following order: the flower heads, stems, leaves, buds and, finally, the details (thorns on the stem and veins on the leaves).

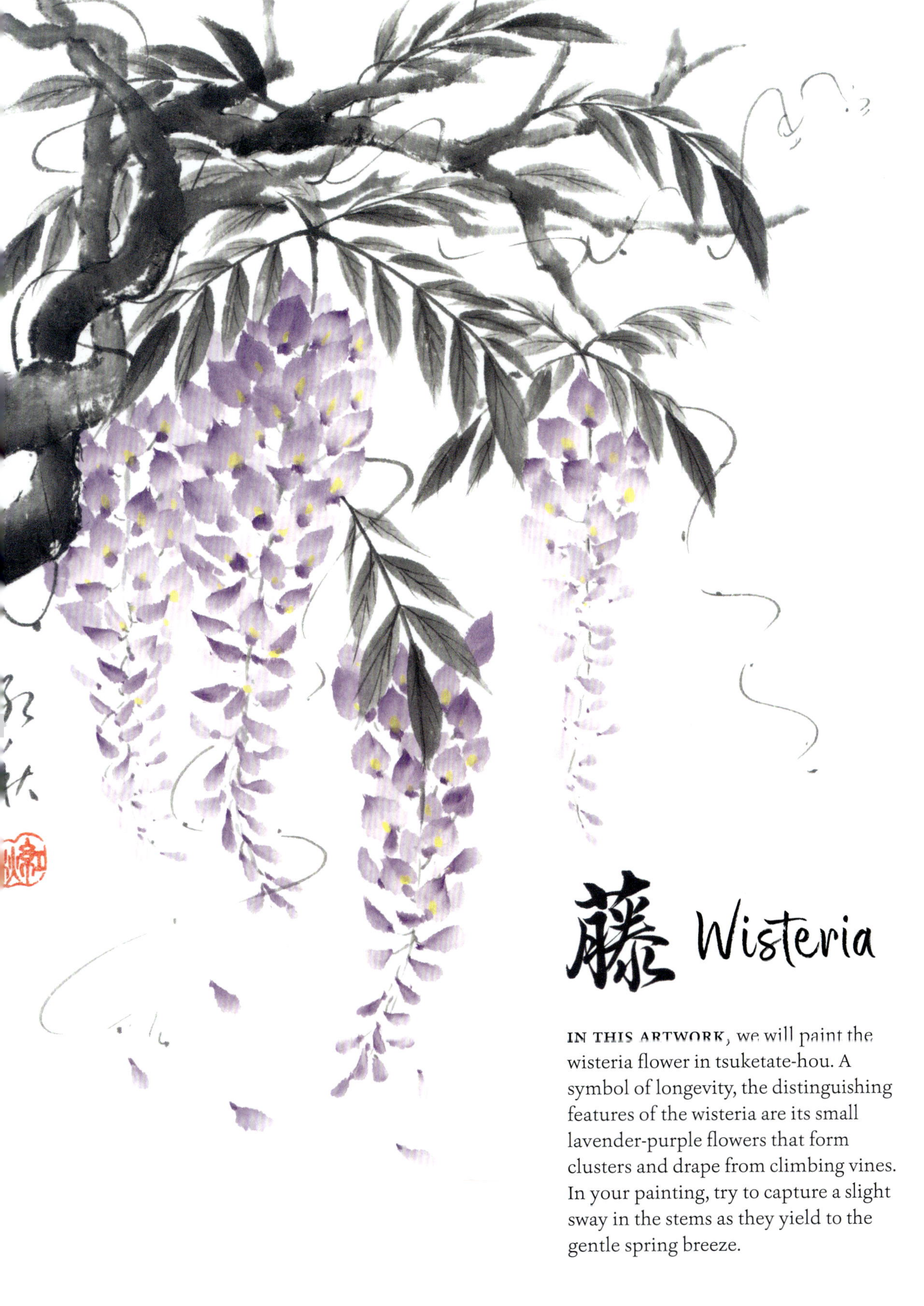

藤 Wisteria

IN THIS ARTWORK, we will paint the wisteria flower in tsuketate-hou. A symbol of longevity, the distinguishing features of the wisteria are its small lavender-purple flowers that form clusters and drape from climbing vines. In your painting, try to capture a slight sway in the stems as they yield to the gentle spring breeze.

WISTERIA FLOWER

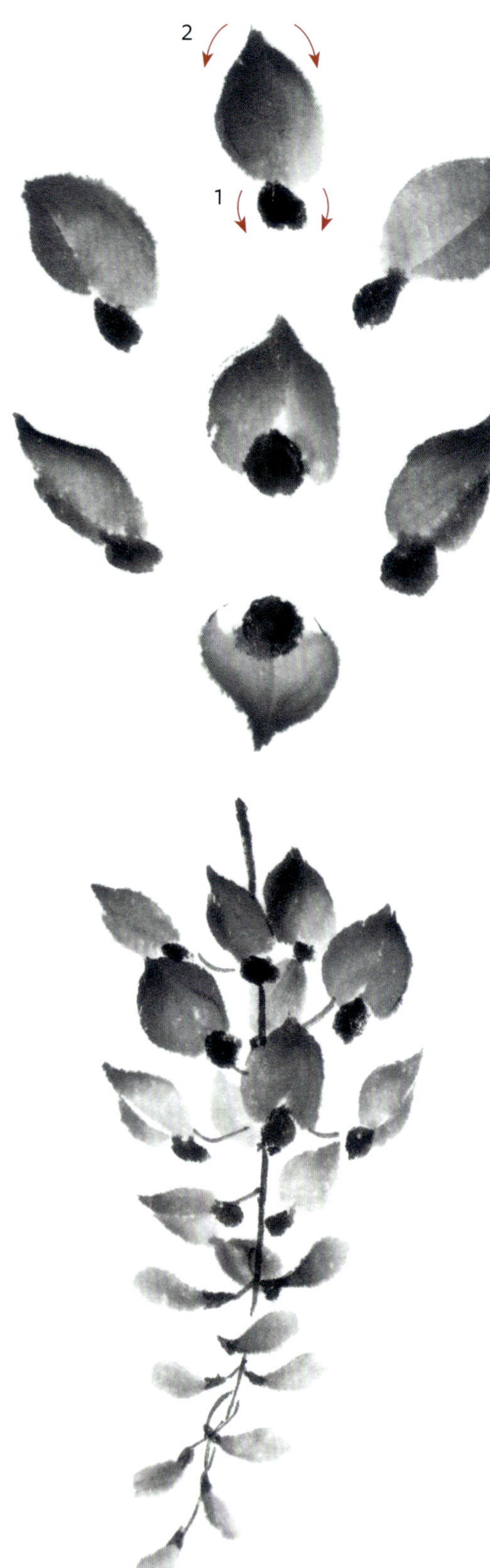

1. Load the ōfude with nouboku and paint a small, rounded shape with the tip of the brush – this represents the keel.

2. Load the brush with tanboku, prepare the tip with chuboku and blend for sanboku-hou. Paint the larger petal structure in two strokes, landing from the tip of the brush.

Practise painting the flowers from different angles.

Colour use

Explore sanboku-hou with different shades of purple and white ink. Once moderately dry, paint a yellow patch on the banner petal (uppermost and largest).

Bud

To paint the buds, point the tip of the brush towards the calyx, and apply a gentle pressure to the body of the brush. Load the menso-fude with nouboku and paint the calyx.

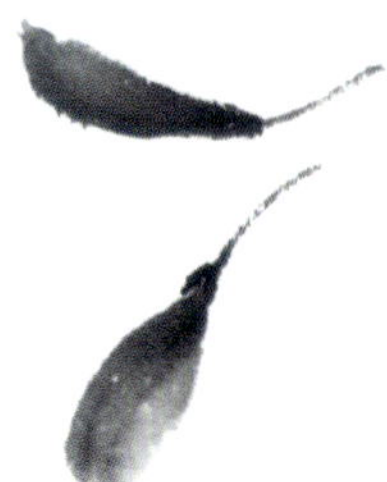

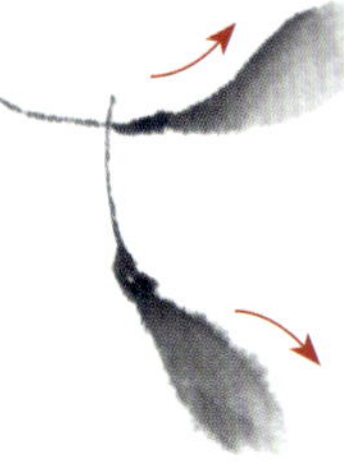

Bring together the flowers and buds to form clusters along the stem.

Paint all the darker keels first in a random arrangement, followed by the larger petals.

Paint the flowers towards the top of the cluster in a darker shade and use larger strokes. As you move down the cluster, use a lighter shade and smaller strokes.

Load the menso-fude with nouboku and paint the slender stems, running through the centre and connecting all the flowers and buds together.

Finally, to convey depth, paint the flowers in the back in a lighter shade of ink.

LEAVES AND BRANCHES

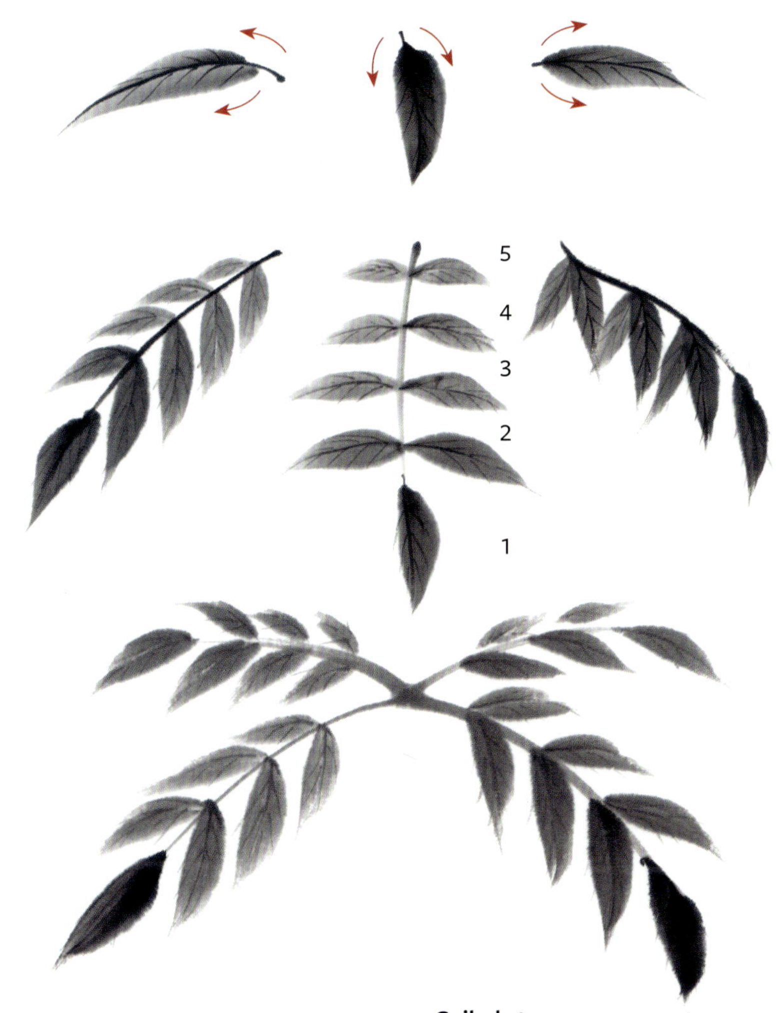

Leaves

The wisteria leaves are arranged symmetrically along the axis, often with a single leaf at the tip of the stem. Load the ōfude with tanboku, prepare the tip with nouboku and blend for sanboku-hou. Paint each leaf in two thin, elongated strokes, starting with the leaves towards the bottom of the stem. Once moderately dry, load the menso-fude with nouboku and paint the veins.

Trunk and branches

Following the composition on p. 103, paint the twisted woody trunk and branches. Adapt the techniques covered to paint the plum blossom trunk (see p. 66) and introduce curves and bends.

Coiled stems

To paint the thread-like, coiled stems, prepare the kofude with nouboku and use sweeping strokes in chokuhitsu – hold the brush in tankou-hou and position the arm in teiwan-hou. Embrace dynamic and flowing brushwork to bring to life the windy movement of the scene.

Bring together the various elements in the following order: the woody trunk and branches, leaves, petals, details (veins of the leaves and texture of the trunk and branches) and, finally, the coiled stems.

牡丹 Peony

THE PEONY FLOWER has many varieties and colours, with large, lush petals and voluminous foliage of dark green, lobed leaves. This particular artwork uses Chinese paint.

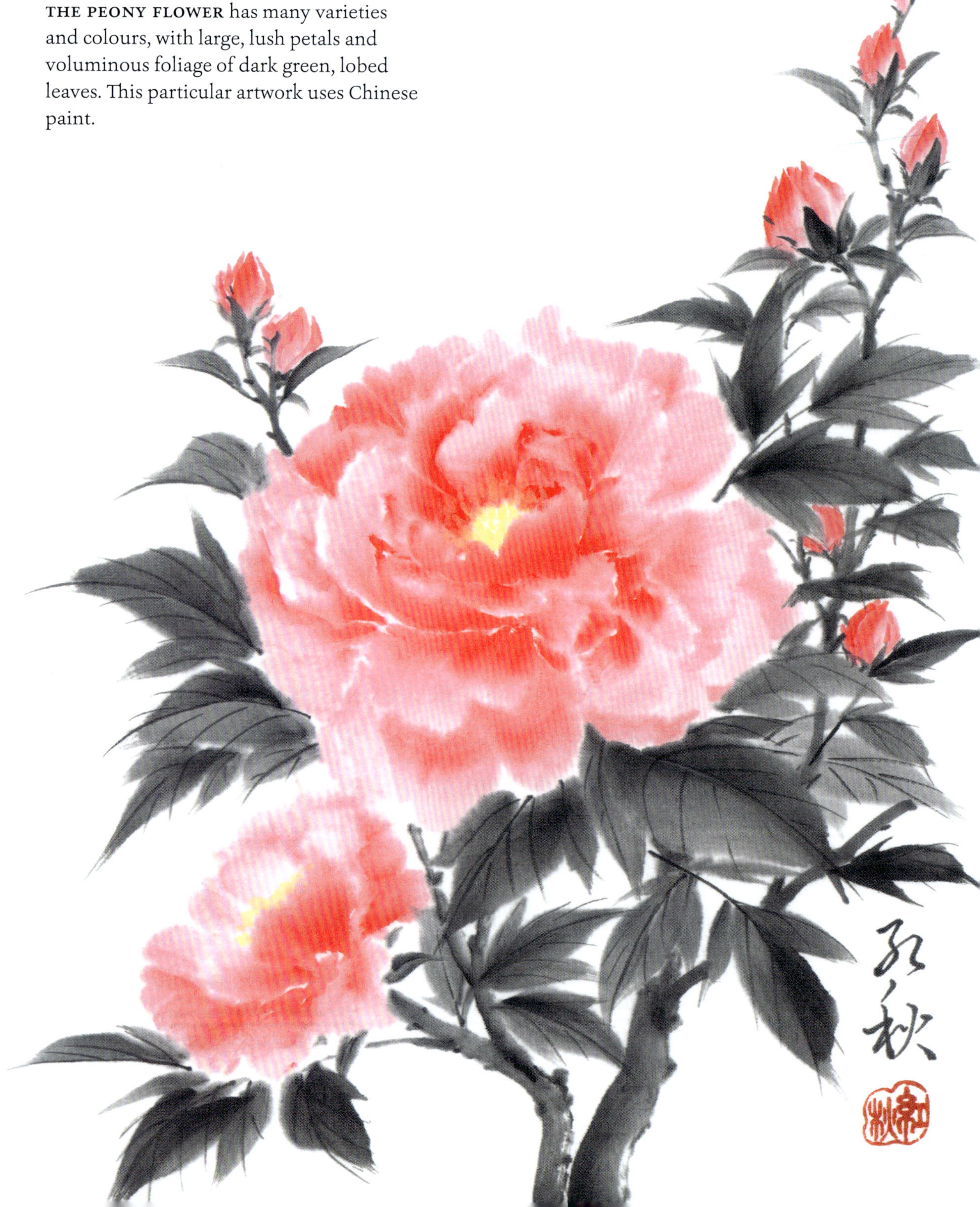

PEONY FLOWER

Load the ōfude (ideally a soft-hair brush to capture the soft petals) with tanboku, prepare the tip with chuboku and blend for sanboku-hou.

1. Begin by painting the front centre petals in two strokes with the tip of the brush pointing downwards. Keep the brush in sokuhitsu and use a gentle up-down motion to create the soft edge of the petals.

2. With the tip of the brush, paint a layer of thinner, wider petals in front, with the tip of the brush pointed towards the centre.

3. Again, with the tip of the brush pointed towards the centre, paint another layer of petals on the other side of the centre point.

4. Lower the angle of the brush, and paint wider petals.

5. Continue building layers of petals in lighter ink.

6. Add more petals on the left and upper section, ensuring the tip of the brush points towards the centre.

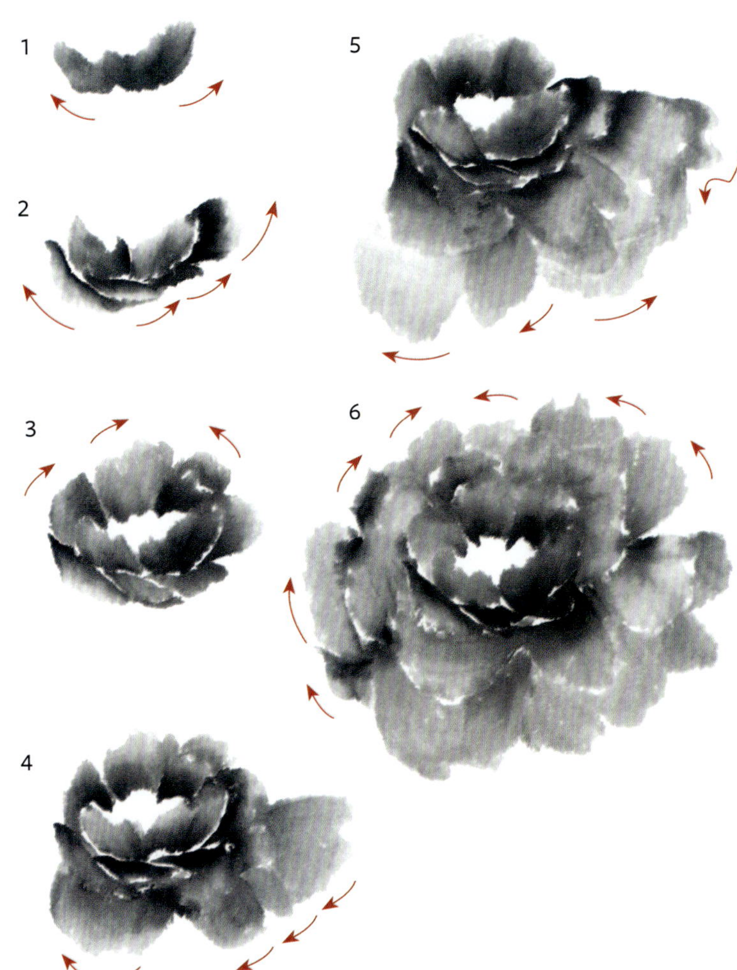

Once you have painted the petals and the ink is moderately dry, load the kofude with nouboku and paint the pistils and stamens in the centre.

Colour use

The peony illustrated on p. 106 exemplifies the use of a single colour: red. Load the brush with light red ink, prepare the tip with dark red ink and blend for sanboku-hou. To paint the central pistils and stamens, load the kofude with undiluted yellow.

This particular artwork uses Chinese paint, which creates a more vibrant and rich finish compared to Gansai paint (see p. 72).

However, peony flowers come in a wide range of colours, including white, pink and red. Some are bicoloured and exhibit a combination of hues. Experiment with different colours and embrace the natural palette the peony offers.

PEONY BUDS AND LEAVES

Bud

To paint the calyx, load the ōfude with chuboku, prepare the tip with nouboku and blend for sanboku-hou. To paint the petals, prepare for sanboku-hou using goku-tanboku and tanboku. The key is to create a colour contrast between the petals and the foliage.

Leaves

Peony leaves are glossy and lobed.

1. In sanboku-hou (using the same shades of ink as the bud calyx), paint the centre lobe first in two strokes, with the tip of the brush pointed towards the centreline.

2. Paint the side lobes, again using two strokes per lobe.

3. Finish off the leaves by painting the veins in nouboku.

Practise different variations of the leaves. (See p. 84 for guidance when painting the leaves.)

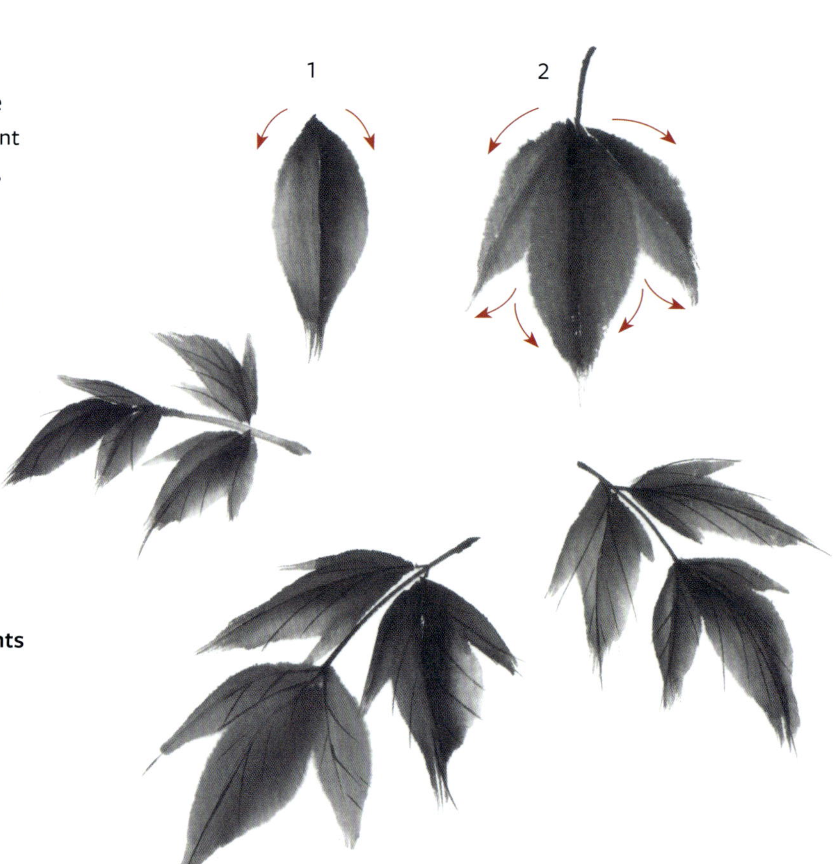

Bring together the various elements in the following order: the flower petals, primary leaves, stem, buds, secondary leaves and, finally, the veins.

KEY POINTS

- For suibokuga using black ink only, using the darkness of the ink to allude to the colour of the flower, while maintaining a contrast between the flowers and foliage.
- When depicting a red peony, for example, use a darker shade of ink for the flower and a lighter shade for the foliage.
- If you are depicting a white-pink peony, use a lighter shade for the flower and a darker shade for the foliage.

秋桜 Cosmos and Dragonfly

INFUSE YOUR ARTWORK with movement and life by incorporating insects and birds into your composition, portraying the symbiotic relationship between different elements of the natural world.

In this artwork, we will cover the techniques to paint a cosmos flower in tsuketate-hou and a dragonfly.

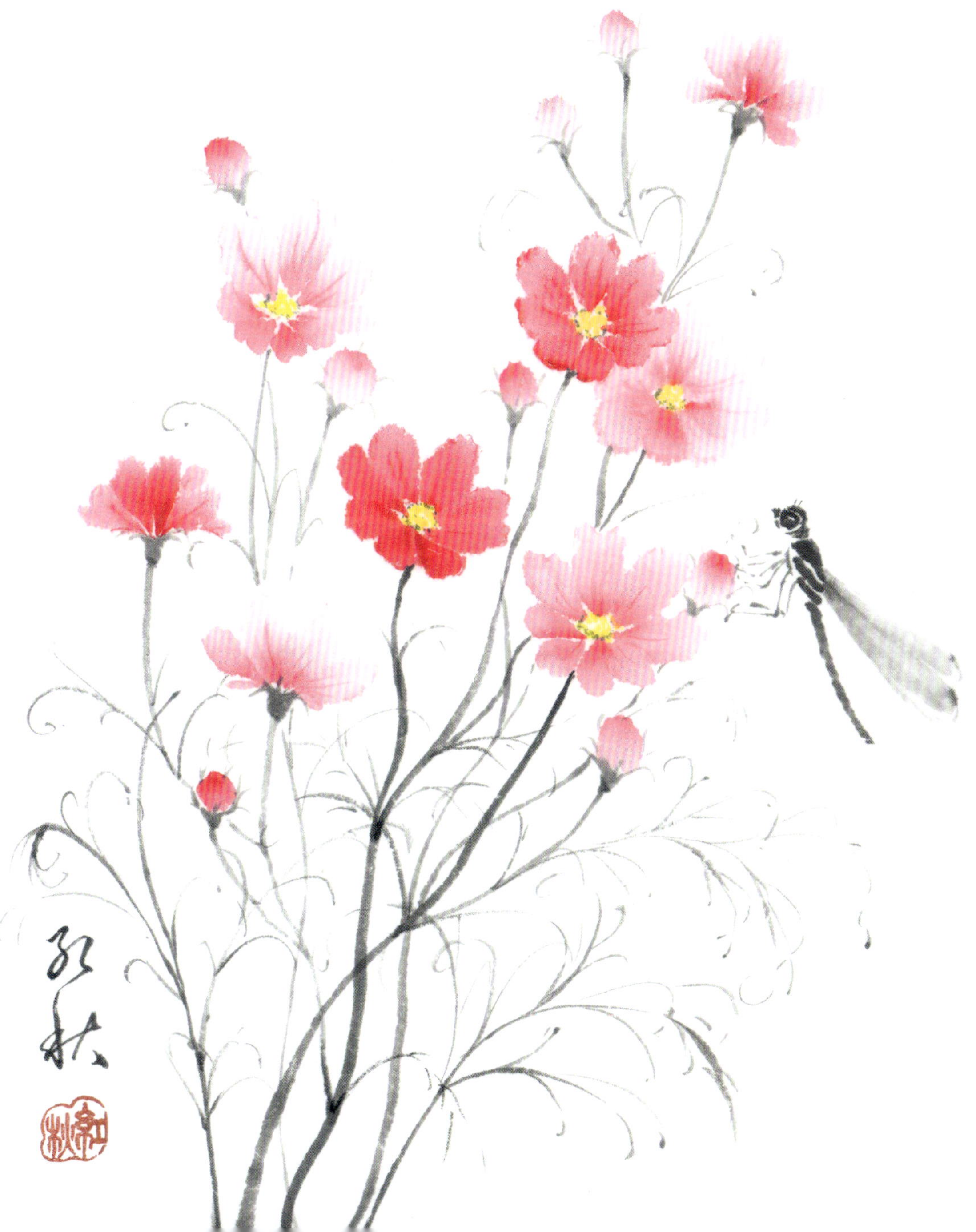

COSMOS FLOWER

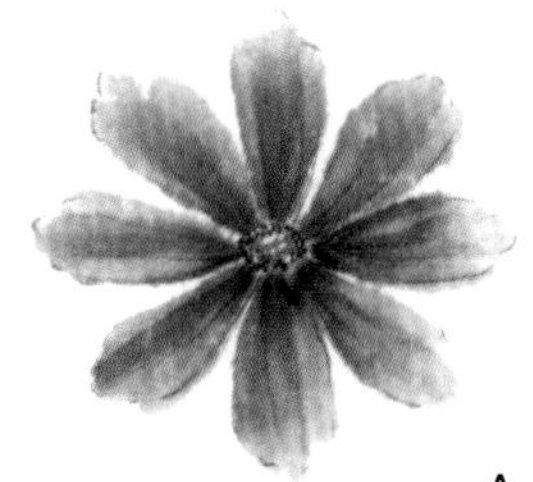

A

Flower A

Load the kofude with nouboku (for colour, use yellow) and begin by painting a cluster of dots to represent the disc florets in the centre of the flower.

Load the ōfude with tanboku (light pink or red), prepare the tip with chuboku (medium-dark red or pink) and blend for sanboku-hou. Next, paint the eight surrounding petal-like structures (ray florets) that radiate outwards. Allow the disc florets in the centre to guide a symmetrical arrangement.

Paint three thin strokes side by side to create each 'petal'. With the tip of the brush pointed towards the centre, push the brush outwards while increasing the pressure to create a thicker stroke. Lift the brush upwards to create a rounded finish. Repeat the same stroke on the left- and right-hand side to complete one petal.

B

If finding balance is difficult, mirror the same strokes on the other side of the central point to create petals marking the twelve and six o'clock positions on a clock, followed by the three and nine o'clock positions. Finally, paint the petals in between, spacing them evenly around the central disc.

To define the petals, prepare the kofude with chuboku and outline the edges and contours.

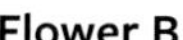

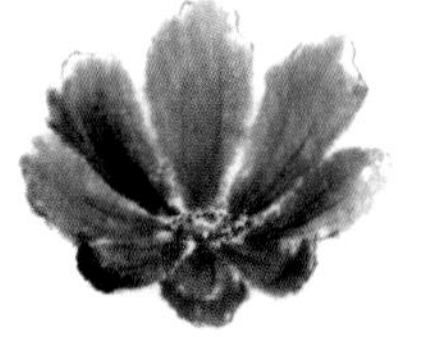

C

Flower B

For this variation, follow the techniques for painting flower A, using shorter strokes for the front three petals. For the remaining petals, use slightly curved, longer strokes to follow the natural cup shape of the flower.

Flower C

Follow the same techniques for painting flower B, however, use even shorter strokes for the front three petals and paint the edges of the petals that curve upwards.

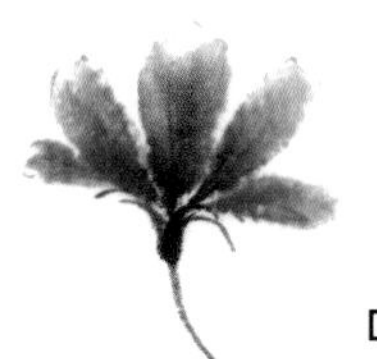

D

Flower D

Load the kofude with nouboku and paint the calyx. Switch to the ōfude and paint four or five petals from the centre outwards.

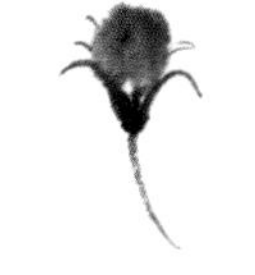

E

Bud E

Follow the same techniques for painting flower D and paint a circular shaped bud.

Stem and leaves

To paint the slender stems and feathery leaves, apply chuboku or tanboku to the tip of the brush, and use light and soft strokes.

Bring together the various elements in the following order: the flowers, buds, stems, leaves and, finally, the dragonfly (optional).

KEY POINT
In your painting, incorporate flowers of different hues, such as pink and red, to mimic the natural clustering of flowers where different colours intermingle.

DRAGONFLIES

1. Load the kofude with nouboku and paint the head, followed by the thorax in three diagonal strokes.

2. Paint the abdomen in chokuhitsu, pausing at regular intervals to faintly mark the segments.

3. Use the tip of the brush to paint the legs.

4. Switch to the ōfude and paint the wings in goku-tanboku, pushing the brush from the outside towards the thorax.

5. Optional: once the ink is moderately dry, use the tip of the brush to paint faint outlines around the wings.

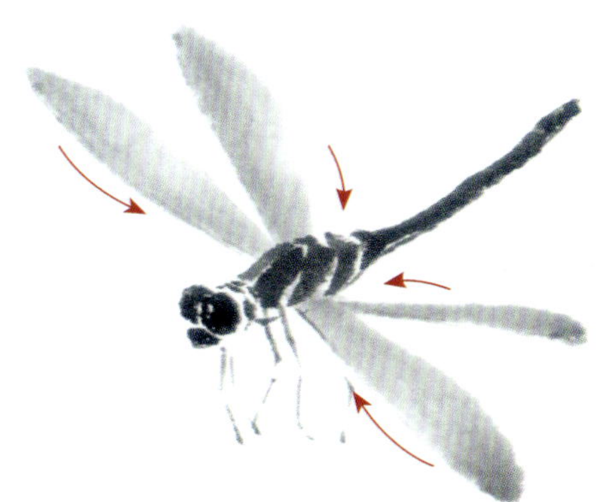

Practise painting the dragonfly from various angles.

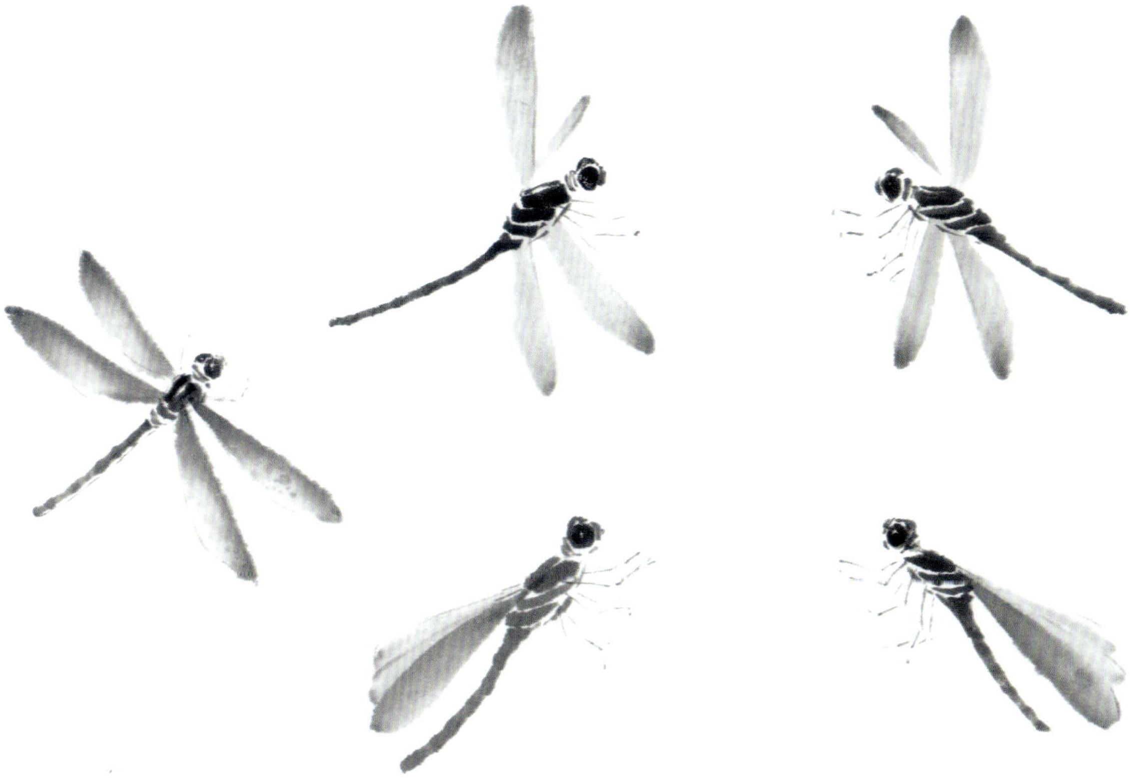

チューリップ
Tulips and Butterfly

IN THIS ARTWORK, we will express the vibrant, velvety petals of the tulip flower and learn how to paint butterflies.

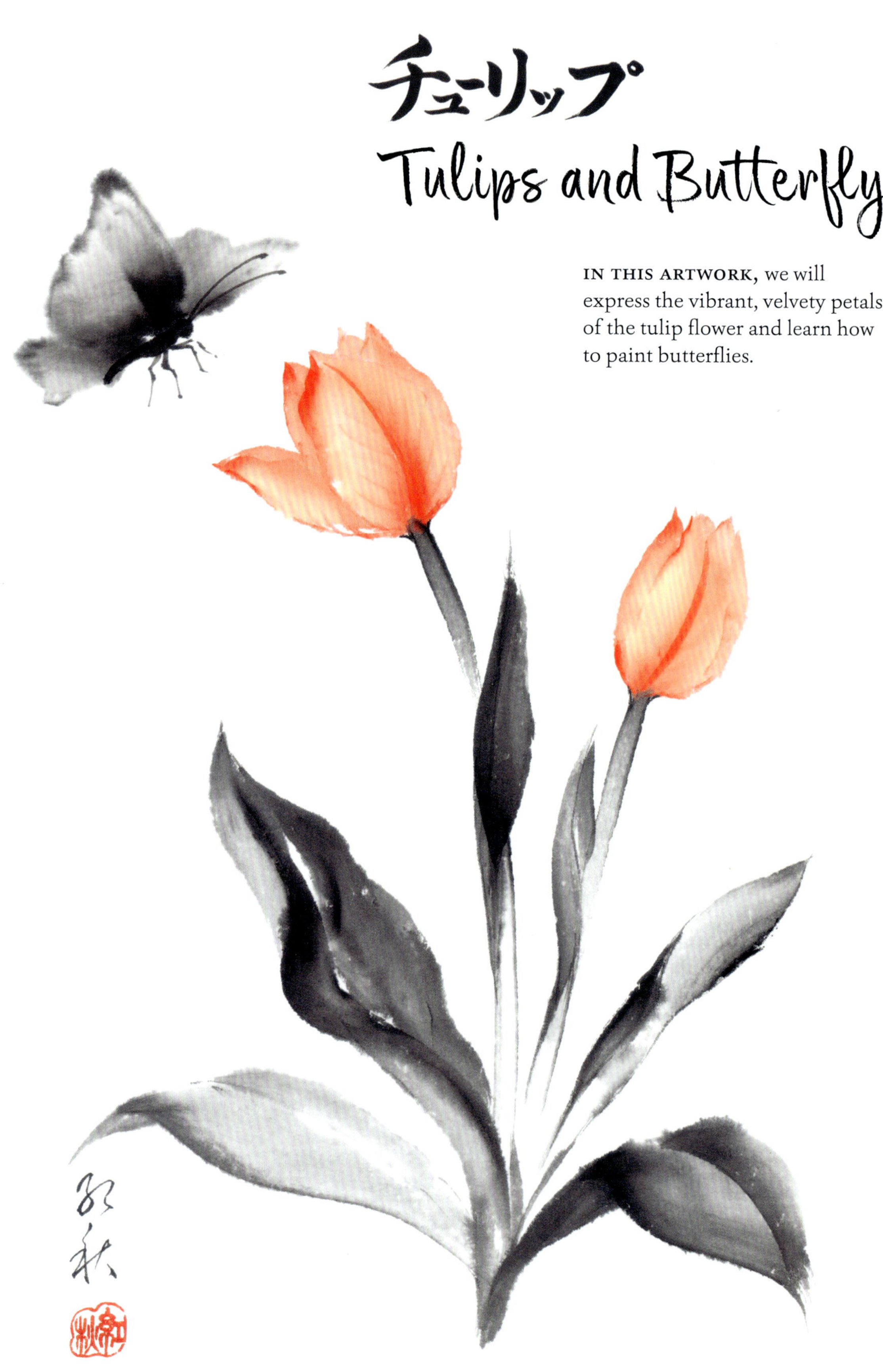

TULIP FLOWER

1. Load the ōfude with tanboku, prepare the tip with nouboku and blend for sanboku-hou. Paint the centreline from the bottom upwards in chokuhitsu.

2. With the tip of the brush positioned towards the centreline, push the brush upwards in sokuhitsu, while varying the pressure to create the wavy edge of the petal.

3. With the tip of the brush pointing outwards, paint the open petal.

4. Following the same technique as step 2 with the brush pointed towards the centreline, push the brush from the base to the tip of the petal.

5. Paint the side petal from the tip to the base.

6. Create a layer of back petals, moving the brush from the tip of the petals towards the base.

7. Finally, flatten the tip of the brush and paint the stem in chokuhitsu in one continuous, flowing stroke (for additional detail, paint the stem in ryoguma).

Switch to the kofude and paint the veins on the petals from the centre outwards.

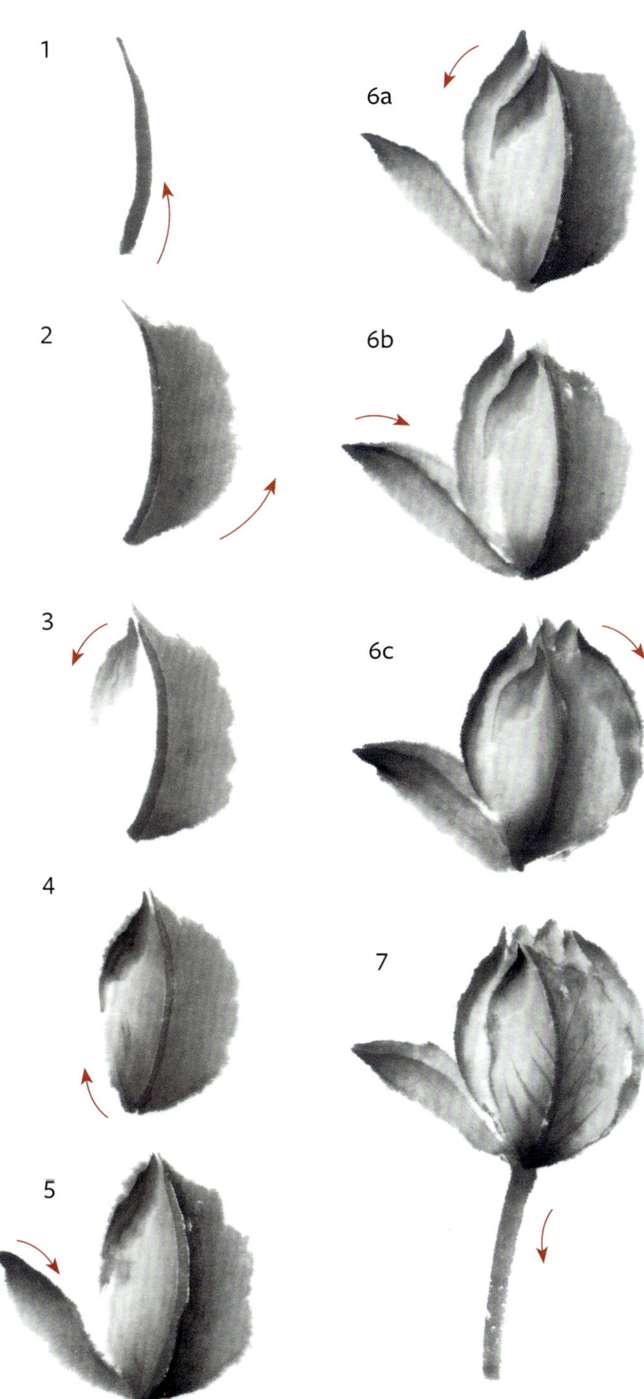

Colour use

Load the brush with yellow ink, prepare the tip with orange ink and blend for sanboku-hou.

For the veins, create a shade of orange ink that is subtly darker than the petals.

TULIP LEAVES

Here, we will paint different variations of the long, slender tulip leaves that grow from the base of the plant.

Load the ōfude with chuboku, prepare the tip with nouboku and blend for sanboku-hou. Follow the stroke order as illustrated below.

To determine the positioning and direction of the brush for each stroke, observe the areas where darker tones are present. Since the tip of the brush is darker than the body when painting in sanboku-hou, the darker tones indicate where the tip of the brush has traced over.

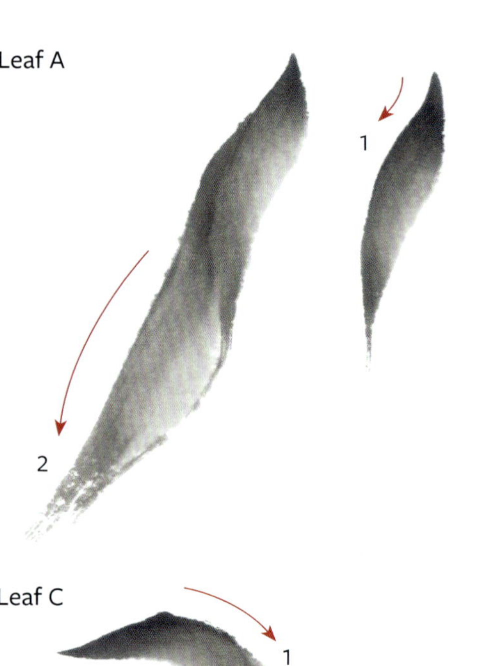

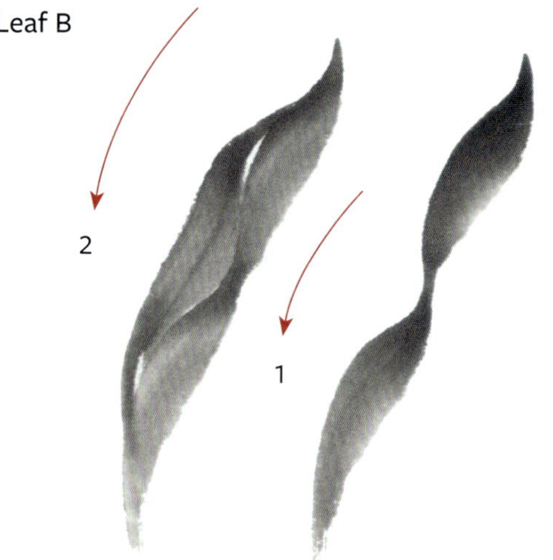

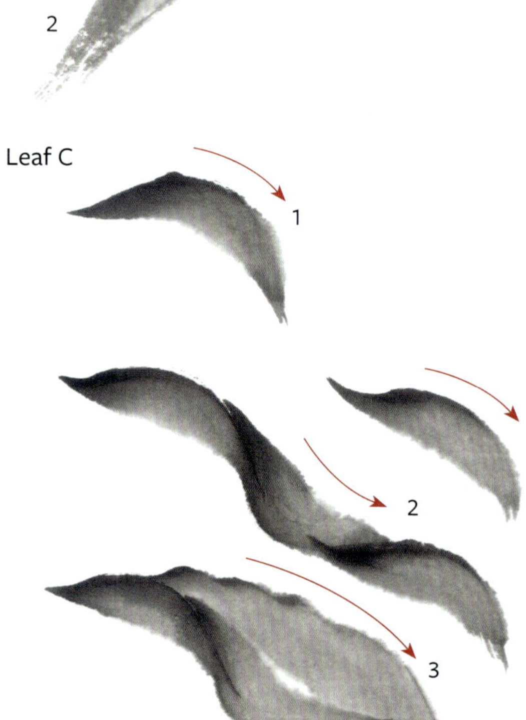

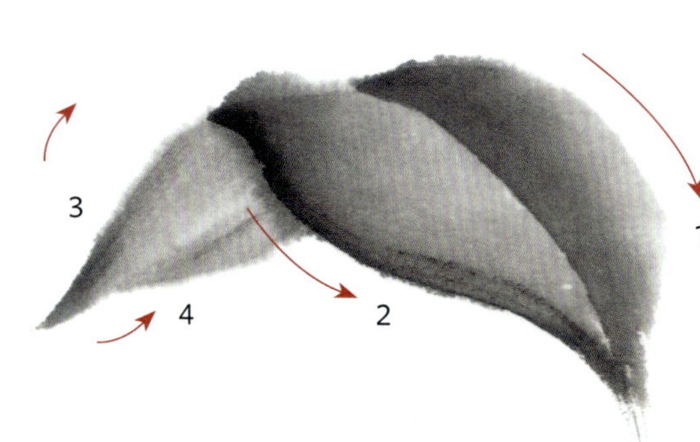

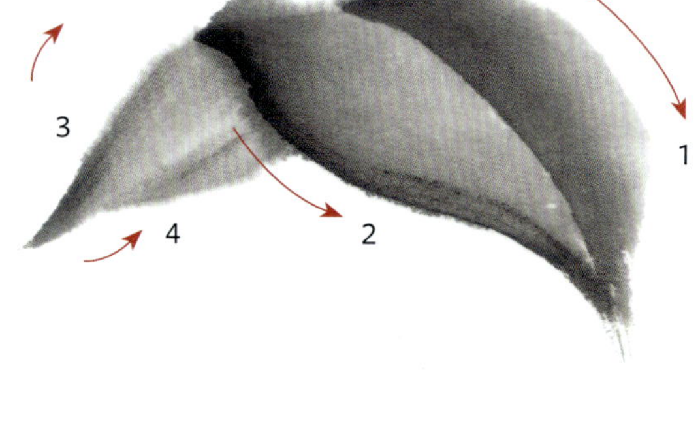

Bring together the various elements in the following order: flowers, stems, leaves, details (veins of the flowers) and, finally, the butterfly (optional).

BUTTERFLIES

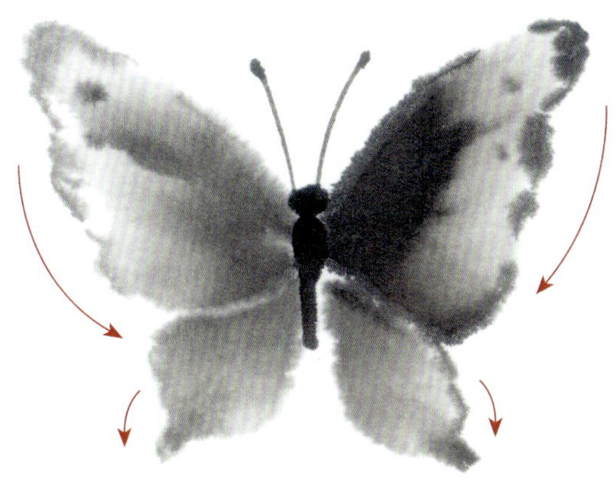

1. Load the kofude with nouboku and use the tip of the brush to paint the head, body and antennae.

2. Load the ōfude with tanboku, prepare the tip with nouboku and blend for sanboku-hou. Paint the forewing. With the tip of the brush pointed towards the butterfly's body, pivot the brush downwards while keeping the position of the tip fixed. At the same time, gently push the brush back and forth sideways to emulate the wavy edges of the wing. Repeat this technique to paint the smaller hind wing. Mirror these wings on the other side of the body.

3. Apply darker ink to the tip of the brush and wipe off excess ink. Using haboku-hou, paint the edge of the wings while the ink is still wet to create the nijimi effect (see on p. 31)

Paint the butterfly from different angles.

Paint the front wings first, followed by the back wings in a lighter shade of ink.

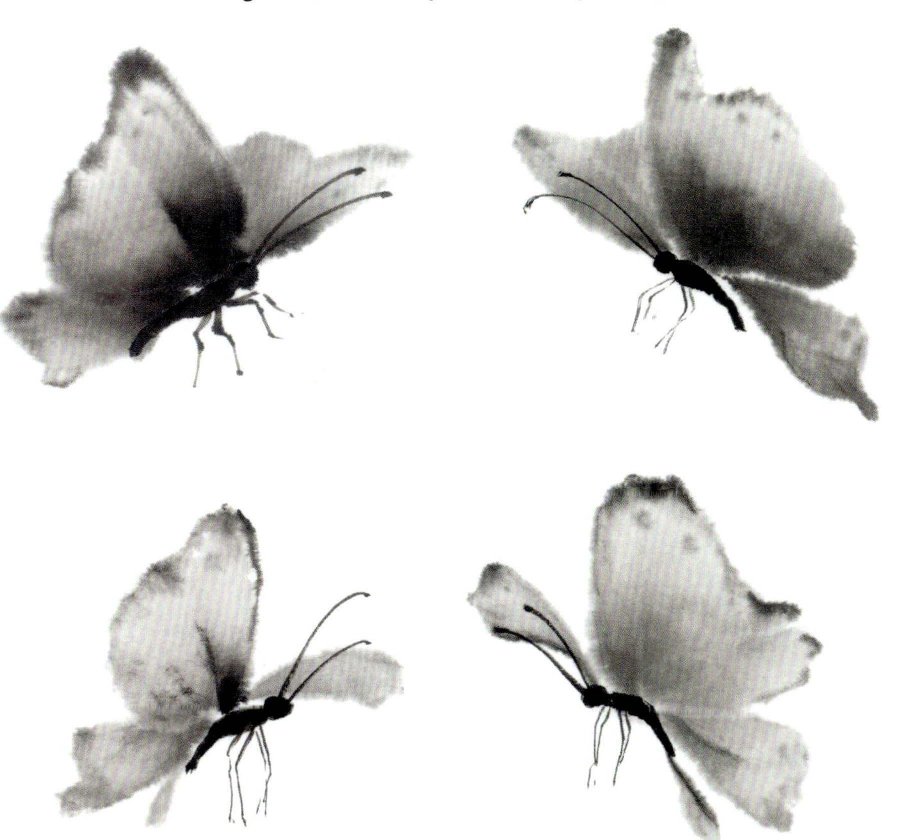

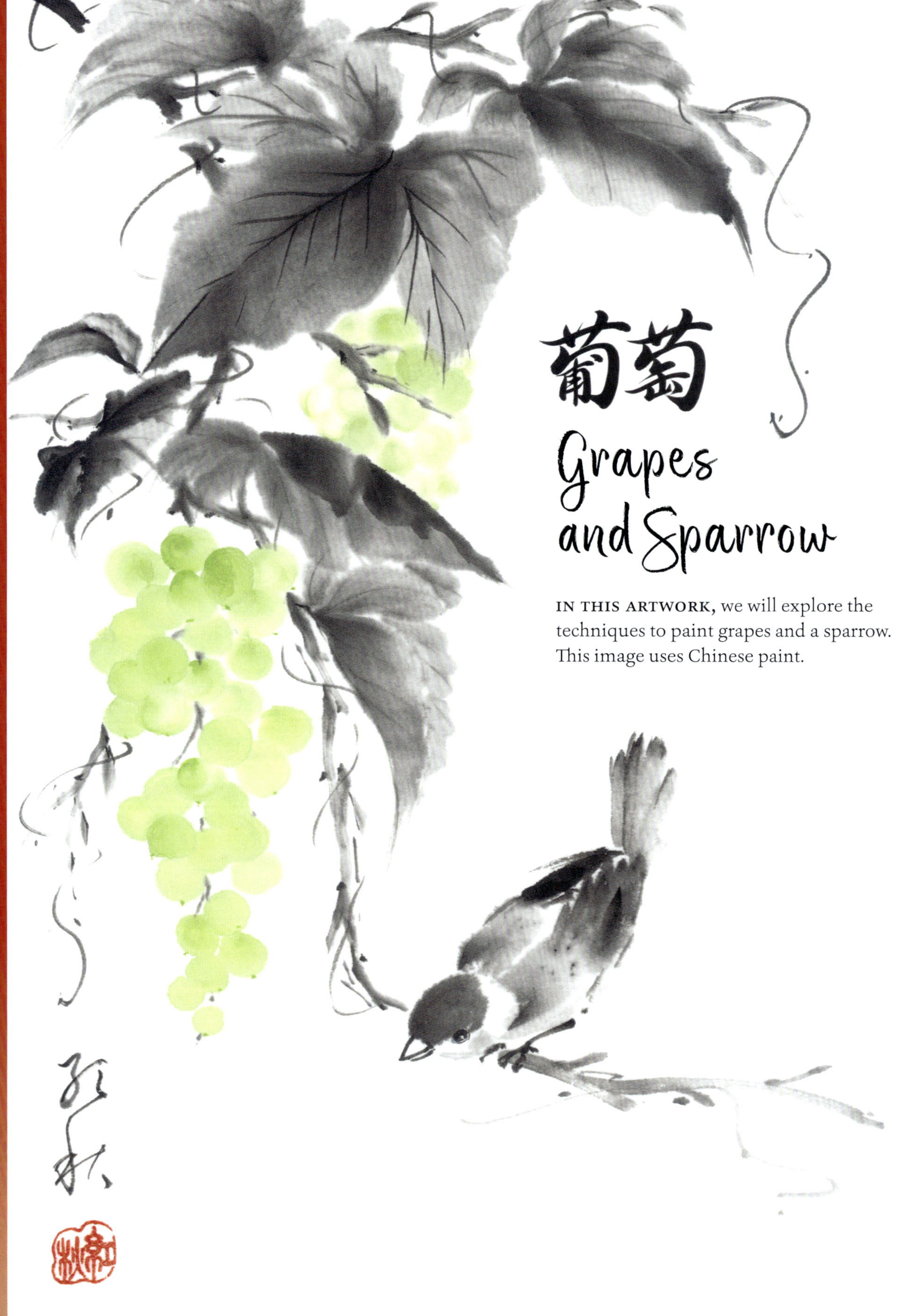

葡萄
Grapes and Sparrow

IN THIS ARTWORK, we will explore the techniques to paint grapes and a sparrow. This image uses Chinese paint.

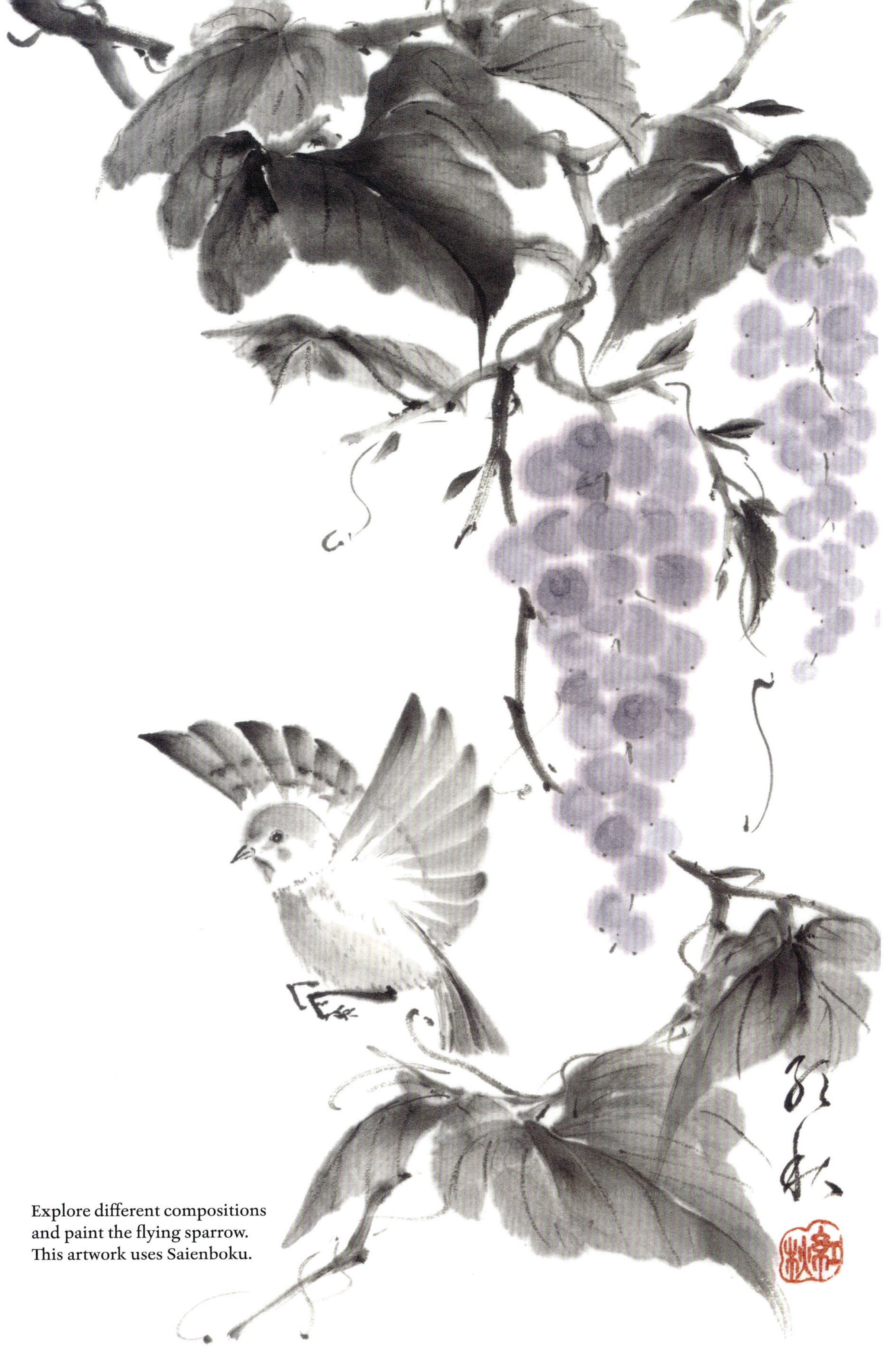

Explore different compositions
and paint the flying sparrow.
This artwork uses Saienboku.

GRAPES

Load the ōfude with tanboku, prepare the tip with nouboku and blend for sanboku-hou. The uchiguma (see p. 27) and motoguma (see p. 30) techniques can also be used, depending on your preference.

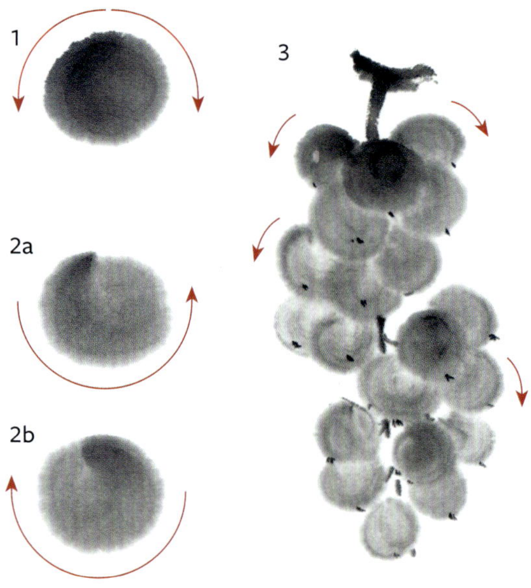

1. **Front grapes**: with the tip of the brush positioned at the top, turn the brush anticlockwise to create a semi-circle. Position the tip of the brush at the top again and turn clockwise to complete the circle. Ensure that the tip of the brush traces the outline throughout the stroke.

2. **Back grapes:** with the tip of the brush positioned at the top:

   a: Turn the brush anticlockwise to create a full or semi-circle for grapes positioned on the left-hand side

   b: Or turn the brush clockwise to create a full or semi-circle for grapes positioned on the right-hand side.

3. Bring together the circles to paint a bunch of grapes. Create a few full circles using step 1, then paint layers behind using step 2.

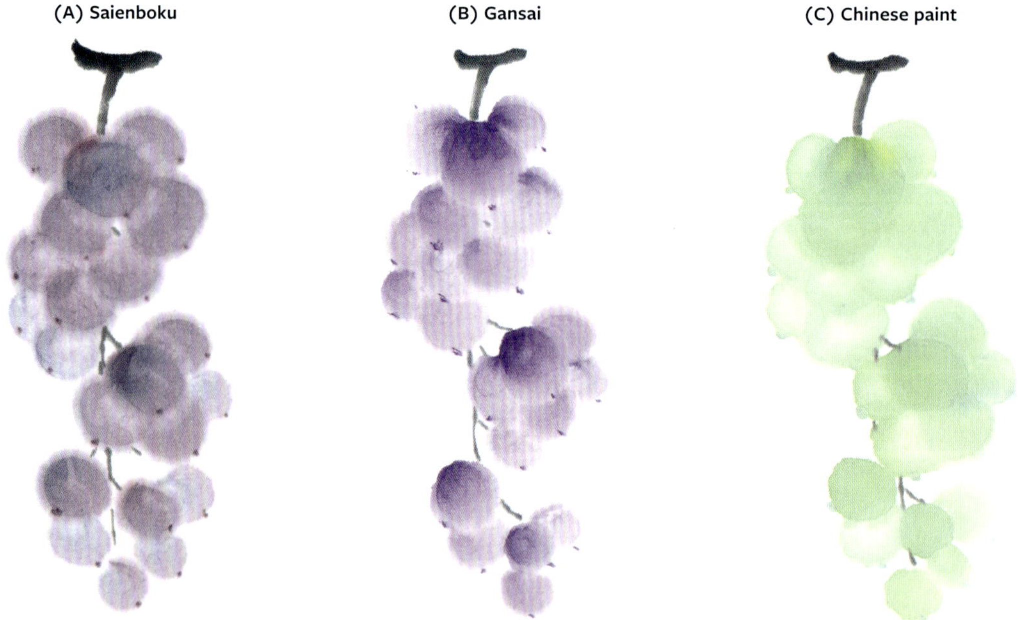

Colour use

The grapes above have been painted in sanboku-hou and illustrate the distinct characteristics that can be produced by different types of coloured ink (see p. 72). To achieve clear brush marks and create a more pronounced three-dimensional effect, similar to that depicted in image A, it is recommended to use Saienboku. Otherwise, to create a softer appearance, you can use Gansai (B) or Chinese paint (C).

GRAPE LEAVES

Prepare the ōfude for sanboku-hou using chuboku and nouboku. Paint the five lobes of the grape leaf.

1. Paint the centre ('terminal') lobe of the leaf in two strokes. To create the serrated edge of the grape leaves, push the body of the brush down at intervals, alternating between heavy and light pressure as you push your brush.

2. Paint the lower lobes on the left- and right-hand side of the centre, again using two brushstrokes for each lobe.

3. Next, paint the upper lobes on the left- and right-hand side, using one brushstroke for each lobe. Once the ink is moderately dry, load the kofude with nouboku and paint the veins.

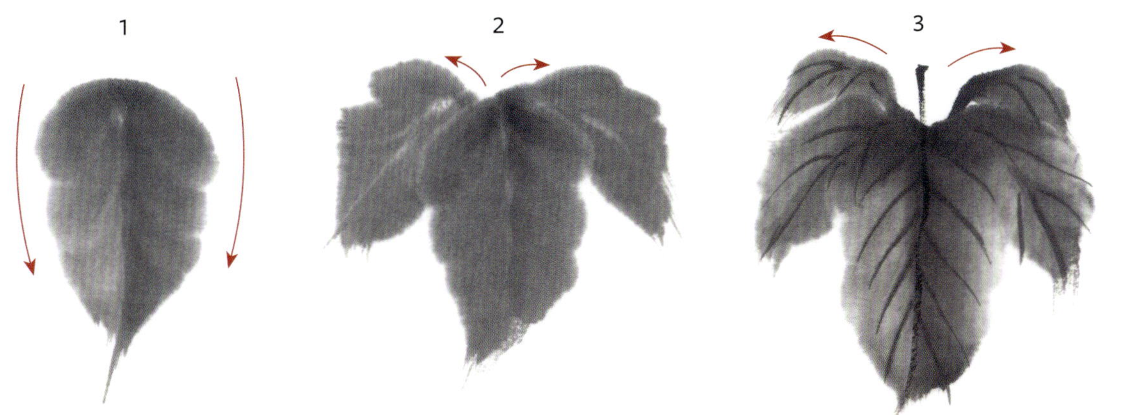

Practise painting the grape leaves from different angles.

Leaf A and B: paint the upper section of the leaf first using a darker shade of ink (this represents the front side), followed by the lower section of the leaf in a lighter shade (this represents the rear side).

Leaf C: paint the front side first, then the back.

Branches

Paint the woody branches following the composition on pp. 116 and 117. In chokuhitsu, paint short and light overlapping strokes while introducing slight curves and bends to mimic the growth habits of the grapevine.

To paint the thread-like, coiled stems, prepare the kofude with chuboku and use light and swift movements in chokuhitsu. Hold the brush in tankou-hou and position the arm in teiwan-hou.

Bring together the various elements in the following order: the leaves, woody branches, grape bunches and sparrow (optional), followed by the details (veins of the leaves and coiled stems).

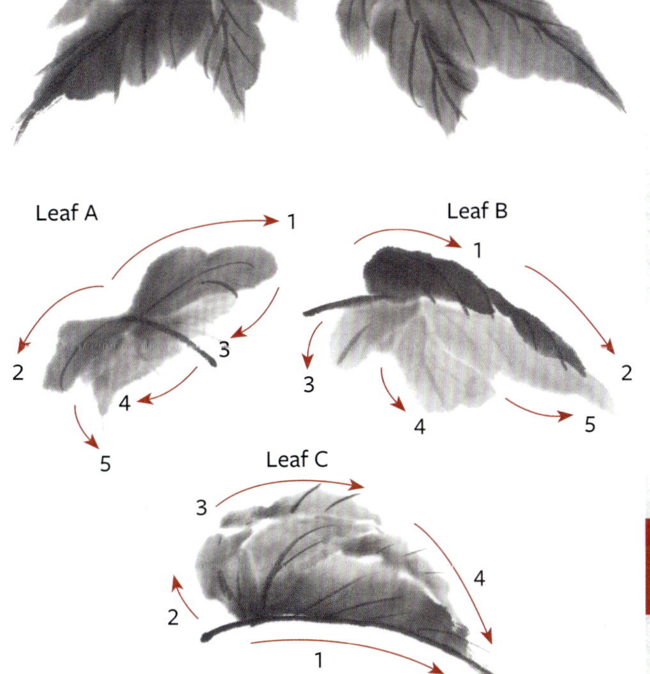

SITTING SPARROWS

1

2

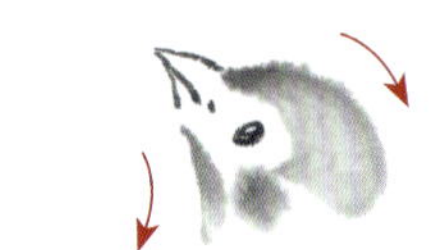

3

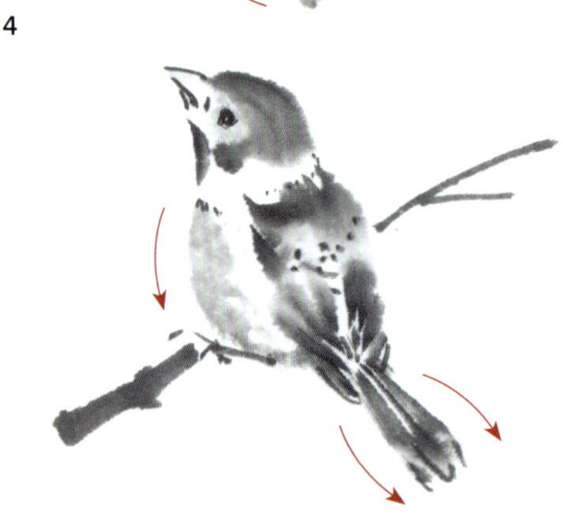

4

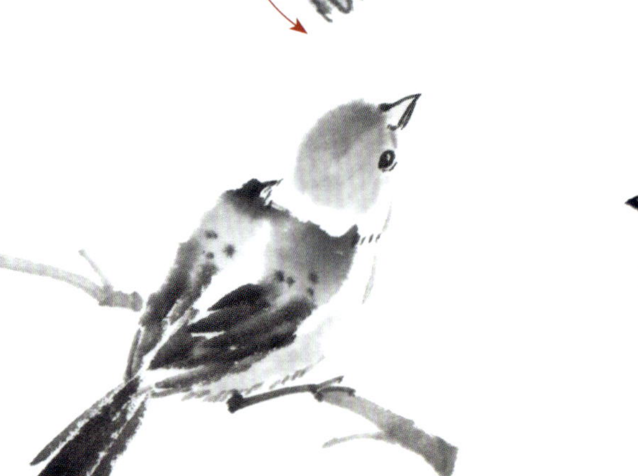

1. Load the kofude with nouboku and use the tip of the brush to paint the eye and beak.

2. Prepare the ōfude for sanboku-hou using tanboku and chuboku. Paint the head with the tip of the brush pointed towards the beak (the darker tones indicate where the tip of the brush points towards).

3. Reapply nouboku to the tip. In sokuhitsu, paint the upper wings from the left to the centre and the right to the centre with the tip of the brush pointed towards the head. Next, paint the lower wings in light and swift bottom-up strokes.

4. With the tip of the brush, paint several strokes in semi-sokuhitsu to create the tail. Prepare the brush with goku-tanboku and paint a rounded line in sokuhitsu, pushing the brush downwards to create the abdomen. Load the kofude or menso-fude with nouboku and paint the legs and feet, followed by the patches on the back.

Practise painting sitting sparrows from different angles.

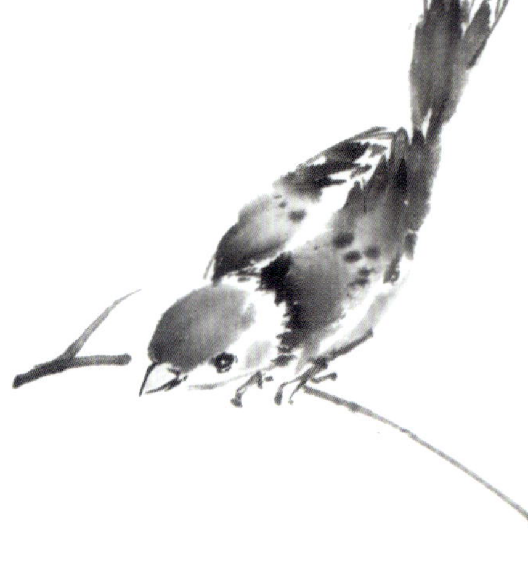

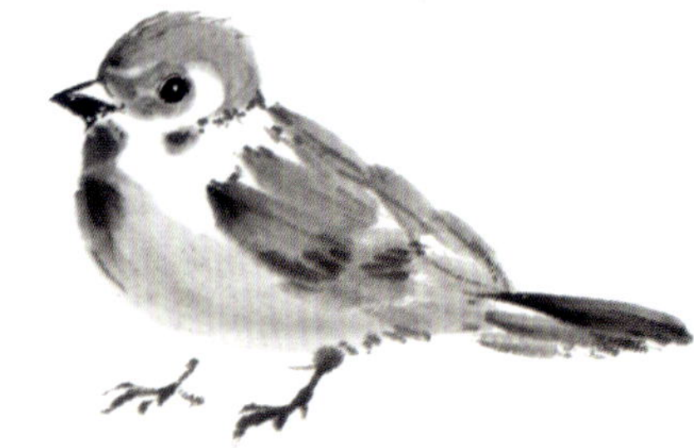

FLYING SPARROW

1. Load the kofude with nouboku and use the tip of the brush to paint the eye and beak.

2. Prepare the ōfude for sanboku-hou using tanboku and chuboku and paint the head with the tip of the brush pointed towards the beak.

3. Continue to paint the opened sparrow wings starting with the underside. Push the brush from the outside inwards.

4. Next, prepare the brush in sanboku-hou using chuboku and nouboku and paint the outer side of the wing in a darker shade of ink following the same brush movements.

5. Reshape the tip of the brush and paint the tail in several top-down strokes.

6. Prepare the brush with tanboku and paint a rounded line in sokuhitsu, pushing the brush downwards to create the abdomen. Load the kofude or mensofude with nouboku and paint the legs and feet.

Finally, add details on the abdomen and wing using the kofude.

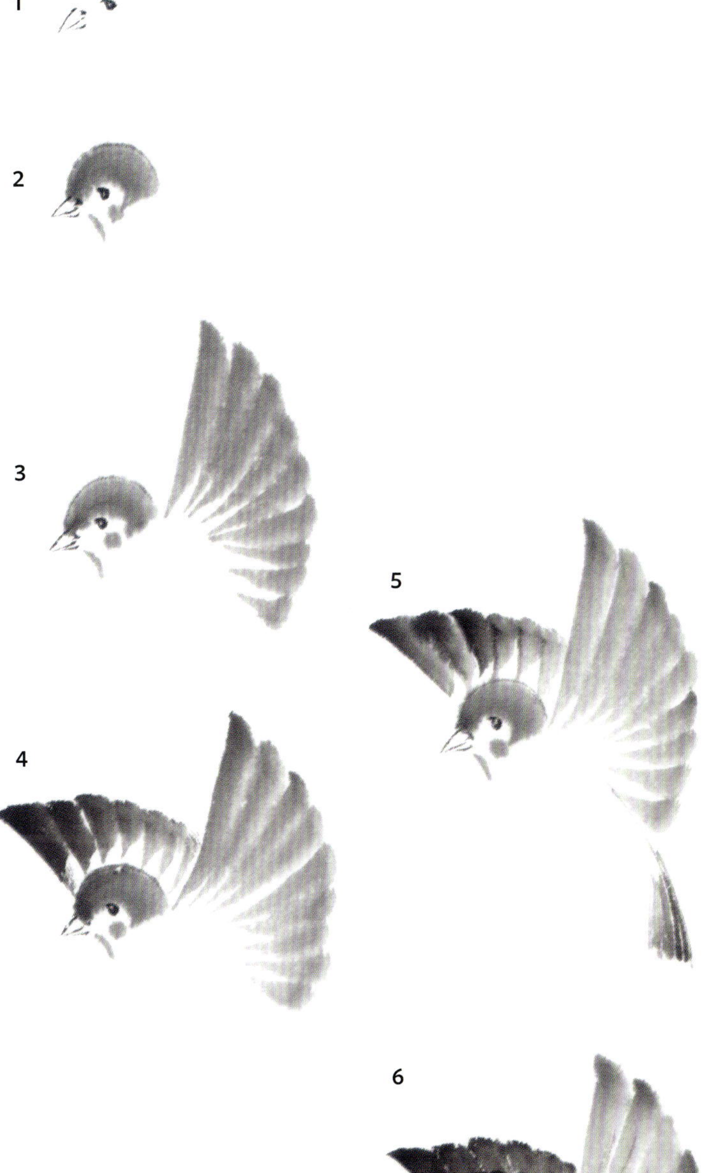

SPARROWS

Refer to the images below and practise painting sparrows from different angles.

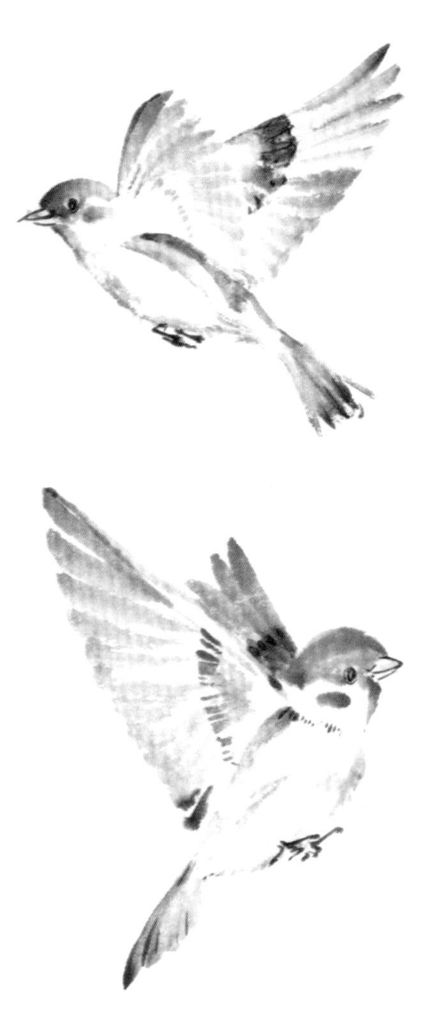

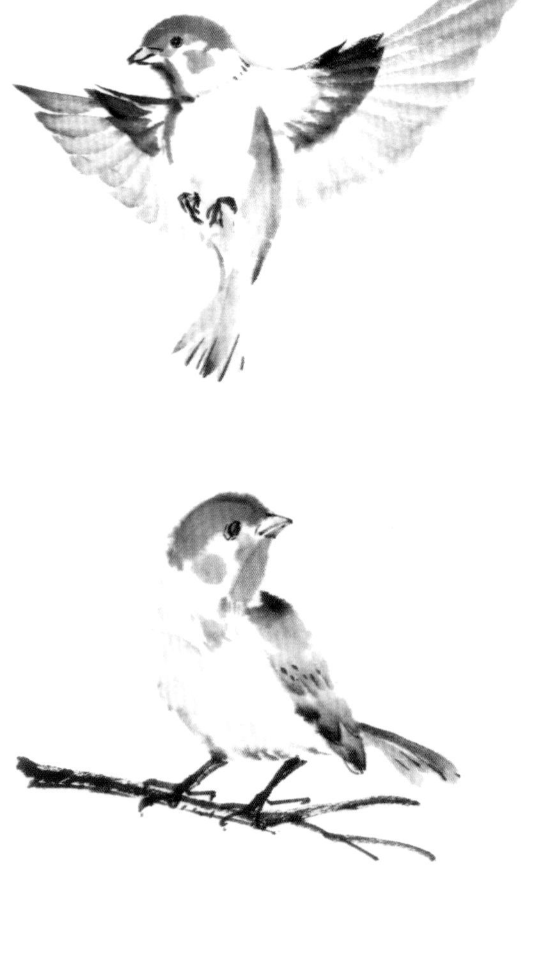

KEY POINT
The basic principles acquired to paint the sparrow can be applied to paint other bird species.

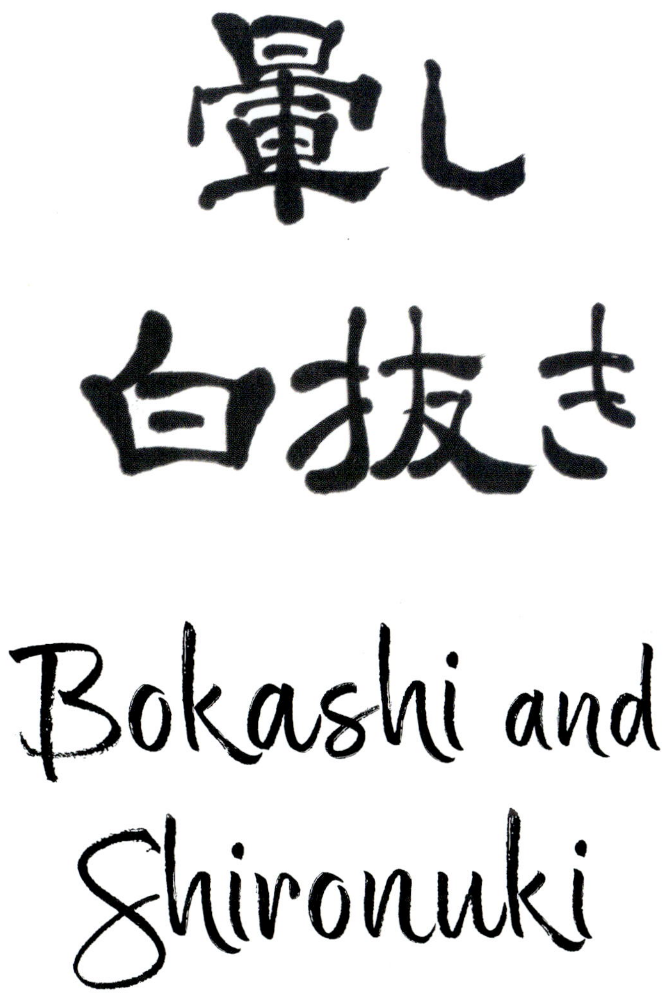

Bokashi and Shironuki

Exploring bokashi and shironuki to paint the sunset, moon, water, rain and snow

HAVING EXPLORED the techniques of painting an array of flowers, plants, insects and birds, we will now integrate the bokashi and shironuki techniques to convey the evocative shifts in weather patterns and the cyclical dance of seasons. With these tools, we will enhance our background by capturing the tranquillity of moonlit nights, the warm nostalgia as the sun descends, or the calm contemplation that the water inspires.

AMI BOKASHI

Bokashi collectively refers to ink-blurring techniques. This chapter will introduce two methods: ami bokashi (net bokashi) and mizu bokashi (water bokashi).

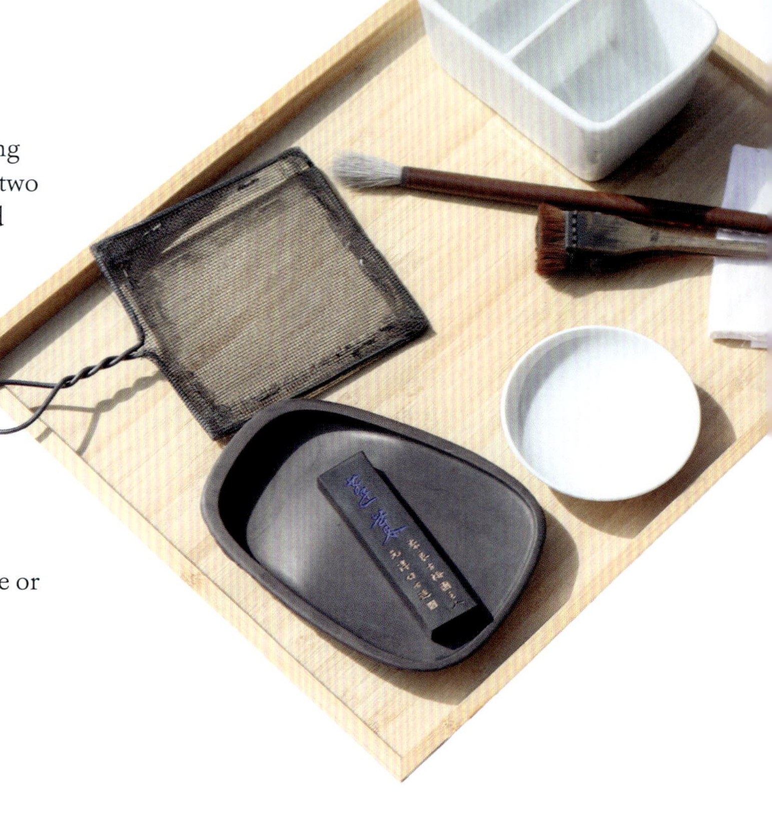

Materials

- **BOKASHI AMI:** fine net or mesh (alternative tool: kitchen sieve)
- **SURIKOMI-BAKE:** grinding brush (alternative tool: toothbrush)
- **ŌFUDE:** large soft-hair brush
- **SUMI AND SUZURI:** ink and inkstone or liquid ink
- **EZARA:** small plate
- **HISSEN:** water jar
- **FUKIN:** cloth or kitchen paper

1

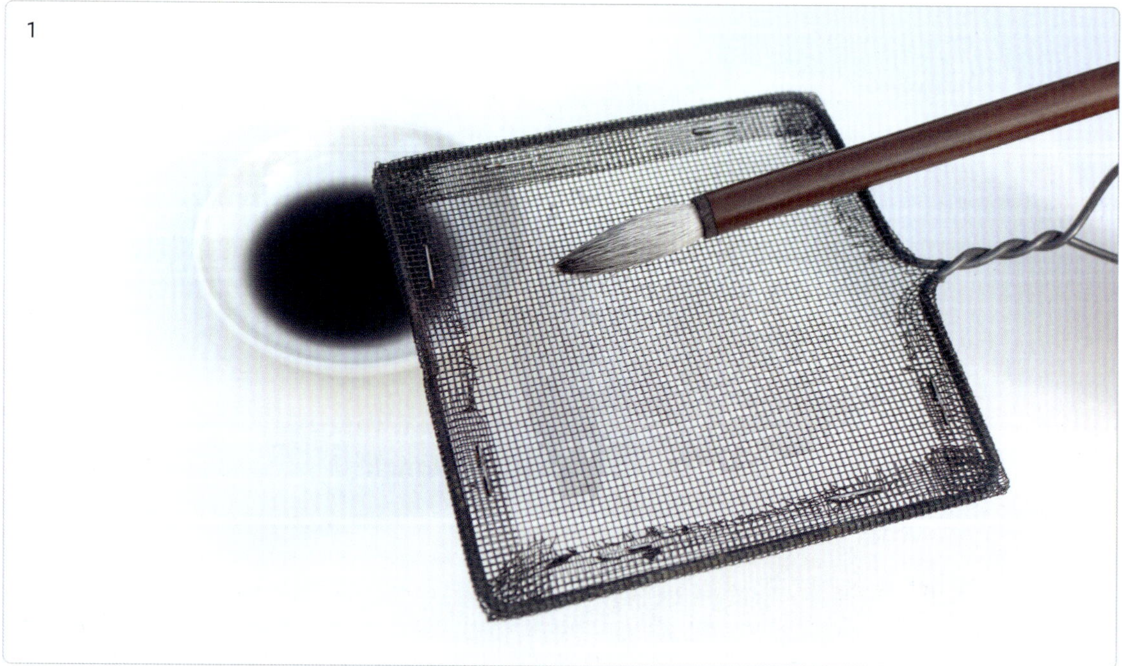

1. Use the brush to apply goku-tanboku or tanboku (choose the shade of ink according to the desired darkness of the sky) evenly across the surface of the net. This step should be done away from your artwork to prevent any splatters of water droplets.

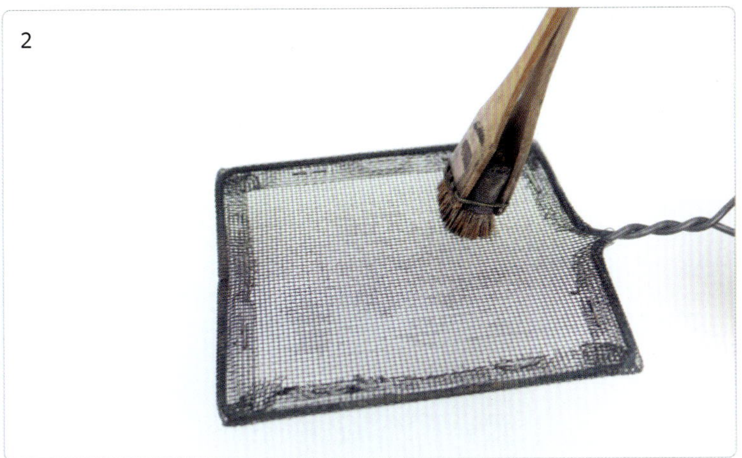

2. Prepare the surikomi-bake brush and gently push it over the surface of the net. This will result in a spray-like effect for subtle shading, which is particularly effective for creating soft, diffused transitions in landscapes. Test this technique on a piece of paper to ensure the desired effect before applying it to the final artwork.

Moon

Cut a circular or crescent shape in a piece of cardstock or prepare a round plate and position it in the desired location for the moon. Paint the sky around it using the bokashi technique – the negative space will give form to the moon.

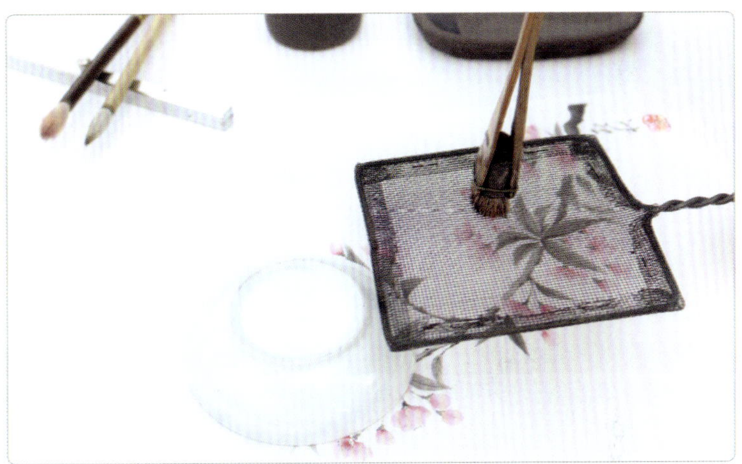

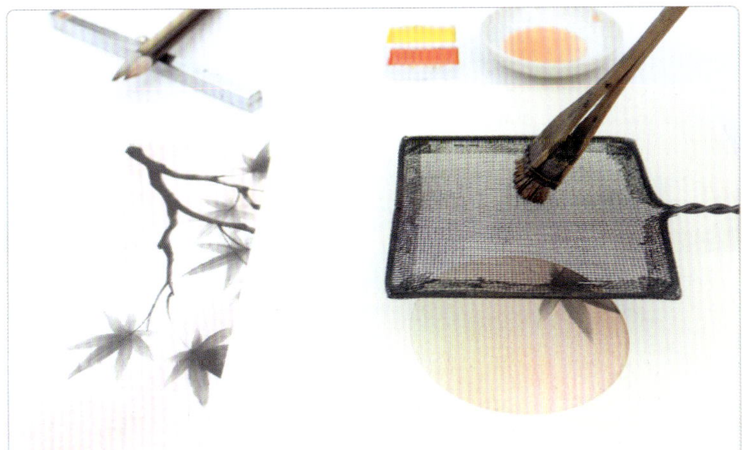

Sun

Cut a circular hole in a piece of cardstock and position the hole in the desired location for the sun. Paint the sun using the bokashi technique. You could try applying coloured ink in the same way.

紅葉 Sunset Maple Tree

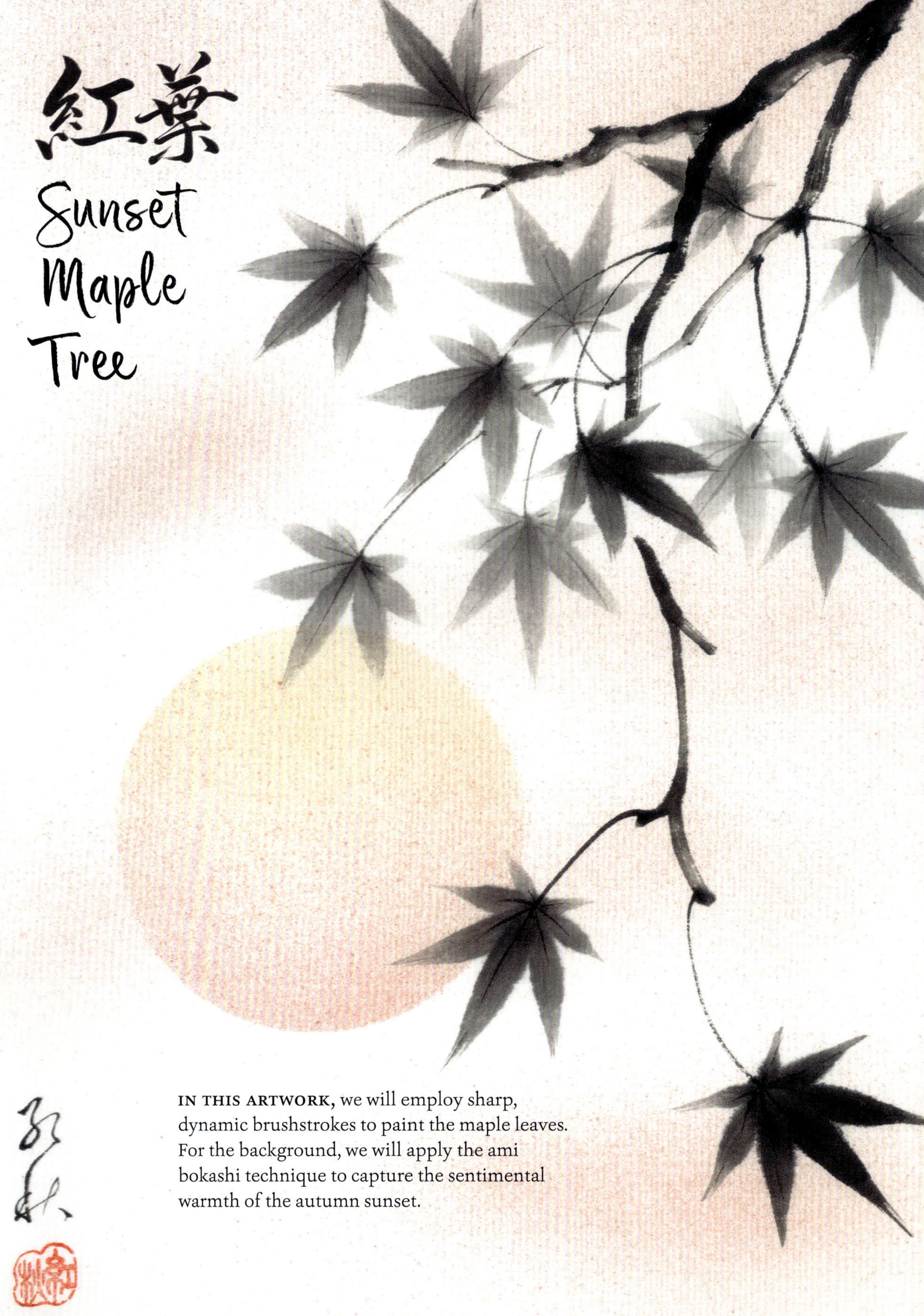

IN THIS ARTWORK, we will employ sharp, dynamic brushstrokes to paint the maple leaves. For the background, we will apply the ami bokashi technique to capture the sentimental warmth of the autumn sunset.

MAPLE LEAVES

Prepare the ōfude for sanboku-hou using chuboku with nouboku, or tanboku with chuboku to allow for a more subtle and seamless gradation. If you choose to incorporate colour for the leaves, load the brush with a light orange-red ink and a deep red ink and blend for sanboku-hou (see p. 139).

1-4. The brushstrokes that mark each lobe resemble those of the orchid petal or bamboo leaf. Position the tip of the brush at the base of the leaf, apply gentle pressure and then swing the brush outward to create a pointy finish. Start with the central lobe of the leaf and work your way outwards, creating shorter lobes.

5. Load the menso-fude with nouboku and use the tip of the brush to create thin, sharp lines for the stems and veins that run through the centre of each lobe. To facilitate swift, controlled strokes, it is advisable to hold the brush in tankou-hou and position the arm in teiwan-hou.

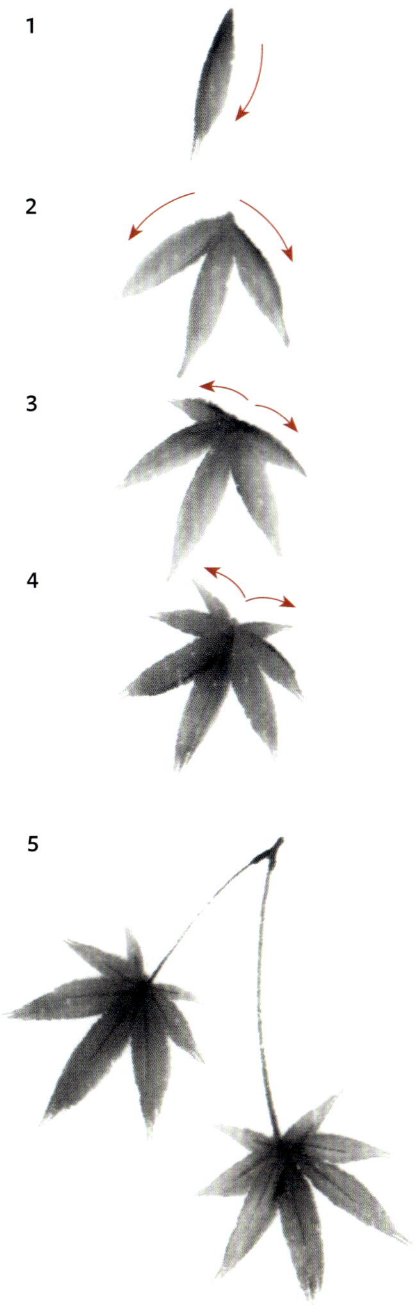

Branches

To paint the branches, load the ōfude with nouboku and remove excess ink to bring out the kasure effect. Create the thicker branches in semi-sokuhitsu and transition to chokuhitsu to create the thinner branches.

Bokashi sun

Use the ami bokashi technique outlined on p. 125 to create a sunset. Capture the various shades of the sunset by using different colours and intensities – use warm colours, such as shades of red, orange and yellow. The sunset illustrated on p. 126 uses yellow for the upper section of the sun, orange for the midsection and darker orange for the lower section.

Optional: apply the same ami bokashi technique to add colour to the background and convey the scattering of sunlight.

Bring together the various elements in the following order: the branches, maple leaves, slender stems and veins. Finally once the ink is moderately dry, paint the sunset with the ami bokashi technique.

KEY POINT

To introduce depth, use a darker shade of ink to paint the leaves that are positioned in front of the other elements, and use a lighter shade for the background leaves.

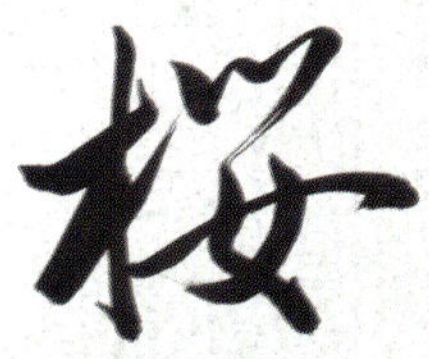

Moonlit Cherry Blossom

IN THIS ARTWORK, we will paint the cherry blossom tree and its abundant blossoms, often associated with the arrival of spring and a symbol of renewal and the impermanence of life. We will expand on the techniques covered for the plum blossom tree in the Shikunshi section.

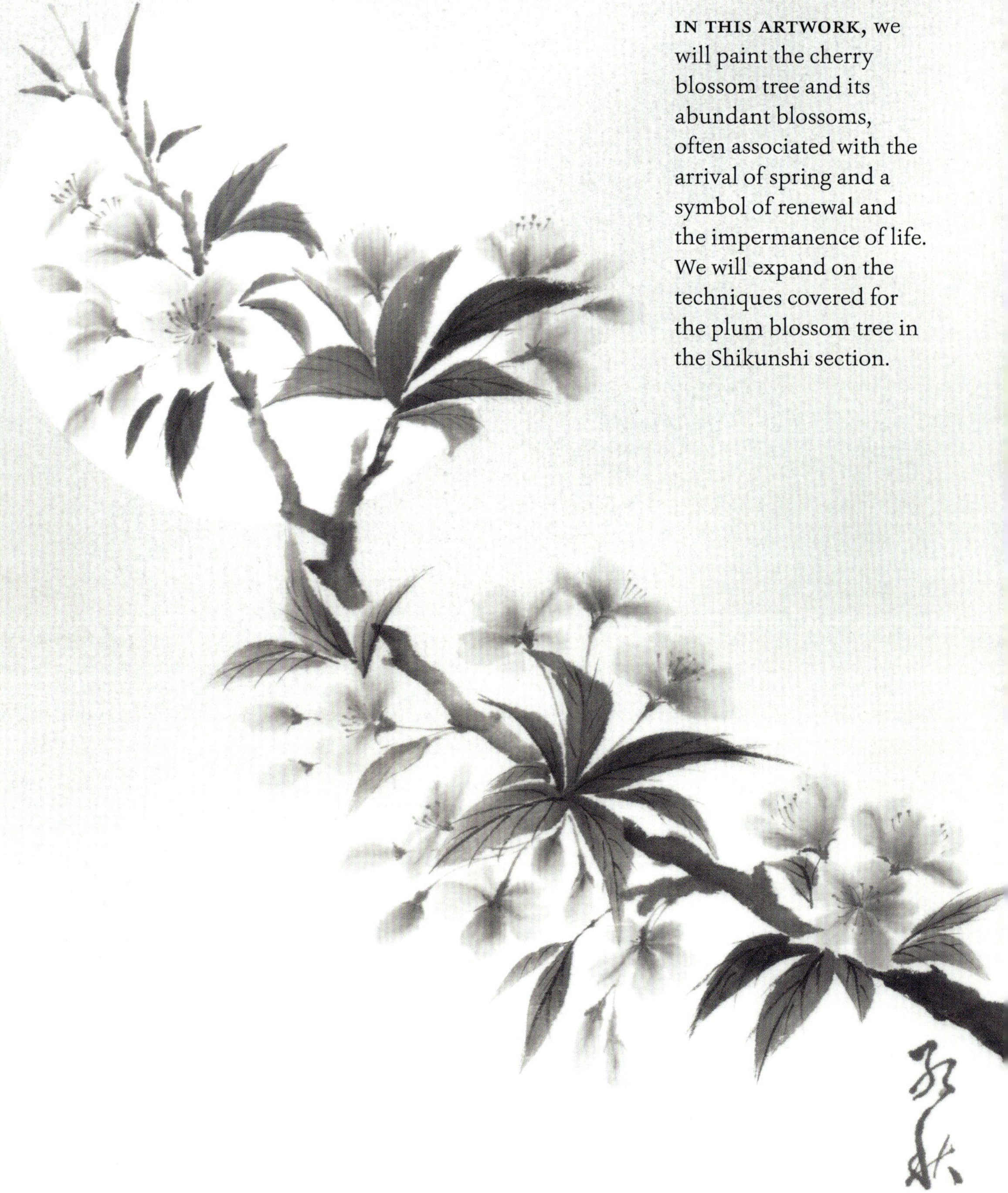

枝垂れ桜

Moonlit Weeping Cherry Tree

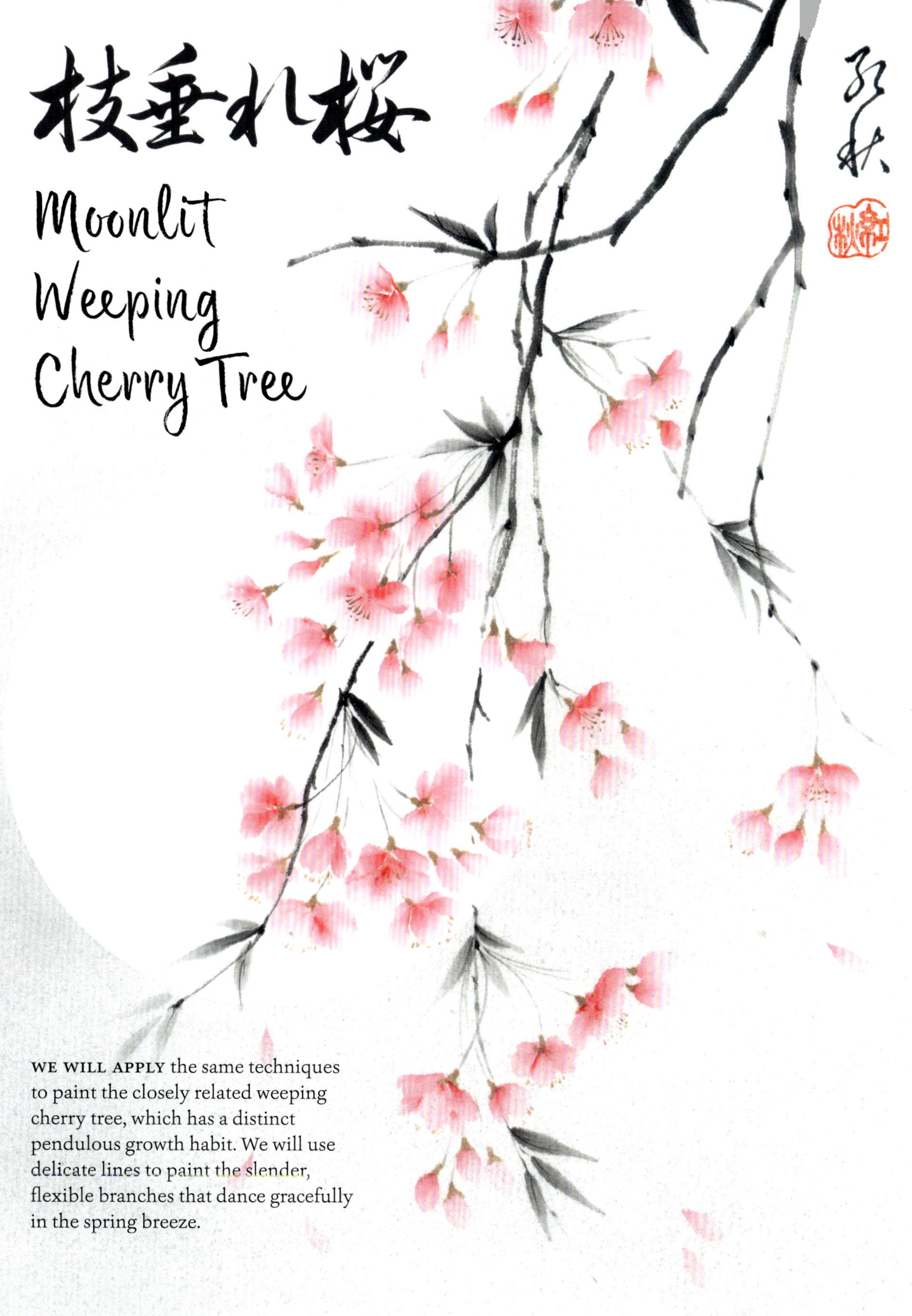

WE WILL APPLY the same techniques to paint the closely related weeping cherry tree, which has a distinct pendulous growth habit. We will use delicate lines to paint the slender, flexible branches that dance gracefully in the spring breeze.

CHERRY BLOSSOM FLOWERS

The flowers of the cherry blossom tree bloom in clusters around a node, covering the branches with a profusion of delicate flowers. Unlike the plum blossom flower, the base of each cherry blossom flower is connected to the branch via a slender structure called the pedicel ('kahei'). The cherry blossom flower petals are also more elongated compared to the plum petals and form a notch at the tip.

Load the ōfude with goku-tanboku, prepare the tip with chuboku and blend for sanboku-hou.

Flowers A and B

Paint five petals evenly around the centre point. Position the tip of the brush at the centre, and use two outward strokes to paint each petal, leaving a notch at the tip.

Once the ink is moderately dry, prepare the menso-fude with chuboku to paint the pistil and stamens.

Vary the angle of the bloom by adjusting the lengths of the petals and the length and direction of the pistil and stamens.

Flowers C, D, E and F

Paint the flower from the side angle or from behind. Once the ink is moderately dry, load the kofude with nouboku and paint the calyx and pedicel.

Flowers G and H

Follow the same brush movements to paint the buds.

Colour use

Load the brush with very light pink ink, prepare the tip with light pink ink and blend for sanboku-hou.

To paint white cherry blossoms on white paper, use the senbyou-hou technique (see p. 32).

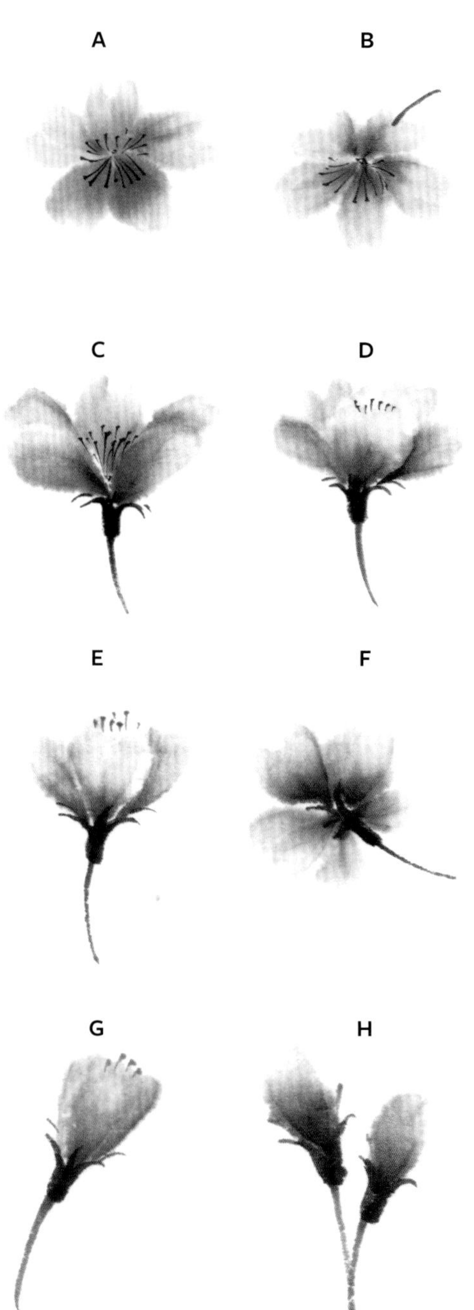

CHERRY BLOSSOM LEAVES

The colloquial term 'cherry blossom' is often used to refer to various species and cultivars of cherry, each showcasing unique coloured blossoms, varying numbers of petals, and distinctive leaf shapes, growth habits and blooming seasons. The most commonly found variety in Japan is the Somei Yoshino, which is particularly popular as they produce a cloud of blossoms that cover the branches in clusters.

Another variety that holds prominence in Japanese poems and songs is the Yamazakura, which is native to Japan and grows in the mountainous regions of Honshu, Shikoku and Kyushu. In this variety, the flowers and the leaves emerge simultaneously. The image on p. 128 is a Yamazakura tree.

Leaves for the Yamazakura and weeping cherry tree.

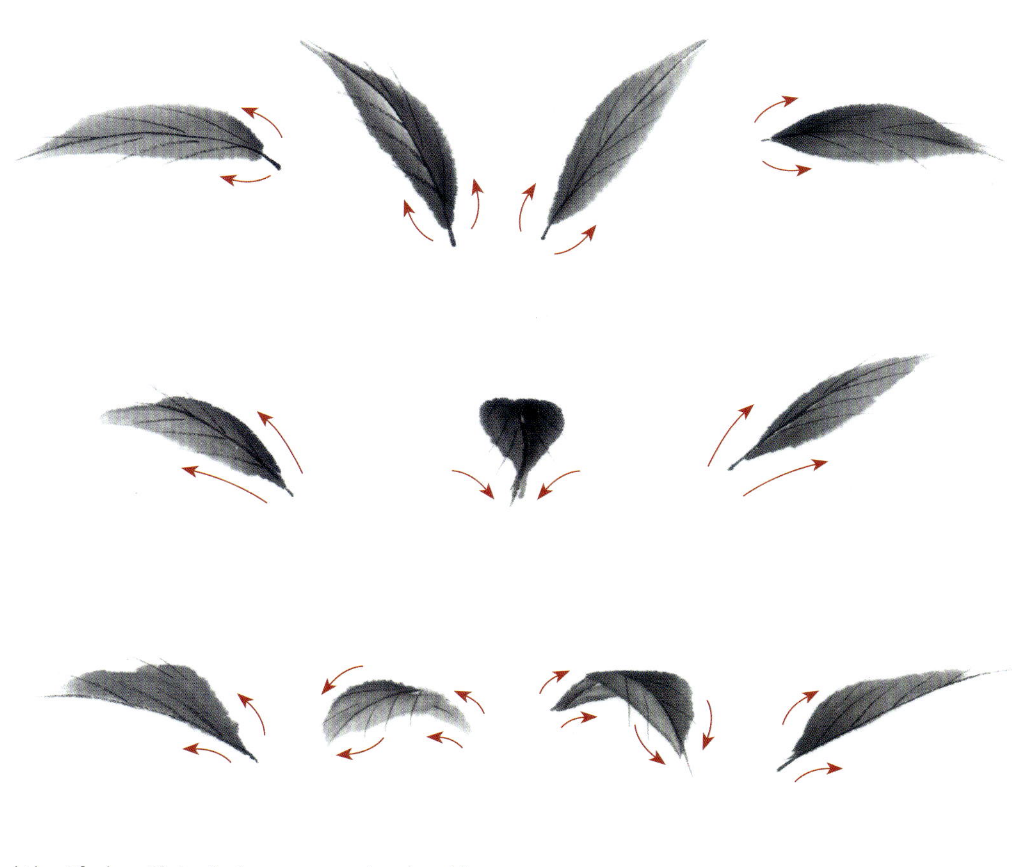

Load the ōfude with tanboku, prepare the tip with nouboku and blend for sanboku-hou. Paint each leaf in two strokes.

Similar to the flowers, clusters of leaves grow from the same node. Bring the leaves together in a close arrangement, and once moderately dry, load the kofude with nouboku and paint the veins.

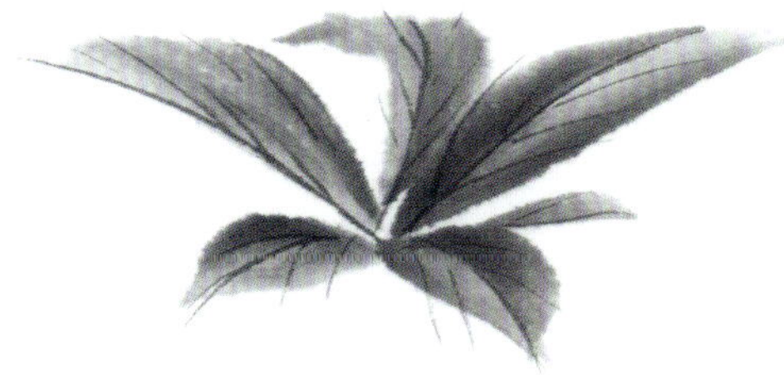

Yamazakura branches

Load the ōfude with chuboku, prepare the tip with nouboku and blend for sanboku-hou. Apply similar techniques used to paint the plum blossom tree (see p. 66) to paint the yamazakura branches. Create a line in semi-sokuhitsu, with the tip of the brush facing down to shade the lower section of the branch. Capture the natural irregularity found in cherry blossom branches by changing the rhythm of the stroke, alternating between fast and slow movements and reducing the pressure as you reach the end of the branch. Make sure to leave a blank space within the branch to accommodate the front flowers and leaves. Finally, paint dots along the branches and twigs to represent the axillary buds.

Optional: for the final touch, use the nijiri-fude or wari-fude techniques to give the tree trunk a rugged organic finish (see p. 67).

Bring together the various elements in the following order: the branches, primary leaves, flowers, secondary leaves, details (veins of the leaves, pistils and stamen) and, finally, the moon (optional).

Weeping cherry blossom branches

Load the kofude or the tip of the ōfude with nouboku. In downward strokes, create slightly arched lines in chokuhitsu, which narrow towards the end. Paint dots along the branches and twigs to represent the axillary buds.

When preparing the brush, make sure to remove excess ink and complete the stroke without reapplying ink. Naturally, the kasure effect will show.

Bring together the various elements in the following order: the flowers, branches and twigs, pedicels, leaves, details (veins of the leaves, pistil and stamen) and, finally the moon (optional).

Bokashi moon

Finish off the composition by painting the sky and moon. Apply the ami bokashi technique (see pp. 124–5). Embrace the brownish-black hues of yuenboku to create a warm, gentle moonlit sky, or the bluish-black hues of shouenboku to create a serene, cool atmosphere. If you prefer a hue that is not achievable by using yuenboku or shouenboku alone, add coloured ink to the black sumi to create your desired hue.

KEY POINT
Shading of the sky using the ami bokashi technique should be subtle and soft, to make sure the delicate features of the flowers are visible. It is also important to note that the bokashi ink becomes more prominent once the supporting paper is applied to your artwork (see p. 157).

MIZU BOKASHI

Materials

- WATER SPRAY
- ŌFUDE: large soft-hair brush
- HAKE: flat brush (optional)
- SUMI AND SUZURI: ink and inkstone or liquid ink
- EZARA: small plate
- HISSEN: water jar
- FUKIN: cloth or kitchen paper

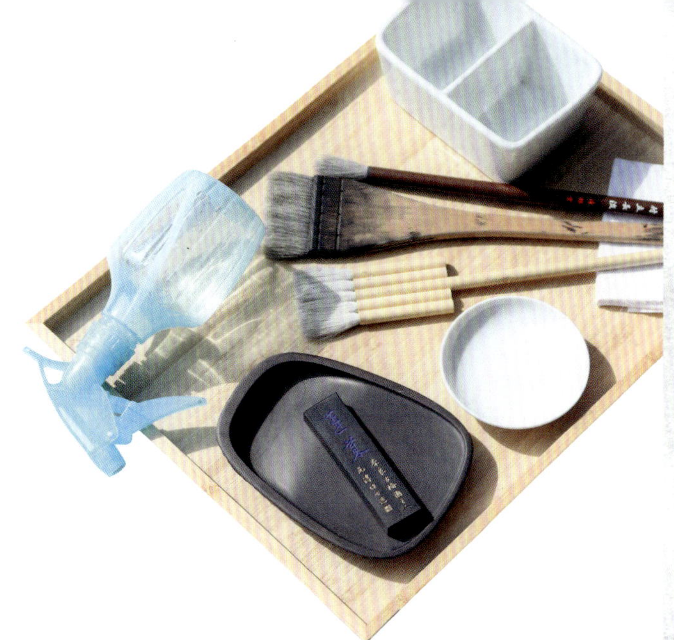

Place your dried artwork on the shitajiki (felt cloth), either face down or face up. When painting using traditional inksticks or Saienboku, the nikawa glue prevents bleeding and blurring, therefore either option is acceptable. However, when using Gansai or Chinese paint, place the artwork face down to prevent smudging or blurring. The result will also depend on the paper type, thickness and absorbency – test before completing your final artwork.

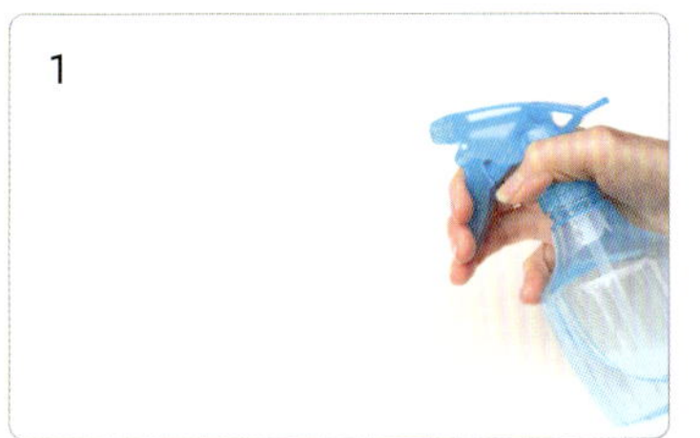
1

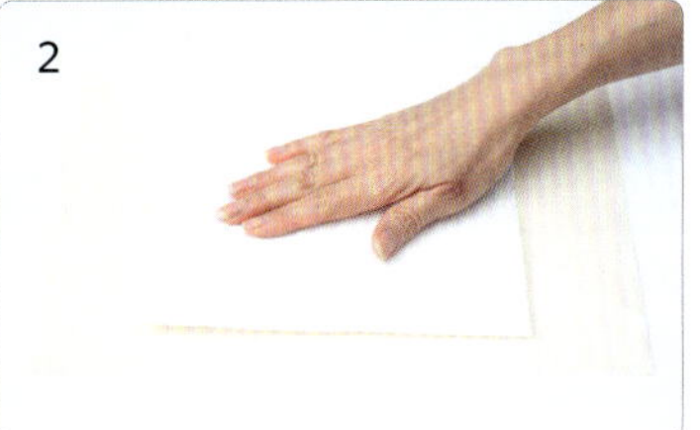
2

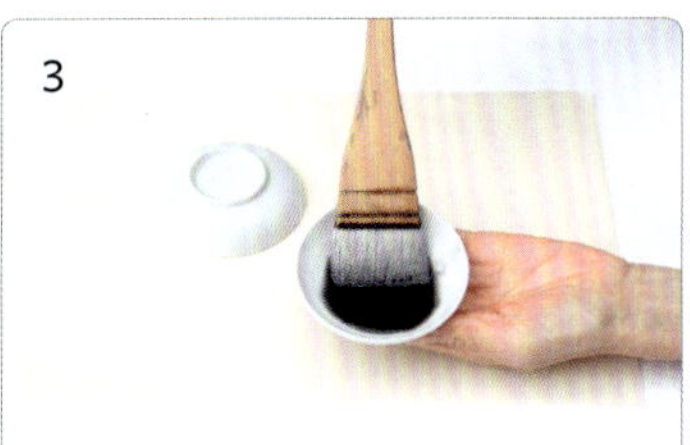
3

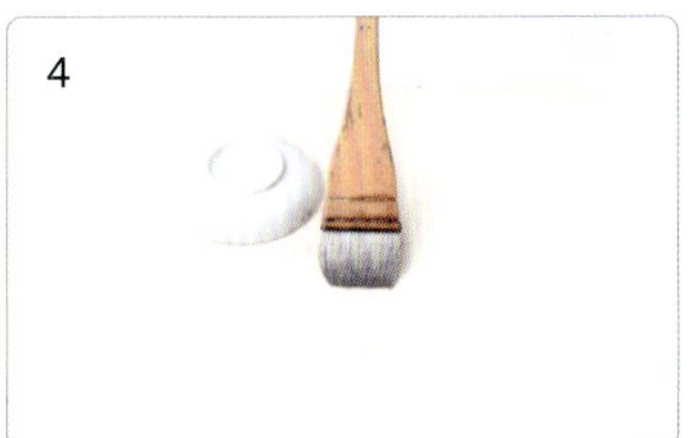
4

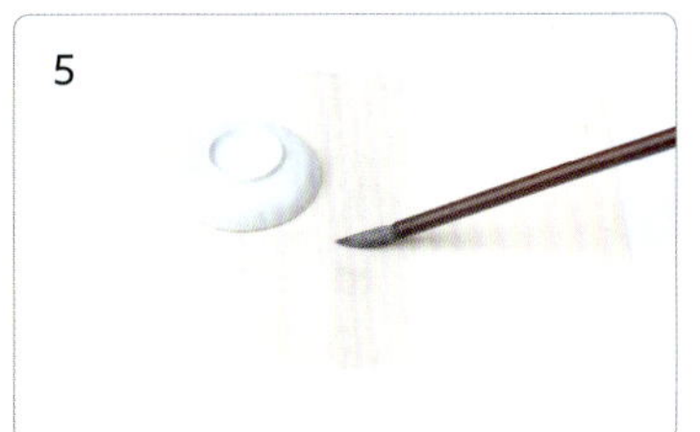
5

1. Spray water evenly across the entire piece of paper or on specific areas as desired.

2. Use kitchen paper to gently blot and remove excess water from the paper's surface.

3. Prepare goku-tanboku in the ezara and load the ōfude or hake with ink. If painting the moon, place a round plate in the desired location and paint around it.

4. For a larger area, paint with the hake or the ōfude positioned in sokuhitsu.

5. For a smaller area or specific patterns like clouds, shadows or water reflections, paint with the ōfude or another soft-hair brush. You can also apply tanboku or chuboku to add different shades.

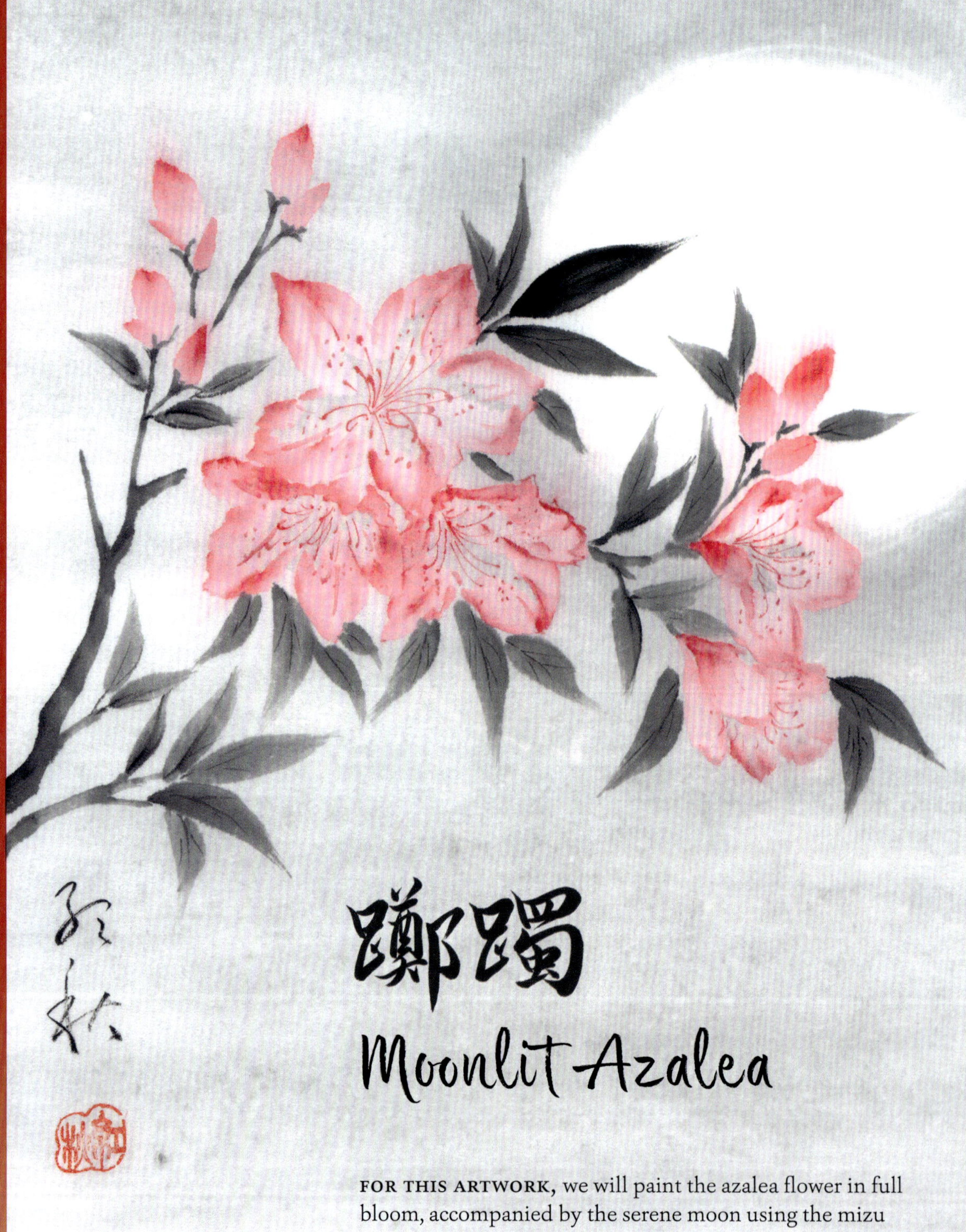

躑躅

Moonlit Azalea

FOR THIS ARTWORK, we will paint the azalea flower in full bloom, accompanied by the serene moon using the mizu bokashi technique.

AZALEA PETALS AND LEAVES

Load the ōfude with tanboku and prepare the tip with chuboku for sakiguma.

Paint each petal in two strokes. Position the tip of the brush at the tip of the petal and rotate downwards in sokuhitsu towards the base. Ensure the tip of the brush traces the petal's margin – this will create a kataguma effect. At the same time, push the brush up and down to create the undulating curves of the petal.

Repeat for the other half of the petal, then repeat for the remaining four petals to complete the flower.

Once you have painted the five petals and the ink is moderately dry, load the menso-fude with nouboku and paint the pistil and stamens.

Optional: paint a dotted pattern to adorn the petals.

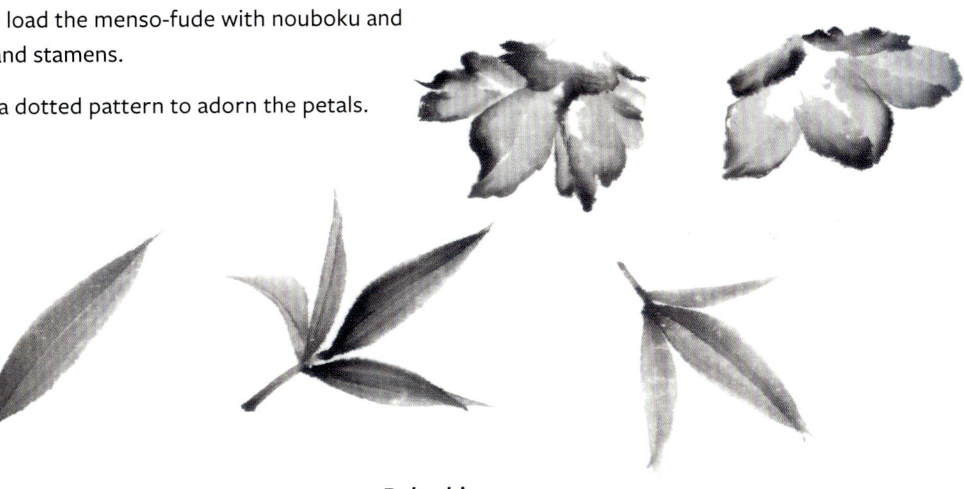

Colour use

To paint the petals, prepare the brush for sanboku-hou using lighter pink and darker pink ink.

For the pistil and stamens, prepare the brush with dark pink or red ink.

Following the composition on p. 134, apply the same techniques covered in the cherry blossom artwork to paint the branches and leaves.

Bring together the various elements in the following order: the flowers and buds, branches, leaves, details (veins of the leaves) and, finally, the moon (optional).

Bokashi moon

Once the ink of the azalea flower, leaves and branches is completely dry, you can paint the moon with the mizu bokashi technique (see p. 133). If using Gansai paint, as in the image on p. 134, place your dried artwork on the shitajiki face down, spray water evenly across the entire piece of paper and gently blot and remove excess water with kitchen paper.

Place a round plate in the desired location for the moon. Prepare goku-tanboku in the ezara and use the hake or ōfude to apply ink to the wet artwork. Begin by applying ink around the plate first, followed by the rest of the paper.

To make the sky darker or to add clouds, apply an additional layer of darker ink. Once the artwork is dry, if you find that the intensity of the sky is lacking, you can repeat the bokashi step to make it darker.

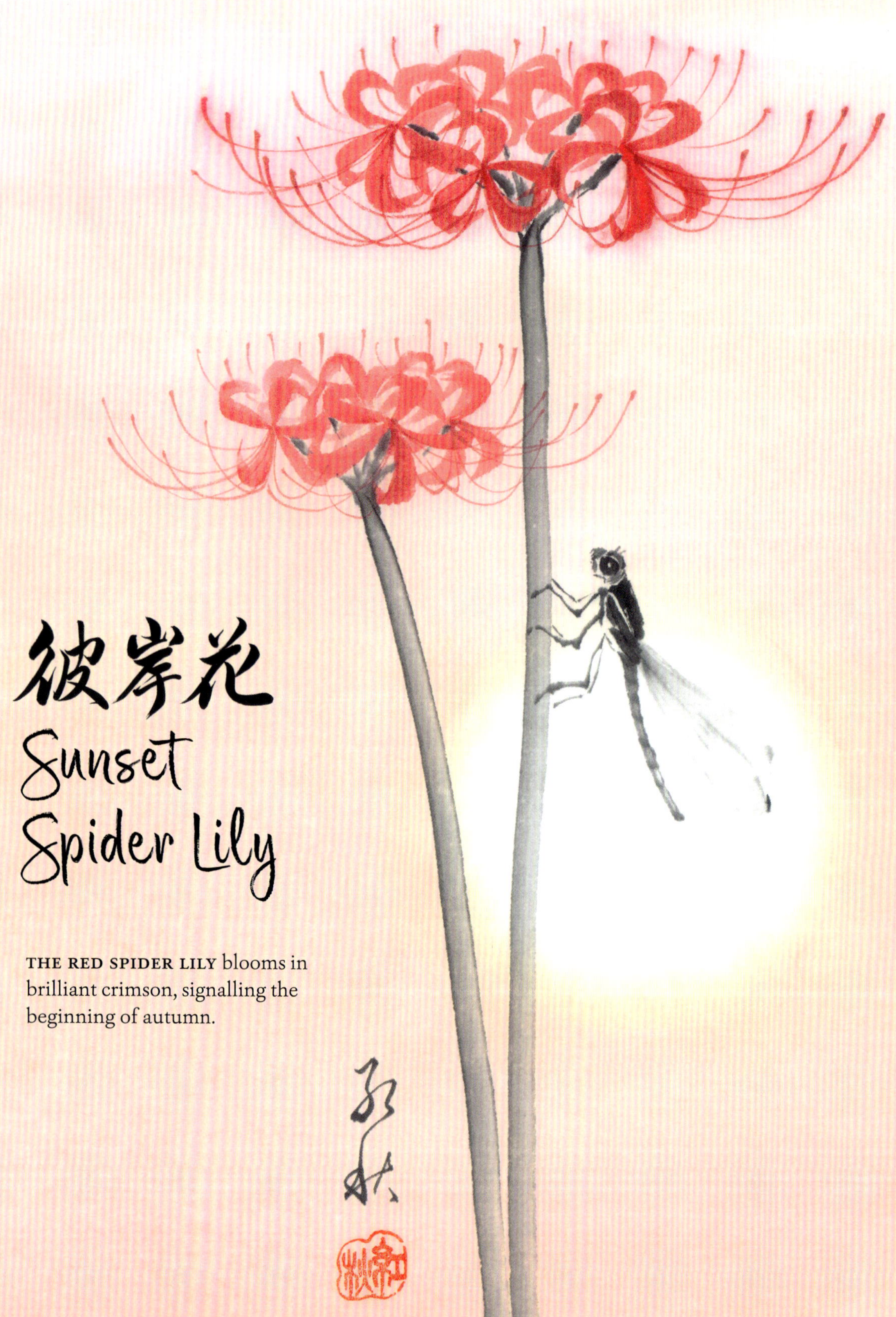

彼岸花 Sunset Spider Lily

THE RED SPIDER LILY blooms in brilliant crimson, signalling the beginning of autumn.

SPIDER LILY FLOWER

The red spider lily flower has five to six slender petals that curl outwards, as well as a prominent pistil and stamens in the centre that extend beyond the petals and resemble spider legs. Five to eight flowers cluster together around one stalk, creating a striking and alluring display.

1. Load the ōfude or kofude with tanboku, prepare the tip with nouboku and blend for sanboku-hou. Paint each petal in two brushstrokes from the centre outward. Repeat this step to paint five or six petals radiating outwards.

2. To create slightly wavy petals, repeat step 1 but jiggle the brush back and forth sideways as you paint each line.

Using either the straight or wavy line techniques, now paint the flower petals with a fold.

3. To curl the petals inwards, paint the tip of the petal first in two strokes, followed by the centre part of the petal, again in two strokes. Repeat for the remaining petals.

4. To curl the petals outwards, paint the centre part of the petal first in two strokes, followed by the tip of the petal again in two strokes. Repeat for the remaining petals.

5. Bring together the cluster of flowers, starting with the front flowers (flower variation 4).

6. Paint the flowers in the back (flower variation 3) using tanboku and chuboku to show depth. Then, paint the main flower stalk in ryoguma (refer to p. 27) and connect each flower to the stalk with slender stems.

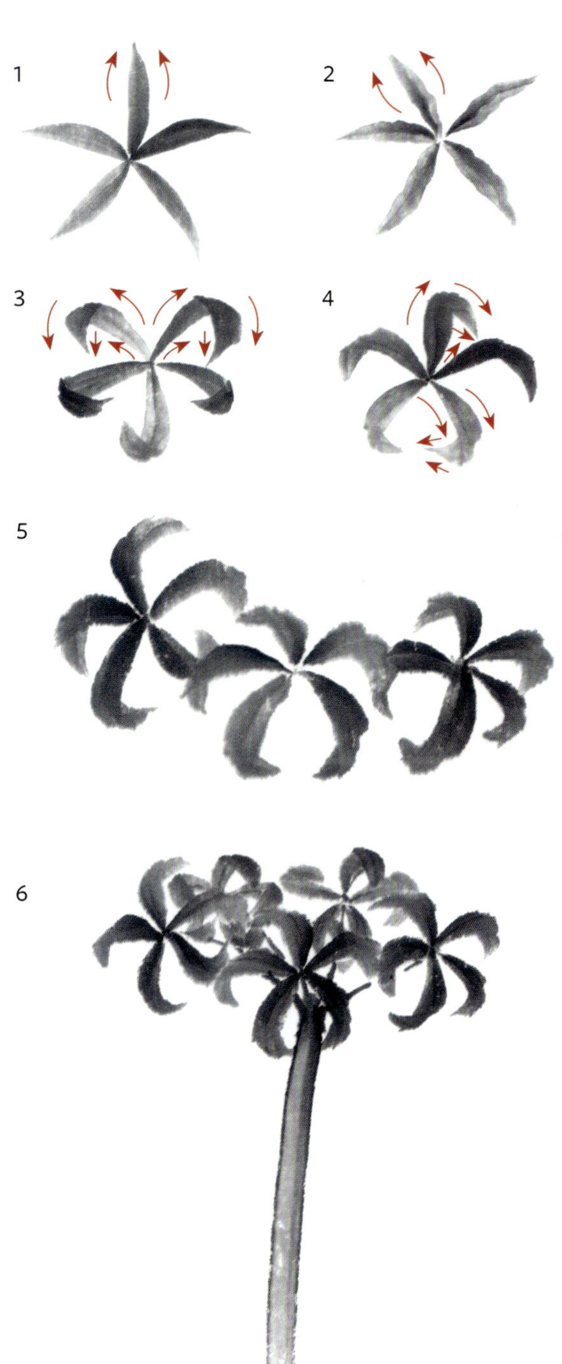

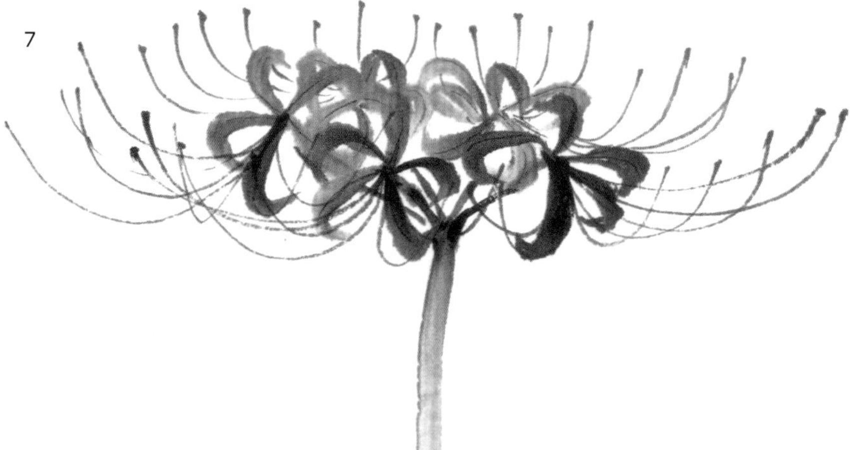

7. Finally, load the menso-fude with nouboku and paint sharp, thin lines extending from the centre of the flowers outwards to represent the pistil and stamens. I recommend holding the brush upright in tankou-hou and positioning the arm in teiwan-hou (see p. 24).

To enhance the autumnal feel, paint a dragonfly on the stalk (see p. 111).

Colour use

Load the brush with light red ink, prepare the tip with medium-dark red ink and blend for sanboku-hou.

To paint the front flowers, prepare the brush for sanboku-hou using light red and dark red ink.

To paint the back flowers, prepare the brush for sanboku-hou using light red and medium-dark red ink.

KEY POINTS

- When using the mizu-bokashi technique, it is advisable to use water-resistant papers such as kozo or bamboo to avoid tearing.
- The thickness of the paper will also effect the visibility of the mizu-bokashi technique. When using thin paper, I recommend applying ink from the back side of the paper. When using thick paper, I recommend applying ink from the front side.

Finally, to paint the pistil and stamens, prepare the brush with dark red ink.

Bokashi sun

Once the artwork is completely dry, paint the sunset in colour using the mizu bokashi technique (see p. 133).

Place your dried artwork on the shitajiki face down, spray water evenly across the entire piece of paper and gently blot to remove excess water using kitchen paper. Prepare two shades of ink in the ezara: one light yellow and one light orange. On the wet artwork, position the round plate in the desired location for the sun, paint a light yellow ring around the plate with the ōfude, to allow the colour to bleed, and then continue to paint the light orange sky. To intensify the colour of the sky, apply an additional layer of darker orange ink.

Bring together the various elements in the following order: the flowers, stems, dragonfly and, finally, the sunset (optional).

鯉 Koi Fish in a Stream

IN THIS ARTWORK we will paint the koi fish, a symbol of strength, courage and resilience. We will also incorporate the mizu-bokashi technique to paint shadows.

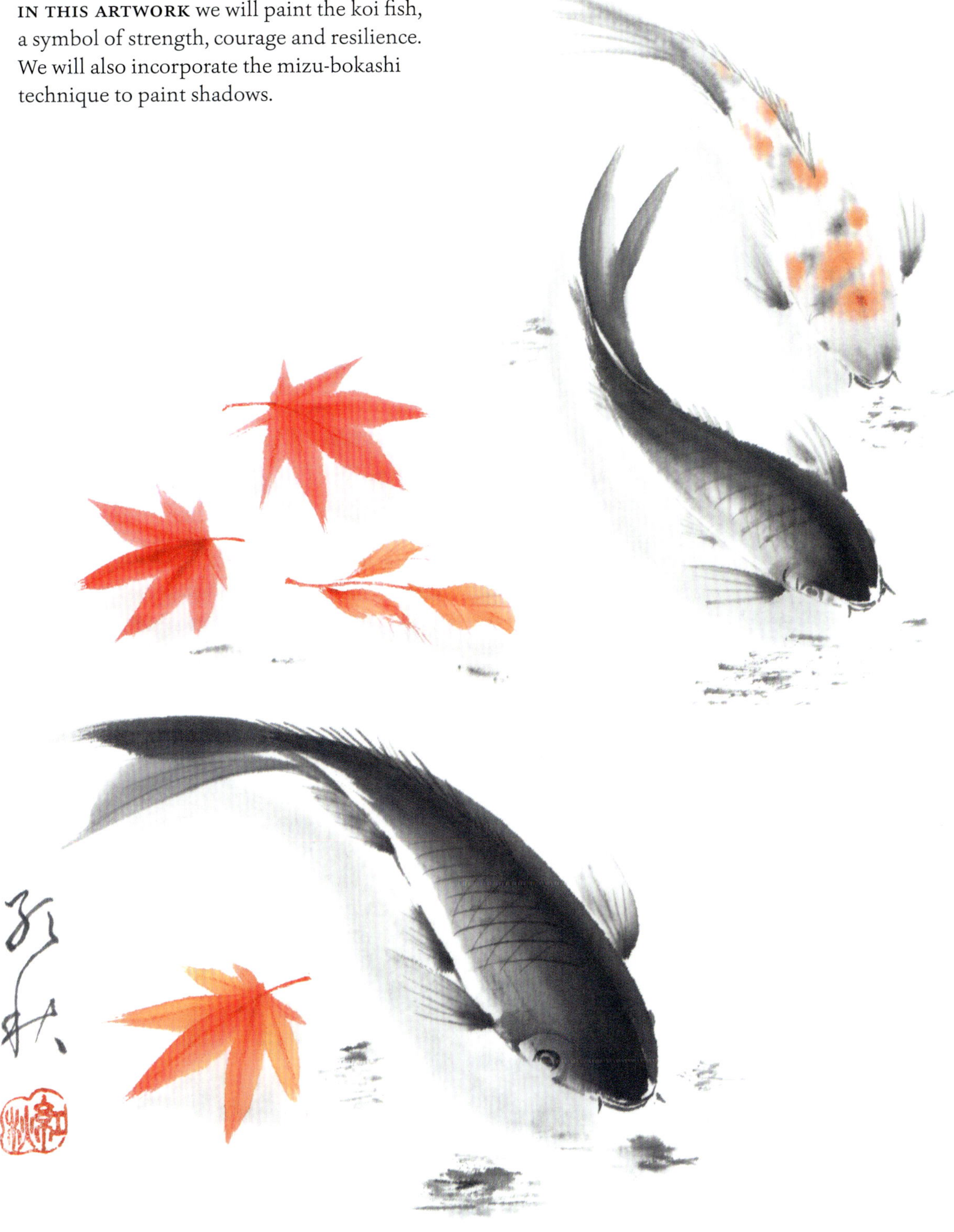

KOI

Koi A and B

1. Load the ōfude with chuboku, prepare the tip with nouboku and blend for sanboku-hou. Starting from the head of the fish, paint a line in semi-sokuhitsu, with the tip of the brush pointing towards the centreline of the body. Swing the brush as you reach the end of the line. Adjust the orientation of the paper to ensure comfortable brush movements. Repeat the same brush movement for the upper section of the body, again with the tip of the brush pointing towards the centre.

2. Prepare the brush for sanboku-hou using tanboku and chuboku, then paint the caudal/tail fin in two strokes, followed by the other fins.

3. Load the kofude with chuboku and paint some thin lines on the fins, as well as some lines to represent the dorsal fin.

4. Once the ink is moderately dry, load the kofude with nouboku and paint the eyes and operculum. Wash the brush, apply chuboku and paint the mouth and diagonal lines on the body to represent the scales. Finish by painting some dots where the lines intersect.

Following the same steps and brush techniques, paint fish (B) with the tail pointing in another direction.

Colour use

To create the reddish-orange patches of colour, first create the body of the fish in a light grey shade. Prepare the brush for sanboku-hou using goku-tanboku and tanboku and repeat steps 1–4. Using haboku-hou (see p. 31), while the ink is still wet, paint some light orange patches followed by some darker orange patches. This will create a natural nijimi effect. To complete the pattern, paint some grey patches on the body with tanboku.

To complete the composition, paint some red and yellow maple leaves and other foliage to complement the colour of the koi fish. Load the ōfude with yellow-orange ink, prepare the tip with red ink and blend for sanboku-hou. Paint the leaves (see p. 127 for how to paint the maple leaves).

Remove excess ink from the ōfude and using the nejiri-fude technique (refer to p. 31), push the brush from side to side to paint the textured ground under the stream.

Bring together the various elements in the following order: foreground fish, background fish (grey then coloured fish), foliage, ground texture and, finally, once dry, the shadows.

Bokashi shadows

Once the artwork is completely dry, place your artwork on the shitajiki face up (as we are only applying ink to detailed areas), spray water evenly across the entire piece of paper and gently blot to remove excess water. Finally, paint the shadows of the fish and leaves underwater in tanboku.

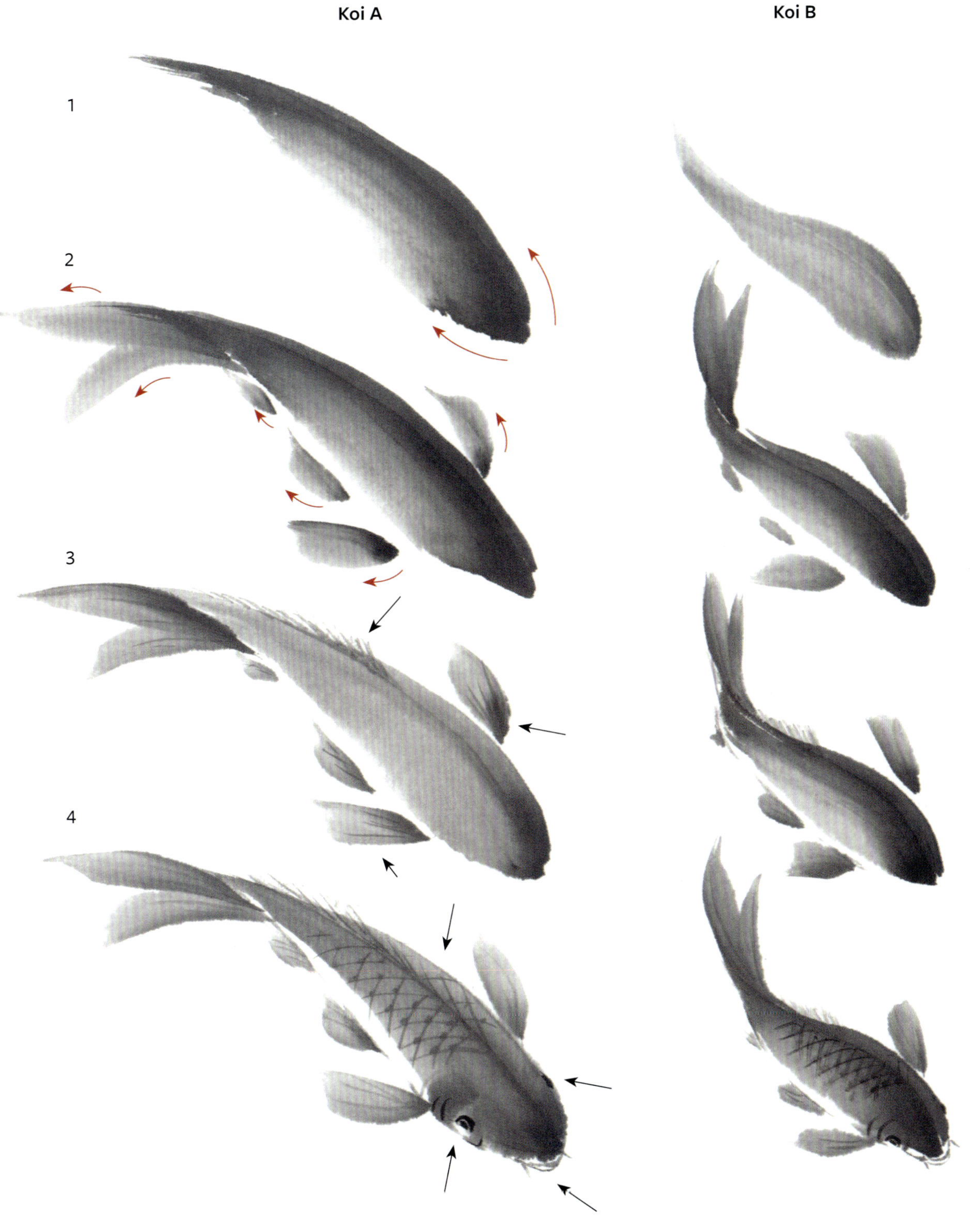

Koi A
Koi B
1
2
3
4

蓮 Lotus Flower in a Pond

IN JAPAN, the lotus flower is held in deep reverence as a symbol of purity and transcendence. In this artwork, we will combine the various techniques we have covered so far to create petals that appear translucent and reflective, along with large, round leaves that adorn the water's surface.

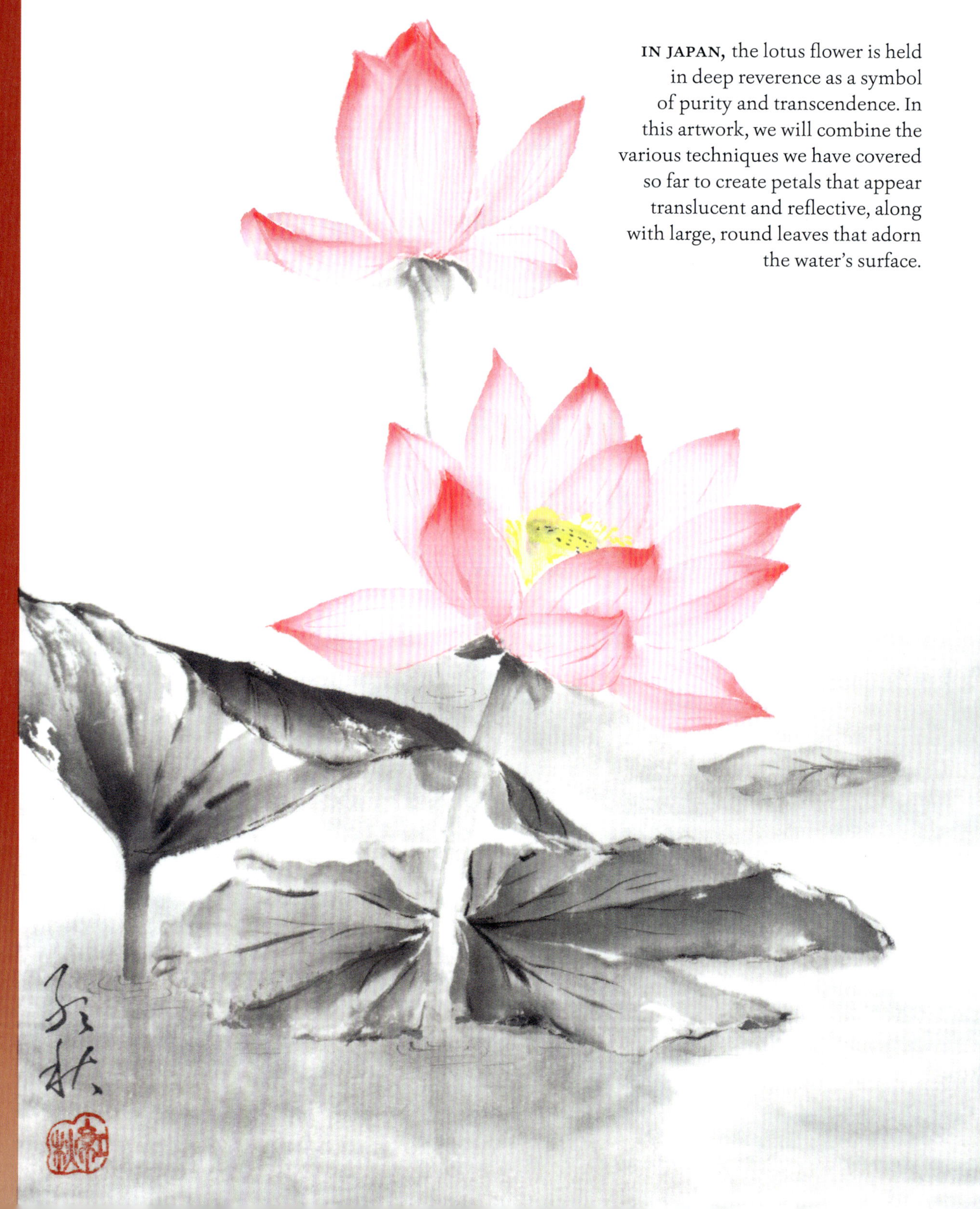

LOTUS FLOWER

Load the ōfude with tanboku and prepare the tip with chuboku for the sakiguma technique.

Paint each petal in two strokes, positioning the tip of the brush at the tip of the petal and tracing the outline with the brush's tip. Mirror the same stroke on the other side to finish the petal (the darker tones indicate where the tip of the brush should trace over).

Practise the petals individually first and from various angles.

Combine the petals in a cup-shaped arrangement, following the image on the right. Start with the petals that are closer to you and explore painting both open and closed flowers.

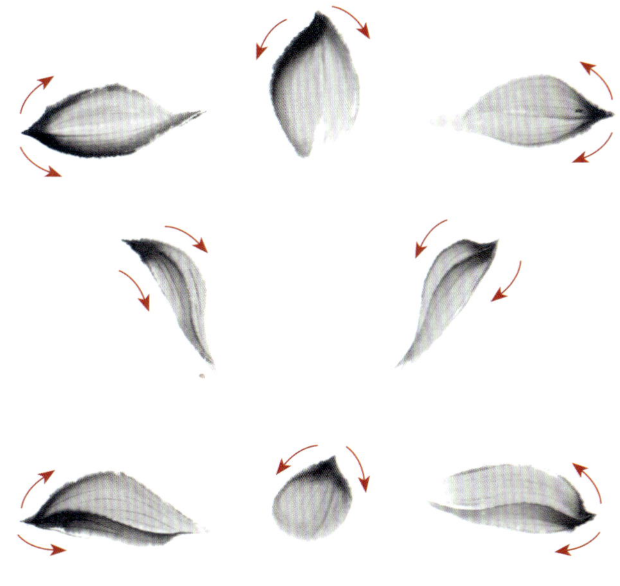

Colour use

To paint the petals, load the ōfude with light pink ink and prepare the tip with dark pink ink for the sakiguma technique.

For the pistils and stamen, paint a circular ring in tanboku, followed by small dots in nouboku arranged in a circular formation. Finally, shade in the centre with undiluted yellow ink.

Once the ink is moderately dry, prepare the menso-fude with darker pink ink and paint light, delicate lines from the bottom-up to mark the contours on the petals.

Finally, flatten the tip of the ōfude and paint the stem in either ryoguma or sanboku-hou, similar to the poppy (p. 89) or the spider lily stem (p. 136).

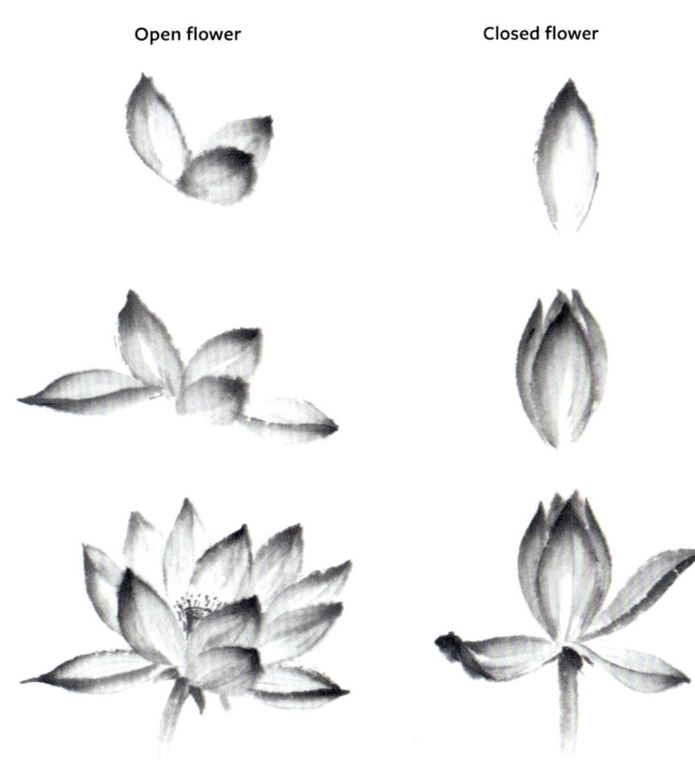

LOTUS LEAVES

Floating lotus leaf

Load the ōfude with chuboku, prepare the tip with nouboku and blend for sanboku-hou. Painting a large circular leaf in one stroke can be challenging, so instead, paint the leaf in multiple strokes. The segmentation introduced by the brush marks will represent the veins and natural folds of the leaf.

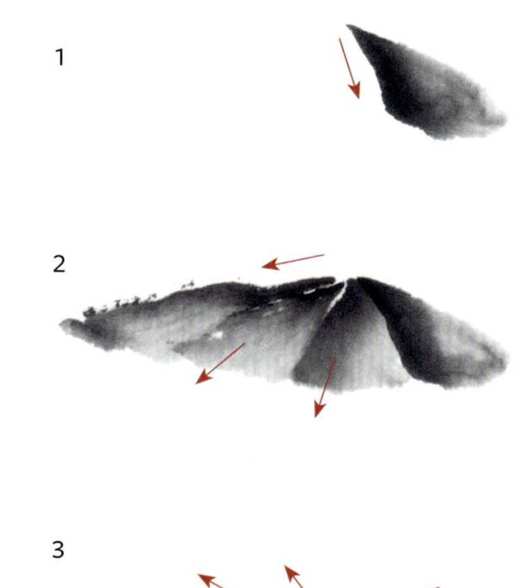

1. Position the tip of the brush at the centre of the leaf, and in sokuhitsu, push the brush outwards while incrementally increasing the pressure and introducing a slight rotation of the brush to create a triangular segment. Then, press the brush firmly down to create a rounded finish.

2. Repeat this movement for the remaining leaf segments starting with the front segments . . .

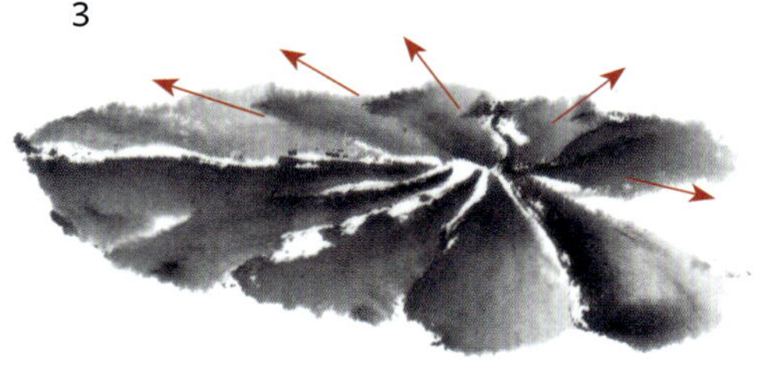

3. . . . Then use shorter brushstrokes to paint the segments in the back, creating an oval shape for the leaf.

4. Once the ink is moderately dry, load the kofude with nouboku and paint the veins.

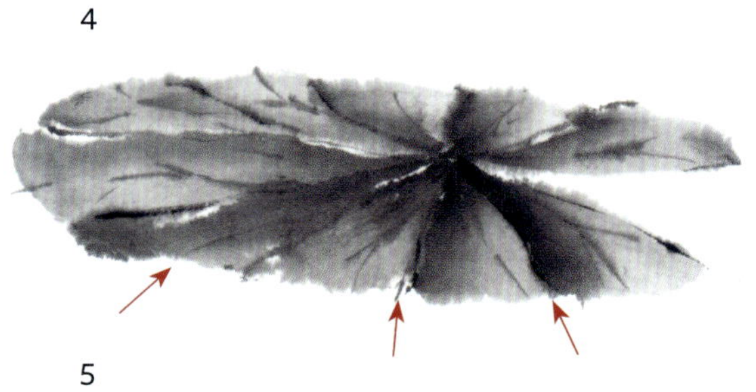

5. Final touch: load the kofude with chuboku or nouboku. With a light touch, outline the front edge of the leaf, marking the shadow that the leaf casts as it meets the surface of the water (refer to the sample artwork on p. 142).

Floating small lotus leaf

Load the ōfude with Tanboku prepare the tip with chuboku for sanboku-hou, and create a small leaf with two strokes (see image on p. 142).

Emerging lotus leaf that rises above the surface of the water

Load the ōfude with chuboku, prepare the tip with nouboku and blend for sanboku-hou.

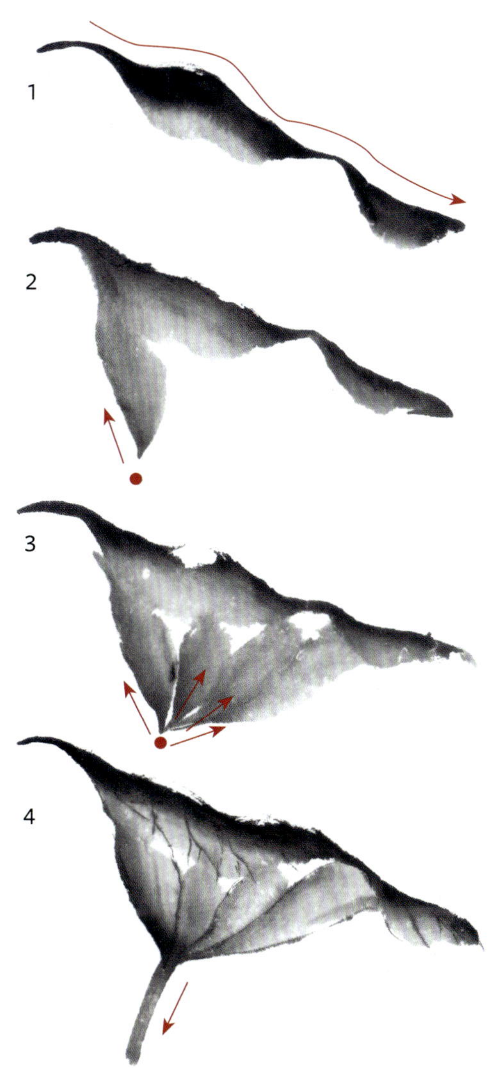

1. To paint the top edge of the leaf, push the brush from left to right in sokuhitsu, with the tip of the brush pointing upwards. Begin by applying light pressure with the tip of the brush, then press the whole body of the brush down on the paper before lifting it again, then finally apply full pressure once more. This pressure control will create an undulating edge that mimics the natural drooping of the leaf edge. (When you create the artwork [p. 142], the leaf should be positioned behind the front flower. Leave a blank space in the leaf for the stem.)

2. Decide where the stem will emerge from (indicated by the red dot). From this position, slide the brush upwards in sokuhitsu towards the top part of the leaf, while incrementally increasing the pressure and introducing a slight rotation of the brush to create a triangular segment (the same technique used to create the segments in the floating lotus leaf).

3. Repeat the same motion to create the remaining segments.

4. Shape the tip of the brush flat and paint the stem emerging from the centre of the leaf to the surface of the water. Once the ink is moderately dry, load the kofude with nouboku and paint the veins.

Reflection

Prepare the brush with a lighter shade of ink and continue the stem in the water's reflection, gradually lifting the brush to allow the reflection to fade.

Bring together the various elements in the following order: the primary flower, secondary flower, stem, emerging lotus leaf, floating lotus leaves and, finally, the water.

Bokashi water

Once the artwork is completely dry, you can apply the mizu bokashi technique to paint the pond water.

Place your dried artwork on the shitajiki face up, as we will not be applying ink over the coloured ink.

Spray water evenly across the lower half of the paper and gently blot to remove excess water.

Paint the pond water with goku-tanboku, followed by tanboku or chuboku to paint the shadows cast by the leaves and flowers.

SHIRONUKI

Shironuki is a unique technique that involves painting with a whitening agent. When the shironuki solution is applied to the paper, it leaves a white mark that repels ink. This allows the painted area to remain white, even when ink is layered on top.

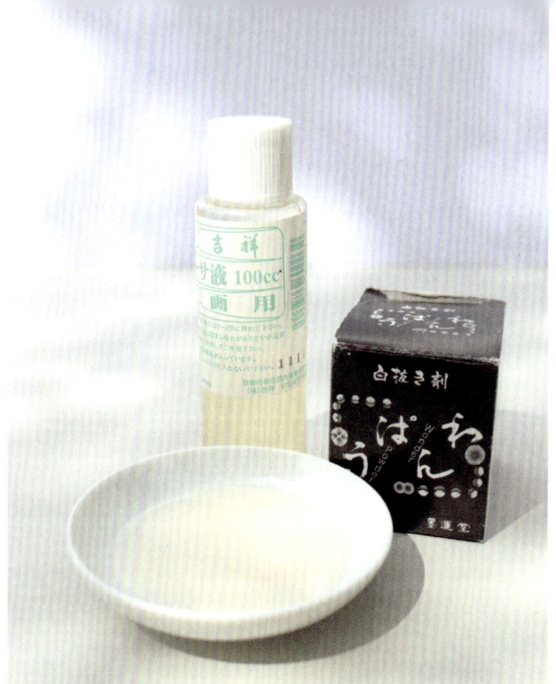

Materials

There are a few options for whitening agents:

A. **WHOLE MILK**
B. **WANPAU** or 'wonder powder' (add lukewarm water to create a liquid)
C. **DOSA** liquid (undiluted or diluted with water)

Apply these solutions to a piece of paper, allow the paper to dry completely, and then paint a layer of dark ink. This layer of dark ink can be applied on either side of the paper.

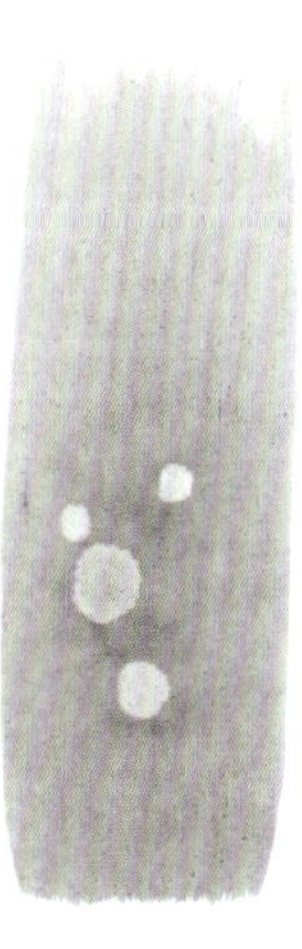

A

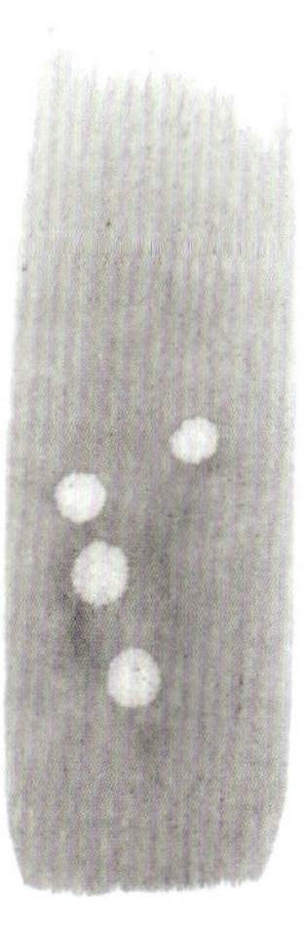

B

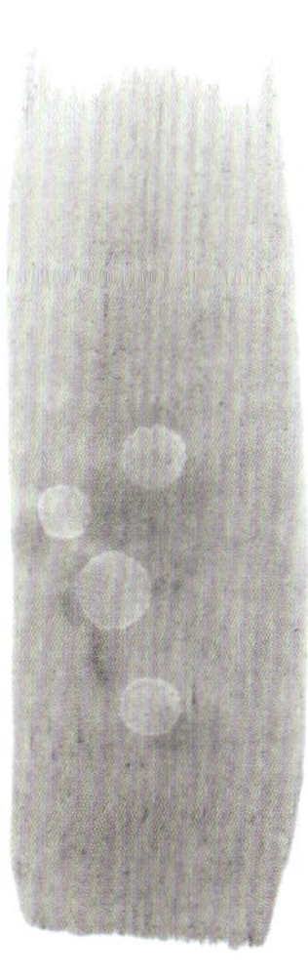

C*

The shironuki effect depends not only on the solution applied, but also on the paper type and texture, and whether the ink is applied on the same or different side of the paper.

The applied shironuki mixture becomes transparent once dried on paper, so remember which side of the paper you painted on.

* While Image C exemplifies dosa whitening without heat application, the effect of the shironuki technique using dosa can be enhanced by pressing the painted area with an iron before applying sumi ink.

To ensure a transparent effect, reserve a clean brush for the shironuki technique.

Shironuki technique: rain

Load a clean kofude with either milk, wanpau or dosa. Hold the brush upright and paint short, sharp lines in chokuhitsu to express the rain. As the whitening agent is transparent, first practise painting rain with sumi ink.

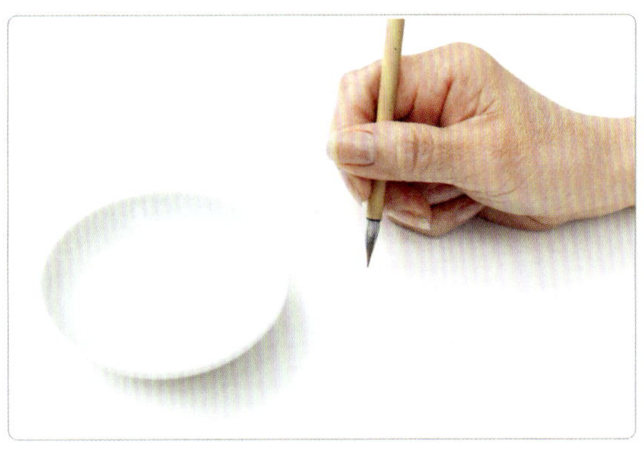

A. Create thin sharp lines in chokuhitsu. Allow variety between the strokes – some should cross over each other sporadically to break the uniformity of the lines.

Avoid creating lines as illustrated in:

B. Brushstrokes created in sokuhitsu will create excessively thick lines.

C. These lines are too uniform and parallel.

A

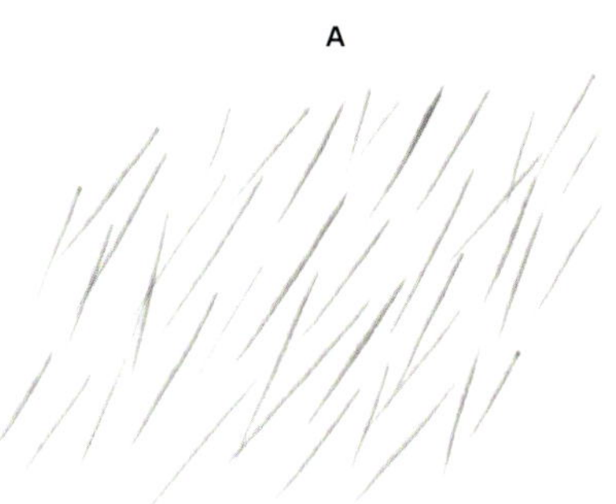

B

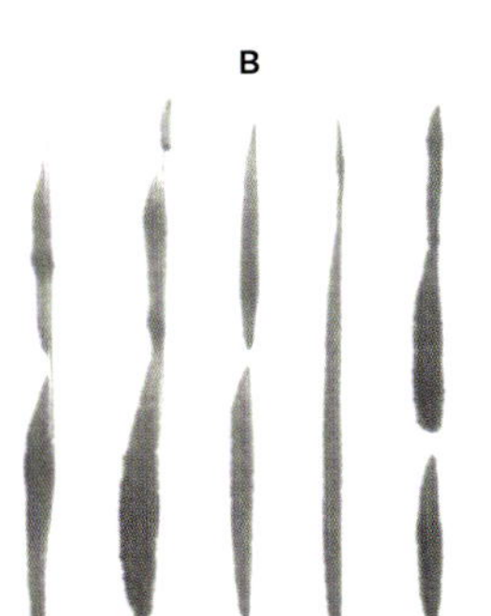

C

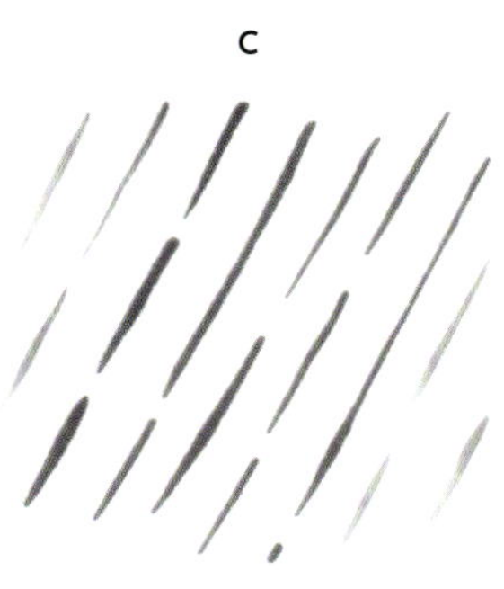

Shironuki technique: snow

We will now apply the same shironuki technique to paint snow and convey a cold wintery atmosphere.

1

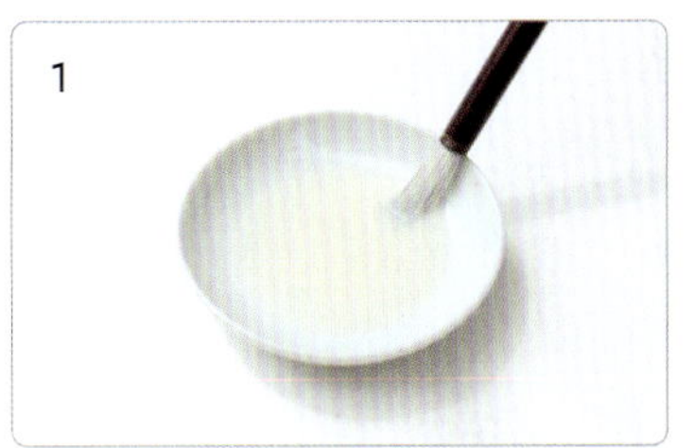

2

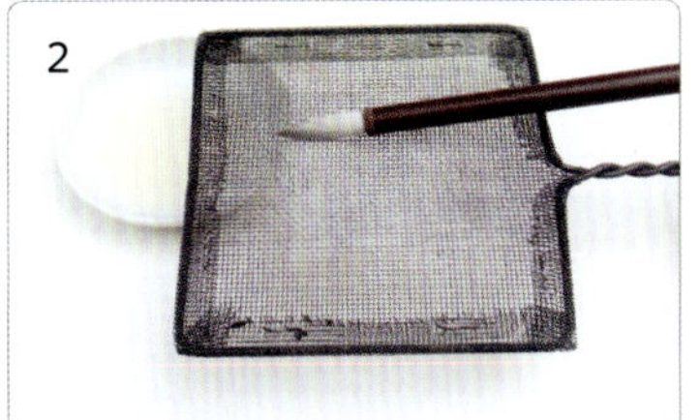

3

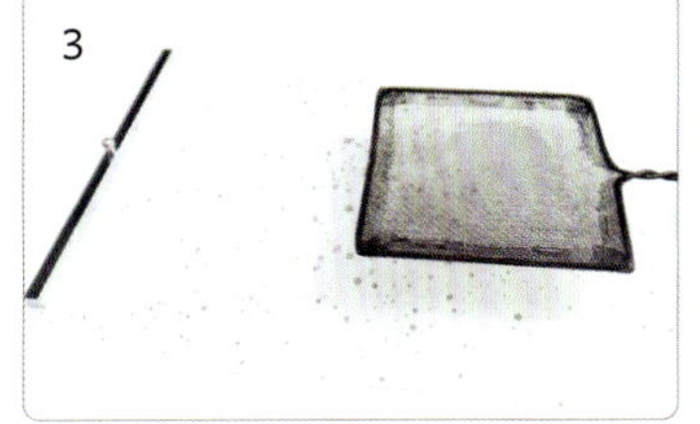

1. Load a clean ōfude with a whitening agent (milk, wanpau or dosa).

2. Prepare the ami (net). Glide the brush sideways over the ami, ensuring the whitening agent is spread evenly on the surface.

3. Bring the ami above the piece of paper and blow gently from above the net, allowing the whitening agent to 'spray' over the paper.

Practise on a test piece of paper to gain a better understanding of the effect and make necessary adjustments before proceeding with the actual artwork. Allow the whitening agent to dry completely and then paint on the same side of the paper.

紫陽花

Hydrangea on a Rainy Day

IN THIS ARTWORK, we will paint the hydrangea, which blooms during the rainy season in Japan. We will use the shironuki technique to paint the rain.

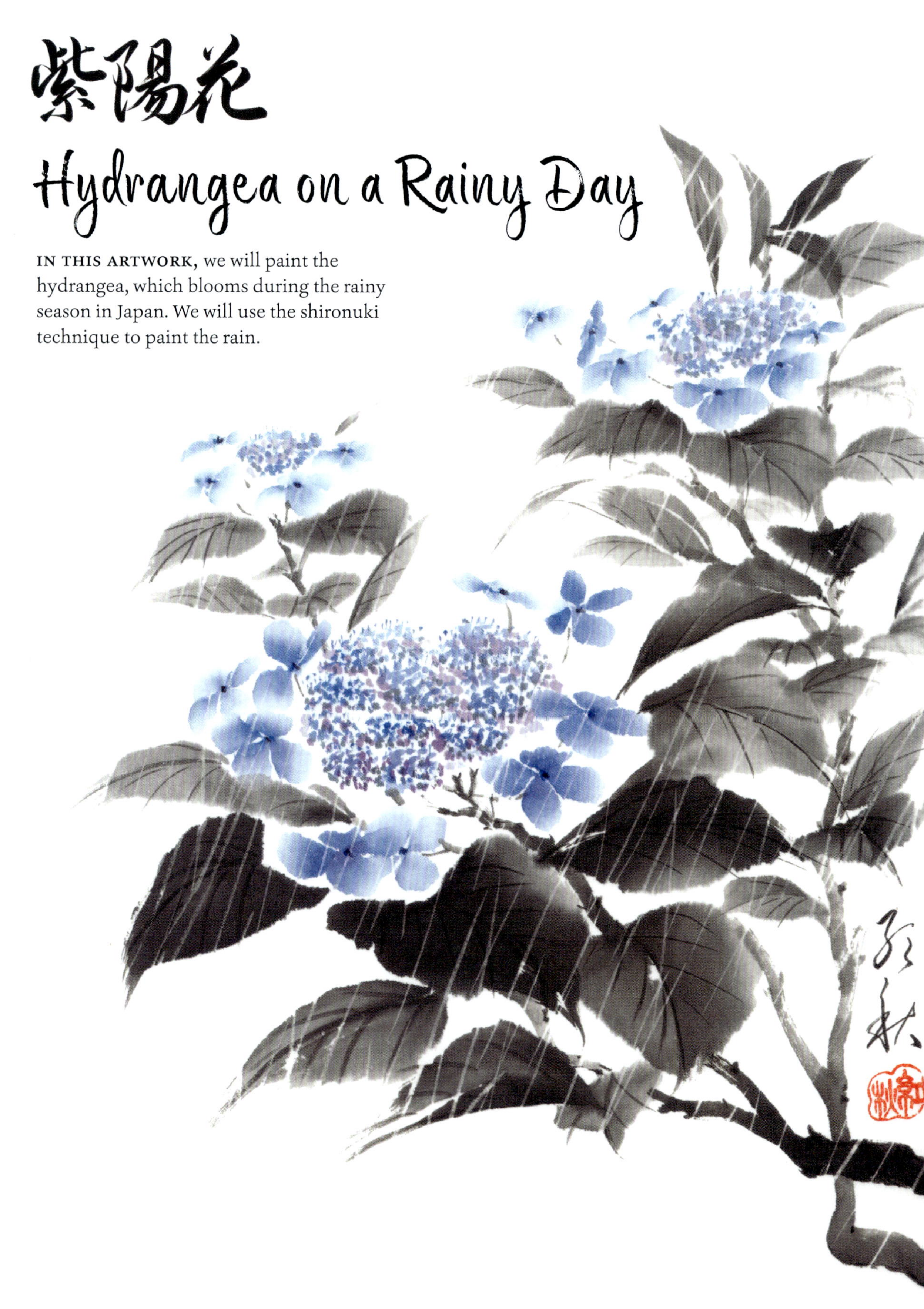

HYDRANGEA FLOWER AND LEAVES

Flower

First apply the Shironuki technique to paint the rain (see p. 147). Allow the paper to dry completely before proceeding to paint the hydrangea.

Here, we paint the 'Gaku Ajisai', a popular hydrangea species that is native to Japan. This variety is composed of many small flowers that cluster in the centre, enclosed by a frame ('gaku') of decorative flowers.

Load the ōfude with tanboku, prepare the tip with chuboku and blend for sanboku-hou (for colour, use two shades of blue ink). Begin by painting the decorative flowers.

1

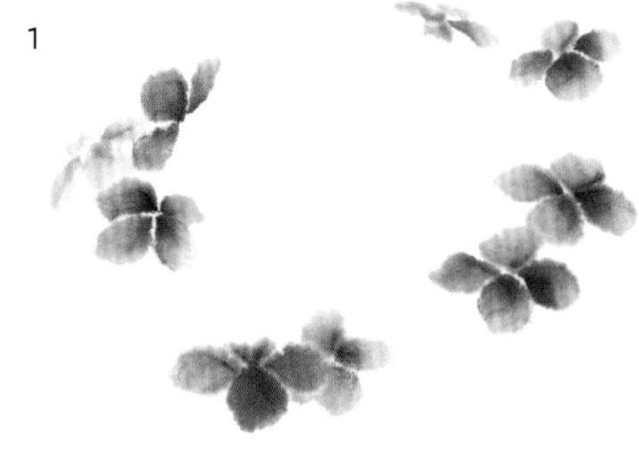

2

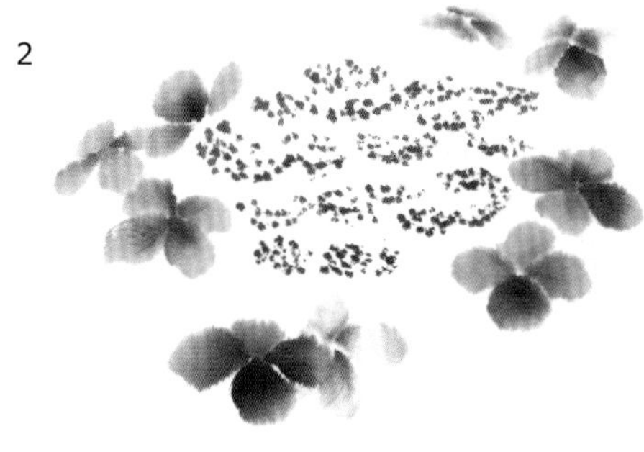

3

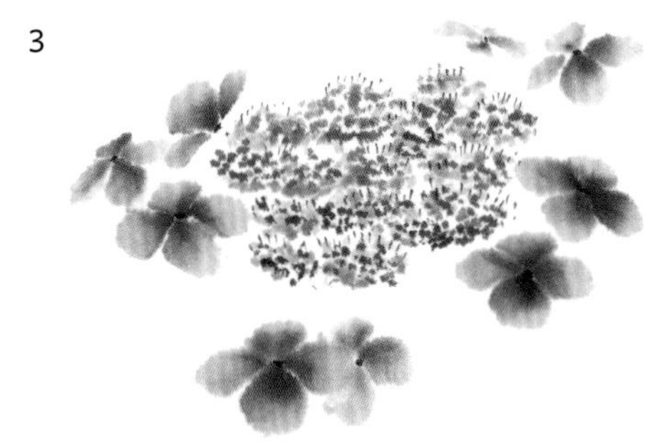

1. Paint each sepal in one gentle sideways pivot of the brush in sokuhitsu and repeat to create a four-sepal arrangement. Bring the flowers together at various angles, painting the front flowers first in darker shades of ink, then the flowers in the back in a lighter shade.

2. Paint the lace-like cluster of flowers in the centre. Prepare two or three different shades of ink (for colour, use navy, royal blue and purple) and paint small, dotted patterns by dabbing the tip of the brush. Begin with the darker ink shades, then apply the lighter shades.

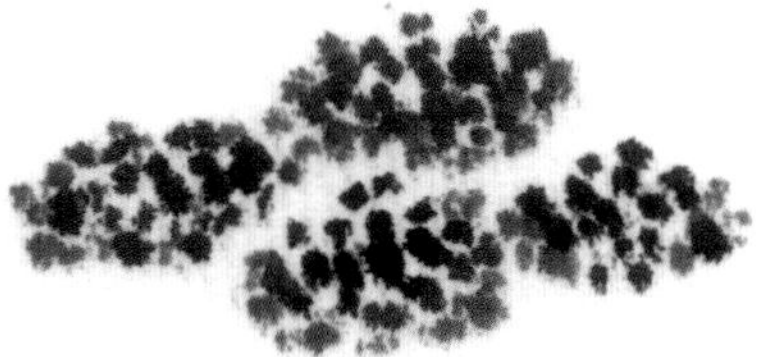

3. Once the ink is moderately dry, load the menso-fude with nouboku (for colour, use dark blue) and paint short lines to represent the pistils and stamens.

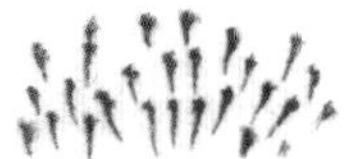

Leaves

These are typically large, broad and have serrated edges. Following the same techniques as for the persimmon leaves, use a greater surface of the brush to create larger and broader leaves (refer to p. 84).

Bring together the various elements in the following order: the rain, flowers, leaves, stem and, finally, the details (veins of the leaves).

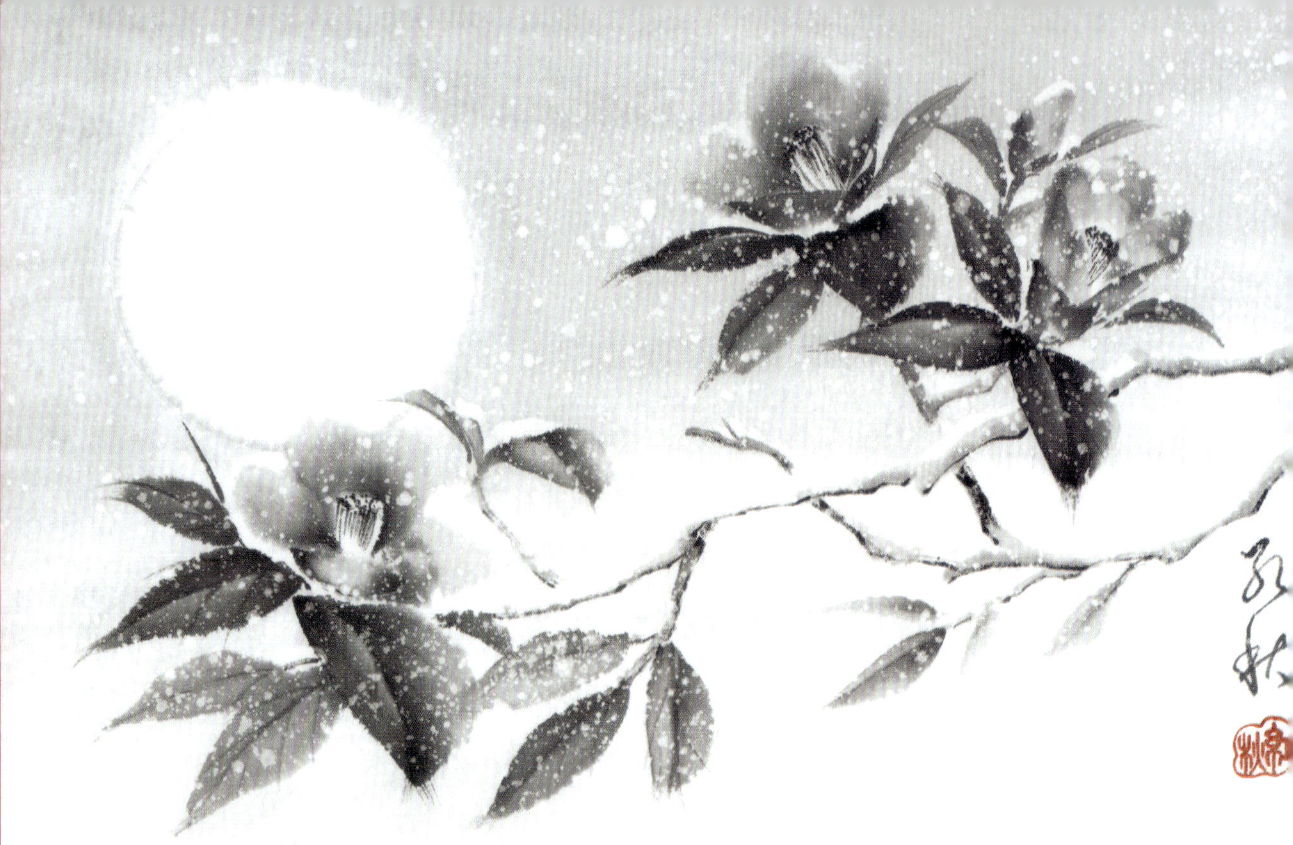

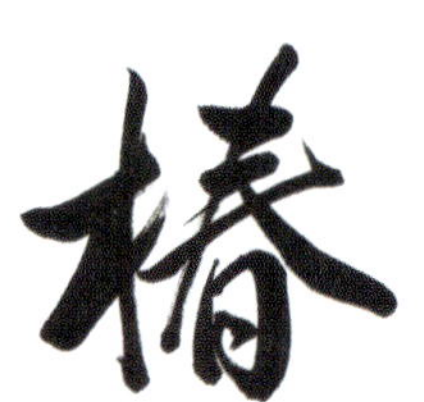

Camellia on a Snowy Night

FOR THE FINAL ARTWORK, we will integrate the various brush and ink control techniques that we have explored in the preceding chapters to convey the beauty of the camellia flower. Additionally, we will incorporate both the shironuki and mizu bokashi techniques to paint the serene winter landscape enveloped by the moonlight.

This particular artwork uses black sumi ink to capture the still, silent atmosphere.

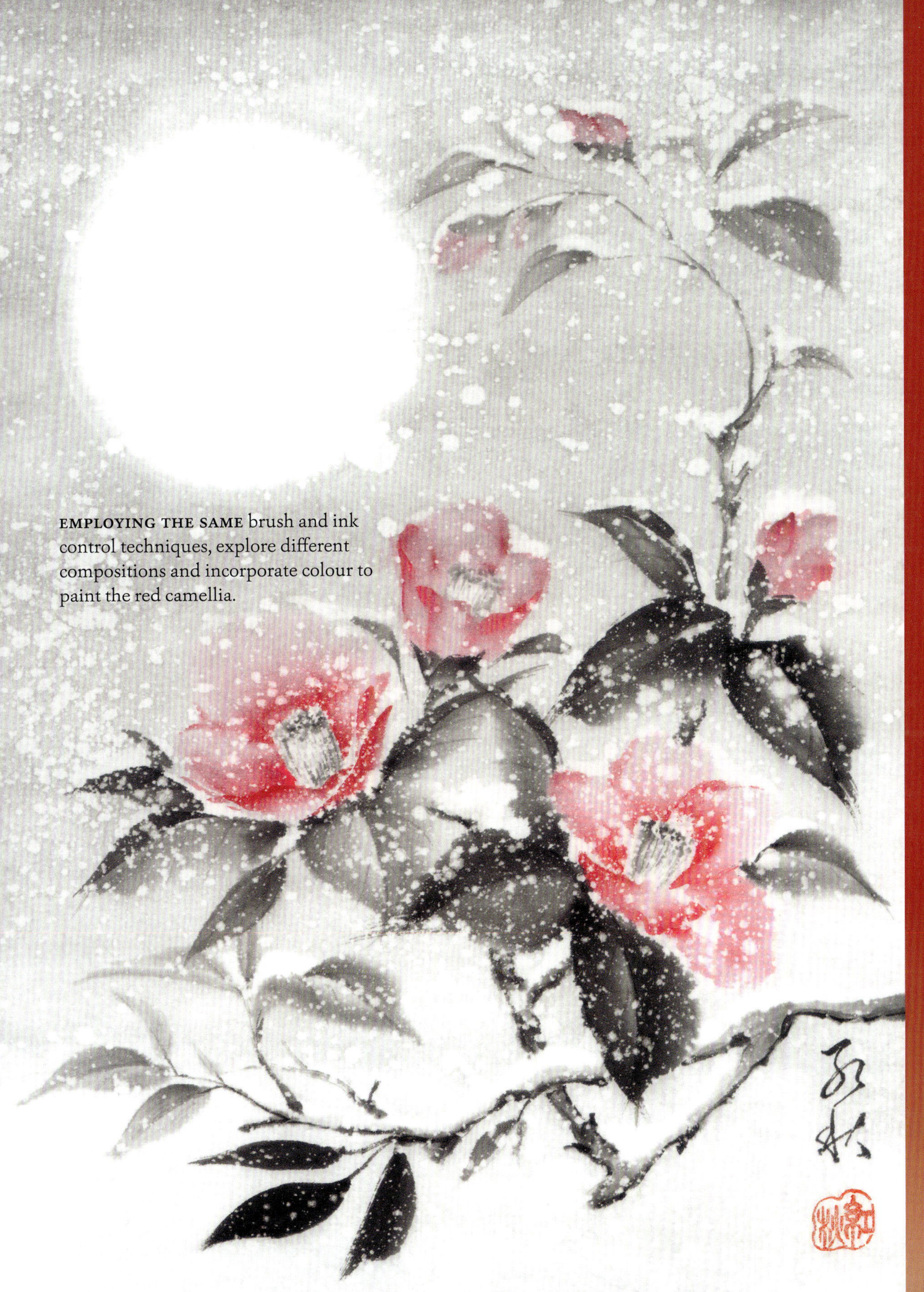

EMPLOYING THE SAME brush and ink control techniques, explore different compositions and incorporate colour to paint the red camellia.

CAMELLIA FLOWER

Flower A

1. Load the ōfude with tanboku, prepare the tip with chuboku and blend for sanboku-hou. Push the tip of the brush from right to left to paint the front petal.

2. Create another overlapping front petal with the tip of the brush, from left to right.

3. Load the kofude with chuboku and paint the pistils and stamens that cluster in the centre.

4. Switch back to the ōfude, and with the tip of the brush pointed towards the centre, push upwards in sokuhitsu while increasing the pressure, then press the body of the brush down to create a rounded finish.

5. Repeat step 4 to create the petal on the other side.

6. Repeat step 4 to create the centre petal, with the tip of the brush pointed towards the centre, push the brush sideways from left to right, or right to left.

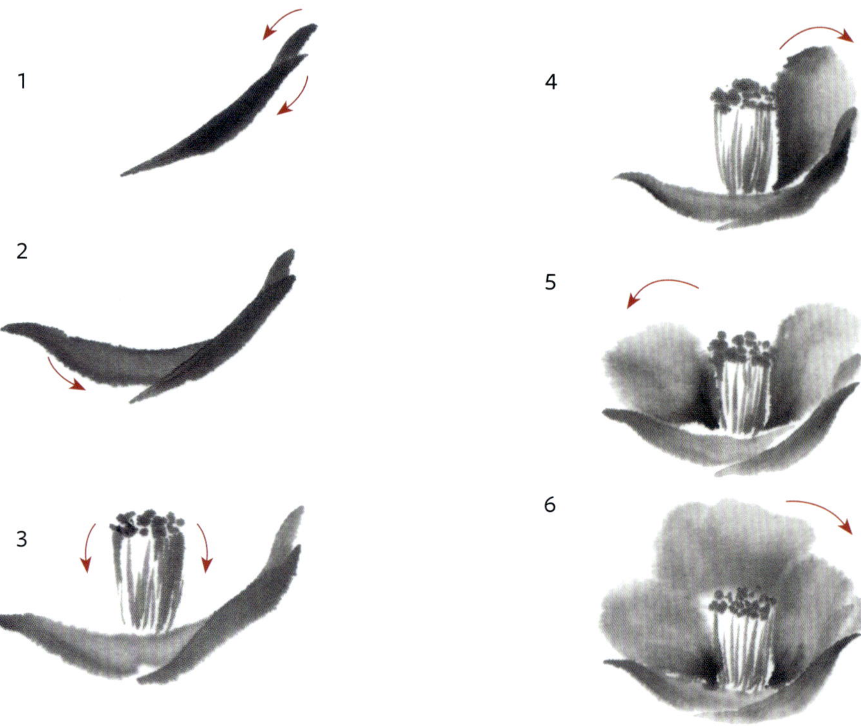

Practise variations of the open flower.

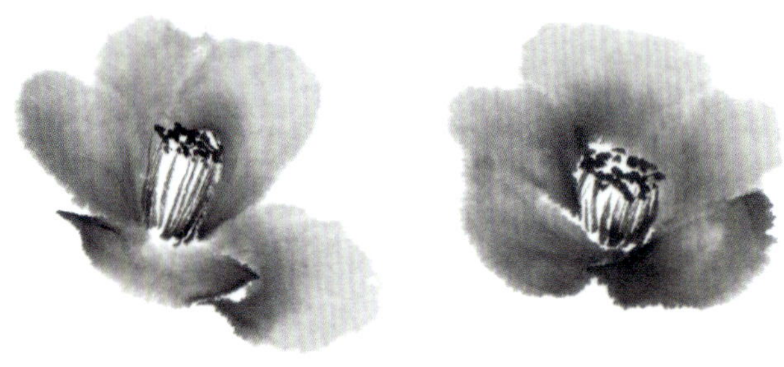

Flower B

1. Load the kofude or ōfude with nouboku and paint the calyx.

2. Load the ōfude with tanboku, prepare the tip with chuboku and blend for sanboku-hou, then paint the first petal. Position the tip of the brush at the tip of the petal, incrementally increasing the pressure while rotating to ensure that the tip of the brush traces the left margin of the petal.

3. Use the same technique to paint the petal on the right-hand side and centre.

4. Prepare the kofude with chuboku and paint the pistils and stamen in the centre.

5. Finish off by painting the petals behind the pistils and stamen on both sides.

6. Then the centre petal in the back.

Colour use

The camellia illustrated on p. 151 exemplifies the use of a single colour: red. Load the brush with light red ink, prepare the tip with medium-dark red ink and blend for sanboku-hou.

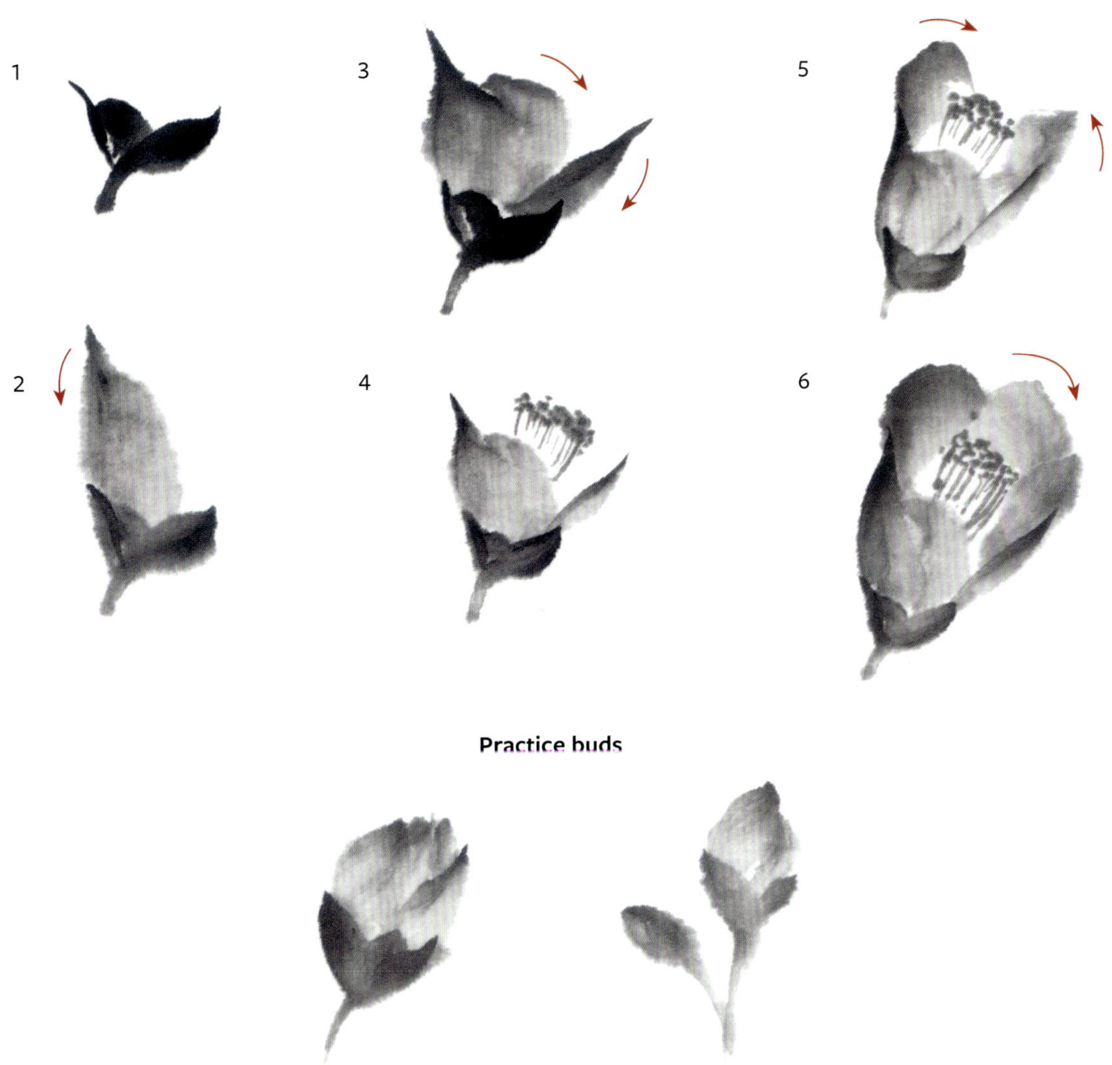

Practice buds

CAMELLIA LEAVES AND BRANCHES

Leaves

The camellia leaves are dark green and glossy. Load the ōfude with chuboku, prepare the tip with nouboku and blend for sanboku-hou.

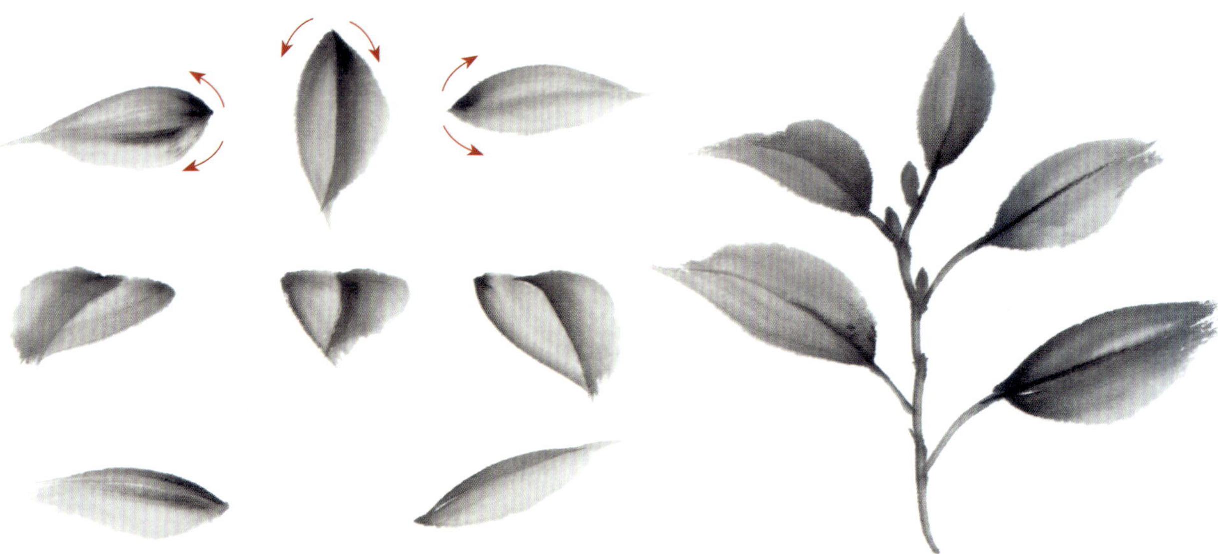

Paint each leaf in two brushstrokes but ensure that the tip of the brush points in the same direction for both strokes (this technique contrasts with previous techniques where the tip of the brush was pointed towards the leaf's centreline for both strokes). This will capture the leaf's natural lustre.

Once the ink is dry, paint the veins faintly and bring the leaves together with a stem.

Branches

Load the ōfude or kofude with tanboku and paint the branch. Then, while the ink is still wet, paint over the lower section of the branches in nouboku, allowing the darker ink to bleed. Alternatively, prepare the brush for kataguma and allow the darker side of the brush to trace the lower section of the branch to create the same effect. Where the branches intersect, leave a blank space on top of the branch positioned below to depict the settled snow (see pp. 150–1).

Bring together the various elements in the following order:

1. **Shironuki falling snow**: before painting, prepare the paper with falling snow using the shironuki technique (see p. 147). Allow the paper to dry.

2. Paint the flowers, buds, leaves and branches, followed by the veins on the leaves. Incorporate smaller leaves into the composition (optional).

3. **Shironuki settled snow**: to further convey the settled snow, paint a blanket of snow sitting on top of the branches, using the shironuki liquid. Allow this to dry.

4. **Bokashi moon**: finally, flip over the paper and spray water evenly across the entire piece of paper. Paint the sky in goku-tanboku using the bokashi technique. To include the moon in your composition, position a round plate in the desired location for the moon (see p. 125) before the bokashi step.

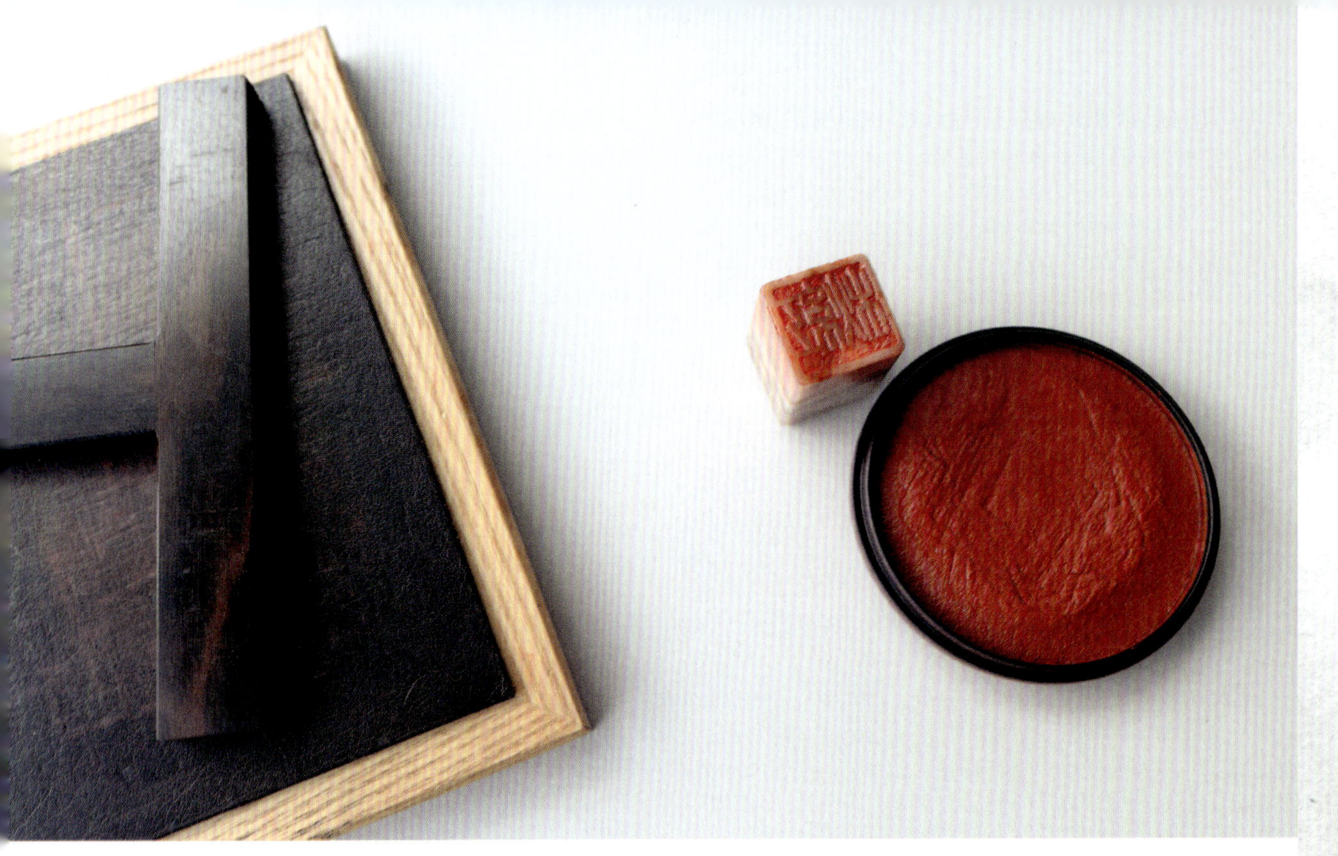

FINISHING TOUCHES

Seal placement ('rakkan')

THE FINAL STEP that unifies a calligraphy or sumi painting artwork is the addition of a signature and/or seal, collectively referred to as 'rakkan' (落款). Its presence signifies the completion of the artwork and a sign of authentication.

The signature and seal are integral elements of the final artwork and can take various forms, such as your name, artist name, or a word or symbol that holds personal value. Selecting the right location for the signature and seal is crucial in order to leave the original brushwork intact and preserve the balance in composition. Every painting has a beginning and an end; a direction in which the narrative unfolds. Placing the seal in the path of the unfolding space will disrupt the composition, therefore, it is recommended to place it where the artwork 'begins'. Additionally, it is important to select the right seal size according to the dimensions and composition of the artwork.

There are two primary methods of seal carving: Hakubun (白文) and Shubun (朱文). Hakubun involves carving the letters themselves, which, when applied, creates white letters surrounded by red borders. Shubun, on the other hand, involves carving the inverse of the letters, creating red letters surrounded by white borders.

When selecting a seal, it is advisable to use hand-engraved seals referred to as 'tenkokuin' (篆刻印), which complement your artwork, rather than machine-made seals. You can commission specialised seal artisans, known as 'tenkokushi', to create your unique seal. Alternatively, you can purchase the necessary tenkoku materials to carve your seal and learn the basic method in the Domestika course: 'Sumi Painting with Colour: Unit 4' (see the link on p. 160).

In Suibokuga, the calligraphic style of the seal stone, as well as the shape, size, and method of carving, are a matter of artistic preference.

Whichever seal you use, the application technique is the same. Press the seal stone in the ink paste (known as 'indei'), which typically comes in various shades of red, from bright vermillion to dark burgundy. Then, place your completed artwork on the rubber mat (known as 'injyokudai'). Use the T- or L-shaped ruler (known as 'inku') to guide the seal placement, and press the seal firmly and straight down.

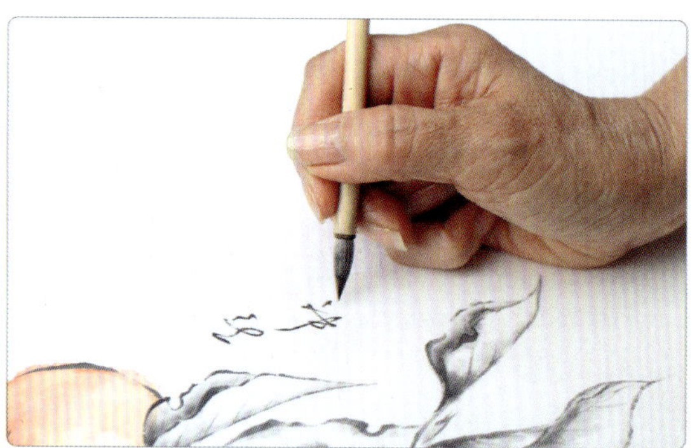

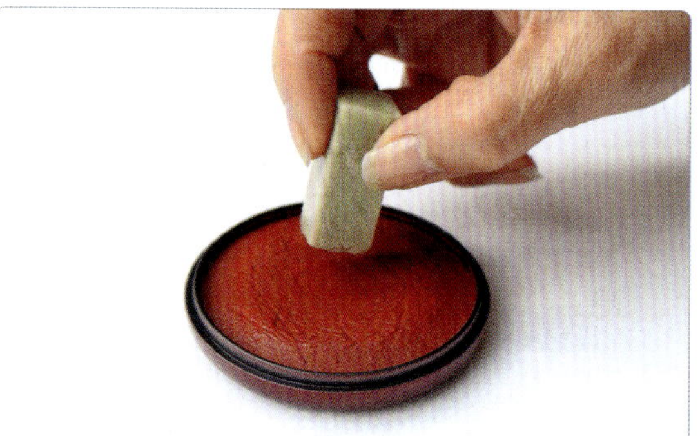

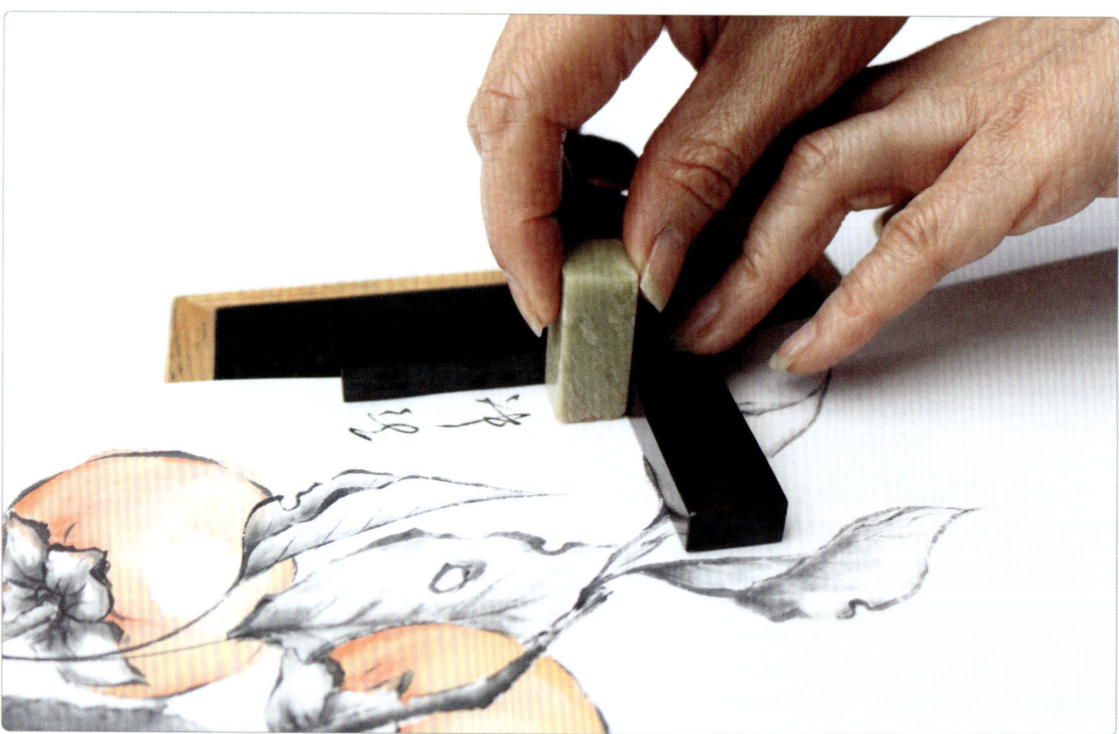

KEY POINT

The drying time of indei (paste) can vary, and in some cases may take a few days. Once the artwork has been finalised with a seal, store the artwork in a safe and dry place and avoid handling until dry.

SUPPORTING PAPER (URAUCHI)

Japanese calligraphy and sumi painting papers shrivel and crease when ink is applied. To strengthen and straighten the artwork and prepare for framing, the final step is to apply the supporting paper. This process, known as urauchi (裏打ち), involves dampening the artwork, flattening out the creases and reinforcing it with another piece of supporting/backing paper known as urauchi gami (裏打ち紙) or urauchi youshi (裏打用紙). In Japan, Kozo-shi is the most commonly used paper for urauchi, as the long fibres are resistant to tearing.

Traditional method (1):

1. Lay the dry artwork face down on a clean, flat surface and use a mist sprayer to moisten the artwork evenly. Gently brush over the artwork with the nadebake (smoothing brush) from the centre outward, to remove any creases in the paper.

2. Place the urauchi paper (i.e., kozo paper that is one size larger than the artwork) separately on a flat clean surface and use a mist sprayer to moisten the paper evenly.

3. Prepare diluted starch glue ('shofunori') and use the noribake (paste brush) to spread the glue evenly across the surface of the damp urauchi paper.

4. Carefully lift the urauchi paper with a ruler, ensuring that the paper remains taut. During this step, allow the inner margin of the paper to adhere to the table surface to ensure it is fixed in place. Gently lower the paper onto the artwork, pressing it down with the nadebake to remove air bubbles at the same time.

5. Lift the artwork and urauchi paper together and place them on a smooth wooden board or panel with the artwork facing towards the board. Insert a small piece of scrap paper between the artwork and the board to facilitate easier removal once dry. Allow the artwork to dry naturally for a day or two.

6. Once the artwork is dry, use a painting knife or spatula to peel it off the board.

7. Trim the margins of the backing paper to achieve a neat finish.

However, this method requires the right tools and extensive experience with the technique – for this reason, it is usually undertaken by mounting artisans or technicians specialising in urauchi and scroll making.

Alternative method (2):

As a more accessible alternative, there are supporting papers available that come with pre-applied glue, known as noritsuki urauchi gami (糊付き裏打紙). These supporting papers adhere directly to the artwork and smooth out creases when pressed with an iron – this method is suitable for framed artworks.

1. Once the artwork is completely dry, spray water across the entire surface to dampen it, and let it sit for 10–15 minutes.

2. Place the artwork face down on a hard surface covered with a shitajiki cloth or layers of paper.

3. Take the urauchi paper and position it on top of the artwork, ensuring that the glued surface is facing down.

4. Iron the paper (without steam) at a temperature of 120–130°C. Start from the centre and gradually push outwards, applying gentle pressure to remove any air bubbles.

5. Flip the artwork over and allow it to cool down.

6. If the edges of the paper haven't adhered sufficiently, turn over the artwork and iron the edges from the front side of the artwork. Make sure to place a piece of standard calligraphy/sumi painting paper on top of the artwork to avoid direct contact with the iron.

Take the Domestika course, 'Sumi-e Introduction: Unit 5' for more details on the noritsuki urauchi technique (see the link on p. 160).

MAINTENANCE AND TIPS

Brushes

The following advice is from Mr Junichi Fujino, a brush craftsman at Hankeidou.

Key brush characteristics to look out for:

The bristles of the brush should be resilient. They should come together without fraying and without individual hairs coming loose. When painting, the bristles should move in unison.

Key points for maintenance and long-term use:

After each use, make sure to remove the ink thoroughly from the brush. Ink can accumulate at the base of the bristles, which can lead to stiffening or splitting of the brush. To avoid this, rinse it under clean water, massaging the bristles to remove any ink residues, and then hang the brush from the handle to dry in a well-shaded area. Finally, wrap the brushes in a fude-maki (a brush holder made of bamboo) or newspaper.

With proper care, a high-quality brush will last a long time. However, if the brush splits, it is time to purchase a replacement. For small brushes used to paint intricate details, the tip of the brush is particularly important. Replace the brush when the tip is worn out.

Inkstone

The following advice is from Mr Yoichi Hieda, an Akama inkstone craftsman and researcher at Hieda Gyokuhoudou.

Key suzuri characteristics to look out for:

A good inkstone should have a surface that allows for easy grinding of the inkstick without requiring excessive force or physical effort. You should be able to create thick ink within 30 minutes or less, depending on the desired consistency and amount. The surface of the inkstone should have a slightly coarse texture, referred to as houbou.

Key points for maintenance and long-term use:

To avoid the build-up of ink and glue residues, rinse the inkstone with lukewarm water (20–25°C) after each use, using a soft sponge or your hand to gently clean the surface. After washing, press a cloth or paper towel against the surface of the inkstone to remove excess moisture. Avoid rubbing or scratching the surface, and do not dry the inkstone in direct sunlight. If possible, store the inkstone in a wooden box in an area with minimal temperature fluctuations.

Even with proper care, after repeated use, the surface of the inkstone will lose its coarse texture from the nikawa glue build-up. When this occurs, purchase a grindstone/whetstone to polish the surface and create Houbou.

Inkstick

The following advice is from Mr Atsushi Nagano, a Kinkoen Nara Sumi craftsman.

Key characteristics to look out for:

Each inkstick can produce a variety of hues and shades, and selecting an inkstick comes down to artistic preference. There are, however, a few points to consider.

Select an inkstick that has a straight, clean appearance. During the drying stage of the manufacturing process, low-quality inksticks will lose their straight and clean shape and become twisted or warped.

A high-quality inkstick can be ground into a rich liquid without excessive force, effort or time when grinding. This, however, also depends on the quality of the inkstone.

Key points for maintenance and long-term use:

Wipe the inkstick after each use, and where possible, store in a paulownia or other wooden box away from direct sunlight, heat and humidity.

Coloured inkstick

The following advice is from Mr Masao Horiike, a Kishu Shouen inkstick artisan and the only remaining Shouenboku specialist in Japan.

For students seeking to enhance their colour use in Sumi-e, it is advisable to use Saienboku or similar coloured paints that contain nikawa glue.

Some coloured paints use gum arabic as an adhesive. While the inclusion of nikawa glue is not essential if the objective of colour use is merely to add colour, it becomes indispensable when aiming to create a three-dimensional world. nikawa glue alters the ink's viscosity and allows for the creation of layers, introducing depth and dimension. If you are seeking high-quality, handmade coloured or black ink, there are a few features to consider. Firstly, look for inksticks that specify the manufacturer's name rather than the seller's name, and secondly, search for inksticks that have letters engraved in their bodies.

Similar to the inkstick maintenance, wipe after each use.

The specialist advice was personally given by Rimpamura, a boutique shop featuring artisan sumi painting materials (https://shop.rimpamura.com/about).

RESOURCES

Links

Koshu Japanese Art

www.koshujapaneseart.co.uk /
www.koshujapaneseart.com

Domestika online courses

Introduction to Sumi-e Painting:
www.domestika.org/en/courses/
2174-introduction-to-sumi-e-painting

Sumi-e painting with colour for floral illustrations:

www.domestika.org/en/courses/3909-sumi-e-painting-with-color-for-floral-illustrations

Suppliers and materials

While by no means exhaustive, below is a list of recommended suppliers for Sumi-e tools and materials.

United Kingdom

AKASHIYA, VIA JAPAN HOUSE, LONDON
https://www.japanhouselondon.uk (Japanese calligraphy set, papers)

CHOOSING KEEPING, LONDON
www.choosingkeeping.com (brushes, pallets, Gansai paint)

L. CORNELISSEN & SON, LONDON
https://www.cornelissen.com/drawing-and-calligraphy.html (Chinese ink sticks, ink stones and liquid ink)

ORIENTAL ARTS, BRIGHTON
https://www.orientalartsbrighton.co.uk (Chinese brushes, papers, inkstick, inkstone, felt, pallets, sealstones)

Japan

PIGMENT TOKYO
https://pigment.tokyo/en (Everything)

RIMPAMURA
www.shop.rimpamura-ec.com (brushes, inkstick, inkstone)

SHOUGETSUDO, HIROSHIMA
www.shop.sgd-fude.net/items/42890739 (Kumano fude)

KURETAKE, NARA
https://item.kuretake.co.jp/kuretake-web/DispCate.do?volumeName=00002 (Gansai watercolors, inks, brushes)

USA

INKSTON
www.inkston.com (Chinese brushes, papers, inkstick, inkstone, pallets, coloured paints, sealstones and paste)

ORIENTAL ART SUPPLY, HUNTINGTON BEACH, CA
www.orientalartsupply.com (Chinese brushes, inks, papers and various accessories)

SUMIESTORE, VIRGINIA BEACH, VA
www.sumiestore.com (Chinese brush, inks, papers and various accessories)

KURETAKE ZIG, SACRAMENTO, CA
www.kuretakezig.us (Gansai watercolors, pens)

GLOSSARY

AMI BOKASHI 網暈し(あみぼかし)
Ink blurring effect that involves pressing a brush against a fine mesh net to spray ink, pp. 124–32

ATARI あたり
A form of Ringa practice that involves tracing the compositional skeleton of the artwork in charcoal and using the line drawing as a guide before painting with ink, p. 33

BOKASHI 暈し(ぼかし)
Ink blurring effect, pp. 123–45

BOKUSAIGA 墨彩画(ぼくさいが)
A style of painting that involves the use of colour as a means to complement and enhance the sumi ink, while using the same brush and ink control techniques as Suibokuga, pp. 71–154

CHOKUHITSU 直筆(ちょくひつ)
Brush movement where the tip of the brush runs through the centre of the line, p. 25

CHOUBOKU 調墨(ちょうぼく)
Techniques to control ink density, pp. 17, 23, 26–30

CHUBOKU 中墨(ちゅうぼく)
A medium dark shade of ink, p. 23

FUDE 筆(ふで) Brush, pp. 18, 20

GOKU-TANBOKU 極淡墨(ごくたんぼく)
A very light shade of ink, p. 23

HABOKU-HOU 破墨法(はぼくほう)
Ink effect technique that involves painting with light ink and layering on dark ink to create a bleeding/blurring effect, p. 31

HAKE 刷毛(はけ) Flat brush, p. 133

HANSOKUHITSU 半側筆(はんそくひつ)
Brush movement where the brush is in half chokuhitsu and half sokuhitsu, p. 25

JUNPITSU-HOU 潤筆法(じゅんぴつほう)
Ink control technique that involves painting with a wet brush or painting on wet paper, p. 31

KAMI 紙(かみ) Paper, pp. 18, 19

KAPPISTU-HOU 渇筆法(かっぴつほう)
Ink control technique that involves painting with a dry brush, p. 31

KASURE 掠れ(かすれ)
Dry brush technique used to create coarse, broken and asymmetrical lines, p. 31

KATAGUMA 片隈(かたぐま)
Ink control technique and effect of creating a line with one light and one dark side, p. 26

KENWAN 懸腕(けんわん)
Arm position where the elbow is held midway between the table and the shoulder, p. 24

KOFUDE 小筆(こふで) Small brush, p. 20

MENSO-FUDE 面相筆(めんそうふで)
A small brush designed with a sharp tip, typically made from hard weasel, badger or deer hair, pp. 20, 133–45

MIZU BOKASHI 水ぼかし(みずぼかし)
Ink blurring effect that involves painting on moistened paper, p. 127, 133–45

MOTOGUMA 元隈(もとぐま)
Ink control technique and effect that involves loading the brush with dark ink and then rinsing the tip of the brush to remove ink, p. 30

NEJIRI-FUDE 捻り筆(ねじりふで)
A painting technique using a brush with dry and twisted bristles, p. 31

NIJIMI 滲み(にじみ) Ink bleeding effect, p. 19, 31

NOUBOKU 濃墨(のうぼく)
A dark shade of ink, p. 23

ŌFUDE 大筆(おおふで) Large brush, p. 20

RAKKAN 落款(らっかん)
Seal and signature placement, pp. 155–6

RINGA 臨画(りんが)
To study and copy an example painting as closely as possible to gain insight into brushwork, ink control techniques and compositional principles, p. 33

RYOGUMA 両隈(りょうぐま)
The ink control technique and effect of creating a line with two dark edges and a lighter centre, pp. 27, 28

SAIENBOKU 彩煙墨(さいえんぼく)
Coloured sumi inkstick, p. 72

SAKIGUMA 先隈(さきぐま)
The ink control technique and effect of creating a line with a dark tip and a lighter body, p. 26

SAKUYO-FUDE 削用筆(さくようふで)
A small mixed-hair brush typically made with a core of strong weasel and white racoon dog hair, surrounded by soft goat hair, p. 20

SANBOKU-HOU 三墨法(さんぼくほう)
The ink control technique and effect of creating a gradation of light to dark. Load the brush with light ink, apply dark ink to the tip and blend the brush to create a gradation of three ink shades, p. 29

SENBYOU-HOU 線描法(せんびょうほう)
Method of painting that gives form to the subject through outlines or contours (also referred to as Kouroku-hou), p. 32

SHIKUNSHI 四君子(しくんし)
A traditional motif in Suibokuga referred to as The Four Gentlemen, which includes the wild orchid, bamboo, chrysanthemum and plum blossom, pp. 35–70

SHIRONUKI 白抜き(しろぬき)
A technique that involves painting with a whitening agent that repels ink, pp. 146–54

SHOUENBOKU 松煙墨(しょうえんぼく)
An inkstick made from burnt pinewood soot, that produces ink with a distinctive bluish-black hue, p. 21

SOKUHITSU 側筆(そくひつ)
Brush movement where the brush angle is lowered, and the tip of the brush marks one edge of the line, p. 25

SOTOGUMA 外隈(そとぐま)
The ink control technique and effect of creating a circle with a darker inner ring and blurred lighter outer ring, p. 27

SOUKOU-HOU 双鉤法(そうこうほう)
Method of holding the brush with the thumb, index finger and middle finger in front to grip the brush, and the ring and little fingers in the back for support, p. 24

SUIBOKUGA 水墨画(すいぼくが)
Monochrome ink painting that uses black ink washes to create a rich spectrum of shades, pp. 13–15

SUJIME 筋目(すじめ)
The white streak that forms when ink touches and repels, creating an effect of visual separation between brush strokes, p. 19

SUMI 墨(すみ) Ink, pp. 21, 22

SUMI-E 墨絵(すみえ)
Monochrome ink painting that uses only black ink balanced with negative space, p. 15

SUZURI 硯(すずり) Inkstone, pp. 18, 21, 22

TANBOKU 淡墨(たんぼく)
A light shade of ink, p. 23

TANKOU-HOU 単鉤法(たんこうほう)
Method of holding the brush with the thumb and index finger in front to grip the brush, and the middle, ring and little fingers in the back for support, p. 24

TEIWAN 提腕(ていわん)
Arm position where the wrist rests gently on the table, p. 24

TSUKETATE-FUDE 付立筆（つけたてふで）
A mixed-hair brush commonly made with a combination of soft and flexible sheep hair and hard deer, horse and racoon dog hairs, p. 20

TSUKETATE-HOU 付立法（つけたてほう）
Method of painting that gives form to the subject through shading and layering, rather than outlines or contours (also referred to as Mokkotsu-hou), p. 32

UCHIGUMA 内隈（うちぐま）
The ink control technique and effect of creating a circle with a darker outer ring and blurred lighter inner ring, p. 27

URAUCHI 裏打ち（うらうち）
Method of straightening and strengthening the artwork before framing or scroll making, p. 157

WARI-FUDE 割筆（わりふで）
A painting technique using a brush with dry and spread-out bristles, p. 31

YUENBOKU 油煙墨（ゆえんぼく）
Inkstick made from a blend of rapeseed or camellia soot and glue, that produces ink with a rich, brownish-black hue, p. 21

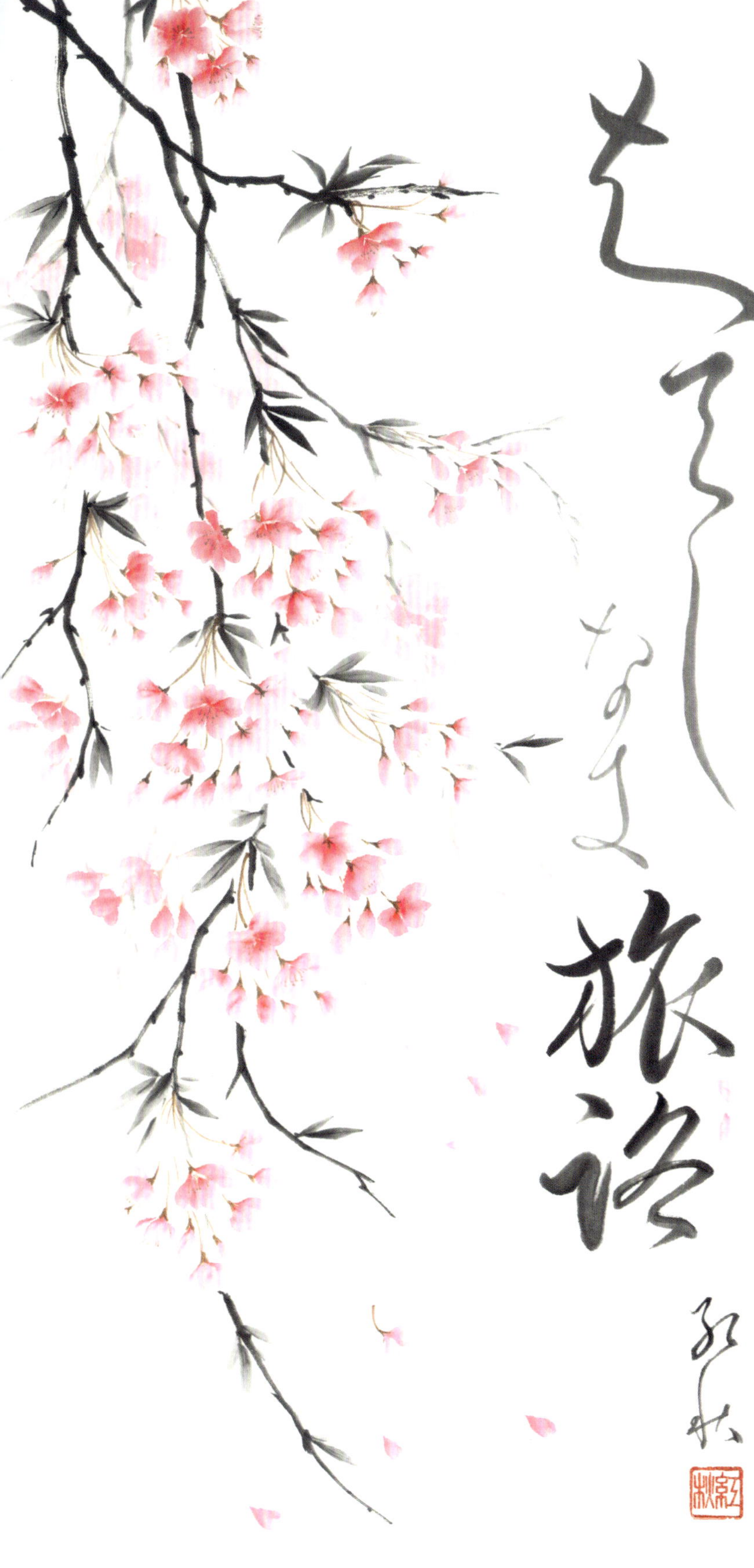

ENDLESS JOURNEY

はてしなき旅路

Over my years of training, my teacher Seizan compiled the best pieces of my basic practice without my knowing and bound them into a book. On its cover, he painted the words, 'Endless Journey' (はてしなき旅路). At first, I thought he meant that my training as a calligrapher would be an endless journey. Only as time passed did the meaning of his words unveil itself to me: each step and each stroke is the journey.

MIRROR-LIKE WISDOM

汚れのない鏡のような智慧

While tempests stir the surface waves, the deep blue remains serene and still, unmoved by what it reflects. This is the mirror-like wisdom of Buddha Akshobhya, the unshakeable one.

Each artwork you create is a faithful reflection of your subconscious – the light, shadows and darkness hidden within the recesses of your mind, embodied by each stroke.

Allow your practice to guide you through the landscape of your emotions and thoughts. Meditate on the rhythmic grinding of the ink and cultivate complete focus in each stroke. With time, the noise of the tempests surrounding you will fade, and your artwork will mirror the purity of your mind.

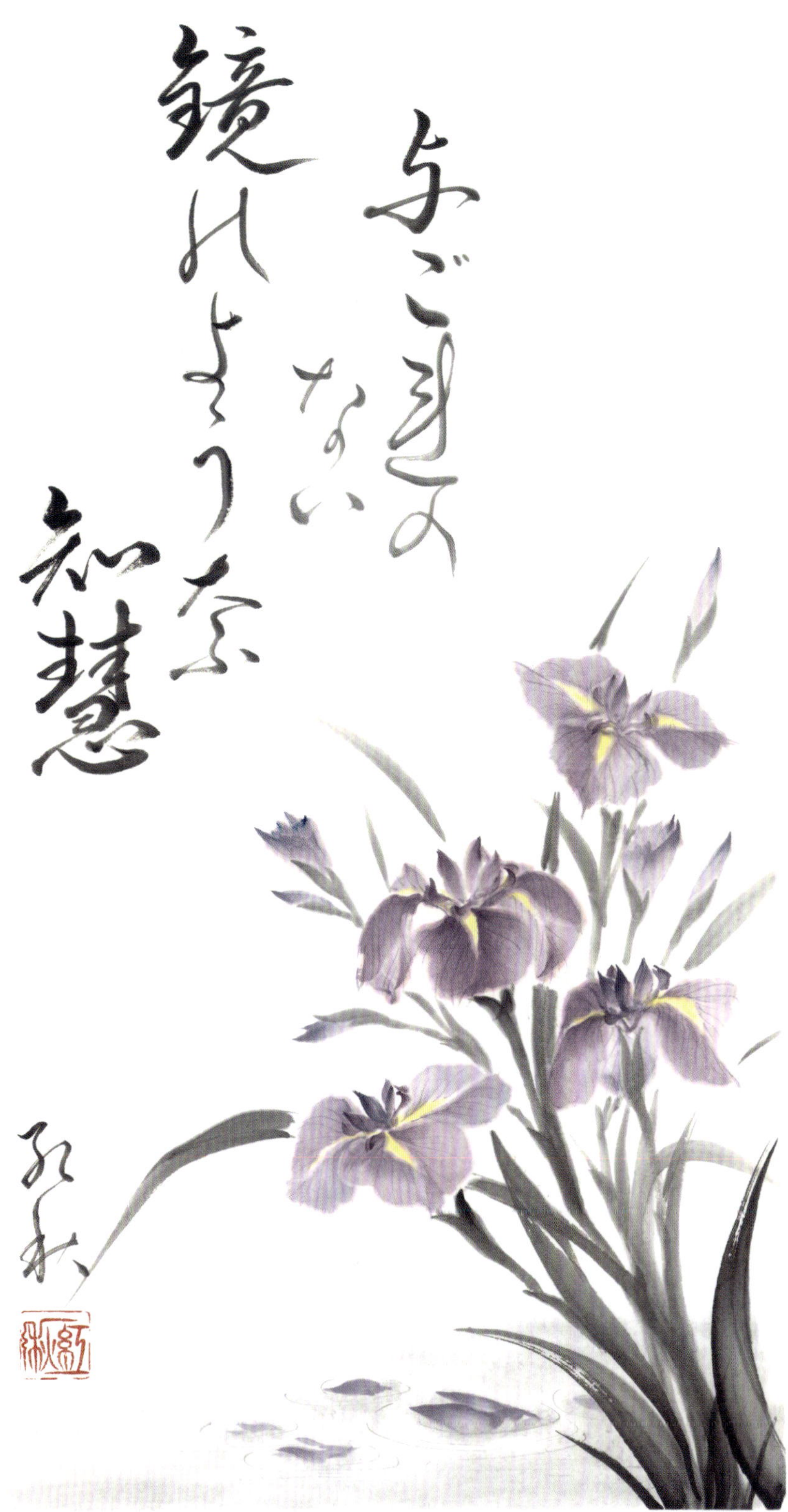

EVERY DAY IS A GOOD DAY

日日是好日

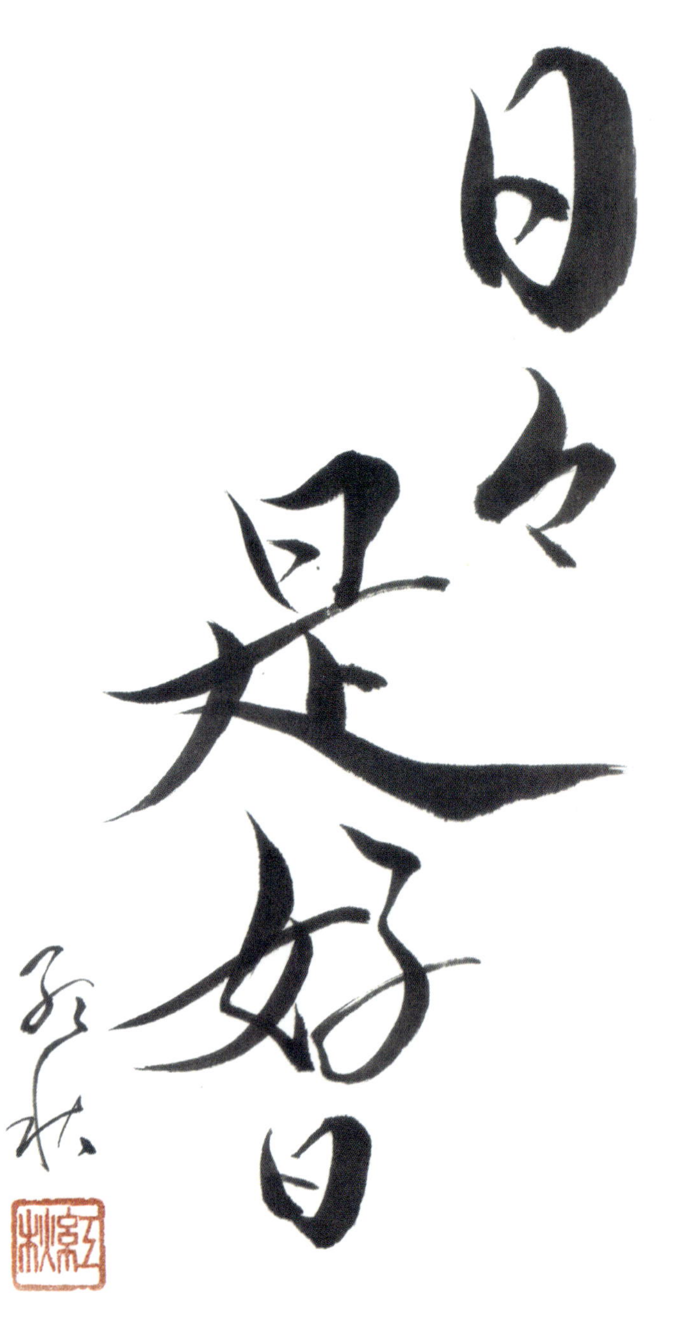

Every day unveils a new practice.

You may retrace the very same composition, guiding your brush through a familiar choreography. Still, day by day, the ink's hues subtly transform, a hint of blue or a depth previously absent. The essence of the brushstrokes shifts, echoing your evolving mindset. Embrace each unfolding day as an opportunity to practise.

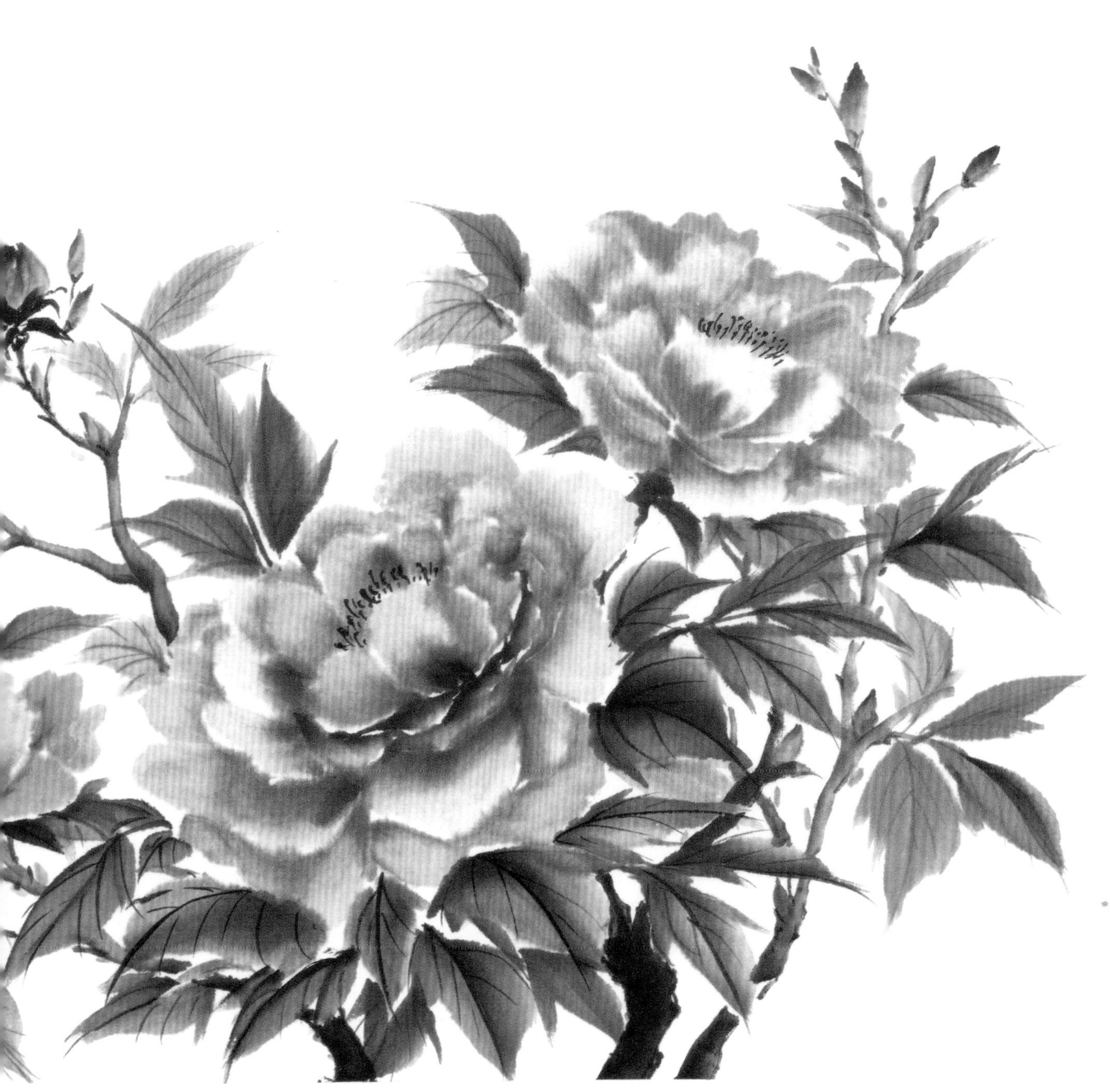

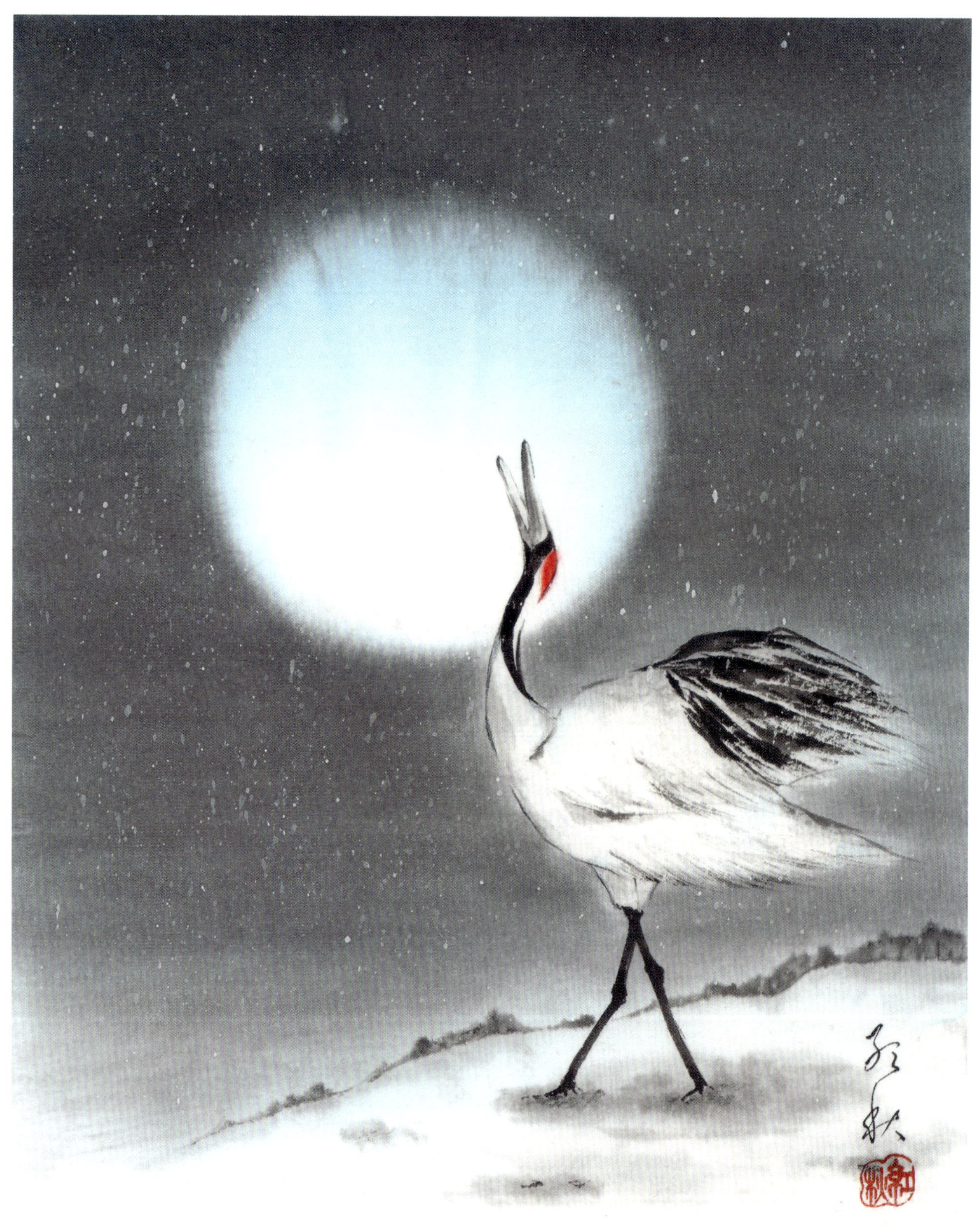

A CRANE UNDER THE MOONLIGHT – You are never truly alone.

SAMPLE SHEETS FOR ATARI

The line drawings on pp. 169–72 can be used for the Ringa practice using Atari. Scan, print and trace over the lines using charcoal before you begin your painting. Refer to p. 33 for more details.

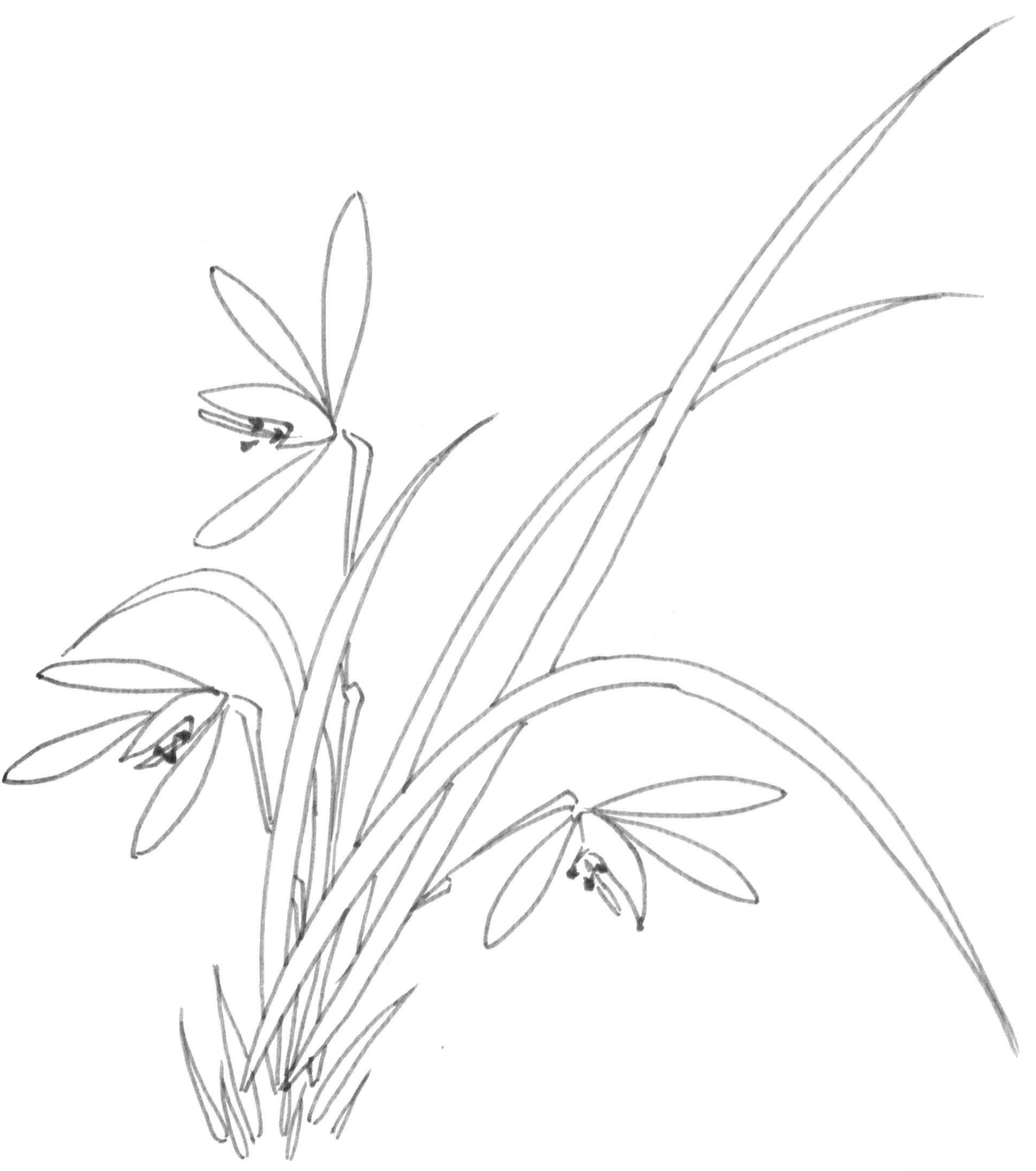

ORCHID

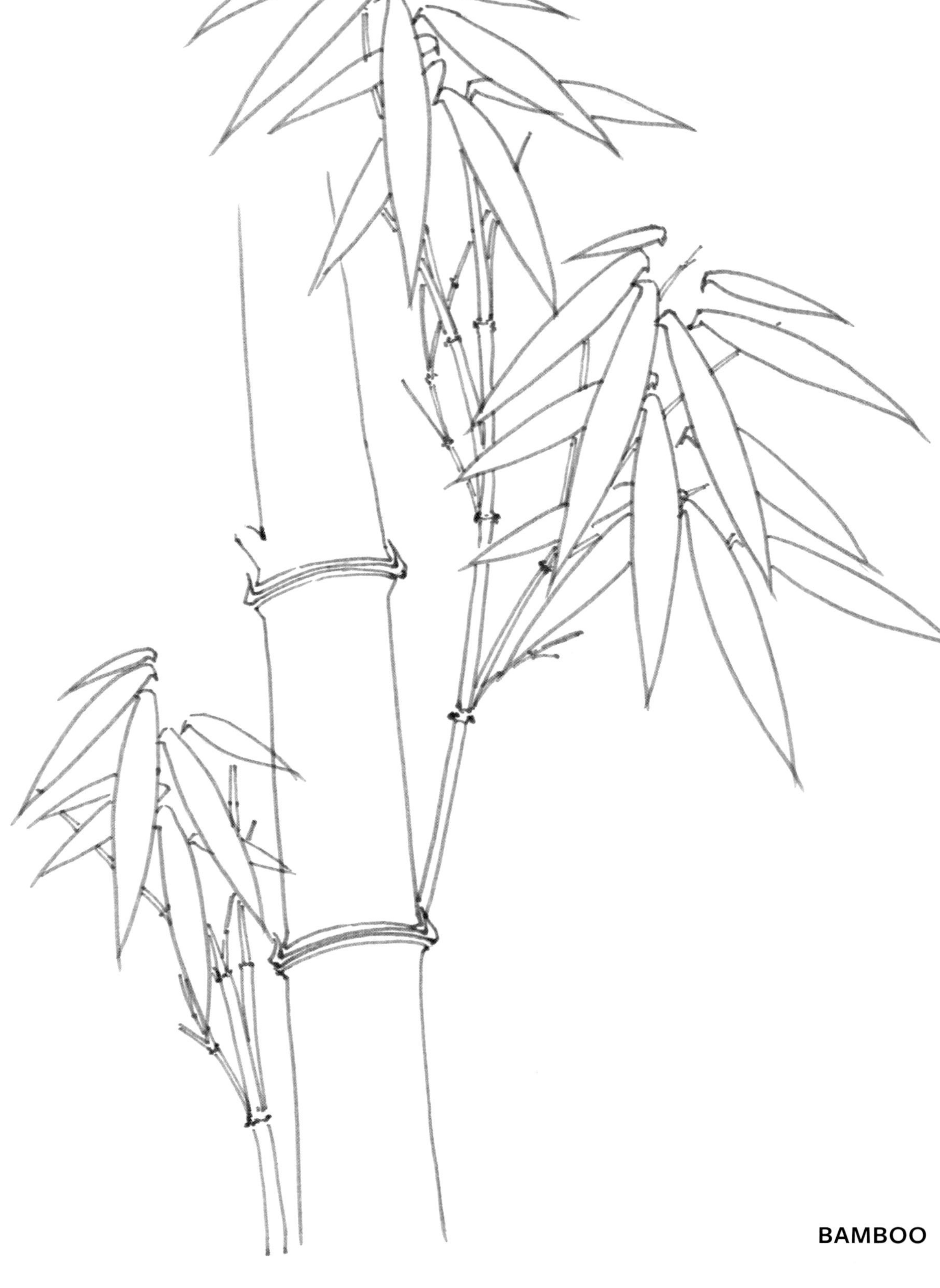

BAMBOO

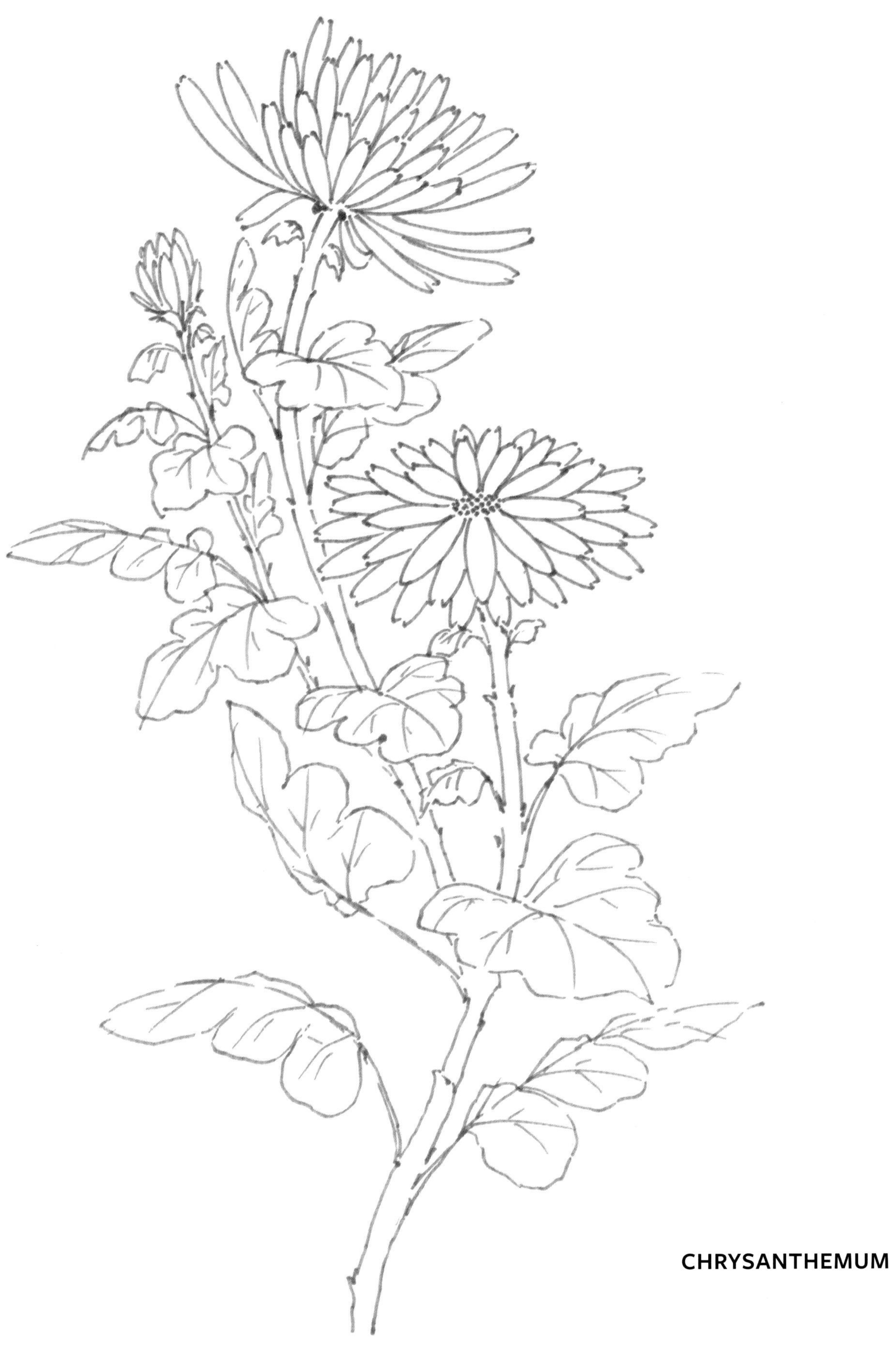

CHRYSANTHEMUM

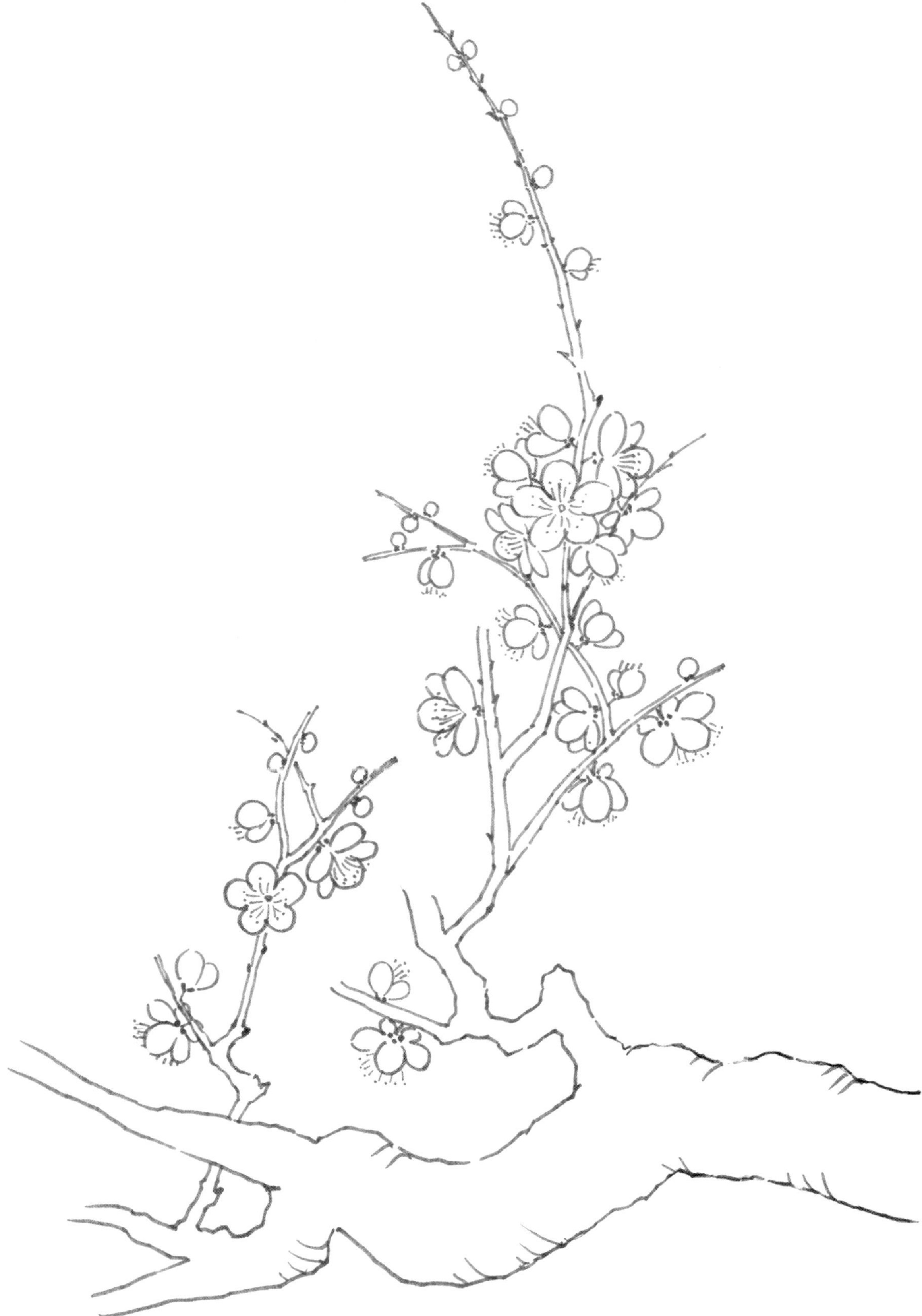

PLUM BLOSSOMS

QUICK VISUAL REFERENCE

These two pages are a quick visual reference for regularly used terms and might be cut out for quick reference - where this reference is not sufficient, please refer to the pages in brackets for fuller instruction.

BRUSHES:

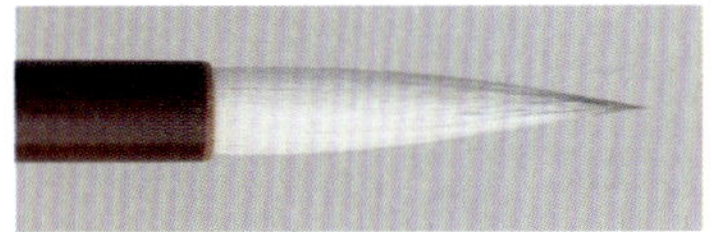

Ōfude (big brush)
(p. 20)

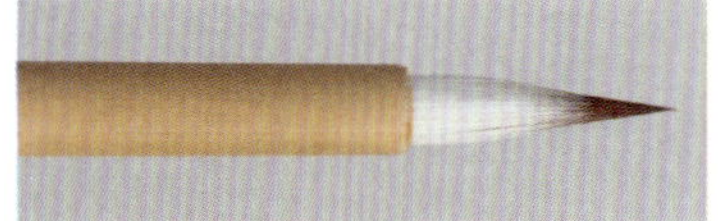

Kofude (small brush)
(p. 20)

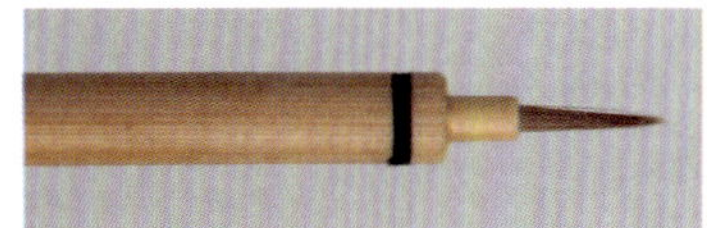

Menso-fude
(p. 20)

BRUSH GRIP:

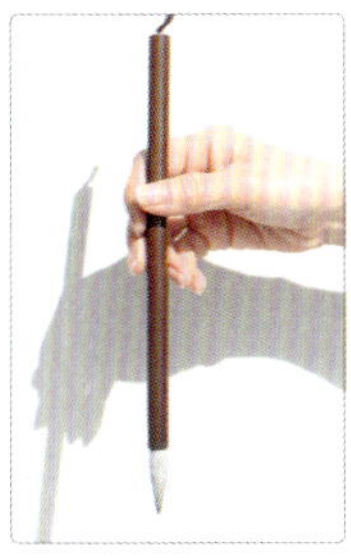

Soukou-hou
(p. 24)

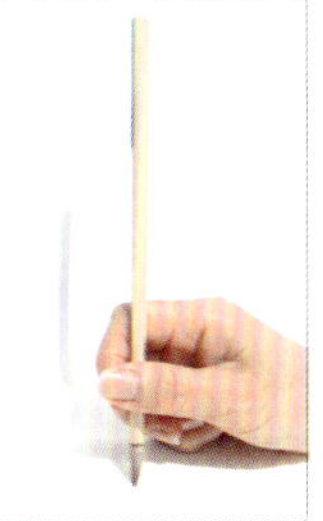

Tankou-hou
(p. 24)

POSTURE:

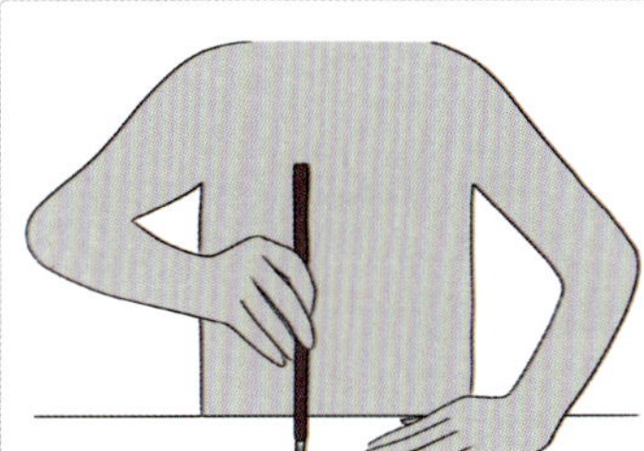

Kenwan-hou
(p. 24)

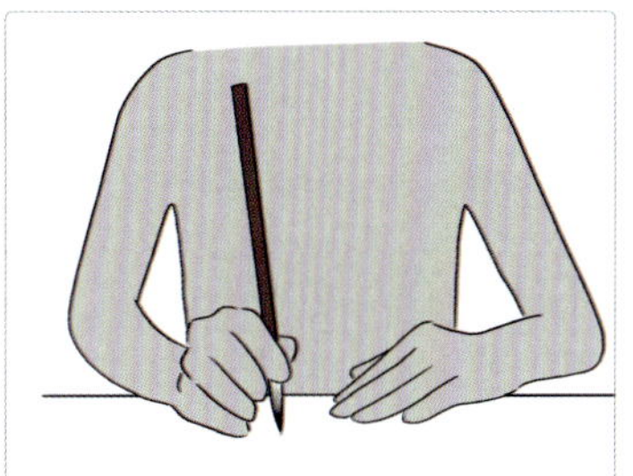

Teiwan-hou
(p. 24)

INK DENSITY:

Nouboku Dark ink
(p. 23)

Chuboku Middle ink
(p. 23)

Tanboku Light ink
(p. 23)

Goku-tanboku Very light ink
(p. 23)

BRUSH MOVEMENT:

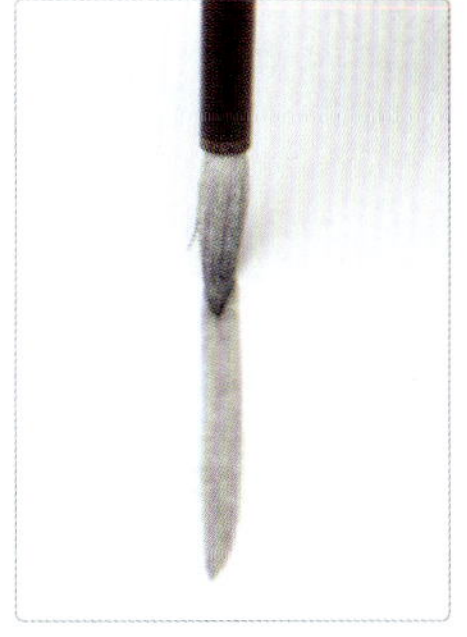

Chokuhitsu (p. 25)
Tip of brush moves through centre of line.

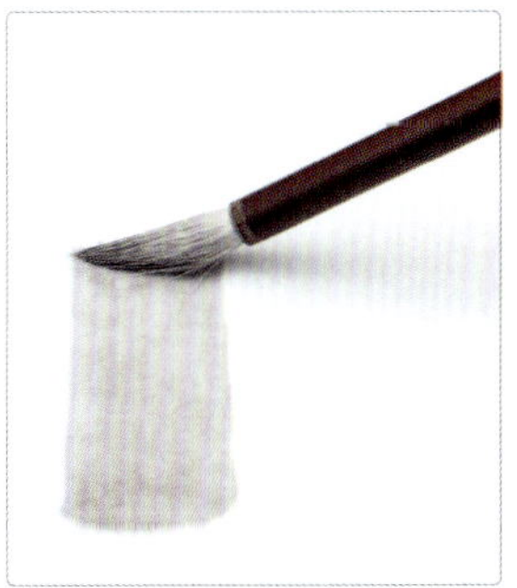

Sokuhitsu (p. 25)
Tip of brush is angled to create one edge of line.

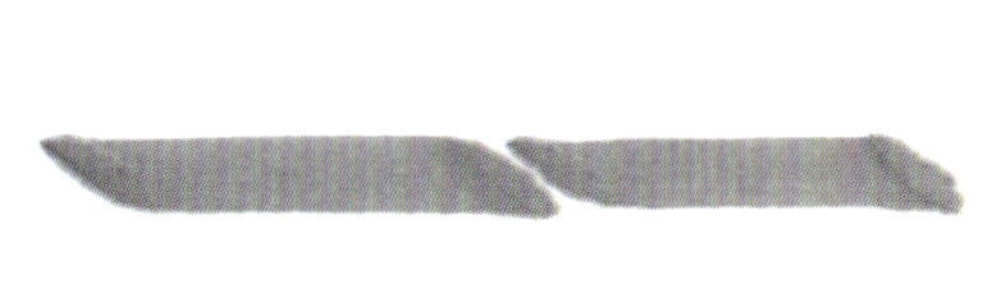

Hansokuhitsu (p. 25)
Half chokuhitsu and half sokuhitsu at an angle.

CHOUBOKU (INK CONTROL) AND BRUSH TECHNIQUES

Sakiguma (p. 26)
Brush preparation: load the brush with light ink and apply dark ink to the tip
Line: a chokuhitsu line with a dark tip and lighter body.

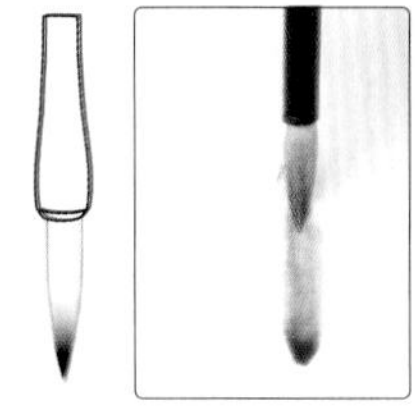

Kataguma sokuhitsu (p. 26)
Brush preparation: load the brush with light ink and apply dark ink to the tip.
Line: a sokuhitsu line with a dark edge and lighter body.

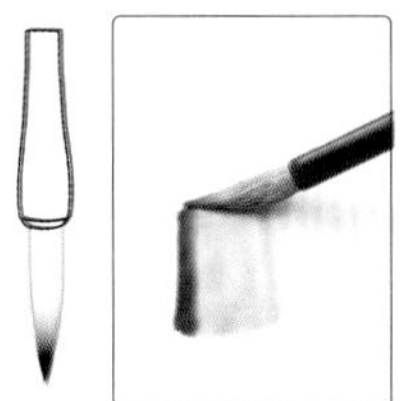

Kataguma chokuhitsu (p. 26)
Brush preparation: load the brush with light ink and apply dark ink to one side of the brush.
Line: a chokuhitsu line with one dark edge.

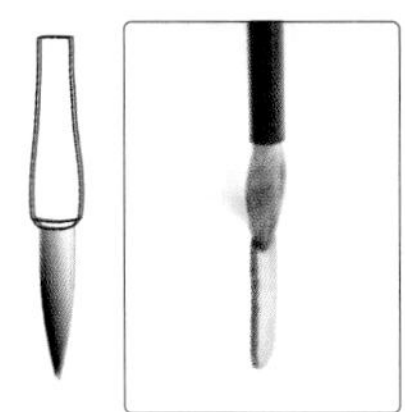

Uchiguma (p. 27)
Brush preparation: load the brush with light ink and apply dark ink to one side of the brush.
Line: a circle with a dark outer border and a lighter inner ring.

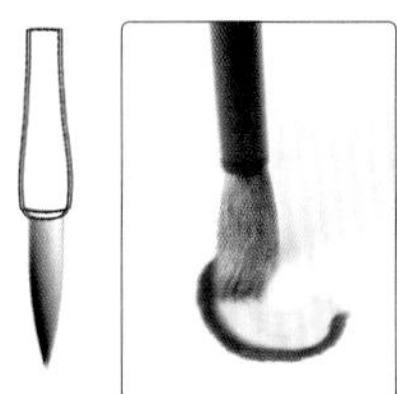

Sotoguma (p. 27)
Brush preparation: load the brush with light ink and apply dark ink to one side of the brush.
Line: a circle with a light outer border and a darker inner ring.

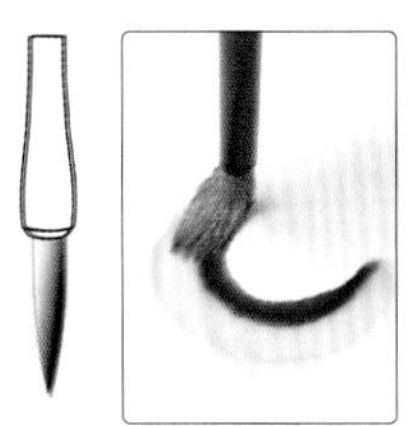

Ryoguma (p. 27)
Brush preparation: load the brush with light ink and apply dark ink to both sides of the brush.
Line: a chokuhitsu line with two dark edges.

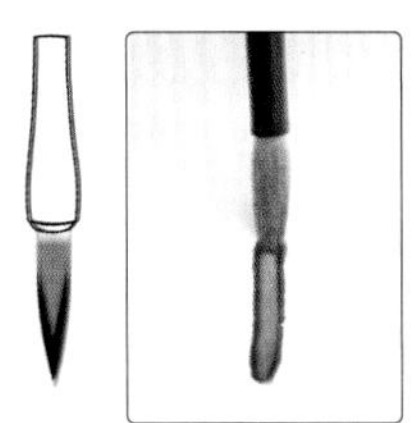

Soft ryoguma (p. 28)
Brush preparation: load the brush with light ink, apply dark ink to one surface of the brush and flip over.
Line: a chokuhitsu line with two subtly darker edges and a lighter centre.

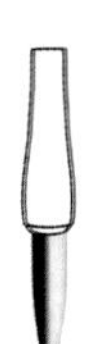

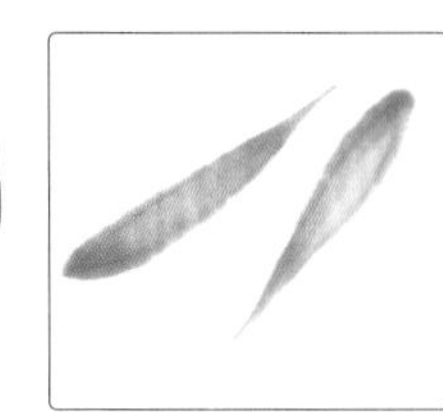

Sanboku-hou (p. 29)
Brush preparation: load the brush with light ink, apply dark ink to the tip of the brush and blend.
Line: a chokuhitsu or sokuhitsu line with a gradation of dark to light.

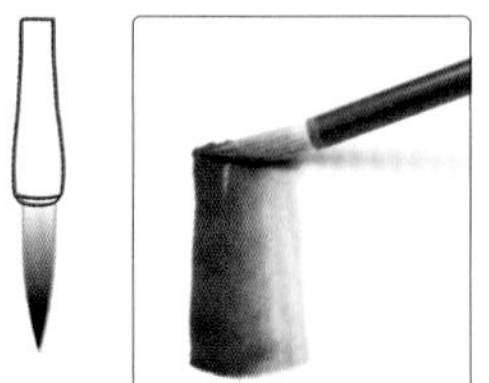

Motoguma (p. 30)
Brush preparation: load the brush with dark ink and wash the tip to remove ink.
Line: a chokuhitsu or sokuhitsu line with a gradation of light to dark.

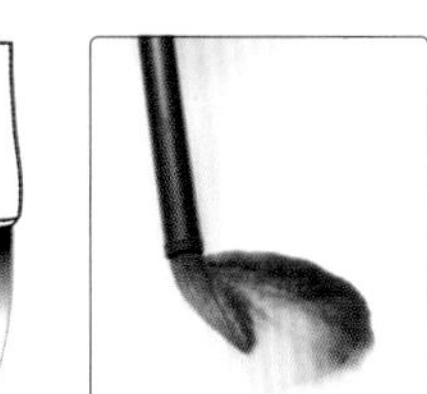

Haboku-hou (p. 31)
A wet-brush technique that involves painting with light ink, and layering darker ink while it is still wet to create a bleeding and blurring effect.

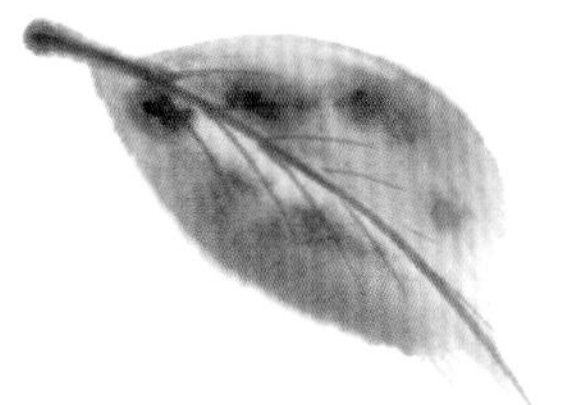

Nejiri-fude (p. 31)
A kasure technique that involves painting with dry, twisted bristles.

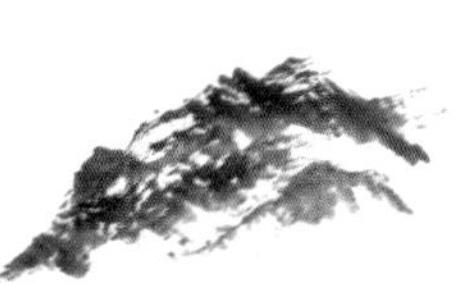

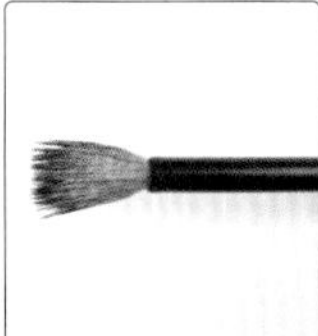

Wari-fude (p. 31)
A kasure technique that involves painting with dry, spread-out bristles.

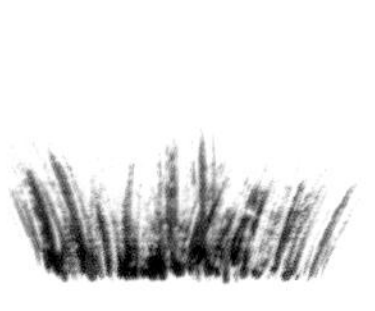

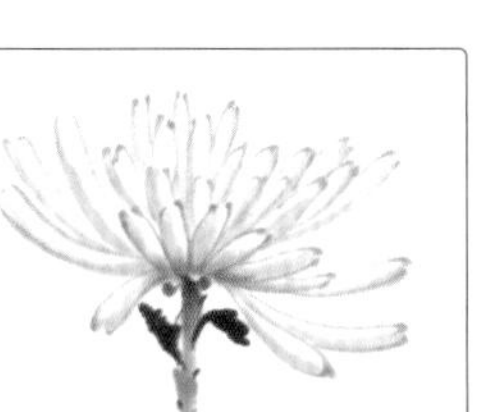

EXPRESSIONS:
Senbyou-hou (p. 32)
Paint controlled outlines with the tip of the brush.

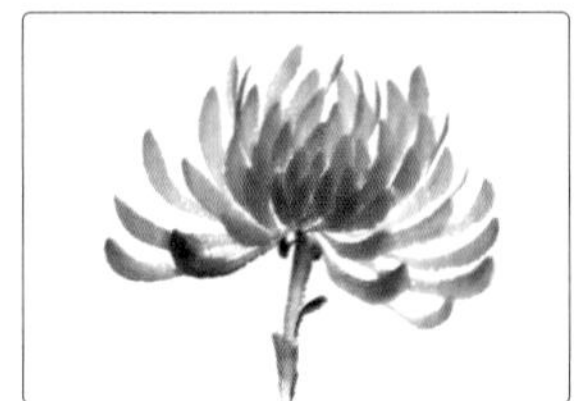

Tsuketate-hou (p. 32)
Create form through shading and layering.

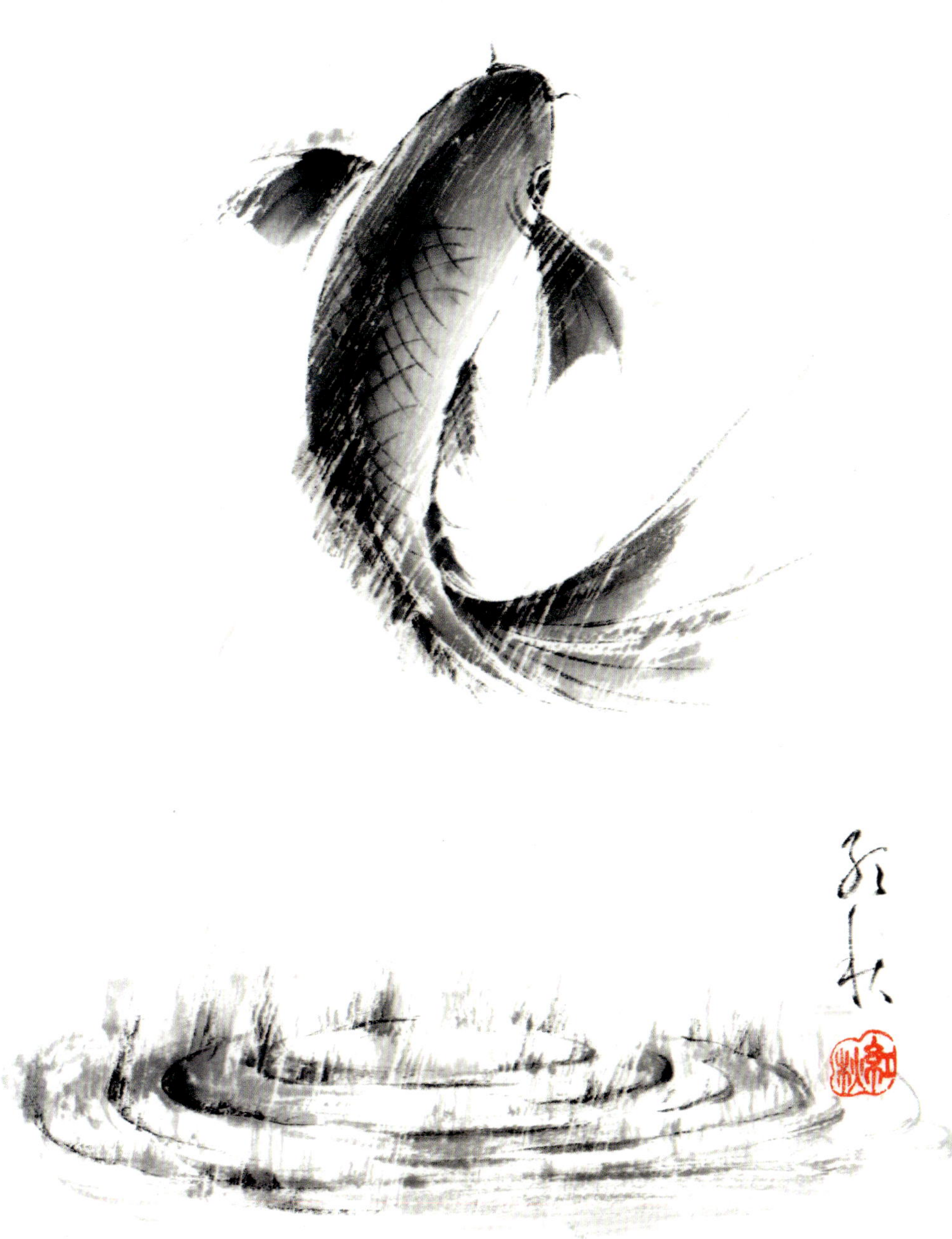

THE STORY OF THE KOI

Chinese folklore tells the tale of a school of koi swimming in the Yellow River. At the end of the river, they encounter a formidable waterfall. Some koi retreat and flow with the river's current, while others persevere and attempt to swim upward against the current.

Trying again and again for one hundred years, one lone koi makes it to the top. The gods who witness this achievement reward the koi for its unwavering spirit, transforming it into a golden dragon.